Methods for Teaching in Early 1

Methods for Teaching in Early Education is a comprehensive textbook offering a thorough introduction to early childhood teaching methods, with a particular focus on inclusive practices.

Aligned with both NAEYC standards and CEC's Division for Early Childhood recommended practices, this text explores various early childhood teaching principles and strategies, providing useful guidance for identifying and choosing between approaches. Covering topics from child-directed strategies to working with professionals in early childhood, the authors provide extensive support to prepare teachers for classroom planning and instruction. Each chapter opens and closes with representative vignettes of the challenges faced by today's early educators, and helpfully highlights key terms and objectives to inform learning goals. With the addition of sample worksheets, suggested exercises and helpful references, this book fully supports future teachers in understanding how they might implement these strategies in practice.

Methods for Teaching in Early Education will prove indispensable for students of teaching methods courses in both general and special education programs, providing a comprehensive introduction to early childhood teaching strategies relevant for today's inclusive classrooms.

Jennifer Ledford is Assistant Professor of Special Education at Vanderbilt University, USA.

Justin D. Lane is Assistant Professor of Special Education at the University of Kentucky, USA.

Erin E. Barton is Associate Professor of Special Education at Vanderbilt University, USA.

"This text by Ledford, Lane, and Barton fills a big void in resources for students studying young children with disabilities. This volume combines what we know about effective instruction, child development, data-based decision making, and inclusive education into a volume that is going to be an instant classic. I can't wait to add it to my book shelf and my required reading lists."

— Ilene Schwartz, *University of Washington, USA*

"Ledford, Lane, and Barton have produced a text that successfully infuses behavior analytic practice into the early childhood context and offers a wealth of evidence-based procedures using easy to read and example-rich descriptions. This is a powerful and pragmatic text for both teachers and the children they serve. Well done!"

— **Robert Pennington**, *University of North Carolina-Charlotte, USA*

"Ledford, Lane, and Barton have filled a gap in the instructional literature with this text by providing readers with contemporary research on skill acquisition alongside clear, detailed explanations of how to implement procedures. This will be a foundational text for behavior analytic courses in skill acquisition for young children because of the clarity and thoroughness of the authors."

— **Kevin M. Ayres**, *University of Georgia, USA*

"*Methods for Teaching in Early Education* is an invaluable resource for anyone working with young children, and especially young children with special needs. The systematic presentation of material mirrored by the equally systematic instructional methods will enhance practitioners' understanding of recommended and developmentally appropriate practice, leading to improved outcomes for all children with whom they interact."

— **Brian Reichow**, *University of Florida, USA*

"Ledford, Lane and Barton have produced the proverbial 'lightning in a bottle' with *Methods for Teaching in Early Childhood*. This volume is an elegant, coherent and accessible collection of evidence-based practices in action. If I had one choice for a text in teacher preparation in EC and ECSE this would be the clear winner."

— **Phillip Strain**, *University of Denver, USA*

Methods for Teaching in Early Education

Jennifer Ledford, Justin D. Lane
and Erin E. Barton

Routledge
Taylor & Francis Group

NEW YORK AND LONDON

First edition published 2019
by Routledge
52 Vanderbilt Avenue, New York, NY 10017

and by Routledge
2 Park Square, Milton Park, Abingdon, Oxon, OX14 4RN

Routledge is an imprint of the Taylor & Francis Group, an informa business

© 2019 Taylor & Francis

Library of Congress Cataloging-in-Publication Data
Names: Ledford, Jennifer R., author. | Lane, Justin D., 1982–, author. |
Barton, Erin Elizabeth, author.
Title: Methods for teaching in early education / Jennifer Ledford,
Justin Lane and Erin Barton.
Description: First edition. | New York, NY : Routledge, 2019. |
Includes bibliographical references and index.
Identifiers: LCCN 2018052181 (print) | LCCN 2019002438 (ebook) |
ISBN 9781315109800 (eBook) | ISBN 9781138088535 (hbk) |
ISBN 9781138088542 (pbk) | ISBN 9781315109800 (ebk)
Subjects: LCSH: Early childhood education–Study and teaching. |
Early childhood special education–Study and teaching. | Inclusive education.
Classification: LCC LB1139.23 (ebook) |
LCC LB1139.23 .L377 2019 (print) | DDC 372.21–dc23
LC record available at https://lccn.loc.gov/2018052181

ISBN: 978-1-138-08853-5 (hbk)
ISBN: 978-1-138-08854-2 (pbk)
ISBN: 978-1-315-10980-0 (ebk)

Typeset in Sabon
by Newgen Publishing UK

We dedicate this work to Mark Wolery and David Gast, who taught us everything we know about good instruction.

Contents

1 Theoretical Approaches and General Guidance in Early Childhood and Early Childhood Special Education

Key Terms

Ecological approach	*Microsystem*	*Mesosystem*
Exosystem	*Macrosystem*	*Behavioral approach*
Inclusion	*Segregation*	*Multi-tiered systems of support*

Chapter Objectives

After completing this chapter, readers should be able to:

- Describe two approaches relevant to development and instruction in early childhood.
- Describe how ecological and behavioral theories are helpful for planning instruction.
- Describe why high-quality environments are a critical foundation for intervention in early childhood.

Dimitri is interviewing for a job as an education assistant (sometimes called a paraprofessional) at a local early childhood center. The center includes children with and without disabilities from infants through kindergarten, and has a reputation for being a high-quality environment for young children. Dimitri does not have a background in child development, so during his job interview, he asks what principles the teachers use to support children's learning and what "high quality" means.

In the early childhood years, children grow and develop at an incredible and astonishing rate—a phenomenon that is often questioned and examined. What exactly contributes to optimal growth and development? What are the impacts of nature and nurture? How do we determine what we should teach children and how we should teach it? These are all critical questions whose answers are driven, in part, by theoretical orientation. Before detailing teaching and learning in early childhood, we will briefly review two theoretical orientations that guide our work. Then, we will outline broad guidelines provided by national early childhood organizations. Finally, we will outline several assumptions about early childhood instruction that guide our beliefs and the procedures outlined in later chapters of the book. Although many of the procedures discussed were developed for or with children with disabilities, the content of the book is relevant for a wide range of practitioners who serve young children in school- or center-based settings. That is, the procedures are pertinent for children who have typical development, children with identified disabilities, and children who are at-risk for developing disabilities based on biological or environmental factors.

Theoretical Approaches Helpful for Guiding Instruction

Ecological Theories of Development

Ecological approaches to development focus on the interactions between a child and their environments, including the **microsystem** (the child's immediate environment, such as the classroom and home) and more distant ecologies (**mesosystems, exosystems,** and **macrosystems** (see Figure 1.1)). Bronfenbrenner asserted that the most significant influences on child development were the behaviors of other people in a child's immediate and distal environments; these behaviors in turn influenced other environmental factors (e.g., relationships, resources) and a child's continued growth. He described development as occurring in the context of increasingly complex reciprocal interactions between children and their environments. Inherent to this model is the understanding that these interactions can be facilitative or inhibitive. Bronfenbrenner later updated his theoretical contributions and referred to a "bioecological model" (Bronfenbrenner, 1999), accounting for the individual biological characteristics that impact development. According to this model, individual differences across children *and* the behavior of adults in their immediate and distal environments (e.g., classrooms, schools, communities) influence child development. Thus, even given fixed individual characteristics, influencing a child's environments can result in considerable changes in child development. Ecological approaches can be used to design individualized assessment and intervention. That is, assessment and intervention approaches may not focus on supporting a child to engage in a behavior that is "next" in a given sequence, but instead plan and design interventions by determining to what extent children have the skills they need to successfully participate in current and future environments.

Behavioral Theories of Development

Behavioral approaches are complementary to ecological systems theory; the focus is generally on the microsystem—the environmental contexts in which the child is directly involved (e.g., his or her classroom). Skinner (1953) referred to behaviorism as the *science of human behavior*; it is generally concerned with observable behaviors and the relationships

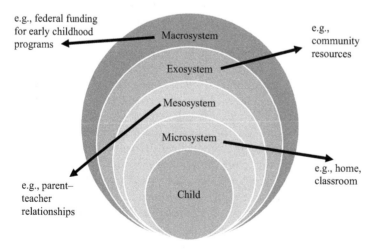

Figure 1.1 Systems Involved in the Ecological Theory of Development.

of those behaviors with the observable environmental events that precede and follow them. Behaviorism, like ecological systems theory, is not in conflict with theories related to biological differences. However, the theory of behaviorism suggests that environmental changes, regardless of biology, should result in changes in child behaviors. Interventions based on the science of behavior are highly individualized and most often rely on the principle of reinforcement as the primary driver behind learning. Relatedly, criticisms of behaviorally based interventions are oftentimes rooted in the notion that behaviorism ignores or devalues internal states, which are highly valued by other theoretical perspectives (e.g., constructivism). Behaviorism does not discount such views, but instead attempts to explain human behavior. The primary drive behind this approach is communicating that actions, whether observable or private, are more tangible than abstract ideas. Applied behavior analysis (ABA) is concerned with applying behavioral principles to behaviors that are socially important; it is not a specific practice or type of intervention.

Typical and Atypical Development

A common dichotomy in early childhood settings is differentiating children with **typical development** (meeting milestones; quantitatively or qualitatively displaying skills similar to those of same-age peers) from those who, in some capacity, display **atypical development** (considered at-risk for a disability or diagnosed with a disability, generally indicating deviation from the developmental trajectory of same-age peers). We do not argue against the value of a proper or provisional diagnosis, especially in regards to narrowing the universe of options when identifying appropriate interventions for capitalizing on strengths and remediating deficits and delays in children. We do highlight the importance of encouraging all early childhood educators to recognize that diagnosis or risk status does not necessarily mean that children without such labels are devoid of needs and require additional support, outside of behaviors commonly targeted in routine activities in the classroom (e.g., diapering, being a good friend during centers). That is, all children display a range of skills and challenges, regardless of their identification as a child with an educational eligibility for special education services. Typical and atypical development is a wide-reaching and multi-leveled continuum. For example, in terms of cognitive ability, the continuum might be conceptualized as ranging from children who display atypical advanced cognitive development to those classified as displaying severe to profound intellectual disability. Even two children who are relatively similar on this rudimentary continuum may have considerably different strengths and needs that should be considered across developmental domains. Similarly, children can range from having advanced social skills to needing considerable supports to engage in prosocial interactions; and while social skills can be influenced by cognition, children who have significant delays in social skills may have advanced cognition (and vice versa). Understanding the complexities of development across domains, typical variation in typical development, and deviations from expected developmental sequences provides early childhood educators with a basis from which they can plan and conduct appropriate instruction for all children.

General and Special Education

Related to developmental differences, general and special education services may be viewed as co-existing but separate services for children with typical development and those at-risk for or with disabilities. For example, an inclusive preschool program may adopt a specific curriculum that focuses on embedding developmentally appropriate targets into centers and related activities. Oftentimes, such curricula provide a scope (depth and breadth) and sequence (order) to ensure educators have a clear guide for planning instruction and monitoring progress; the expectation is that most children will benefit from this class-wide approach to instruction. Challenges arise when children with varied needs enroll in the class-room and do not necessarily respond to this approach or learn in a way that corresponds with recommended guidelines, especially for children who do not readily display learning-to-learn behaviors (e.g., consistently attend to staff and peers). This example highlights the importance of individualizing instruction for all children instead of basing instructional decisions against a particular scope and sequence. Such information is helpful for guiding instruction but will likely require modification to ensure all children benefit from planned activities. Adopting a curriculum framework may remedy some of the challenges associated with a single curriculum. A curriculum framework refers to the "idea that a curriculum is not a single resource or feature but rather a set of concepts or structure for classifying and organizing the many elements and processes involved when creating learning ecologies for young children" (Grisham-Brown, Hemmeter, & Pretti-Frontczak, 2005, p. 20). In addition, collaboration among professionals trained in early childhood education and early childhood special education is critical for further ensuring socially meaningful goals and objectives are targeted across the day. The burden of ensuring all children make meaningful gains should not lay on the shoulders of a single individual, but, more so, within an interdisciplinary model of education, capitalizing on strengths of all professionals who serve young children. Similar to the point made when discussing typical and atypical development—children may need a variety of supports to successfully engage in early childhood environments (e.g., general education) regardless of their designation as a child who is eligible for special education services. Likewise, a child's eligibility for special education services or specific disability diagnosis does not designate what types of special education supports they will need.

Sources of Information about Instruction in Early Childhood Contexts

Ecological and behavioral theories provide a foundation for understanding and explaining behavior–environment relations and their influence on child development and learning. A number of organizations have introduced guidelines to maximize rigorous educational practices that respect the culture, beliefs, and backgrounds of all children, regardless of exceptionality. These guidelines warrant attention when developing instructional programs, designing classrooms, effectively interacting with parents and other professionals, and advocating for appropriate practices for all children.

National Association for the Education of Young Children (NAEYC)

NAEYC is a national organization devoted to promoting high-quality early learning for children ages birth through 8 years, via work in the areas of practice, policy, and research (NAEYC, n.d.). NAEYC is important in early childhood for its work in identifying **developmentally appropriate practices** and advocating for high-quality early childhood experiences (Copple & Bredekamp, 2009). In collaboration with the Division of Early Childhood of the Council for Exceptional Children (DEC), NAEYC developed a joint position statement on inclusion (described below). NAEYC has identified principles of development and learning that guide early childhood intervention, which are listed in Table 1.1.

Division for Early Childhood (DEC) of the Council for Exceptional Children (CEC)

DEC is a non-profit organization whose purpose is to promote policies and evidence-based practices that promote the development of children who have disabilities, developmental

Table 1.1 National Association for the Education of Young Children (NAEYC) Principles of Child Development and Learning that Inform Practice

1. All the domains of development and learning—physical, social and emotional, and cognitive—are important, and they are closely interrelated. Children's development and learning in one domain influence and are influenced by what takes place in other domains.
2. Many aspects of children's learning and development follow well-documented sequences, with later abilities, skills, and knowledge building on those already acquired.
3. Development and learning proceed at varying rates from child to child, as well as at uneven rates across different areas of a child's individual functioning.
4. Development and learning result from a dynamic and continuous interaction of biological maturation and experience.
5. Early experiences have profound effects, both cumulative and delayed, on a child's development and learning; and optimal periods exist for certain types of development and learning to occur.
6. Development proceeds toward greater complexity, self-regulation, and symbolic or representational capacities.
7. Children develop best when they have secure, consistent relationships with responsive adults and opportunities for positive relationships with peers.
8. Development and learning occur in and are influenced by multiple social and cultural contexts.
9. Always mentally active in seeking to understand the world around them, children learn in a variety of ways; a wide range of teaching strategies and interactions are effective in supporting all these kinds of learning.
10. Play is an important vehicle for developing self-regulation as well as for promoting language, cognition, and social competence.

Table 1.2 Guiding Principles and Values for NAEYC and DEC

1. A belief in civic and democratic values, including respect, equality, and a participatory approach to decision-making.
2. A commitment to ethical behavior on behalf of children.
3. The use of educationally and developmentally significant goals as guides in designing and implementing curriculum, assessment, and program evaluation.
4. Coordinated systems that connect curriculum, assessment, and program evaluation.
5. Support for children as individuals and as members of families, cultures, and communities.
6. Respect for children's abilities and differences, so that systems of curriculum, assessment, and program evaluation promote the development and learning of all children.
7. Partnerships and communication with families.
8. Respect for evidence, including research as well as professional consensus.
9. Shared accountability for giving all children opportunities to reach essential goals—including accountability of programs, staff, administrators, and policymakers.

delays, or who are at-risk for future problems (DEC, 2012). In collaboration with NAEYC, DEC has developed a list of guiding principles and values (DEC, 2007) shared by the organizations (see Table 1.2). In addition, DEC has established Recommended Practices in Early Childhood and Early Intervention (see Table 1.3, p. 8), which are designed to assist practitioners to make theoretically sound and research-based decisions about their practices (DEC, 2014).

Research Literature

In addition to professional organizations, professional journals are excellent sources of information on evidence-based practices in early childhood. These journals often include research studies conducted to determine whether a given intervention was effective for changing a specific behavior for children with particular characteristics. They also often contain reviews or meta-analyses, which synthesize all of the available research on a given topic. Journals that often publish intervention research specific to early childhood, or early childhood special education, include *Young Exceptional Children, Journal of Early Intervention, Topics in Early Childhood Special Education,* and *Early Childhood Research Quarterly.* Table 1.3 includes information gleaned from a synthesis of interventions designed to improve outcomes for children with autism spectrum disorders.

Other Resources

A number of organizations and research teams have synthesized, and continue to synthesize, the larger intervention literature for purposes of identifying practices that have been evaluated in studies that adhere to contemporary guidelines for methodological rigor and demonstrate evidence of effectiveness. The *Early Childhood Technical Assistance Center* (ECTA) provides resources and links to information for those in the field who want to identify and learn more about evidence-based practices relevant to early childhood. Other technical assistance centers provide useful information in specific areas relevant to early childhood such as intensive intervention (National Center on Intensive Intervention) and social-emotional development (National Center for Pyramid Model Innovations). In addition, the *What Works Clearinghouse* (WWC) through the *Institute for Education Sciences* (IES) has evaluated a number of programs and approaches to instruction. Also, the *United States Department of Education, the Office of Special Education Programs* (OSEP) has provided funding for those who conduct syntheses of published studies.

Critical Issues for High-Quality Early Childhood Settings

Educational Placement

Inclusion refers to the participation of individuals with a wide variety of characteristics in a single setting or activity; **segregation** refers to the separation of individuals based on certain characteristics. For children with disabilities, federal law dictates that placement should be determined on an individualized basis, with children participating in environments with typically developing peers to the maximum extent possible. NAEYC and DEC's joint position statement on inclusion stated that children of all abilities have the right to "participate in a broad range of activities and contexts as full members of families, communities, and society" (NAEYC, 2009). In this statement, they also identified steps that should be taken by early childhood programs to promote inclusion of all young children, including: (a) creating high expectations for all children, (b) developing a program philosophy on inclusion, and (c) developing a system of supports for children. In 2015, the U.S. Departments of Health and Human Services and Education issued a policy statement on the inclusion of children with disabilities into early childhood programs. The policy statement highlighted the research on inclusion and the importance of high-quality inclusive environments for young children with and without disabilities, called for states to focus on high-quality inclusion in early childhood, set clear expectations for increasing the rates of inclusion and the availability of high-quality inclusive environments, and provided specific recommendations for states to advance high-quality inclusion. In 2017, the U.S. Department of Education, Office of Special Education Programs, issued a Dear Colleague letter which reaffirmed the position of the U.S. Department of Education (ED or Department) that all young children with disabilities should have access to inclusive high-quality early childhood programs where they are provided with individualized and appropriate supports to enable them to meet high expectations.

(Ryder, 2017, p. 1)

Although consideration of least restrictive environment (LRE) is required, safeguards for ensuring children receive appropriate services in inclusive preschool programs vary considerably from those for children in K-12 settings. For example, preschool-aged children at-risk for or with disabilities who display challenging behaviors are more likely than school-age children to be suspended or expelled from a program, leading to deleterious outcomes related to academic and social development. Such practices have short- and long-term implications for young children, including delayed social-emotional development and failure to obtain a high school diploma (U.S. Department of Education Office of Civil Rights, 2014). These data are even more troubling when considering the racial and gender disparities that also exist (i.e., boys, especially Black boys, are most likely to be suspended or expelled). Unfortunately, kindergarten teachers report that such issues carry over when children enter the school system, negatively impacting early K-12 experiences (Lane, Stanton-Chapman, Jamison, & Phillips, 2007; Rimm-Kauffman, Pianta, & Cox, 2000). Such practices oftentimes, independent of LRE, lead to young children receiving services in segregated settings or lead to the provision of instruction in a one-to-one arrangement, without same-age peers present. The level of support required for children to be successful should be individualized by each child's need with arrangements individualized by skill sets or clusters of related behaviors (e.g., one-to-one arrangement for learning isolated letter sounds, small group direct instruction for learning when and how to share). Within inclusive early childhood settings, these supports can occur and vary *within* the classroom and related settings—for example, (a) related service providers conduct sessions in the early childhood setting (e.g., speech-language pathologist runs sessions with a small group of children during centers; a Board Certified Behavior Analyst conducts a trial-based functional analysis or trains the teacher on how to implement procedures in a more controlled setting); (b) early childhood educators can utilize heterogeneous group arrangements—children with varying levels of academic and social needs serve as peer models, as well as create opportunities for observational learning; (c) a balance of naturalistic and systematic teaching is used for all children; (d) paraprofessionals and related individuals are trained on how to implement strategies and procedures with fidelity. These examples simply highlight potential options for capitalizing on supportive arrangements and settings, instead of a segregated versus an inclusive setting.

Evidence-Based Practices

Guidelines provided by NAEYC (2009) and DEC (2014) emphasize the importance of practitioners identifying and using developmentally appropriate and recommended practices in early childhood to address differential developmental gains between children with or at-risk for disabilities and those who display typical development. The overarching goal of the developmentally appropriate and recommended practices is providing an enriched early childhood environment that includes high-quality teaching and, in turn, subsequently decreases the ever-widening gap that appears when children with or at-risk for disabilities do not receive adequate supports. Although adherence to recommendations is crucial for success, early childhood educators typically require support when identifying recommended and evidence-based practices. A common and detrimental issue that continues to plague the field of education is bridging the gap between

Table 1.3 DEC's *Instruction*-Recommended Practices and Evidence-Based Practices

DEC Recommended Practices from the Instruction Topic	Evidence-Based Practices for Children with ASD
1. Practitioners, with the family, identify each child's strengths, preferences, and interests to engage the child in active learning.	1. Antecedent-based intervention
	2. Differential reinforcement
	3. Discrete trial teaching
2. Practitioners, with the family, identify skills to target for instruction that helps the child become adaptive, competent, socially connected, and engaged and that promote learning in natural and inclusive environments.	4. Exercise
	5. Extinction
	6. Functional behavior assessment
	7. Functional communication training
3. Practitioners gather and use data to inform decisions about individualized instruction.	8. Modeling
	9. Naturalistic intervention
4. Practitioners plan for and provide the level of support, accommodations, and adaptations needed for the child to access, participate, and learn within and across activities and routines.	10. Parent-implemented intervention
	11. Peer-mediated intervention
	12. Picture exchange communication system
5. Practitioners embed instruction within and across routines, activities, and environments to provide contextually relevant learning opportunities.	13. Pivotal response training
	14. Prompting
6. Practitioners use systematic instructional strategies with fidelity to teach skills and to promote child engagement and learning.	15. Reinforcement
	16. Response interruption/redirection
	17. Scripting
7. Practitioners use explicit feedback and consequences to increase child engagement, play, and skills.	18. Self-management
	19. Social narratives
8. Practitioners use peer-mediated intervention to teach skills and to promote child engagement and learning.	20. Social skills training
	21. Task analysis
9. Practitioners use functional assessment and related prevention, promotion, and intervention strategies across environments to prevent and address challenging behavior.	22. Technology-aided instruction
	23. Time delay
	24. Video modeling
	25. Visual supports

Note: Evidence-based practices listed are those with evidence for 0–5-year-old children with ASD, as identified by Wong et al., 2015.

research and practice. Defining evidence-based practices is a complicated endeavor, given several different guidelines have been published in recent years. Rather than highlight a single set of guidelines, we want to broadly define the overarching expectations for designating a practice as *evidence-based*. Evidence-based practice refers to a single practice that has been identified as successfully improving or remediating a specific behavior for a specific population, based on high-quality experimental studies. Federal guidelines and relevant professional organizations require teachers to use these practices (also called research-supported practices) when planning instruction for young children with and without disabilities. Table 1.3 lists DEC's recommended practices in the instruction topic for young children with disabilities and evidence-based practices for children with autism spectrum disorders, identified via literature review by Wong and colleagues (2015). Note that the recommended practices are rather broad in scope, while Wong and colleagues' evidence-based practices are more specific. Recommended practices highlight overarching expectations to guide practitioners, but are relatively broad to allow for individualization in regards to classroom roles and expectations, instructional programs, etc. In contrast, the evidence-based practices specify for whom and under what conditions an intervention or set of practices may or may not be effective. This was done in an effort to help practitioners navigate the literature and reduce uncertainty when identifying appropriate practices. Additional DEC Recommended Practices were developed for other topic areas (e.g., transition, leadership, assessment, interactions); documents describing the practices are available for free online at www.dec-sped.org/dec-recommended-practices. We also note that evidence-based practices should be used based on both previous research support *and* ongoing data collection. That is, even practices identified as evidence-based cannot be used without ongoing assessment regarding the evidence that the practice is working in a particular context, for teaching a specific behavior to an individual child.

Multi-Tiered Systems of Support

Multi-tiered systems of support (MTSS) refers to a framework for identifying the extent of support needed by individual children for reaching specific goals. Levels of support are oftentimes represented within a three-tiered framework, existing along a continuum of individualization, intensity, and number of opportunities to learn a behavior or skill set. Within MTSS, children are not assigned to a single tier of support, but receive services that are commensurate with the level of support required for them to be successful (e.g., Pyramid Model; Hemmeter, Ostrosky, & Fox, 2006). Within the early childhood literature, MTSS is more likely to be effective for improving social-emotional development in preschool-age children when educators are (1) provided with multiple hours of training on strategies and interventions and (2) provided with coaching on implementation in a one-to-one format (Shepley & Grisham-Brown, 2018).

In MTSS models, Tier 1 supports are comprised of universal instructional practices meant to support learning in most children who attend preschool, oftentimes thought of as representing high-quality instruction as part of a curriculum framework (developmentally and culturally appropriate targeted goals and expected outcomes of instruction in the classroom; Grisham-Brown & Hemmeter, 2017). Tier 2 supports are utilized when data indicate a child or multiple children are displaying difficulties learning a target behavior (behavior is absent or less robust than same-age peers in the classroom). Although a clear definition of what differentiates Tier 2 from Tier 3 is lacking in the literature, children who require Tier 2 supports typically (1) require individualized learning outcomes (e.g., child will appropriately tap a peer on the shoulder to gain attention); (2) require supplements to current classroom practices (e.g., visual schedule for transitioning between activities); or (3) need additional opportunities to learn and practice a behavior in context (e.g., three peer confederates ask the target child to share a marker during art). In contrast, Tier 3 supports will typically involve adaptations in all three areas for children who require the most intensive supports to make gains in developmentally and culturally appropriate behaviors that are valued in early childhood classrooms. Within this tiered approach, children who require intensive services are likely to require systematic instruction. **Systematic instruction** refers to an individualized instructional program that includes a plan to promote stimulus control by implementing a procedure that highlights the critical features of a stimulus, shows the child how to respond, and leads to reinforcement under tightly controlled conditions. Data are collected to monitor progress with the specific program, with a plan to remove adult supports as the child is successful. Common examples of systematic instructional procedures include constant time delay, progressive time delay, and system of least prompts. Systematic instruction is ultimately a procedure that can occur throughout the day in various formats, including during common activities such as free play during centers, the playground, small group instruction, and mealtimes. DEC- (2014) and NAEYC- (2009) recommended practices emphasize the importance of providing systematic instruction during age-appropriate activities for purposes of promoting short- and long-term success in children.

MTSS provides an interdisciplinary framework for determining the extent to which children receive individualized services in early childhood classrooms (joint statement provided by DEC, NAEYC, and National Head Start Association [NHSA], 2014). Assessment and evaluation are considered core processes of MTSS, reflecting the iterative and ongoing process of collecting data to determine what level of support a child needs to be successful in his or her environment.

Program Quality

Program quality is an all-encompassing term associated with the physical, temporal, and social aspects of a classroom. Program quality also includes appropriate use of instructional practices and ensuring procedures are implemented as intended (procedural fidelity). A number of options are available for rating program quality, such as the *Classroom Assessment Scoring System* (CLASS) and the *Early Childhood Environment Rating Scale, Revised Edition* (ECERS-R). In addition, DEC (2014) provided guidelines that are oftentimes related to, or associated with, program quality. These resources highlight the importance of considering all aspects of the environment. Assessing quality indicators provides guidance in regards to determining if an aspect of the setting requires modification, which includes not only the physical layout of the indoor space but people within the space (e.g., paraprofessionals require additional training). If one or more indicators of program quality are lacking it could explain a child's lack of progress and should be considered before introducing more intensive or restrictive interventions. For example, a first-year teacher is well trained in response-prompting procedures, preference assessments, and behavior management. She meets all students and conducts assessments to identify goals and instructional objectives for the academic year. She develops data sheets, written procedures, and has a plan to collect reliability data on target behaviors and procedural fidelity data. After two weeks, the teacher is unable to meet the needs of her students. Expectations for self-care routines are unclear to paraprofessionals and children, paraprofessionals leave the classroom at unplanned times to take breaks or personal phone calls, centers are undefined, etc. Each of these issues hinders instruction and requires attention from the teacher to ensure all aspects of the environment are meeting the needs of adults (e.g., established schedules and expectations) and children (e.g., age-appropriate materials, clearly defined centers, expectations and classroom rules).

Guiding Assumptions

In addition to the guiding principles provided by NAEYC and DEC, we would like to outline several assumptions that guide our approach to intervention and instruction in early childhood, and thus the remainder of this book:

1. All children deserve consistent access to high-quality early childhood settings that are staffed with nurturing and responsive adults. We explicitly believe children should not be suspended or expelled from these settings; instead, they should receive sufficient levels of support, systematic instruction, and adequate opportunities to learn the skills needed to fully participate and engage appropriately in these settings.
2. All children deserve to spend time in typical settings, with other children. Federal law indicates that children with disabilities be served in the least restrictive environment (LRE); some children may require individual instruction or some supports that occur outside of typical settings. For example, some children might require intermittent supports in hospital or home settings due to healthcare needs. However,

instruction should focus on providing appropriate access and supports to ensure participation in typical settings. All supports that *can* be provided in typical settings, should be. For example, special instruction and related services generally should not occur in a pull-out, one-to-one format; early childhood professionals (e.g., teachers, related service providers) should consider push-in or small group instruction whenever possible.

3. All children deserve frequent and consistent access to appropriate, effective, systematic instruction to enable them to learn and use a variety of functional behaviors.

4. Practitioners should use evidence-based and recommended practices. This requires two things. First, practitioners need to learn how to use evidence-based practices and to be familiar with resources which will allow them to remain up-to-date as research evidence is accumulated (e.g., DEC, NAEYC, WWC). Second, practitioners should collect and use data to inform instruction. Data should be used to make changes to child goals, instructional practices, environmental supports, and so on.

5. Practitioners should use a variety of evidence-based strategies, including both child- and adult-directed strategies, and individual and group-based teaching.

6. Practitioners should include families and other stakeholders in important decision-making.

7. Practitioners cannot be expected to be successful without ongoing, effective professional development and support. Early childhood systems, agencies, and programs should develop and implement professional development systems that ensure practitioners have the technical assistance and ongoing supports needed to deliver effective instruction to all children.

During the interview, Maria, the director of the school, and Sarah, a teacher there, shared a number of resources from NAEYC and DEC with Dimitri. They also shared their professional development plans and explained how those plans ensure staff stayed up to date on the latest information about evidence-based practices. While he was touring the school, he saw lots of different teaching styles and a number of different activities, and was impressed with how responsive and caring the teachers were. He had a better idea about what "high quality" meant and accepted the job offer on the spot!

Resources

http://ectacenter.org
www.pyramidmodel.org/about/ncpmi_pmc/
https://intensiveintervention.org
https://ies.ed.gov/ncee/wwc/
www.dec-sped.org
www.naeyc.org

References

Bronfenbrenner, U. (1999). Environments in developmental perspective: Theoretical and operational models. In S. L. Friedman & T. D. Wachs (Eds.), *Measuring environment across the life span: Emerging methods and concepts* (pp. 3–28). Washington, DC: American Psychological Association Press.

Copple, C., & Bredekamp, S. (2009). *Developmentally appropriate practice in early childhood programs serving children from birth through age 8.* Washington, DC: National Association for the Education of Young Children.

DEC (Division for Early Childhood) (2007). Promoting positive outcomes for children with disabilities: Recommendations for curriculum, assessment, and program evaluation. Arlington,

VA: DEC. Retrieved from http://docs.wixstatic.com/ugd/38a114_79c24e0dd77f4cffad2a722f 9ff98794.pdf.

DEC. (2012). Bylaws of division for early childhood. Arlington, VA: DEC. Retrieved from http:// docs.wixstatic.com/ugd/38a114_79c24e0dd77f4cffad2a722f9ff98794.pdf.

DEC. (2014). DEC recommended practices. Arlington, VA: DEC. Retrieved from https:// divisionearlychildhood.egnyte.com/dl/tgv6GUXhVo.

DEC/National Association for the Education of Young Children (NAEYC). (2009). NAEYC standards for early childhood professional preparation programs. Retrieved from www.naeyc. org/resources/position-statements/standards-professional-preparation.

DEC, NAEYC, & National Head Start Association. (2014). Frameworks for response to intervention in early childhood: Description and implications. *Communication Disorders Quarterly*, 35, 108–119.

Grisham-Brown, J., & Hemmeter, M. L. (2017). *Blended practices for teaching young children in inclusive settings* (2nd ed.). Baltimore, MD: Brookes.

Grisham-Brown, J., Hemmeter, M. L., & Pretti-Frontczak, K. (2005). *Blended practices for teaching young children in inclusive settings*. Baltimore, MD: Brookes.

Hemmeter, M. L., Ostrosky, M., & Fox, L. (2006). Social and emotional foundations for early learning: A conceptual model for intervention. *School Psychology Review*, 35, 583–601.

Lane, K. L., Stanton-Chapman, T., Roorbach Jamison, K., & Phillips, A. (2007). Teacher and parent expectations of preschoolers' behavior: Social skills necessary for success. *Topics in Early Childhood Special Education*, 27, 86–97.

National Association for the Education of Young Children (NAEYC). (n.d.). Strategic direction. Washington, DC: NAEYC. Retrieved from www.naeyc.org/sites/default/files/globally-shared/ downloads/PDFs/about-us/people/NAEYC_Strategic_Direction.pdf.

Rimm-Kaufman, S. E., Pianta, R. C., & Cox, M. J. (2000). Teachers' judgments of problems in the transition to kindergarten. *Early Childhood Research Quarterly*, 15(2), 147–166.

Ryder, R. (January 9, 2017). Dear Colleague Letter. United States Department of Education, Office of Special Education and Rehabilitative Services. Retrieved from: www2.ed.gov/policy/speced/ guid/idea/memosdcltrs/preschool-lre-dcl-1-10-17.pdf

Skinner, B. F. (1953). *Science and human behavior*. New York: Simon and Schuster.

Shepley, C., & Grisham-Brown, J. (in press). Multi-tiered systems of support for preschool-aged children: A review and meta-analysis. *Early Childhood Research Quarterly*.

U.S. Department of Education Office for Civil Rights. (2014). Civil rights data collection: Data snapshot: School discipline. Retrieved from http://ocrdata.ed.gov/Downloads/CRDC- School-Discipline-Snapshot.pdf.

Wong, C., Odom, S. L., Hume, K. A., Cox, A. W., Fettig, A., Kucharczyk, S., … & Schultz, T. R. (2015). Evidence-based practices for children, youth, and young adults with autism spectrum disorder: A comprehensive review. *Journal of Autism and Developmental Disorders*, 45, 1951–1966.

2   Considerations for Selecting Behaviors for Instruction

Key Terms

High-priority learning objectives *Discrete behaviors*   *Chained behaviors*
Discriminative stimulus   *Topography*   *Reliable*
Function   *Response class*   *Response patterns*
Task analysis   *Immediate imitation* *Delayed imitation*
Instructional control   *Functional*   *Measurable*

Chapter Objectives

After completing this chapter, readers should be able to:

- Identify domains of behavior and examples within each.
- Differentiate between discrete and chained behaviors, and provide examples of each.
- Define response class, and give examples of response classes.
- Identify several response patterns that may be associated with favorable outcomes for young children.
- Name one chained and one set of discrete behaviors that could be task-analyzed; describe the potential steps.
- What are some common behaviors that are necessary for optimal learning outcomes for children?

Marti is ready to begin her second year in a public-school classroom for three- to five-year-old children with disabilities. She feels confident going into the year that she has developed some good routines and activities that are developmentally appropriate and engaging for children. She wants to be more thoughtful this year about what behaviors she targets for teaching, but she finds that her undergraduate preparation program did not provide many opportunities for her to carefully consider what goals are most important for young children to learn. She begins to peruse the literature to determine whether there is guidance available for her choices.

Given limited time and other resources, teachers and other practitioners are often tasked with providing systematic instruction and progress monitoring on a relatively small number of objectives per child. Thus, an important job of early childhood practitioners is to decide which child behaviors should be considered **high-priority learning object-ives** (HPLOs); we define HPLOs as behaviors that are considered important for the child to learn, necessitating instruction and progress monitoring by the practitioner. For children with disabilities who receive special education services, these HPLOs should be identified on individualized education programs (IEPs; for children aged three or older) or individualized family service plans (IFSPs; for children birth to age three); for children who do not receive such services, these objectives can be specified via a formal or informal learning plan. We suggest identifying HPLOs for every child, with the help of their family, rather than only for children with identified delays or disabilities; this ensures that purposeful teaching occurs that allows all children to develop in important ways.

Domains of Behavior

Many practitioners consider behavior in domains defined by federal law in relation to developmental delay—social, communication, physical, adaptive, and cognitive skills (IDEA, 1997; IDEIA, 2004). In the early childhood years, all of these domains are areas of substantial growth for children—perhaps more so than at any other time in their lives. The wide range of behaviors that practitioners must consider is made even more complicated by the fact that many behaviors could fall into multiple domains—for example, greeting peers could be considered both a social and a communication behavior. Likewise, engaging in increasingly complex play could be considered an adaptive or social skill. Similarly, handwashing could be considered both a motor and an adaptive behavior. Below, we outline six slightly different domains relevant to early childhood settings; additional domains may be important for some children in some settings, and many behaviors important in early childhood settings may be categorized as occurring in multiple domains. Domains include: social-emotional, prerequisite behaviors for school success, pre-academic, play and leisure, self-help, and movement and physical activity behaviors. Table 2.1 includes a list of sample behaviors important for young children in each domain.

Critical Prerequisite Behaviors

In addition to behaviors in the six domains listed above, several behaviors are important prerequisite behaviors to learning in early childhood environments. We describe five of

Table 2.1 Common Behaviors Across Domains

Domain	Sample Behaviors
Social-Emotional	Sharing and taking turns with toys; appropriately requesting, protesting, and commenting; engaging in increasingly complex conversations; engaging in appropriate social problem solving with peers
Prerequisites for School Success	Imitating peers; following routine directions; engaging in classroom activities; initiating to adults and peers; persisting during difficult activities
Pre-Academic	Using age- and content-appropriate vocabulary, naming letters and letter names; sorting by form and function; ordering items by size; counting small sets of items; engaging in scientific inquiry by posing questions and testing hypotheses; repeating and extending patterns; recognizing environmental print
Play and Leisure	Engaging in increasingly complex pretend play behaviors with objects; playing functionally with toys; playing near and then with peers; playing games with rules; using increasingly complex language to describe play
Self-Help and Completion of Routines	Engaging in the toileting routine; self-feeding; hand-washing; cleaning up materials; putting away and retrieving personal items during arrival and dismissal routines
Movement and Physical Activity	Ambulation (crawling, walking, running); accessing appropriate structures on the playground (swings, ladders, slides); engaging in prolonged moderate-to-vigorous physical activity; using fine and gross motor skills to access and use classroom materials (e.g., drawing a line with a paintbrush; grasping and placing blocks)

these behaviors below—imitation, waiting for a prompt, visual discrimination, picture–object correspondence, and ready behaviors. These behaviors are sometimes called pivotal behaviors (or keystone behaviors; Wolery & Hemmeter, 2011), and are those which impact a child's ability to efficiently learn from typical instruction. Other behaviors (not discussed below) can be considered pivotal behaviors because they open up opportunities for additional learning—for example, teaching children to engage in more complex play behaviors may increase the number of opportunities to interact with peers.

Imitation. Imitation is mimicking a behavior that another person has engaged in, either right after they do so (**immediate imitation**) or later (**delayed imitation**). A strictly behavioral definition of imitation would include only imitation that occurs immediately after the model; we think it is useful to consider a broader definition including copying the behavior of a model regardless of timing. Generally, we think of imitation as occurring in three different ways: (a) verbal imitation, or saying what someone else says; (b) gestural imitation, or doing what someone else does with their body; and (c) object imitation, or doing an action that someone else does with a material. Imitation is an important process by which all children learn how to engage in new behaviors (Ledford & Wolery, 2011). Verbal imitation is critical for learning language, while gestural and motor imitation are critical for learning other new skills, such as play and self-help behaviors. Imitation proficiency has been associated with a number of positive outcomes (Rogers, Hepburn, Stackhouse, & Wehner, 2003; Thurm, Lord, Lee, & Newschaffer, 2007). However, some children with disabilities have deficits or delays in imitation when compared to their typically developing peers (Rogers et al., 2003; Stone, Ousley, & Littleford, 1997). When children can imitate, you can teach them using models, rather than physical guidance, which is less intrusive and restrictive (see Chapter 8). Moreover, children who readily imitate their peers are likely to benefit from observational learning (see Chapter 12). Imitation should be directly taught and reinforced for children who do not learn this skill in typical contexts; imitation of adults and peers has been successfully taught using response prompting procedures such as progressive time delay (Venn et al., 1993) and system of least prompts (Barton & Ledford, 2018).

Waiting for a prompt. To benefit from some prompting procedures, children must be able to wait for a prompt when they are unable to answer independently. For example, if you asked a question, and the child did not know how to respond correctly, it is preferable for a child to refrain from guessing and indicate they need a prompt by *waiting* for help. This prevents errors and allows children to receive help when they need it. Wait training can be taught using procedures similar to progressive time delay procedures (see Chapter 8).

Visual discrimination. Children must be able to visually discriminate between a range of icons to engage in many receptive and expressive identification tasks, to effectively benefit from some visual supports, and to use icons to communicate (such as picture exchange or a speech-generating device). You can teach visual discrimination by using a systematic response prompting procedure (see Chapters 8–11) to teach children to discriminate between examples and non-examples of icons via matching tasks. For example, if you want to teach a child to name letters, you first need to confirm that they can independently match identical letters given a field of the identical letter and non-identical letters (sometimes called distractors). This ensures that the child is attending to the salient differences among letters. If they are unable to match, visual discrimination should be taught prior to expressive identification (see Chapter 8).

Picture–object correspondence. Use of two-dimensional representations to communicate expectations is common in early childhood settings. Practitioners may use photos to depict classroom rules or line drawings to represent the daily schedule. For children to benefit from these depictions, they must demonstrate picture–object correspondence. That is, they must associate each icon with the corresponding activity. It is important to note that some children need to be taught that pictures can correspond with items or activities, but all children need to be taught to what the specific icons refer. For example, at the beginning of the school year, children will not instinctively understand that a line drawing that shows a pencil and some written text refers to a daily sign-in activity. Similar to the above skills, picture–object correspondence and specific relations between icons and activities can be taught via response prompting procedures (see Chapters 8–11).

Ready behaviors. Prior to using direct instructional procedures, it is helpful to have **instructional control**—that is, to teach children the behaviors that are expected and reinforced when direct instruction occurs. For example, you might need to teach a child that when you say his or her name, they should pause and look in the general direction of the speaker. Teaching and reinforcing these behaviors can occur on an individual or class-wide basis (Beaulieu, Hanley, & Roberson, 2012); doing so prior to attempting instruction is likely to make instructional interactions more predictable and successful for the child, and more efficient.

Research Abstract

Sweeney, E., Barton, E. E., & Ledford, J. R. (2018). Using progressive time delay to increase levels of peer imitation during sculpting play. *Journal of Autism & Developmental Disorders*. doi: 10.1007/s10803-018-3638-2.

In this single case design study, authors taught four children with disabilities to imitate actions modeled by their peers in the context of sculpting play. Children were recruited because they demonstrated adequate accuracy for imitating adults but did not yet accurately imitate peers. During play activities, the first author used progressive time delay with full physical prompts (see Chapter 8) to prompt children to imitate a peer's sculpting action (e.g., rolling Play-Doh™). All children demonstrated an increase in unprompted peer imitation behaviors, indicating progressive time delay was effective for teaching peer imitation.

Critical Issue for Teaching: Access to Communication

Some young children may display difficulties in using oral language to communicate (delayed speech or absence of speech) and, as such, augmentative and alternative communication (AAC) should be considered. Having a way to communicate requests, protests, comments, and other ideas *is critical for all children*. If a child does not yet have a way to functionally and appropriately communicate these things, it is essential that they immediately and consistently receive support and instruction to learn to do so. Some children may use AAC as the primary mode of communication, while others may use a form of AAC as a supplement or support to other modes of communication, such as speech. First, if you are considering using AAC with a child we recommend collaborating with a speech and language pathologist (SLP). A number of options are available and an SLP will likely be aware of the full spectrum of choices. Second, AAC can be further categorized into one of two categories: (1) unaided AAC—refers to gestures, signs, and related behaviors that do not involve additional supports outside of the individual, and (2) aided AAC—refers to use of items or devices such as picture cards, fixed displays, and dynamic display devices (Romski & Sevcik, 2005; Romski, Sevcik, Barton-Hulsey, & Whitmore, 2015). Aided AAC can be subdivided into (1) no-tech (e.g., picture cards), (2) low-tech (e.g., switches), and (3) high-tech (e.g., speech generating devices) options. If utilizing a total communication approach, children may use a mixture of speech, signs, gestures, and AAC to communicate; each communicative behavior should be honored.

When considering using aided AAC with a child, a number of considerations warrant attention. First, studies have found that AAC is an effective mode of communication for a variety of children across ages and diagnoses. These data negate the outdated belief that AAC may inhibit the development of oral language (Romski & Sevcik, 2005). Second, contemporary studies recommend that a social partner use AAC when interacting with children who are learning to use aided AAC (Romski, Sevcik, Cheslock, & Barton-Hulsey, 2017; Sennott, Light, & McNaughton, 2016). That is, social partners (child and communication partner) use AAC to communicate with one another. This occurs when the adult models how to use AAC, in conjunction with speech, on the child's device or on another device. We also note that effective use of an AAC device requires systematic teaching, and is *not* the same thing as facilitated communication (also called by other names, such as rapid prompting), which is a pseudoscientific procedure that may result in unintended harm (see Tostanoski, Lang, Raulston, Carnett, & Davis, 2014).

Sources for Identifying HPLOs

We list some important behaviors that might be valuable for young children to learn in Table 2.1. However, practitioners will likely need to teach a wide variety of behaviors to children with a wide range of needs. Practitioners can identify critical behaviors to be taught using a variety of sources. Common ones include early learning standards, curricula, ecological assessments, and formal plans (i.e., IEPs, IFSPs). Identifying HPLOs ensures consistency in teaching children by all members of a team, provides a guide for evaluating growth in important areas, and assists in communicating expectations and progress to others. However, even when a child has a formal plan—an IEP—her IEP goals should not be the only focus of instruction; she also should have access to instruction related to the general curriculum and relevant early learning standards.

Early Learning Standards

All 50 states have early learning standards for children who are aged 3–5 years, and most states have standards for infants and toddlers. These standards identify important learning goals that are developmentally appropriate for young children. The National Association for the Education of Young Children (2002) identified both potential benefits and possible risks of the proliferation of standards for young children. Benefits include the presence of clear expectations about learning and increased consensus on important skills for young children. Risks include possible negative outcomes for children who do not meet standards, and teaching to standards instead of teaching based on what each child needs to improve short- and long-term outcomes. They also identified recommendations for standards: (a) emphasis of significant and developmentally appropriate outcomes across domains; (b) development and revision of standards based on feedback from experts and stakeholders; (c) aligned systems that ensure adequate implementation and assessment;

and (d) adequate resources. The Early Childhood Technical Assistance Center (ECTA) provides updated information about state standards, including links to standards for each state: http://ectacenter.org/portal/ecdata.asp#standards. Standards can be particularly important for assisting practitioners in determining whether certain behaviors are developmentally appropriate and for sharing that information with other stakeholders such as parents. For example, it may be important to share with parents when they have behavioral or learning expectations that are too developmentally advanced or to show parents which prerequisite skills are important for improving future learning.

Curricula

A curriculum is a tool that includes the content for teaching. Many curricula also include specific strategies and a criterion-referenced assessment tool. A curriculum specifies the scope (what is taught) and the sequence (when it is taught) of instruction. The NAEYC recommends that a curriculum promotes learning across domains (social, emotional, physical, language, and cognitive skills; NAEYC, 2018). Generally, curricula are professionally published and available for purchase. Some commonly used early childhood curricula include High Scope, Creative Curriculum (Teaching Strategies, 2010), and the Assessment, Evaluation, and Programming System (Bricker, 2002), which are comprehensive curricula including sequences of skills across a variety of domains, guidance regarding teaching strategies, and assessments. Generally, these curricula are used to guide instruction for a group of children (e.g., a class), although modifications should be made as needed. Some comprehensive curricula also exist specifically for children with disabilities; these curricula are commonly individual in nature—that is, they specify the scope and sequence of learning for a single child rather than a group of children. Examples of commonly used individual curricula are the STAR program and the Verbal Behavior Milestones Assessment and Placement Program (VB-MAPP). However, even when individual curricula are used, consideration should be given to *individualized* selection of the target goals that are important for each child and their family.

Ecological Assessments

In coordination with learning standards and curricula, ecological assessments are helpful tools for determining which behaviors would be useful for a child to demonstrate in their current contexts. Ecological assessments focus on the environment and how children's behaviors influence, and are influenced by, the environment around them. An ecological congruence assessment (Wolery, Brashers, & Neitzel, 2002) is designed to determine what activities a child engages in during the school day, whether their participation is different from their peers', whether they require more support than their peers, what supports might be needed, and whether the child lacks skills needed to engage in the activity. Then the team can determine to what extent differences are acceptable, what supports are needed, and what skills the child needs to learn. This process is highly individualized, and prioritizes the behavior of the child in contexts in which they typically learn, rather than according to a pre-determined sequence. See Appendix 2.1 for a sample data collection form for the ecological assessment process.

Family Priorities

In combination with the above procedures, family priorities should always be considered when identifying HPLOs. When teaching children in their own homes, the Routines-Based

Interview (McWilliam, Casey, & Sims, 2009) can be used to identify family priorities for teaching their children in the context of typical routines. When determining objectives to be taught in a different setting such as in school, teachers should explicitly ask parents for specific information about their priorities for their child's learning. These will vary quite widely by family—for example, for two 4-year-old students in the same classroom, one family might be highly interested in their child acquiring pre-academic skills and pre-requisite behaviors while another might be primarily concerned with social-emotional skills and peer interactions.

Categorizing Behavior

Most behaviors across domains can be categorized as *discrete* or *chained*. After discussing these types of behaviors, we discuss behavioral definitions that are topographical versus functional in nature and describe the importance of response patterns.

Discrete behaviors are single, observable actions that are brief in duration. Many pre-requisite, pre-academic, and social behaviors are discrete in nature. **Chained behaviors** are series of discrete behaviors that are combined in specific ways. Many movement, self-help, and play behaviors are chained. For these behaviors, completion of one step serves as a **discriminative stimulus** for the initiation of the next step (e.g., it signals that the next step should be started). For example, turning off the water during handwashing is the stimulus that cues an individual to get a paper towel, and putting a baby doll in a bathtub can serve as the discriminative stimulus to pick up the sponge to "wash" the baby. Table 2.2 provides examples of specific discrete and chained behaviors that are common in early childhood settings.

It is important to carefully define desirable behaviors, regardless of whether they are discrete or chained; thus, practitioners should carefully consider the **topography** of these behaviors, which refers to what the behaviors look like. For example, if desirable behavior is for a child to request desired items during play, the desired topography might be for the child to vocalize "I want that, please" while physically pointing to the object. This topography should be carefully defined, so that implementers can teach and reinforce the desired behavior and so that changes in the behavior can be reliably measured. Generally, **reliable** measurement means that two people could measure the same behavior and come to the same conclusion. For example, without that specific topographical definition, one observer might determine that a child vocalizing "That?" was an instance of the desired behavior while a different observer might determine that the behavior was *not* an instance because it was not sufficiently clear.

Although topography is critical to determining what exactly is being taught and how it should be measured, **function** is also important. Function can be thought of as the reason

Table 2.2 Common Discrete and Chained Behaviors

Discrete Skills	Chained Behaviors
Naming colors	Handwashing
Selecting a named picture from an array of 3	Putting toys in bins and then on the shelf
Imitating an action with an object	Putting a spoon in a pot, stirring, and
Responding to a peer greeting by saying "hi"	putting the spoon near a doll's mouth
Responding to a peer request for a share by handing the object or saying "OK, when I'm done"	Using a slide (climbing up stairs, sitting at top, pushing self down)

for the behavior or the change the behavior causes in the environment. Behaviors that serve the same function are referred to as a single **response class**. For example, you might greet a friend by waving, giving a hug, or saying "Hi!"—these are members of the same response class although they are topographically different. We sometimes want children to engage in a behavior with a specified function (e.g., greet peers, select a stimulus from an array) but find a variety of topographies acceptable (e.g., wave or say "hi," point to or pick up the correct stimulus). All topographies of the response class that are considered correct should be specified in the behavioral definition.

Response patterns refer to a generalized pattern of responding—that is, given certain contexts, a child demonstrates a certain type of reaction. Many behaviors in the *prerequisites for school success* category are response patterns, such as demonstrating persistence and independence. These behaviors are topographically different across situations (e.g., to demonstrate persistence, a child builds a new block tower when an original tower falls or uses a different request when an initial one was misunderstood by teachers). When measuring progress over time, it is more difficult to quantify response patterns in comparison to specific discrete and chained behaviors. However, practitioners may measure a proxy of the response pattern by identifying and defining specific situations in which children can be taught to engage in behaviors indicative of the pattern. For example, a practitioner could specify a learning objective that involves a child attempting to repair a communication error by using different words or gestures (persistence), or could specify that a child followed at least three different group directions across at least three different classroom activities (following directions).

It may be somewhat difficult to set expectations regarding response patterns. For example, following verbal directions is an important response pattern that helps teachers safely supervise multiple children at once, as is common in early childhood settings. However, too narrow a focus on compliance could leave young children, especially those with additional risk factors such as communication delays, at-risk for bullying or abuse. Similarly, persistence can be an important response pattern, but it is also important to teach children that there are alternatives to persistence in some contexts (e.g., asking for help rather than continuing to attempt an action alone, moving to a different activity when frustrated by a block tower that falls rather than continuing to repair the tower).

Task Analysis

Task analysis refers to the process of breaking down complex skills into smaller parts (Szidon & Franzone, 2009). It can also refer to the resulting list of smaller parts. Task analysis was a major breakthrough in the early years of educating individuals with considerable motor or cognitive disabilities; it allowed practitioners to teach students (usually those residing in institutions) who were previously considered "uneducable" (Schworm, 1979). Even skills that seem somewhat simple to adults such as moving from a seated to a standing position actually involve numerous steps, all of which are critical to the success of the behavior. Most references to task analysis (Schuster, Gast, Wolery, & Guiltinan, 1988; Smith, Shepley, Alexander, & Ayres, 2015) in the literature refer to the task analysis of chained behaviors—also referred to as perceptual-motor task analyses. However, task analysis is also relevant when teaching complex objectives that involve multiple discrete behaviors—also referred to as symbolic-conceptual task analyses (Schworm, 1979). Table 2.3 below shows examples of the task analysis of one chained behavior and one pre-academic skill involving discrete behaviors. When task-analyzing chained behaviors, there are several potential avenues for producing steps (Wolery, 2012).

1. *Observing another child.* Especially when complex motor movements are involved, this option is a preferable one—for example, if you are interested in teaching a 4-year-old with motor delays to transition from sitting to standing, it would be beneficial to watch another young child who has recently become proficient in this behavior because this child is likely to engage in some compensatory strategies that adults do not need or could not engage in.

2. *Observing an adult or yourself.* In some cases, you might not have access to observing another child engage in the desired behavior. In this case, it might be helpful to observe an adult engage in the behavior, or to engage in the behavior yourself, and write down all of the steps used to complete the task. This might be especially appropriate when teaching children to engage in classroom activities, such as opening a specific program on the classroom computer.

3. *Use published curricula or resources.* Some curricula offer task analyses for commonly taught behaviors (e.g., Links, Verbal Behavior Milestones Assessment and Placement Program [VB-MAPP]). These are appropriate, especially as initial references, although you might find that modifications are needed. For example, task analyses for washing hands necessarily differ based on the mechanisms for turning on the water and accessing a paper towel or hand dryer.

4. *Use a logical analysis.* In some instances, you might want to task-analyze a behavior for which observations or other resources are not available. For example, you might want to teach children to engage in a specific classroom routine at the beginning of the school year, such as lining up on the playground and walking inside or putting away materials and signing in during the morning routine. Rather than observation or using published materials, you can analyze what steps are needed to successfully complete these behaviors.

When task-analyzing complex sets of discrete skills, you should generally use a logical analysis. The following steps should be used to complete the task analysis:

1. *Define the behaviors to be taught* (e.g., name all letters in the alphabet, point to eight different shapes from a field of three).

2. *Determine the size of the group to be taught simultaneously.* For example, for a child who is having difficulty learning letter names, teaching all or even half of the letters simultaneously is unlikely to be effective. Instead, start with a small set (two or three letters). You should always teach at least two discrete behaviors at the same time (Doyle, Wolery, Ault, Gast, & Wiley, 1989). For example, never teach a child to only name one letter or only point to one shape; teach them to name two letters or point to two shapes, using alternating trials (e.g., sometimes ask them to name the letter R and sometimes ask them to name the letter N). You should choose the initial group by identifying two stimuli (or behaviors) that are very different. For example, when choosing two letters to teach, A and K would be difficult initial letters because they share some visual similarities (diagonal lines) and auditory similarities (i.e., they "sound" alike). O and K or A and P would be better initial pairs. Note that in Table 2.3, two easily discriminable colors are taught first, with more similar colors (blue/purple, black/brown) taught later.

3. *Set a mastery criterion.* This will determine when you can add new stimuli to the teaching set. For example, you might teach the letters O and K until the child demonstrates 100 percent correct naming of those two letters for three consecutive days.

4. *Determine the order of introduction of the remaining behaviors.* For example, after a child has met the mastery criterion for the first two letters, in what order will the remaining letters be introduced for teaching?

Table 2.3 Task Analysis of Chained and Discrete Behaviors

Handwashing (Chained)	Naming 8 Colors (Discrete)
1. Turn knob to turn water on 2. Put one hand under soap dispenser 3. Push soap dispenser button with other hand 4. Rub hands together for 3–5 seconds 5. Put hands under water 6. Continue to rub hands together 7. When soap is removed, turn knob to turn water off 8. Pull paper towel from dispenser 9. Rub paper towel over hands 10. Place paper towel in trashcan	When presented in isolation, with intermixed trials: 1. Name "red" and "yellow" 2. Name "red," "yellow," "green," and "purple" 3. Name "red," "yellow," "green," "purple," "blue," and "orange" 4. Name "red," "yellow," "green," "purple," "blue," "orange," "brown," and "black"

5. *Determine the schedule of instruction for mastered behaviors.* Following mastery, teachers should consider intermittently including mastered behaviors into instruction. For example, if a child reached mastery for naming the letters O and K, a teacher might move on to teaching letters A and P. The teacher should consider intermittently including O and K during instruction on A and P, to provide additional opportunities to respond to learned material.

It is important to note that task analysis is *not* a teaching strategy. Instead, it is a strategy for organizing and ordering behaviors to be taught, prior to teaching.

Assessing Chained Behaviors

Before beginning teaching, as part of some teaching strategies (i.e., simultaneous prompting, see Chapter 9), and to assess maintenance of a behavior once instruction has stopped, practitioners need to assess the extent to which children can engage in targeted behaviors, without any assistance. Discrete behaviors can be assessed in a relatively straightforward manner—that is, you provide an opportunity to respond, and record whether the behavior occurred correctly. For chained behaviors, assessment is more complex. For example, if you only provide the initial discriminative stimulus for the chain, and the child does not engage in the first behavior correctly, you might consider reporting that the child engaged in 0 percent correct responding. This type of assessment is called a **single opportunity probe** (SOP), and it ends immediately when a child performs the first step incorrectly. However, given this type of assessment, it is possible that you underestimate a child's performance—for example, given the example in Table 2.3, it might be possible that the child can engage in 90 percent of the steps correctly but does not yet initiate turning the water on (Step 1). To prevent this underestimation, you can conduct a **multiple opportunity probe** (MOP). MOPs involve providing an opportunity to complete all steps to measure whether the child correctly completes each one. Given the handwashing example, if the child did not turn the water on, the assessor would complete Step 1 (the discriminative stimulus for Step 2) and provide an opportunity to complete Step 2. If the child completed Step 2, then the assessor would determine whether the child completed Step 3. If not, the assessor would complete Step 3 to provide the discriminative stimulus to complete Step 4 (and so on). This assessment is more conservative than an SOP, but requires additional time. In terms of research studies, authors have probably avoided MOP because it provides the student with opportunities to learn the task observationally; however, in practice, it is efficient and desirable if a child learns during assessment. A third option, the

natural opportunity probe (NOP), has been suggested (Alexander, Ayres, Shepley, Smith, & Ledford, 2017). During this probe, rather than providing a brief interval for completion of the first step, the assessor would provide a longer interval and would record any steps completed correctly. For example, during the SOP, the assessor would discontinue the assessment if the child attempted to retrieve a paper towel as the first step. But, during an NOP, the child would be allowed to continue the process—if he followed retrieving the towel by turning on the water, that step would be considered correct. NOPs may provide reasonable estimates of behavior occurrence under typical conditions. All three procedures for assessing chained behaviors are depicted in Figure 2.1.

As you may have noticed given the NOP and SOP descriptions, when assessing the performance of chained behaviors, the sequence of behaviors is an important consideration. For example, in Table 2.3, handwashing could be correctly completed if the child put hands under water both before and after getting soap (complete step 5, then 3 and 4, then 5 again), and the child could get a paper towel and use it to turn off the water (complete

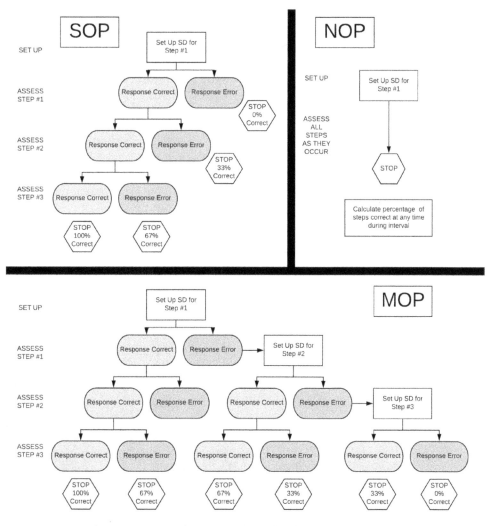

Figure 2.1 Steps for Assessing a Three-step Chained Behavior via the SOP (Single Opportunity Probe), NOP (Natural Opportunity Probe), and MOP (Multiple Opportunity Probe).

step 8 and then 7). Generally, you should teach chained behaviors in a specific sequence, but also plan in advance to count as correct reasonable variations in responding. As we discuss in Chapter 4, it is also important to plan for generalization—that is, to teach children to correctly complete steps with stimuli with a range of characteristics (for example, teaching handwashing given a soap dispenser that requires pushing a lever versus pulling a lever, or teaching color-naming in the context of simple pictures in a book and with toy cars).

Writing Objectives

Once a behavior has been selected as an HPLO, teachers should write measurable objectives so that progress can be regularly assessed. Pretti-Frontczak and Bricker (2000) provide four characteristics of high-quality individualized objectives. First, objectives should be **functional**—that is, they should be meaningful in the child's everyday life. Second, objectives should be *general* rather than specific—for example, rather than specifying that a child take a turn with a specific toy, goals should target turn-taking more generally, so that the skill is useful in a variety of contexts. Third, the *context of instruction* should allow for frequent opportunities for the child to learn the behavior. Finally, the goal should be **measurable**—that is, an observer could watch and reliably determine whether it happened. Similarly, Boavida, Aguiar, and McWilliam (2014) specify that goals should be *measurable* and *functional*. They also indicate that objectives should contain criteria related to *acquisition* (i.e., how we will know when it is mastered) and *timeframe* (i.e., when mastery is expected). Some authors have used the acronym SMART to determine whether objectives have the necessary components—*specific* (e.g., contains acquisition criterion), *measurable*, *attainable*, *relevant* (i.e., functional), and *time-based* (i.e., contains a timeframe criterion). We should note that some objectives might require a higher mastery criterion than others—having a single criterion (e.g., 80 percent accuracy across three days) for all objectives is not reasonable. After selecting HPLOs for children and writing measurable objectives, you can begin to consider reinforcement and select teaching procedures, the focus of the next several chapters.

After reading the early learning standards for her state, Marti decides to talk with the parents of each child in her classroom to determine family priorities. She also conducts an ecological assessment for each child, noting their strengths and needs throughout the school day. After doing this, she feels more confident in identifying some prerequisite behaviors to teach some children right away to improve their ability to learn, and some additional skills that she hadn't previously considered teaching, especially in the social-emotional and play domains. She feels that this process has allowed her to identify more meaningful goals for each child, which will lead to more focused teaching and better child outcomes.

References

Alexander, J. L., Ayres, K. M., Shepley, S. B., Smith, K. A., & Ledford, J. R. (2017). Comparison of probe procedures in the assessment of chained tasks. *The Psychological Record*, 67, 547–557.

Barton, E. E., & Ledford, J. R. (2018). The effects of reinforcement on peer imitation in a small group play context. *Journal of Early Intervention*, 40, 69–86.

Beaulieu, L., Hanley, G. P., & Roberson, A. A. (2012). Effects of responding to a name and group call on preschoolers' compliance. *Journal of Applied Behavior Analysis*, 45, 685–707.

Boavida, T., Aguiar, C., & McWilliam, R. A. (2014). A training program to improve IFSP/IEP goals and objectives through the routines-based interview. *Topics in Early Childhood Special Education*, 33, 200–211.

Bricker, D. (2002). *Assessment, evaluation, and programming system*. Baltimore, MD: Brookes.

Doyle, P. M., Wolery, M., Ault, M. J., Gast, D. L., & Wiley, K. (1989). Establishing conditional discriminations: Concurrent versus isolation-intermix instruction. *Research in Developmental Disabilities*, 10, 349–362.

IDEA (Individuals with Disabilities Education Act) of 1997, 20 U.S.C. § 1400 *et seq.* (1997).

Individuals with Disabilities Education Improvement Act (IDEIA) of 2004, 20 U.S.C. § 1400 *et seq.* (2004).

Ledford, J. R., & Wolery, M. (2011). Teaching imitation to young children with disabilities: A review of the literature. *Topics in Early Childhood Special Education*, 30, 245–255.

McWilliam, R. A., Casey, A. M., & Sims, J. (2009). The routines-based interview: A method for gathering information and assessing needs. *Infants & Young Children*, 22, 224–233.

National Association for the Education of Young Children (NAEYC). (2018). The 10 NAEYC Program Standards. Retrieved from www.naeyc.org/our-work/families/10-naeyc-program-standards.

Pretti-Frontczak, K., & Bricker, D. (2000). Enhancing the quality of individualized education plan (IEP) goals and objectives. *Journal of Early Intervention*, 23, 92–105.

Rogers, S. J., Hepburn, S. L., Stackhouse, T., & Wehner, E. (2003). Imitation performance in toddlers with autism and those with other developmental disorders. *Journal of Child Psychology and Psychiatry*, 44, 763–781.

Romski, M., & Sevcik, R. A. (2005). Augmentative communication and early intervention: Myths and realities. *Infants & Young Children*, 18, 174–185.

Romski, M., Sevcik, R. A., Barton-Hulsey, A., & Whitmore, A. S. (2015). Early intervention and AAC: What a difference 30 years makes. *Augmentative and Alternative Communication*, 31, 181–202.

Romski, M. A., Sevcik, R. A., Cheslock, M. A., & Barton-Hulsey, A. (2017). The system for augmenting language. In R. J. McCauley, M. E. Fey, & R. B. Gillam (Eds.), *Treatment of language disorders in children* (2nd ed.) (pp. 155–186). Baltimore, MD: Brookes.

Schuster, J. W., Gast, D. L., Wolery, M., & Guiltinan, S. (1988). The effectiveness of a constant time-delay procedure to teach chained responses to adolescents with mental retardation. *Journal of Applied Behavior Analysis*, 21, 169–178.

Schworm, R. (1979). Task analysis in special education: Definition and clarification. *Journal of Special Education Technology*, 2, 37–44.

Sennott, S. C., Light, J. C., & McNaughton, D. (2016). AAC modeling intervention research review. *Research and Practice for Persons with Severe Disabilities*, 41, 101–115.

Smith, K. A., Shepley, S. B., Alexander, J. L., & Ayres, K. M. (2015). The independent use of self-instructions for the acquisition of untrained multi-step tasks for individuals with an intellectual disability: A review of the literature. *Research in Developmental Disabilities*, 40, 19–30.

Stone, W. L., Ousley, O. Y., & Littleford, C. D. (1997). Motor imitation in young children with autism: What's the object? *Journal of Abnormal Child Psychology*, 25, 475–485.

Sweeney, E., Barton, E. E., & Ledford, J. R. (2018). Using progressive time delay to increase levels of peer imitation during sculpting play. *Journal of Autism and Developmental Disorders*. doi: 10.1007/s10803-018-3638-2.

Szidon, K., & Franzone, E. (2009). Task analysis. Madison, WI: National Professional Development Center on Autism Spectrum Disorders, Waisman Center, University of Wisconsin.

Teaching Strategies (2010). *The creative curriculum* (4th ed.). Bethesda, MD: Teaching Strategies.

Thurm, A., Lord, C., Lee, L., & Newschaffer, C. (2007). Predictors of language acquisition in pre-school children with autism spectrum disorders. *Journal of Autism and Developmental Disorders*, 37, 1721–1734.

Tostanoski, A., Lang, R., Raulston, T., Carnett, A., & Davis, T. (2014). Voices from the past: Comparing the rapid prompting method and facilitated communication. *Developmental Neurorehabilitation*, 17, 219–223.

Venn, M. L., Wolery, M., Werts, M. G., Morris, A., DeCesare, L. D., & Cuffs, M. S. (1993). Embedding instruction in art activities to teach preschoolers with disabilities to imitate their peers. *Early Childhood Research Quarterly*, 8, 277–294.

Wolery, M. (October, 2012). Task analysis. Unpublished presentation. SPED 3400, Vanderbilt University.

Wolery, M., & Hemmeter, M. L. (2011). Classroom instruction: Background, assumptions, and challenges. *Journal of Early Intervention*, 33, 371–380.

Wolery, M., Brashers, M., & Neitzel, J. C. (2002). Ecological congruence assessment for classroom activities and routines: Identifying goals and intervention practices in childcare. *Topics in Early Childhood Special Education*, 22, 131–142.

APPENDIX 2.1

Observer: _____ Child name: _____ Date: _____

General Notes, including number of adults and children present.

Time	Activity	Assistance	Congruence	Skills Needed
Use a new row each time a child's activity, assistance, or congruence changes	Name of what is happening.	How much help is provided? Is the help individual or group? Are other children receiving similar help?	Is the child doing the same thing as some or all other children?	What new behaviors does the child need to learn to successfully participate in this activity?

3 Reinforcement, Rewards, and Praise

Key Terms

Behavior	*Challenging behavior*	*Antecedents*
Consequences	*Reinforcement*	*Reinforcer*
Tangible reinforcement	*Attention*	*Escape*
Socially mediated	*Automatic reinforcement*	*Contingent*
Non-contingent	*Reward*	*Preferred*
Non-preferred	*Praise*	*General praise*
Behavior-specific praise	*Preference assessment*	*Reinforcer assessment*

Chapter Objectives

After completing this chapter, readers should be able to:

- Explain the differences among the terms rewards, praise, and reinforcers.
- Identify reinforcement as the primary agent of behavior increases.
- Explain how to introduce and use reinforcement-based procedures.
- Describe circumstances under which praise may and may not function as a reinforcer.
- Justify why reinforcement is a critical consideration in early childhood contexts.
- Describe procedures for conducting paired stimulus, concurrent operants, and multiple stimulus preference assessments.
- Explain how the use of preference and reinforcer assessments is aligned with current recommended practices by national early childhood organizations.

Judy is a teacher in a rural Head Start classroom. Children in her classroom spend much of their day engaging in child-led play activities, but she also conducts some structured, developmentally appropriate small group activities that are teacher-led. She is concerned that Charlie, a young girl with Down syndrome in her classroom, does not participate well in child-led play activities. She often requires frequent prompting and adult involvement to appropriately manipulate materials and communicate with her peers. Judy is particularly worried because Charlie has demonstrated that she can do these things during structured activities, but does not do them on her own.

Given that children are attending high-quality settings and teachers have appropriately identified high-priority learning objectives (HPLOs), the next step is to determine how to teach these valuable behaviors to children. **Behaviors** are any observable actions performed by a student. A behavior may be desirable (e.g., responding to peer initiations, playing appropriately with toys) or problematic/challenging (e.g., biting or grabbing toys from other children). Although some people may refer to *behavior* colloquially as behavior that is problematic, when referring to undesirable behaviors, we will use the more precise term **challenging behavior**—the term *behavior* alone is neutral.

Why do children engage in certain behaviors? To answer that question, we should consider both the events that occur before the behavior (**antecedents**) and after the behavior (**consequences**). Antecedents can take on many topographies, or forms. For example, a child may begin cleaning up immediately after he hears a teacher say, "Time to clean up!" or following observation of a peer engaging in similar behaviors. Alternatively, he might have finished with a specific set of toys, and may clean up because of a history of feedback or other positive consequences occurring after he cleans up (for example, praise from a teacher or permission to engage in a different preferred activity). Children generally engage in voluntary behaviors due to previous contact with associated antecedents and consequences.

Reinforcement

Reinforcement refers to the occurrence of an event (**reinforcer**) immediately following a behavior that increases the likelihood that the same behavior will occur in the future. Note that reinforcement is specific to a behavior: thus, it is correct to say that you reinforce a behavior—not that you reinforce a child. Systematically and contingently providing reinforcing consequences is consistent with Recommended Practices of the Division for Early Childhood of the Council for Exceptional Children (INS7, INT1, INT3).

Reinforcers can take many forms. One common type of reinforcer is access to tangibles, or items (**tangible reinforcement**). Providing stickers, toys, snacks, activities, or other items could serve as tangible reinforcement. Another common type of reinforcement is attention (**social reinforcement**). Provision of praise, verbal comments, hugs, and high-fives are all examples of social events that could serve as reinforcers and might be provided by adults or peers. One type of reinforcement that may not be as obvious is **escape** from attention or activities. For example, allowing a child to leave an activity or allowing him to engage in an activity independently (escaping teacher proximity) may serve as reinforcers. All of these types of reinforcers are referred to as **socially mediated** reinforcers because another human typically provides or mediates access to, or escape from, tangibles or attention. A common class of reinforcers—stereotypy—is often not socially mediated. That is, a child provides that behavior to him or herself. Stereotypy is commonly associated with individuals with autism spectrum disorder (ASD) and refers to repetitive behaviors that appear to be non-purposeful (e.g., rocking, tapping fingers on forehead). Most infants and young children engage in some stereotypy and many adults also do so (e.g., biting fingernails, twirling hair); the extent to which this behavior might be considered undesirable is related to the frequency and intensity with which it is performed and the extent to which it interferes with other activities. We refer to stereotypy as being **automatically** reinforced—this means that the behaviors themselves were preferred rather than being reinforced by an outside source. Although engaging in stereotypy and repetitive behaviors is generally automatically reinforced, these behaviors can also be sensitive to social consequences—that is, some children may engage in stereotypy because of a history of escape (e.g., adults allow a child to avoid other children when they engage in stereotypy) or attention (e.g., adults provide verbal attention when a child engages in stereotypy). Other examples of reinforcers that are not *necessarily* socially mediated are food, drink, and rest, all of which can be self-delivered.

Reinforcement can also be categorized as *positive* or *negative*. Positive reinforcement is the provision of preferred items and activities, such as providing a favorite form of social attention when a child appropriately engages in a non-preferred activity for a certain amount of time. Negative reinforcement is the removal of non-preferred items and activities, such as allowing a child to leave a non-preferred activity after he has appropriately engaged in the activity for a certain amount of time. In both cases, the outcome is that the desirable behavior (appropriate engagement) increases. For example, when a child engages in a non-preferred activity appropriately for several minutes, a teacher might provide him with a preferred toy (*positive* reinforcement) or allow him to leave the activity (*negative* reinforcement). Negative reinforcement *should not be confused with punishment.* Effective practitioners systematically use both negative and positive reinforcement.

Contingent Reinforcement

Anytime a specific consequence results in increased likelihood of a behavior occurring, that consequence is considered to be a reinforcer, regardless of whether the consequence was *intended* to be a reinforcer. Table 3.1 shows three examples of reinforcement in different contexts. Note that reinforcement can occur even when the provider of the consequence is unaware of his or her behavior or intends the opposite effect. Reinforcement occurs on a behavior-specific and individual-specific basis. That is, the same consequence

Table 3.1 Examples of Reinforcement in an Early Childhood Classroom

Child Behavior	Adult Intention	Consequence	Outcome
A child with low social competence has been attempting to initiate appropriate interactions with peers, like offering them toys	Teacher wants to encourage continued use of initiations (increase likelihood initiations will occur)	Teacher begins providing effusive praise for initiations, such as "Wow! Myles! I'm so happy that you are sharing toys with Charlotte!"	Child begins initiating more frequent initiations (praise served as a positive reinforcer for initiations)
A child with a low tolerance for waiting has been frequently taking toys away from peers without requesting them	Teacher wants to discourage grabbing toys (decrease likelihood that child will grab toys without asking for them)	Teacher begins providing a brief "time out" for the child, which consists of a one-to-one conversation with the teacher about why grabbing behavior is unkind	Child begins grabbing toys more frequently (attention from adult in form of conversation served as a positive reinforcer for grabbing)
A toddler throws food on the ground during lunch time	Teacher does not replace food (does not intend to change behavior occurrence)	Child escapes from having non-preferred food on his plate, and from trying it	Child throws non-preferred foods on ground more often and other toddlers start to imitate him (escape from non-preferred food served as a negative reinforcer for throwing)

might result in future increases in one behavior but not another and the same consequence might result in future increases in a behavior for one child but not another. For example, the provision of praise might result in increases in social initiations, but not increases in successful toileting. Likewise, the provision of praise might result in increased independent handwashing for one child but not another—this may occur even for children who are similar in age, temperament, and ability. To make things even more complicated, the same consequence may serve as a reinforcer for a specific behavior for a given child at one time, but may not serve as a reinforcer at a later time. Even preferred items and activities may not consistently serve as reinforcers; see information later in the chapter about assessing preferences and reinforcers.

Reinforcement can be related or unrelated to the desirable behavior it follows. Some approaches, such as activity-based intervention (Johnson, Rahn, & Bricker, 2015) or incidental teaching (Hart & Risley, 1975), require the use of related reinforcers. For example, if a child's most preferred tangible items were small toy cars, and one instructional objective was to name colors, the child might be asked to name the color of a car, and when he provided the name of the color, be given access to the car. In some approaches, such as direct instruction with massed trials, the reinforcers chosen are often unrelated to the instructional task. For example, a teacher might ask a child to name the color of a small manipulative, and might provide a toy car when the child named the color. When possible, use of related reinforcers is generally preferred (e.g., use cars in a color-naming task, rather than counters). For some children with restricted interests, poor play skills, or few identified reinforcers, use of unrelated reinforcers may be more feasible and may result in faster learning. For example, a child with ASD who enjoys lining up cars might become upset if cars were manipulated by adults and provided contingently on correct responding. Similarly, for a child who was primarily interested in cars, it might be difficult to provide related reinforcement when teaching a wide variety of behaviors. Sometimes reinforcers are selected because they do not interrupt the instruction or interactions, which can increase the efficiency of learning. For example, Barton and Ledford (2018) chose to provide reinforcement in the form of stickers during a small group activity designed to promote peer imitation, rather than a more highly preferred item (a toy wand), because the stickers were less likely to interfere with play behaviors during the small group activity. It is important to remember that the *effectiveness* of the reinforcer is more important than the *relatedness* (see information for identifying effective items or activities likely to be reinforcing later in this chapter).

Non-Contingent Reinforcement

Generally, reinforcement is provided **contingent** on a specific behavior—that is, the reinforcer is provided immediately following a behavior. The goal is to increase that behavior's occurrence (desirable behavior). Another, lesser-used, type of reinforcement is **non-contingent** reinforcement (NCR). NCR refers to the provision of a preferred item/activity or removal of a non-preferred item/activity that is unrelated to the occurrence of the target desirable behavior. NCR is particularly helpful when high rates of reinforcement prevent problematic behaviors from occurring. For example, consider two approaches described below:

Scenario #1: Contingent Reinforcement

Charlotte often grabs toys from her peers, resulting in the peer crying or grabbing the toy back *and* teacher attention. The teacher decides to notice and respond when Charlotte requests a toy instead of grabbing. When she does so, the teacher provides verbal and physical attention. Charlotte begins grabbing toys less often.

Scenario #2: Non-Contingent Reinforcement

Charlotte often grabs toys from her peers, resulting in the peer crying or grabbing the toy back *and* teacher attention. The teacher decides to provide frequent attention in the form of playing with Charlotte *regardless of what she is doing*, rather than providing the attention only when she engages in challenging behavior. Charlotte begins grabbing toys less often.

In both approaches, the teacher shifted from providing contingent reinforcement for challenging behavior (providing attention when Charlotte grabbed toys) to providing either contingent reinforcement for desirable behaviors (providing attention for requests) or non-contingent reinforcement (providing frequent attention regardless of behavior). Providing non-contingent reinforcement, especially when the overall rate of reinforcement in a given context is low, is one reinforcement option. When appropriate behavior occurs infrequently, use of contingent reinforcement for those behaviors may not be effective. However, as will be discussed more in depth in later chapters, providing contingent reinforcement may be both preferred by children and more effective when teaching new behaviors.

Reinforcement, Rewards, and Praise: Similarities and Differences

As described above, reinforcement is defined based on the effect a given consequence has on the future occurrence of behaviors. Rewards are different than reinforcers—the term **reward** generally refers to escape from, or access to, tangibles or attention that are intended by the provider to be positive. Thus, rewards are typically based on the provider's expectations regarding items or activities perceived as being preferred by children. **Preferred** items and activities are those that the child would choose to engage with. **Non-preferred** items and activities are those that the child would not choose to engage with—this term is relative; for example, working out may be non-preferred relative to reading a book but preferred relative to commuting to work.

Especially for young children, it is usually most effective to provide preferred items or activities immediately following a desirable behavior. However, in addition to the immediate provision of preferred items or activities (or removal of non-preferred items or activities), rewards can also indicate that preferred activities will be available in the future. For example, teachers can provide a child with a token for each successful and independent classroom transition. This token is not, in and of itself, a preferred item. However, it indicates that a preferred item or activity will be available in the future. For example, after receipt of five tokens, a child might gain access to the opportunity to engage with a preferred game on a tablet or visit a preferred adult in the adjoining classroom. A critical component of these delayed reward systems is that children should be taught how to use them, since tokens themselves are not inherently meaningful or preferred. Teaching token-based systems should include explicit instruction and a systematic procedure for ensuring early access to success, with gradually increasing requirements. Figure 3.1 shows potential steps for teaching young children to use two different token-based systems.

Early childhood practitioners often use **praise** statements, defined as statements that explicitly provide approval for a child's behavior. **General praise** statements provide approval without specifically stating the reason for the approval (e.g., "Good job!").

Example #1: Improving engagement in small group activities	*Example #2: Improving responding during individual instruction*
Goal: Ms. Staisha, a Head Start teacher, would like Kenton to attend and participate during daily 10-minute small group activities related to the unit of study.	**Goal:** Ms. Amey, an itinerant special education teacher, would like Juan correctly name photos of his friends during individual instruction. She will teach generalized use of the behavior during communicative interactions in free play.
Token System: Ms. Staisha will set an interval timer prior to the activity. When the timer vibrates, she will provide a token to Kenton if he is in his assigned area and appropriately manipulating materials, attending to her, or watching his peers.	**Token System:** Ms. Amey will provide a token for correct responses to the question: "Who is this?".
Instruction: Ms. Staisha explains to Kenton that he will earn tokens for appropriate behavior. She plans a practice session during free play, a time when Kenton has high rates of appropriate behavior.	**Instruction:** Ms. Amey plans a practice session similar to an instructional session, but with photos of known adults. When Juan replies correctly to the question "Who is this?" related to the known photos, he earns a token.
Increasing Requirements: Ms. Staisha begins by providing Kenton a token at the first opportunity during a small group activity. She then immediately tells him he can exchange the token for a sticker (an item known to be preferred by Kenton) and he is allowed to leave the activity. She systematically increases the requirement to 2, 3, 4, and then 5 tokens.	**Increasing Requirements:** Ms. Amey begins by providing a token for every correct response and provides the tablet (an item identified as preferred) after Juan earns 5 tokens. Then, she requires 6, 8, and 10 tokens prior to the terminal reward. Finally, she begins thinning reinforcement by giving a token for every *other* correct response.

Figure 3.1 Sample Steps for Using Token Systems.

Behavior-specific praise does provide explicit information (e.g., "I like how you said 'Thank you' to Alicia!"). The argument for using behavior-specific praise is that it provides children with more information; however, some research suggests differences in outcomes when general and behavior-specific praise are used are negligible (Stevens, Sidener, Reeve, & Sidener, 2011; Strain & Joseph, 2004). Moreover, the research on praise suggests mixed effects; that is, praise does not always serve as a reinforcer and in fact, may serve as a punisher (resulting in decreased desirable behaviors; Henderlong & Lepper, 2002). For children who are motivated by positive adult attention (i.e., who prefer praise), the provision of general or behavior-specific praise as reinforcement for desirable behaviors may be a helpful tool. Praise may be more effective for younger rather than older children (Corpus & Lepper, 2007). However, praise will not serve as a reinforcer for all behaviors, for all children, regardless of age.

When using praise, you should consider using the following guidelines:

1. Provide praise for important behaviors. Praise allows children to learn what behaviors are valued in their communities. To provide praise for behaviors that are important within the learning community, practitioners must be thoughtful about praise rather than doling it out liberally. Do you want to increase the extent to which all children in your class show kindness to their peers? Then purposefully and carefully praise those behaviors.

2.   Provide praise on an individual basis. For example, if you would like for one child to improve peer relations by using his peers' names, provide praise for that one child for engaging in that behavior.

3.   Avoid providing praise for behaviors that have already been established and behaviors that are inconsequential. For example, consider a teacher who provides praise each morning for each child who "signs in." While this might be reasonable at the beginning of a school year, it likely has no effect on child behavior as the year progresses. If the teacher intended the praise to serve as consistent positive feedback for children as they start their day, she might consider instead having a different meaningful interaction—for example, providing children with a choice of greeting (hug, high five, fist bump) or presenting a high-interest question of the day.

4.   Do not use praise as a substitute for responsive interactions with children, and ensure your tone is genuine. Rather than saying, for example, "Good job," you might make a comment related to children's ongoing play, such as "I noticed you and Abby were sharing those trucks!" or "It looks like you and Abby may need some more room for all of your trucks." We discuss responsive interactions in depth in Chapter 7.

5.   Provide process praise (praise for specific behaviors), rather than person praise (praise for attributes; Bayat, 2011). For example, instead of "Great job! You're so smart!" you might say "I noticed how long it took you to figure that out. Great job sticking with it!" Or, instead of "Good work. You're so strong," you might say "Good work. That was very heavy and you worked really hard to lift it!"

Schedules of Reinforcement

Good teaching requires the identification of **stimuli** (items or activities) to be used as reinforcers, and systematic use of these stimuli. Reinforcement can be provided according to a number of schedules, or rules. In some situations, reinforcement is provided contingent on desirable behaviors. For example, when a child requests a favorite snack, the snack (the reinforcer) can be provided immediately. Similarly, when a child correctly responds given an opportunity during small group, the teacher can immediately provide a token. Providing reinforcers for the occurrence of specific behaviors is referred to as a **ratio schedule**. Ratio schedules may be fixed or variable, meaning reinforcer delivery is predictable (fixed) or unpredictable (variable). Commonly used ratio schedules are FR1, FR2, and VR3. FR refers to a fixed ratio—under these schedules, reinforcement is provided for every behavior (FR1) or every second behavior (FR2). VR refers to a variable ratio—under these schedules, reinforcement is provided for *approximately* every third behavior (VR3). Variable ratio schedules are not less systematic—they are instead less predictable. If a teacher were conducting a short instructional session with nine opportunities to respond, and she used an FR3 schedule, she might provide a token after the 3rd, 6th, and 9th response. If she used a VR3 schedule, she might provide reinforcement after the 2nd, 6th, and 8th response or the 3rd, 5th, and 9th response. FR schedules may be easier to plan and implement, but VR schedules may encourage more consistent responding over time due to their unpredictability (i.e., children do not know whether their next response will result in provision of a reinforcer).

Effective Use of Reinforcers

General Guidelines

Bailey and Wolery (1992) provided the following guidelines for the use of reinforcement:

1. Identify items and activities that are truly reinforcing (i.e., will increase behaviors they follow).
2. Use embedded reinforcers. For example, if a child is interested in cars, teach color-naming during car play activities, and give the child access to more cars when he successfully names their color.
3. Select reinforcers that are easily delivered.
4. Choose reinforcers that are acceptable to families, teachers, and administrators.
5. Select reinforcers that are likely to be available in a child's typical environments.
6. Use a variety of reinforcers. This was also endorsed as an important strategy by the National Association for the Education of Young Children (NAEYC) and the Division for Early Childhood of the Council for Exceptional Children (DEC, 2014).
7. Provide reinforcement immediately after the child engages in the behavior.

Providing Frequent Choices

Generally, the effectiveness of reinforcers is improved when varied rewards are provided (Egel, 1981). Moreover, providing children with choice-making opportunities results in a number of positive outcomes (Dunlap et al., 1994; Dunlap & Liso, 2004). After identifying some preferred items (see Assessment, below), providing choices of potential reinforcers may result in improved performance relative to providing a single reinforcer for each opportunity, even if the single reinforcer is the most highly preferred. For example, if fish crackers are highly preferred for a child and cereal and raisins are moderately preferred, you might consider always offering a choice of rewards among those three items rather than always providing fish crackers.

Class-wide Reward Systems

Practitioners are often interested in providing reinforcers to several or many children, using a single system. This reduces effort on the part of the teacher, and may make the provision of reinforcement more feasible (Pokorski, Barton, & Ledford, 2017). Effective use of class-wide or other group reinforcement strategies is possible, although it is worth mentioning again that reinforcement is child- and behavior-specific. Below, we discuss two specific strategies: independent and interdependent group contingencies. Before using either type, you should (1) identify behaviors that will result in reinforcement, and (2) teach children to engage in those behaviors. Both independent and interdependent group contingencies are generally conducted via token-based rewards, although that is not necessary. These systems should not be used to identify or punish students who fail to meet a behavioral expectation.

Independent Group Contingencies

When independent group contingencies are used, target behaviors are identified and taught for the group as a whole, but rewards are provided individually. For example, a teacher might provide tokens to children who demonstrate appropriate peer social interaction behaviors during free play. Meeting this criterion may occur differently for different children—for example, a teacher might prompt a child with low social competence to respond to a peer request for sharing by saying "You can have it when I'm finished" and then provide a token contingent on that prompted response. Another child might independently provide a compliment to her peer, and that unprompted response could be reinforced via a token. Thus, all children are provided with rewards based on a targeted behavior, although the specific behavioral topography may be somewhat different for each child. Similarly, you can individualize the reward by providing choices. For example, children may be allowed to choose an item from a "treasure chest" when they receive five tokens.

Interdependent Group Contingencies

Interdependent group contingencies are different than independent group contingencies because reinforcers are provided to the group as a whole. For example, a teacher might provide small marbles to individual or groups of children for engaging in appropriate peer social interaction behaviors during free play. When the class has received a sufficient number of stones to fill a small container, the terminal reward is provided. The reward is class-wide, but should be individualized. For example, the class can earn an opportunity to open a treasure chest, and each child can choose his or her favorite toy or activity. Or, the class can earn a party, with options to play a variety of games, at least one of which is preferred for each child. Moreover, although each child can earn a marble for appropriate social behaviors, the exact behaviors may differ by child—one child may earn a marble for playing in proximity to his peers while another may earn a token for engaging in cooperative play and following game rules.

Guidelines

You should follow these guidelines when using group contingencies:

1. Choose a general target behavior for the group, but identify specific behaviors for each learner, which are within that learner's repertoire.
2. Do not attend to non-attainment. Reward systems can serve as punishment when children are singled out for failure to earn rewards. Instead, **identify reasonable goals for each child such that all children have the opportunity to succeed.**
3. Ensure adequate opportunities to earn tokens for all children. This involves identifying specific target behaviors that are in each learner's repertoire, and noticing and responding when learners engage in those behaviors. A highly socially competent child might interact with peers dozens of times in a school day, while a less socially competent child may interact much less frequently and thus reinforcing his social behaviors might require adults to more carefully plan to set up and support opportunities for success.
4. Ensure frequent access to the terminal reinforcer for all children. Group contingencies are unlikely to work effectively if children access the terminal reinforcer infrequently. Thus, especially in the early stages of implementation, you should provide frequent

opportunities to earn the terminal reinforcer. There is a dearth of research on the topic, but we believe that children should generally earn reinforcers daily, especially when the contingency is new. Over time, teachers may choose to reduce reinforcement opportunities such that children are earning the terminal reinforcers at least weekly, but we caution that too thin a schedule will result in ineffectiveness.

Research Abstract

Pokorski, E., Barton, E. E., & Ledford, J. R. (2017). Assessing the differential effects of known and mystery rewards in a preschool-based group contingency. *Journal of Early Intervention.*

In this single case design study, authors compared the use of known and mystery rewards when implementing group contingencies with groups of preschoolers including children with multiple and severe disabilities. These two variations of group contingency interventions were also compared to a baseline condition in which contingencies were unrelated to social interactions. Following a training session, children were provided with tokens for the first social interaction occurring in each 1-minute interval. During the "known" rewards condition, children were aware of the reward they would earn contingent on earned token. During the "mystery" rewards condition, children did not know what reward would be earned. There were no differences between the two intervention conditions—use of a group contingency with either known or mystery rewards increased initiations to the child with disabilities compared to baseline conditions. This suggests that either known or mystery rewards can be used effectively alongside group contingencies to promote social interactions in inclusive settings.

Assessment

Because reinforcers are individual and behavior-specific, it is important for early childhood practitioners to understand what items and activities are likely to serve as reinforcers for desirable behaviors for children with whom they work (including teacher attention such as praise). Thus, we describe below three procedures for identifying preferred items and activities (preference assessments) and for determining whether preferred items and activities have reinforcing value (reinforcer assessments). Assessing children's preferences are consistent with Recommended Practices of the Division for Early Childhood of the Council for Exceptional Children (INS1, A1).

Preference Assessments

Preference assessments are formal procedures by which practitioners can assess the extent to which a child prefers a certain item or activity relative to others. Below, we discuss three commonly used procedures for assessing preferences—the multiple stimulus without replacement method (MSWO), the paired stimulus method (PS), and the concurrent operant (CO) method. However, all methods require an initial survey of preferences, which we discuss first.

To begin planning a preference assessment, an initial assessment to identify *potential* preferred items or activities is needed. This can be completed in several different ways: (1) direct report from a child, (2) indirect report from adults, and (3) observation. If the child can verbally report his or her preferences, you can request that the child tell you or show you some of his or her favorite things. If not, or in addition, you can ask familiar adults to name items or activities the child enjoys or might enjoy. Finally, you can use observation to identify what items or activities the child chooses when given a choice; you can use these items or items with similar properties to conduct the preference assessment. In addition to including individualized items or activities, you might also want to include common and developmentally appropriate items. For example, many young children enjoy bubbles, small cars, and small light-up toys—even if these are not identified as preferred, they might be appropriate items to include, especially if the child has had limited opportunities to engage with these items.

When identifying potentially preferred stimuli, you may want to categorize these as (a) tangibles (generally, toys or other items), (b) edibles, or (c) social interactions. Generally, separate preference assessments are completed for these types of stimuli. You may be interested in identifying only one type of preferred stimulus—for example, you may be particularly interested in identifying preferred social interactions (e.g., child seems to enjoy physical attention such as high-fives) for a child who engages in problem behavior following verbal redirections. In contrast, you may be interested in identifying small edibles (e.g., fish crackers) that can serve as reinforcers for trying bites of new foods for a child with ASD who eats only a few different items. Table 3.2 could be used to organize information about potentially preferred items. After organizing this information, you should decide whether you are interested in identifying tangible, edible, or social reinforcers—or some combination of those. Then you should identify which stimuli written in the table will be included in the assessment. Including more stimuli in an assessment may provide a more detailed account of a child's preferences—however, in the case of MSWO and PS assessments, including more stimuli results in a longer assessment period.

Before beginning preference assessment procedures, you should determine whether you are interested in assessing preference among different types of attention/social stimuli (e.g., high-fives, hugs, dance party), tangible items (e.g., figurines, spinner toys, bubbles), or edible items (e.g., fish crackers, cereal, dried fruit). Two preference assessments (MSWO and PS, described below) are generally conducted with one stimulus type (e.g., relative preference among five different tangible items). The final assessment (CO) can include stimuli that are both social and tangible in nature; the CO assessment is generally not used for edible reinforcers.

When using the MSWO and PS assessments, you should consider whether you want to use actual items or representations of the items during the assessments. When using actual items, you present an array of the items for the child to choose from. For example,

Table 3.2 Table for Organizing Information about Potential Preferred Items and Activities

	Child-Reported	Adult-Reported	Observation	Commonly Preferred Items
Tangible Items (e.g., small toys)				
Edible Items (e.g., fish crackers, dried fruit)				
Social Interactions (e.g., high-fives, noodle arms)				

you might put apples, banana, and cereal on a table and allow the child to take one. When using *representations* of items, you use symbolic representations (usually photos or 2-D drawings) during the presentation. In this case, you would present an array of representations (e.g., photos of apple, banana, and cereal), and the child would select a photo. In turn, you would present the item represented by the photo. Some items (such as edibles) are easily presented to children. Others, such as social interactions, are more easily presented via representations. However, if photos or 2D drawings are to be used, you should ensure the child understands that these drawings represent actual items.

Multiple Stimulus Without Replacement Preference Assessment

One commonly used preference assessment is the multiple stimulus without replacement, or MSWO preference assessment. The MSWO is appropriate for children who are capable of making choices, given a large array of stimuli. It is appropriate for use with social interactions and edibles, and is appropriate for tangible items *only* when removal of these items is unlikely to result in problem behavior. During this assessment, children are presented with the opportunity to choose preferred stimuli, and, in the case of tangible items, after a short period in which the child is allowed to manipulate the item, removal of that item.

The steps of conducting an MSWO, as outlined in Figure 3.2, include:

1. Choose 5–7 stimuli that may be preferred.
2. Set up a data collection form (see Figure 3.3).
3. Gather materials and begin the assessment by providing access to each item, successively. This may be referred to as "pre-exposure"—it allows the child to access each stimulus to ensure he or she makes informed choices during the assessment (i.e., increases the likelihood that he or she chooses something because it is preferred rather than novel). For example, for an edible assessment with five stimuli, the implementer would provide a small sample of each and allow the child to eat it. For a tangible assessment with six items, the implementer might provide an opportunity for the child to play with each toy for a short period of time (e.g., 30 seconds or 1 minute) before presenting the next toy.
4. Place all items in a straight line on a surface in front of the child and ask the child to choose one.
5. Allow access to that item for a pre-determined amount of time (e.g., 30 seconds or 1 minute), and then indicate that the child should give the item to you. For some children, it might be beneficial to provide a verbal reminder shortly before you request return of the item (e.g., "Maria, it's almost time to put away the bubbles").
6. Present remaining items *with the previously chosen item removed* in a straight line on a surface in front of the child, in a different order, and ask the child to choose one.
7. Repeat steps 5 and 6 until all items have been accessed *or* until a child stops selecting items. For example, if there were six items initially, and the child chooses and plays with four toys in the first four trials, and then does not make a choice for the 5th trial, you can stop the assessment—this indicates that the remaining items are not preferred.
8. Complete this assessment (session) several times, preferably over at least two different days.
9. Rank order items in terms of preference. For each item:
   a. Determine the total number of trials in which an item was presented. For example, if an item was selected first, second, and first across three successive sessions, it was presented only four times (once in the first and third sessions, and twice in the second session). If an item was chosen last (sixth) across all

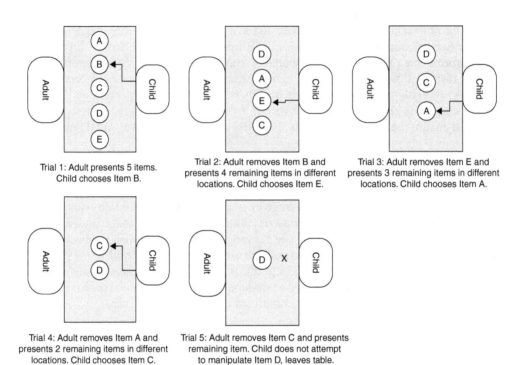

Trial 1: Adult presents 5 items. Child chooses Item B.

Trial 2: Adult removes Item B and presents 4 remaining items in different locations. Child chooses Item E.

Trial 3: Adult removes Item E and presents 3 remaining items in different locations. Child chooses Item A.

Trial 4: Adult removes Item A and presents 2 remaining items in different locations. Child chooses Item C.

Trial 5: Adult removes Item C and presents remaining item. Child does not attempt to manipulate Item D, leaves table.

Figure 3.2 Visual Depiction of Trials in an MSWO Assessment.

three sessions, it was presented 18 times.

b. Determine the total number of times chosen. Across three sessions, this will generally be three for all items. If an item was not chosen (e.g., was not selected even during the final trial), the number may be lower.

c. Divide the number of times chosen by the number of times presented, then multiply by 100. This number represents the percentage of opportunities in which the item was chosen.

d. Order the stimuli, with the most preferred stimuli represented by larger percentages.

As shown in Figure 3.3 and Appendix 3.1, your MSWO data collection form should include information about the child, implementer, and date, as well as data about which items were chosen and the location of the selected item. In Figures 3.3 and Appendix 3.1, the gray cells indicate a decreasing number of items available for each trial. During the first trial, all six stimuli are available, and the number of items decreases by one for each remaining trial. The location of selected items is important because you want to ensure that the child does not have a side selection bias—for example, a child who always chooses the item that is closest to him is unlikely to be making a choice based on preference. In Figure 3.3, the rank of preference is:

1. Bubbles (chosen 2/3 opportunities; 67%)
2. Tie: Slime and Spinner (chosen 2/5 opportunities; 40%)
3. Cars (chosen 2/7 opportunities; 29%)
4. Ball (chosen 2/10 opportunities; 20%)
5. Pretend phone (chosen 0/12 opportunities; 0%).

		Notes:
Date:	1/12/2019	Sp=spinner (40%)
		Ba=ball (20%)
Child:	Muhammad	Bu=bubble (67%)
		Sl=slime (40%)
Teacher:	Alisha	C=cars (27%)
		P=pretend phone (0%)

Trial #	Item Selected	Location Selected							
1	Sp				X				
2	Bu		X						
3	Sl					X			
4	C	X							
5	Ba		X						
6	N/A								

Trial #	Item Selected	Location Selected							
1	Bu	X							
2	Sl		X						
3	C					X			
4	Sp				X				
5	Ba		X						
6	N/A								

Figure 3.3 Sample Data for an MSWO Preference Assessment.

There may be several explanations for differences between the two sessions shown in Figure 3.3. If the spinner was a novel toy, it may be that Muhammed (a) was initially interested due to novelty, but less interested after he was given the opportunity to play with the toy, (b) had the opportunity to play with bubbles immediately preceding Session 1 but not Session 2, or (c) has a relatively equal preference for bubbles, slime, and the spinner. Because the results were somewhat discrepant after two sessions, a third session might be warranted.

Paired Stimulus Preference Assessment

Another commonly used preference assessment is the paired stimulus (PS) preference assessment. The paired stimulus assessment is appropriate for children who are capable of making choices, but who perform more consistently with a smaller array due to motoric or cognitive delays. However, this procedure takes more time than the MSWO, given the same number of stimuli. It is appropriate for use with social interactions and edibles and for tangible items *only* when removal of these items is unlikely to result in problem behavior. During this assessment, children are presented with the opportunity to choose one preferred stimuli given a choice of two. In the case of tangible items, after a short period in which the child is allowed to manipulate the item, the item is removed. Social and edible items have naturally occurring terminations (e.g., social interaction ends, edible is eaten).

The steps of conducting a PS preference assessment include:

1. Choose 5–7 stimuli that may be preferred.
2. Set up a data collection form (see Figure 3.4 and Appendix 3.2).
3. Gather materials and begin the assessment by providing access to each item, successively (described previously for the MSWO assessment).
4. Pair items and order items for presentation. If, for example, six items are to be used, there are 15 possible pairs and thus 15 trials in a PS are required to present each item compared to every other item (compared to six trials in an MSWO).
5. Place two items on a surface in front of the child and ask the child to choose one.
6. Allow access to that item for a pre-determined amount of time (e.g., 30 seconds or 1 minute), and then indicate that the child should give the item to you. For some children, it might be beneficial to provide a verbal reminder shortly before you request return of the item (e.g., "Maria, it's almost time to return the bubbles").
7. Repeat steps 5 and 6 for all remaining pairs.
8. Complete this assessment (session) several times, preferably over at least two different days.
9. Rank order items in terms of preference. For each item, count the number of times chosen and order them, with the item chosen the largest number of times being the most preferred, and the item chosen the fewest number of times being the least preferred.

As shown in Figure 3.4 and Appendix 3.2, your PS data collection form should include information about the child, implementer, and date, as well as all pairs presented and the items chosen. Side bias is also possible in PS assessments, so ensure that you present all stimuli on both sides. In Figure 3.4, the rank of preference is:

1. Fish crackers (chosen 5 times)
2. Cereal (chosen 4 times)

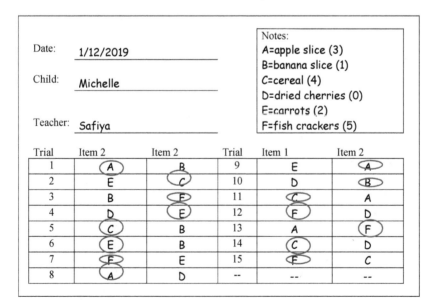

Date:	1/12/2019
Child:	Michelle
Teacher:	Safiya

Notes:
A=apple slice (3)
B=banana slice (1)
C=cereal (4)
D=dried cherries (0)
E=carrots (2)
F=fish crackers (5)

Trial	Item 2	Item 2	Trial	Item 1	Item 2
1	(A)	B	9	E	(A)
2	E	(C)	10	D	(B)
3	B	(F)	11	(C)	A
4	D	(E)	12	(F)	D
5	(C)	B	13	A	(F)
6	(E)	B	14	(C)	D
7	(F)	E	15	(F)	C
8	(A)	D	--	--	--

Figure 3.4 Sample Data for a PS Preference Assessment.

3. Apple slices (chosen 3 times)
4. Carrots (chosen twice)
5. Banana (chosen once)
6. Dried cherries (not chosen).

Concurrent Operants Preference Assessment

A preference assessment that is less commonly used is the concurrent operants (CO) assessment. This assessment is appropriate when a child's potentially preferred items or activities are not easily provided and removed in a trial-based format. For example, a parent might report that a child highly prefers playing on a tablet device, but may also report that the child engages in considerable problem behavior when the device is removed. This type of behavior makes it difficult to conduct MSWO and PS preference assessments. Similarly, you may hypothesize that a child prefers adult conversation, but it may be difficult to assess this in comparison with other stimuli in a trial-based format because the child may attempt to engage the assessor in conversation across trials. In situations such as these, a concurrent operants preference assessment might be preferable.

The steps of conducting a CO preference assessment include:

1. Choose 5–7 stimuli that may be preferred.
2. Set up a data collection form (see Figure 3.5 and Appendix 3.3) and a digital timing device (e.g., a simple sports timer or phone application that can serve as a timer), and determine the length of the session (e.g., 10 minutes).
3. Gather materials and provide contexts for each. For example, place five different materials in five different locations in a room. You might place small interlocking blocks at one table in a corner of the room, an iPad on a rug in another corner, figurines on a table in the center of the room, books near a bean bag chair in the third corner, and an adult in a chair (with a second chair available) in the fourth corner.
4. Orient the child to the available options in the room, and tell the child that he or she can do whatever he or she wishes. Begin the timer when a child begins to manipulate a material or enters an area.
5. Stop the timer when the child becomes unengaged or leaves an area, and record the amount of time spent in the area.
6. Restart the time when the child enters another area or becomes engaged again.
7. Repeat steps 4 and 5 until the session has ended or the child does not engage in any items for a pre-determined amount of time (e.g., one minute).
8. Complete the assessment several times, over at least two different days.
9. Rank order items in terms of preference. Add the number of seconds in which the child was engaged with each item across all opportunities and rank items, with the item with the largest number of seconds being the most preferred item.

As shown in Figure 3.5 and Appendix 3.3, a CO data collection form should include information about the child, implementer, and date, as well as all possible options. In Figure 3.5, the rank of preference is:

1. Tablet (chosen for 4 minutes, 14 seconds)
2. Adult attention (chosen for 31 seconds)
3. Trampoline (chosen for 15 seconds)
4. Figurines, books, and blocks (not chosen).

Date: _____ 1/12/2019	Notes:	
Child: _____ Ashwaq		
Teacher: _____ Gina		

| *Write each activity name. Then write the number of seconds spent at each activity. At the end of the session, add time for each activity.* | Activity 1: **tablet** 2 min 59 s 1 min 15 s | Activity 2: **adult attention** 31 s | Activity 3: **figurines** 0 s |
| | Activity 4: **books** 0 s | Activity 5: **blocks** 0 s | Activity 6: **trampoline** 15 s |

Figure 3.5 Sample Data for a CO Preference Assessment.

For Ashwaq, it seems as though the tablet is clearly the most preferred item. However, the relative preference for figurines, books, and blocks is unclear. If needed, another preference assessment could be conducted, testing the relative preference of items in the absence of the tablet (i.e., with the five other activities only).

Unlike the MSWO and the PS assessments presented earlier, the CO example included potential preferred items from multiple categories (tangibles and attention). This is an advantage of the CO assessment, although CO assessments are generally not used for edibles.

Selecting a Preference Assessment

MSWO, PS, and CO preference assessments all provide information regarding relative preference for specific stimuli. For children who make choices among a large array of items or activities, any of the assessments can be used. Table 3.3 outlines benefits and drawbacks of each assessment and situations in which each should be used. As discussed in the previous two chapters, and highlighted throughout the remainder of the book, individualization is key. Specifically, you should carefully select stimuli and assessment type based on knowledge of the child and the information you hope to gain.

Reinforcer Assessments

Preference assessments are designed to identify *preferred stimuli.* Although this is critical information, you should note that all preferred stimuli will not serve to reinforce all behaviors. The more highly preferred an item is, the more likely it is to reinforce desirable behaviors. A **reinforcer assessment** is designed to determine whether a particular preferred

Table 3.3 Summary of Preference Assessment Types

Preference Assessment	Benefits	Drawbacks	Contexts
Multiple Stimulus Without Replacement (MSWO)	• Fewer trials relative to the PS • Less complex data collection relative to the CO • Assessment of relative preference of all included stimuli	• Requires removal of preferred items	• Child can choose from a large array • One class of reinforcer is of interest (i.e., attention or tangible or edible items)
Paired Stimulus (PS)	• Smaller arrays compared to the MSWO • Less complex data collection relative to the CO • Assessment of relative preference of all included stimuli	• Requires removal of preferred items	• Child requires a smaller array • One class of reinforcer is of interest (i.e., attention or tangible or edible items)
Concurrent Operants (CO)	• Does not require removal of preferred items • Can include stimuli from multiple categories (i.e., attention and tangibles)	• If child chooses only one stimuli, relative preference for others is not assessed	• Multiple classes of reinforcers is of interest • Child engages in problem behavior when preferred stimuli are removed

stimulus (or commonly used reward) results in improvements in a specific target behavior. This provides evidence that a specific preferred item may serve as a reinforcer for similar target behaviors. For example, if a child cleans up items more quickly (e.g., puts more blocks in a bucket during a one-minute period), when a teacher provides verbal praise for every third block than when a teacher provides no praise, we have evidence that praise serves to *reinforce* this cleaning behavior. This information indicates praise may serve as a reinforcer for other behaviors, including behaviors we would like to change. For example, Barton and Ledford (2018) first conducted MSWO or PS preference assessments for three children with disabilities included in a study designed to increase imitation of peers. Then, using a highly preferred tangible item and/or a highly preferred social interaction, they conducted reinforcer assessments to determine whether preferred items served as reinforcers for completion of simple tasks. For all participants, the highly preferred items served as reinforcers, as shown by higher responding during reinforcement conditions of the reinforcer assessment, similar to data shown in Figure 3.5.

To conduct a reinforcer assessment, perform these steps, as outlined in Figure 3.6:

1. Determine what stimuli (e.g., edible, verbal praise) will be tested. You may choose the stimuli by conducting interviews, observations, or formal preference assessments, given that preferred items often serve as reinforcers for some behaviors.
2. Establish the child behavior you will reinforce. This behavior should be one that can be completed by the child with a small or moderate amount of effort—not a behavior that is difficult for the child or that the child cannot yet perform. It should also be a behavior that can be performed repeatedly. Examples include putting an item in a different location (e.g., moving blocks from one shelf to another) or jumping from

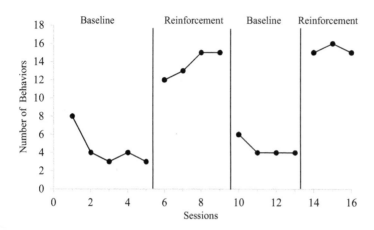

Figure 3.6 Hypothetical Data from Jose's Reinforcer Assessment.

one designated spot to another. The behavior should be neutral rather than highly pre-ferred (something the child would choose to do regardless of consequences) or highly non-preferred (something the child would avoid).

3. Conduct a baseline condition. During this condition, conduct three or more short sessions (e.g., 1 minute) during which you ask the child to engage in the behavior, but provide no consequences for doing so. For example, you might say "Jose, please jump from one square to the other like this [demonstrate] until my timer goes off." Then, set the timer and count the number of behaviors for each session.

4. Graph the behavior across sessions and stop when the levels of the behavior are *stable*, or about the same across sessions. In Figure 3.6, you see that Jose engaged in many jumping behaviors during the first session, but then the number of behaviors stabilized to about 3–4 for the remaining sessions.

5. Conduct reinforcer sessions. During this condition, conduct three or more short sessions (i.e., the same length as your baseline sessions) during which you ask the child to engage in the behavior, and provide the reinforcer for doing so. For example, you might say "Jose, please jump from one square to the other like this [demonstrate] until my timer goes off. Every time you jump, I'm going to clap and tell you that you are doing a good job." Then, set the timer and count the number of behaviors for each session (see Figure 3.7).

6. Repeat step 4 by graphing data from the reinforcer condition. You can find more information about graphing in several peer-reviewed resources (cf. Barton & Reichow, 2012; Barton, Reichow, & Wolery, 2007), and online (www.abainternational.org/journals/bap/supplemental-materials.aspx).

7. Repeat the baseline and reinforcer conditions, graphing all data.

8. Determine whether data are different between baseline and reinforcer conditions. If more behavior occurred when they were reinforced than when no reinforcement was provided, the selected stimulus is likely to serve as a reinforcer. If data are similar between conditions, the selected stimulus is unlikely to serve as a reinforcer.

Judy decides that she should conduct a preference assessment to determine what the most preferred edibles are for Charlie. Because Charlie has demonstrated impulsive behaviors during some activities, Judy decides a PS preference assessment would be more appro-priate, since Charlie might grab an item from a larger array without first considering all of her options. She begins by printing depictions of each of five edibles: fish crackers, raisins,

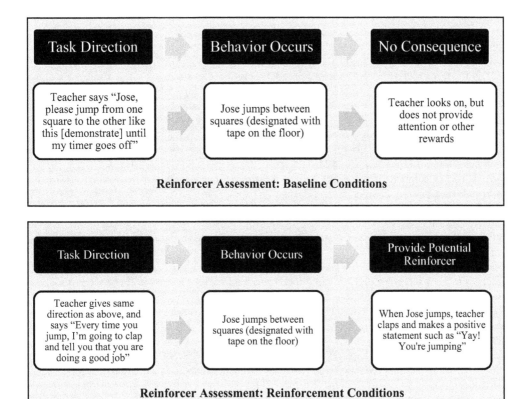

Figure 3.7 Reinforcer Assessment Procedures.

chocolate chips, dried mango, and cereal. She began the assessment by allowing Charlie to have one bite of each, and then presented all pairs (10 trials) three days in a row. Across days, the most preferred edible was raisins. With the help of Charlie's itinerant special education teacher, Judy devised and practiced a token system with Charlie during structured activities, during which she received tokens for initiating to peers or appropriately manipulating materials. Judy then set a 3-minute interval timer for all free play periods, and she provided tokens to Charlie whenever she was appropriately playing or interacting when the timer sounded. At the end of free play sessions, Judy referenced Charlie's token board (affixed to the wall near her favorite center), and gave her one raisin for every five earned tokens, along with behavior-specific praise.

Related Resources

www.naeyc.org
www.dec-sped.org
http://vkc.mc.vanderbilt.edu/ebip/preference-assessments/
http://vkc.mc.vanderbilt.edu/ebip/differential-reinforcement/
http://vkc.mc.vanderbilt.edu/ebip/class-wide-reward-systems/
https://eclkc.ohs.acf.hhs.gov/children-disabilities/article/child-preferences
http://ectacenter.org/~pdfs/decrp/PG_Asm_IdentifyingChildStrengths_prac_print_2017.
   pdf

References

Bailey, D. B., & Wolery, M. (1992). *Teaching infants and preschoolers with disabilities* (2nd ed.). New York: Macmillan.

Barton, E. E., & Ledford, J. R. (2018). Effects of reinforcement on peer imitation in a small group play context. *Journal of Early Intervention*, 40(1), 69–86.

Barton, E. E., & Reichow, B. (2012). Guidelines for graphing data with Microsoft Office 2007, Office 2010, and Office for Mac 2008 and 2011. *Journal of Early Intervention*, 34, 129–150.

Barton, E. E., Reichow, B., & Wolery, M. (2007). Guidelines for graphing data with Microsoft® PowerPoint™. *Journal of Early Intervention*, 29, 320–336.

Bayat, M. (2011). Clarifying issues regarding the use of praise with young children. *Topics in Early Childhood Special Education*, 31, 121–128.

Corpus, J. H., & Lepper, M. R. (2007). The effects of person versus performance praise on children's motivation: Gender and age as moderating factors. *Educational Psychology*, 27, 487–508.

DEC (Division for Early Childhood). (2007). Promoting positive outcomes for children with disabilities: Recommendations for curriculum, assessment, and program evaluation. Missoula, MT: DEC.

Division for Early Childhood of the Council for Exceptional Children (2014). DEC recommended practices in early intervention/early childhood special education. Retrieved from: www.dec-sped.org/recommendedpractices.

Dunlap, G., & Liso, D. (2004). Using choice and preference to promote improved behavior. Center on the Social and Emotional Foundations of Early Learning. Retrieved from http://csefel.vanderbilt.edu/briefs/wwb15.pdf.

Dunlap, G., DePerczel, M., Clarke, S., Wilson, D., Wright, S., White, R., & Gomez, A. (1994). Choice-making to promote adaptive behavior for students with emotional and behavioral challenges. *Journal of Applied Behavior Analysis*, 27, 505–518.

Egel, A. L. (1981). Reinforcer variation: Implications for motivating developmentally disabled children. *Journal of Applied Behavior Analysis*, 14, 345–350.

Hart, B., & Risley, T. R. (1975). Incidental teaching of language in the preschool. *Journal of Applied Behavior Analysis*, 8, 411–420.

Henderlong, J., & Lepper, M. R. (2002). The effects of praise on children's intrinsic motivation: A review and synthesis. *Psychological Bulletin*, 128, 774–795.

Johnson, J. J., Rahn, N. L., & Bricker, D. (2015). An activity-based approach to early intervention (4th ed.). Baltimore, MD: Brookes.

Ledford, J. R., Chazin, K. T., Harbin, E. R., & Ward, S. E. (2017). Massed trials versus trials embedded into game play: Child outcomes and preference. *Topics in Early Childhood Special Education*, 37, 107–120.

Pokorski, E. A., Barton, E. E., & Ledford, J. R. (2017). A review of the use of group contingencies in preschool settings. *Topics in Early Childhood Special Education*, 36, 230–241.

Stevens, C., Sidener, T. M., Reeve, S. A., & Sidener, D. W. (2011). Effects of behavior-specific and general praise, on acquisition of tacts in children with pervasive developmental disorders. *Research in Autism Spectrum Disorders*, 5, 666–669.

Strain, P. S., & Joseph, G. E. (2004). A not so good job with "good job": A response to Kohn 2001. *Journal of Positive Behavior Interventions*, 6, 55–59.

Appendix 3.1 Data Collection Form for MSWO Preference Assessment

Date: _____

Child: _____

Teacher: _____

Notes:

Session #1

Trial #	Item Selected	Location Selected					
1							
2							
3							
4							
5							
6							

Session #2

Trial #	Item Selected	Location Selected					
1							
2							
3							
4							
5							
6							

Session #3

Trial #	Item Selected	Location Selected					
1							
2							
3							
4							
5							
6							

Appendix 3.2 Data Collection Form for PS Preference Assessment

Date: _____

Child: _____

Teacher: _____

Notes:

Trial	Item 2	Item 2	Trial	Item 1	Item 2
1			9		
2			10		
3			11		
4			12		
5			13		
6			14		
7			15		
8					

Appendix 3.3 Data Collection Form for CO Preference Assessment

Date: _____	Notes:	
Child: _____		
Teacher: _____		

Write each activity name. Then write the number of seconds spent at each activity. At the end of the session, add time for each activity.	Activity 1:	Activity 2:	Activity 3:
	Activity 4:	Activity 5:	Activity 6:

4 Introduction to Teaching and Learning

Key Terms

Learning	*Prompting*	*Instructional control*
Environment	*Attending cues and responses*	*Stimulus control*
Teaching	*Discriminative stimulus*	*Differential reinforcement*

Chapter Objectives

After completing this chapter, readers should be able to:

- Describe under what conditions learning occurs.
- Explain the relevance of antecedent and consequent events for learning.
- Describe how discriminative stimuli and prompts differ.
- Define and exemplify acquisition, fluency, maintenance, and generalization.
- Describe procedures for improving acquisition, fluency, maintenance, and generalization.

Finnick is a second-year lead teacher in a preschool classroom housed in an urban elementary school. During his first year he struggled with planning for and improving age-appropriate behaviors in all students. Before students return to the classroom in the fall, he wants to develop a plan of action for how to properly identify and imple-ment interventions for all students, especially those who have individualized education programs (IEP). Although he is well intentioned, Finnick is unsure how to effectively teach his students, who each come to his class with their own set of diverse needs.

The primary purpose of this chapter is to introduce the basic principles of learning and teaching in early childhood contexts. It includes an introduction to essential terminology and procedural steps related to effective teaching, and is essential to understanding the strategies and procedures discussed in the remainder of the text.

Introduction to Underlying Principles of Teaching and Learning

Learning refers to an "enduring change in [a child's] behavior" (Wolery & Hemmeter, 2011, p. 371) that occurs based on experiences and interactions within environments in which they spend time (Wolery, Ault, & Doyle, 1992). Understanding the term learning first requires understanding the terms behavior and environment. As discussed in Chapters 2 and 3, **behavior** refers to the observable actions of a child and can be further subdivided as referring to a single isolated action (or discrete behavior) or a series of actions (or chained behavior) that lead to a specific outcome. Oftentimes in early childhood, we are interested in improving a variety of behaviors for purposes of building a child's skill set or reper-toire. Thus, when planning instruction, we identify and organize opportunities to improve meaningful behaviors that, when learned, will likely lead to increased independence and new experiences in the classroom and community. It is important to understand the inter-relatedness of behavior and environment. **Environment** refers to the physical, social, and temporal aspects of the immediate setting. Each aspect influences the extent to which a child will learn and display a novel behavior under typical conditions. For example, the behavior of independently walking from one center to the next is influenced by the phys-ical layout of the classroom (e.g., furniture, pathways for walking). Improving a child's responses to peer initiations requires an understanding of peers who are available in the classroom and any related training that might be necessary to promote success. A child's engagement in non-preferred activities might be influenced by the order in which preferred and non-preferred activities are temporally interspersed throughout the school day. Finally, teachers must ensure that a child has an adequate number of opportunities to learn—and must individually determine what is "adequate" for a particular child and skill. Some children may learn new behaviors given only a few unstructured opportunities to observe their peers; other children may require many systematically implemented trials before acquiring novel behaviors. Thus, the occurrence, or lack thereof, of a behavior is directly influenced by multiple components of the environment, including physical settings, tem-poral contexts, social opportunities, and adequately planned instructional trials.

Efficient learning of functional skills by young children is the resulting outcome of high-quality teaching. As discussed in Chapter 2, planning instruction initially involves carefully selecting behaviors that are meaningful for a child in their typical environments. Once instructional targets are identified, the process of selecting and implementing an appropriate intervention requires careful attention. **Teaching** refers to arranging the social, temporal, and/or physical environment to support acquisition and use of new behaviors. Teaching relies on the three-term contingency, commonly known as the **Antecedent-Behavior-Consequence** (A-B-C) paradigm. This paradigm is useful for planning changes in observable and measurable behaviors emitted by children. **Antecedent** refers to envir-onmental stimuli that cue a child that he or she can display a specific **behavior**, while **consequence** refers to changes in the environment that immediately follow a behavior (see Figure 4.1). For example, when a child is asked her name by a peer (antecedent) she may respond by verbally stating or signing her name (behavior). The peer in turn may respond by introducing himself or simply walking away to engage in another activity (consequence). These interactions will likely influence how the child responds in the future when encountering similar circumstances. Teaching requires taking advantage of the three-term contingency by systematically planning appropriate antecedents and consequences for student behaviors, to maximize learning opportunities. This contingency also applies to challenging behaviors. For example, when a child has a tantrum when she is told she cannot have an extra cracker, the teacher can ignore the tantrum and not give her the extra cracker. However, if the teacher gives the child extra attention or acquiesces and gives the child an extra cracker, the child learns tantrums often result in desired responses and might be more likely to use tantrums in the future. This paradigm should be used to increase appropriate behaviors and prevent and decrease challenging behaviors.

Building Blocks of Systematic Teaching

Beginning early in life, children are exposed to innumerable opportunities to learn new behaviors—just a few examples include infants learning to vocalize based on their caregiver's consequences (e.g., verbally responding when a baby coos, providing food when they cry), toddlers learning to communicate with more complexity to request and protest, and young children learning to walk given a combination of opportunities to observe

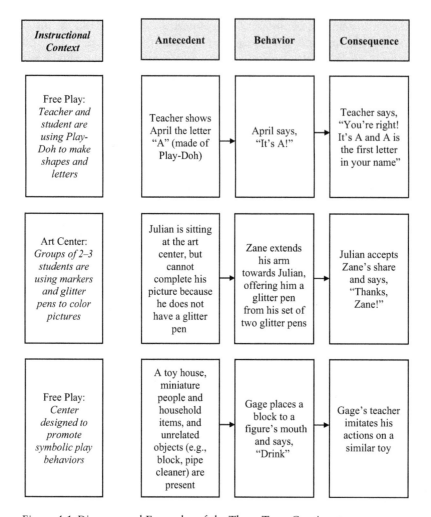

Figure 4.1 Diagram and Examples of the Three-Term Contingency.

others walking and to engage in increasingly complex motor behaviors with support from adults. A single opportunity to engage in a behavior is referred to as a **trial**. The examples above are trials that are generally unplanned or loosely planned. However, many young children, especially those with, or at-risk for, disabilities require carefully planned and monitored instructional trials—with consideration for the antecedents, behaviors, and consequences present for each opportunity. A **session** refers to a collection of trials that occur during a specified time period (e.g., a short 5-minute small group direct instruction activity, a 30-minute lunch period). Adequate **dosage**, or number of learning opportunities, is critical to ensure children learn to engage in **functional behaviors**, or behaviors that are useful to them in their everyday lives. The number of planned and unplanned learning opportunities needed to acquire behaviors varies widely across children and skills, but most children require carefully planned instructional trials to learn at least some types of behaviors. An insufficient number of instructional opportunities may exist in typical contexts; thus, specific, systematic instructional opportunities are needed to ensure children learn the skills they need to learn (Barton, Bishop, & Snyder, 2014; Wolery, 2012).

Generally, two types of sessions are most relevant for teaching children to engage in functional behaviors. **Instructional sessions** are specific times during which a teacher provides instructional trials related to at least one specific **target behavior** (the behavior for which you are providing teaching). For example, a teacher might conduct a 5-minute, individual session each morning during which she teaches a child to match photographs of common items by giving him three opportunities to match each of three different items (an instructional session with nine trials and one target behavior—matching). Or, a teacher might conduct a session each day during lunch time, when she teaches a child to use a spoon during five planned trials and teaches a child to respond to peer initiations during five planned trials (an instructional session with ten trials and two target behaviors—using a spoon and responding to peers). **Baseline sessions** are collections of trials in which a child is given an opportunity to engage the target behaviors in the absence of teaching. Baseline sessions are typically conducted prior to the commencement of teaching, to determine to what extent the child can engage in the behavior independently. This is important because, for example, if a child engaged in 80 percent correct responding on the first day of instruction, with no baseline data collected, we could not be sure whether (a) our teaching procedure was highly effective, or (b) the child was already capable of completing the behaviors with 80 percent accuracy.

Teaching a child when and how to display a behavior involves arranging the environment to highlight the conditions under which to display a target behavior. The unique stimulus condition that cues the child to respond is known as the **discriminative stimulus**. That is, a discriminative stimulus tells the child when to engage in a particular behavior. Within the three-term contingency the discriminative stimulus is a specific type of antecedent condition, which signals to the child that if he or she displays the target behavior, a pleasant consequence will likely follow (reinforcement as part of the consequent event). Examples of discriminative stimuli include task directions, such as adult directives or questions, and subtle or overt changes in the typical environment. For example, one discriminative stimulus for saying "red" might be the presentation of a red item plus the question, "What color is this one?" It is also possible for a child's behavior to serve as a discriminative stimulus for subsequent behaviors. For example, one discriminative stimulus for beginning handwashing is exiting from a bathroom stall. Reliable performance of a behavior in the presence of a discriminative stimulus, and only when one is present, is known as **stimulus control** (see Figure 4.2). Stimulus control is established via **differential reinforcement**, which refers to the reinforcement of a certain behavior only when a discriminative stimulus is present, and the withholding of the reinforcement when the discriminative stimulus is absent. For example, the child may receive a token when he says "red" following presentation of a red item and the teacher question, "What color is this one?" (i.e., in the presence of the discriminative stimulus), but reinforcement is not provided when he says "red" following presentation of the question with a green item (i.e., not in the presence of the discriminative stimulus).

Ensuring reliable stimulus control influences learning across the lifespan. For example, toddlers with typical development commonly learn when and how to reliably obtain attention from their parents and, as such, their behaviors are reinforced by access to attention. Stimulus control is not unique to teaching, but is the goal of teaching, in that we capitalize on what is known about learning and utilize those principles in practice to ensure reliable performance of target behaviors. Teaching typically involves one of three approaches to promote learning: (a) modifying the antecedent condition before the child has an opportunity to respond (e.g., superimposing a picture of a dog over the word "dog" and fading the picture over time); (b) introducing adult supports (or prompts) before a child has an opportunity to respond or after he or she has an opportunity to respond, but

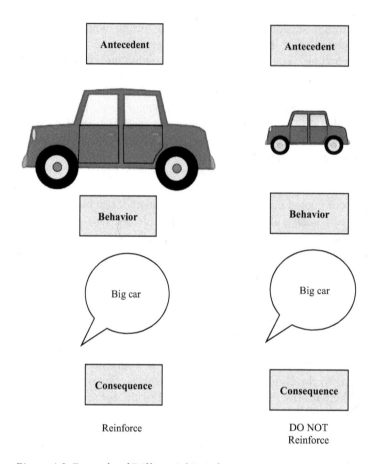

Figure 4.2 Example of Differential Reinforcement.

does not (also known as a response prompt [e.g., adult models how to wash hands]); or (c) providing some form of error correction after a child displays an incorrect behavior (e.g., verbal reprimand or additional practice displaying a target behavior) (see Figure 4.3 for an example of each). Throughout this book we will focus on various types of prompts as a means of promoting learning in young children. **Prompts** refer to changes in the environment that show a child *how* to respond in the presence of a particular stimulus (or antecedent condition; e.g., adult models how to trace a letter). Prompts should not be confused with discriminative stimuli (task direction, question, or other environmental modification or change), which indicates to the child *when* to display a behavior (see Table 4.1). Systematic methods are available for identifying which prompts should be used, and how they should be administered and removed.

Relatedly, in order to ensure a child is attending to the relevant features of a stimulus, an adult sometimes needs to provide an **attending cue**. An attending cue refers to a change in the environment that signals to the child that it is time to pay attention to relevant stimuli. During the course of typical activities, practitioners often provide non-systematic cues that help children attend to certain people, materials, or actions. For example, we might tell one child to watch another child who is doing something particularly interesting with toys, or call a group's attention to one child who has engaged in a desirable behavior. When engaging in direct instruction (see Chapters 8–11), we often use these attending

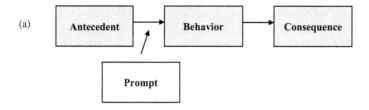

dog   dog   dog   dog

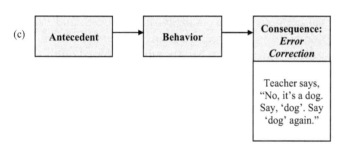

Teacher says,
"No, it's a dog.
Say, 'dog'. Say
'dog' again."

Figure 4.3 Examples of Adult Supports to Promote Learning in Young Children.

Note: (a) response prompt that is provided immediately before a child has an opportunity to respond or once a specified time has passed with no response; (b) antecedent manipulation (e.g., superimposition of a target word over a photograph); (c) error correction immediately following a child providing an incorrect response.

Table 4.1 Differentiating Discriminative Stimuli from Prompts

	Discriminative Stimulus	*Prompts*
Examples	*Tells the child when to display a behavior*	*Shows the child how to be correct*
Question: Non-academic	Peer asks, "What's your name?"	Adult, standing near the child, provides a verbal model of his name.
Question: Academic	Paraprofessional holds up an index card with the letter "B" written in marker and asks, "What letter?"	Paraprofessional provides a verbal model of the letter name.
Directive or Task Direction	Teacher presents toys and says, "Feed the baby."	Adult shows the child the correct action and waits for her to respond.
Environmental Cues	Door to playground open, with opportunity to go outside, it is cold, and the child's coat is hanging up in a cubby.	Teacher says, "It's cold outside," which serves as a verbal reminder (prompt) for the child to obtain her coat.

cues more systematically. A **general attending cue** typically involves an adult providing a gesture (point to an item) or a statement that asks ("Ready?") or tells the child ("Look.") to orient his or her attention to the current activity. The goal when using an attending cue is that the child stops his or her current activity and makes eye contact with the adult, looks at an item(s), or orients his or her body in space toward the instructor or item(s). Such behaviors from the child are referred to as **general attending responses**. A general attending response is considered a proxy for attention or readiness (i.e., child indicating he or she is ready to actively engage in the instructional situation). In addition to a general attending cue and child response, an adult can provide a **specific attending cue**, asking the child to actively engage in a response directly related to relevant aspects or features of the discriminative stimulus. A specific attending cue highlights the critical features of a stimulus and typically involves a child providing a **specific attending response** to an adult's directive or question, either verbally or nonverbally. Like a general attending response, a specific attending response is a representation of attention, but provides an opportunity to indicate they are attending to the *specific stimuli characteristics* that are needed for learning. For example, a "look" cue may result in a child looking in the general direction of the materials, but does not ensure that they are attending to the specific features of the stimulus that require discrimination. Specific cues provide evidence that the child is attending to these features. One example is asking the child to match a green card (the target stimulus) to an identical copy present in an array of red, green, and yellow before asking him to name the color. Following correct matching, you are confident that he has attended to the relevant feature because he matched the stimulus based on this feature. Other examples include tracing a letter with their finger prior to naming the letter, matching three stimuli in an array before being asked to point to one of them, or naming letters before being asked to read a word. These cues may be more effective than general cues, but can result in considerably increased trial duration. Thus, we suggest the use of the cues primarily with children who have demonstrated difficulty exhibiting consistent attention to relevant instructional stimuli. Examples of general and specific attending cues and responses are shown in Table 4.2.

Phases of Learning

Learning is a broad term that refers to a relatively permanent change in behavior. Understanding the basic foundations of teaching, specifically establishing stimulus control and differentially reinforcing target behaviors in the presence of appropriate discriminative stimuli, allows us to further consider the process of learning as defined by its phases: (a) acquisition, (b) fluency, (c) maintenance, and (d) generalization.

1. **Acquisition** refers to the child reliably and appropriately displaying a behavior during instruction. When we colloquially refer to learning, we are often referring to the acquisition stage. Acquisition of a behavior refers to the ability to complete the basic requirements of said behavior, without additional external supports. Thus, a child who can say "red" when presented with a red item and related question and "blue" when presented with a blue item and related question has demonstrated acquisition of these two, basic color-naming skills.

     Acquisition can be promoted via provision of learning opportunities, support (e.g., prompts), and reinforcement.
2. **Fluency** refers to a child displaying a behavior at a natural rate (within an expected time frame) when compared to some normative or functional criterion (e.g., same age peers). A child who is fluently displaying a behavior has (1) acquired the behavior and

Table 4.2 Examples of Attending Cues and Responses in Sequence

General Attending Cue (Adult)	General Attending Response (Child)	Specific Attending Cue (Adult)	Specific Attending Response (Child)	Discriminative Stimulus
"Ready"	Child turns his body and orients toward the adult	"Trace the letter"	Child traces the letters with his finger	"What letter?" + letter written in crayon on a coloring sheet
"Look"	Child orients her body toward the target stimulus.	"Tell me the letters"	Child names each letter in succession	"What word?" + words spelled with magnet letters
"Ready. Look at me."	Child turns her body and orients toward the adult	"Tell me the letters" + adult's verbal model for each letter	Child imitates naming each letter in succession	What word?" + letter made of blocks
"Ready. Look at this" + gesture toward stimuli.	Child orients his gaze toward the materials	"Match"	Child matches the target photograph to an identical photograph in a field size of four	"What is this called?" + gesture to photograph of target object
"Look at me."	Child turns his face and makes eye contact with the teacher.	"We are going to match pictures. What are we going to do?"	Child says, "Match pictures"	Adult presents pictures in a field size of six, gives the child the target stimulus, and says, "Match."

(2) displays the behavior in a manner that can be described as *smooth* and *rapid*. In some cases, a child who does not fluently display a behavior may be provided with fewer opportunities to engage in the behavior (i.e., if a child is slow or awkward when putting on their coat, adults may do it for them more often, to facilitate faster transitions, leaving the child with fewer practice opportunities). Likewise, fluency in academic responding may allow for more practice opportunities when in large groups. For some academic behaviors like reading, fluency may also impact comprehension and the ability to complete complex tasks. A child who quickly responds to questions about color in the context of ongoing activities has demonstrated fluent skill production.

Fluency can be promoted by reinforcing behavior occurrence that meets certain criteria (e.g., completing a task within a few minutes of starting, naming sight words within a few seconds of presentation) and providing frequent practice opportunities.

3. **Maintenance** refers to a child continuing to display a behavior after instruction has stopped. A child has maintained a behavior when he or she displays the behaviors under typical conditions, outside of an instructional situation. It is important to note that it is critical for some behaviors to maintain once instruction stops (e.g., when we teach a child to name colors, we want them to be able to use that skill indefinitely). However, we expect that some behaviors will only continue when interventions are used—for example, a child may need continued use of visual supports to sustain levels of appropriate engagement during small group activities. A child who acquires

color-naming behaviors in the spring, and still exhibits high levels of accuracy the next fall has demonstrated maintenance of behavior change.

Maintenance can be promoted when practitioners: (a) choose functional and meaningful behaviors the child is likely to use often, (b) choose behaviors likely to be reinforced by multiple people who interact with the child, (c) teach to a strict criterion (e.g., 100 percent correct for five consecutive sessions), and (d) vary reinforcement over time (e.g., start by reinforcing all correct behaviors—use an FR1 schedule, then an FR2 schedule, then a VR3 schedule, as described in Chapter 3).

4. **Generalization** refers to the broad and varied use of acquired behaviors. Two types of generalization are possible. **Stimulus generalization** refers to the use of an acquired behavior with a variety of people, in different settings, and with multiple materials that were not part of instruction. For example, a child who learns color-naming with toy cars and who names colors in books has generalized the color-naming skill. **Response generalization** refers to displaying behaviors that are similar, but not identical to those that were targeted during instruction. A child who was taught to *respond* to peer greetings by waving and saying "Hi!" has exhibited response generalization if he begins to *initiate* greetings or respond to greetings by saying "Hey!"

Generalization can be prompted when practitioners teach across multiple contexts (e.g., with different social partners or implementers, with varied materials, in different settings), teach and reinforce varied responding (e.g., response generalization), and teach skills likely to be useful and reinforced in multiple contexts (e.g., at home, at school, in community settings).

Although each phase is commonly referred to and discussed in isolation, simultaneous consideration of each phase when planning instruction increases the likelihood a child will learn and use behaviors that are meaningful to them and their families in their typical contexts. The ultimate outcome of teaching is that a child can independently display a socially meaningful behavior, in contexts in which it is appropriate (generalized), at an adequate rate (fluent), for as long as it is needed (maintained).

Choosing Instructional Procedures and Variations

In the following chapters, we will present numerous specific procedures designed to improve learning via the application of antecedent manipulations and differential reinforcement. These procedures are **evidence-based**—that is, there is considerable research evidence to suggest that they are effective. However, early childhood practitioners must decide if particular procedures are evidence-based *given their particular needs*. For example, graduated guidance (discussed in Chapter 11) is evidence-based for teaching chained behaviors to children with disabilities—it is not evidence-based for teaching word reading to young children without disabilities. Thus, practitioners need to be able to identify and use a wide range of strategies, and need to be able to apply them based on the characteristics of children they care for and the behaviors they are planning to teach (Ledford et al., 2016). Additionally, many of the practices we present in later chapters can be applied in various contexts. Below, we discuss some important procedural variations and some guidelines to consider when determining *what* procedure to choose and *how* to apply it.

Instructional Arrangement

Instructional trials can be delivered in a variety of arrangements—some typical arrangements include one-to-one (1:1) or individual, small group, and large group instruction. Table 4.3 below illustrates some potential instructional arrangements.

Table 4.3 Instructional Arrangements

Arrangement	Illustrative Example
Individual	Using graduated guidance (see Chapter 11) with social praise as a reinforcer, Nora, a preschool teacher, teaches Dante, a young child with Down syndrome, to manipulate his clothing (pull pants up/down) during toileting routines.
Small group	Using progressive time delay (see Chapter 8) with a token reinforcement system, Rahma, a kindergarten teacher, teaches Timothy, a young child with typical development, to name letters alongside two peers, who she teaches to read sight words.
Large group	Using system of least prompts (see Chapter 10) and edible reinforcers, Bralee, a Head Start teaching assistant, teaches Abdi, a child with developmental delays, to respond to "where" questions during storybook reading.

Table 4.4 Benefits and Drawbacks of Different Instructional Arrangements

Arrangement	Benefit	Drawback
Individual: Teacher is providing systematic instruction to a single child	• Distractions can be minimized • Privacy is afforded, which can be important for personal care tasks • Teaching one child at a time is simpler than managing multiple children	• Children are sometimes removed from typically occurring activities for 1:1 instruction (although this is not required; see information about trial arrangement below) • When one practitioner teaches a single child, other practitioners may be required to supervise a large number of non-participating children
Small group: Teacher is providing systematic instruction to several (2–5) children	• Children can learn from their peers • Children may have more frequent opportunities to respond when compared with large group instruction	• Teachers may have difficulty managing multiple children while engaging in effective instruction
Large group: Teacher is providing systematic instruction to a whole group of children (6–10)	• Children can learn from their peers • All supervising adults can be present to assist in behavior management	• Children may get few opportunities to respond, which may slow learning • There may be a substantial number of distractions, reducing salience of instructional stimuli (i.e., children may have difficulty attending)

Many skills can be taught in any of the arrangements listed in Table 4.3, while others, such as self-help skills, should be taught individually. Table 4.4 lists some benefits and weaknesses of each arrangement; discussions regarding small group instruction are also included in Chapter 12.

Trial Arrangement

There are two questions regarding trial arrangement that should be answered prior to instruction: (1) What will occur during inter-trial intervals (i.e., between trials)? (2) How many of the trials will contain known versus unknown stimuli? There are three common ways to manage inter-trial intervals, resulting in three primary variations: **massed trial**

Table 4.5 Trial Arrangements

Arrangement	Illustrative Example
Massed Trial	Using progressive time delay (see Chapter 8) with a token reinforcement system, Rahma, a kindergarten teacher, teaches Timothy, a young child with typical development, to name letters alongside two peers, who she teaches to read sight words. She conducts 8 trials per child, with only a few seconds separating each trial, during a 5-minute instructional session.
Trials Embedded in an Activity	Using system of least prompts (see Chapter 10) and edible reinforcers, a Head Start teaching assistant, teaches Abdi, a young child with developmental delays, to respond to "where" questions while he plays alongside his peers during free play by contriving situations (e.g., putting the toy cars on a shelf out of reach, and asking "Where are the cars?").
Distributed Trials	Each time during the day when children in the classroom are expected to engage in toileting, Nora uses graduated guidance (see Chapter 11) with social praise as a reinforcer to teach Dante, a young child with Down syndrome, to manipulate his clothing (pull pants up/down).

instructional sessions, with very short (e.g., a few seconds) inter-trial intervals; **trials embedded into a single activity**, usually with child-directed play occurring during inter-trial intervals; and **trials embedded in activities across the day**, also referred to as distributed trials, often occurring during transitions or contingent on a typically occurring discriminative stimulus. Table 4.5 above illustrates some potential trial arrangements. Note that all of these types of trials can be conducted individually or in small or large groups.

Embedded instruction. Embedded instruction refers to conducting instructional trials during child-led or play-based activities—an adult capitalizes on a child's interest or his or her initiation to an item or activity and promotes behaviors that may or may not be related to the current activity (Grisham-Brown & Hemmeter, 2017; Grisham-Brown, Schuster, Hemmeter, & Collins, 2000; Ledford et al., 2017; Venn et al., 1993; Wolery, 2012). Of the instructional approaches highlighted in this chapter, embedded instruction is arguably viewed as a more favorable instructional approach in inclusive early childhood classrooms when compared to massed instruction (Wolery & Hemmeter, 2011). Embedded instruction is an effective instructional approach (e.g., Wolery, Anthony, Caldwell, Snyder, & Morgante, 2002) and is typically recommended because it allows the child to explore his or her environment, while an adult embeds instruction into typically occurring activities; the general notion is that the child's exploration is relatively uninterrupted. Like all instructional approaches, embedded instruction requires careful planning and consideration of each child's goals and objectives for the school year, as well as comfort with instructional procedures. For example, a child with autism spectrum disorder (ASD) and cognitive delays may require numerous opportunities to learn when and how to display a target behavior and, as such, it would be necessary for a practitioner to embed multiple opportunities per activity across the day to see meaningful increases in the child's behavior. Thus, it may be difficult for practitioners who serve multiple children to embed a sufficient number of opportunities to teach a variety of skills to all children.

Massed instruction. Massed instruction refers to teaching the behaviors in an instructional session/activity for multiple opportunities, with very short intervals between trials, and is commonly associated with direct instruction. Some refer to massed instruction as "discrete trial instruction" or "discrete trial training" (DTT) but discrete trial simply refers to an adult-directed trial in which an antecedent is presented, a behavior occurs, and a consequence is delivered; this type of trial can occur within the context of massed or embedded instruction, using a number of different teaching procedures. Thus, we avoid the use of the term DTT as it is usually insufficiently descriptive (e.g., instead, we might describe the use of progressive time delay using massed trials or the system of least prompts embedded during play). Massed instruction typically involves using systematic instructional procedures in a one-to-one or small group arrangement (Ledford, Lane, Elam, & Wolery, 2012; Walker, 2008). Contemporary recommendations indicate that instructional sessions should be "relatively short (5–8 minutes)," incorporate "identified reinforcers," and occur with small groups of two to five children (Wolery & Hemmeter, 2011, p. 376). Although a balance of naturalistic and direct instruction is recommended, early childhood educators may be less likely to utilize massed instruction in practice due to philosophical disagreements with behaviorism, a dislike for direct instruction (e.g., false belief that direct instruction cannot promote generalization; Wolery, 2012), and a lack of training in how to effectively implement massed trials. Massed instruction is a defensible choice when teaching children to recognize when and how to respond to specific environmental cues for behaviors, especially given how fleeting such opportunities may be during typical early childhood activities (e.g., opportunity to share with a peer occurred once during a 15-minute music and movement activity). Repeated opportunities to practice skills can lead to more efficient learning of behavior–environment relations compared with less frequent opportunities during typically occurring activities. Further, expecting children to create learning opportunities embedded into their play will likely not produce a sufficient dosage of learning opportunities for them.

Distributed instruction. Distributed instruction typically refers to learning opportunities separated by time, either within an instructional session/activity or across the day. This approach should be selected when targeting behaviors that occur as part of routine activities, such as self-care skills (e.g., handwashing, toileting) and communication (e.g., ask for cup at the snack table), and when targeting behaviors that are appropriate across activities (e.g., initiate peer-to-peer interactions). In addition, distributed instruction may be appropriate when promoting generalized use of behaviors, especially those that may have been targeted in more controlled environments. Within an instructional activity, it is possible to target multiple behaviors within an activity, spacing opportunities to respond across the session. For example, a child's individualized education program (IEP) may include objectives related to verbally naming common items, identifying items by attribute, and requesting preferred materials. The teacher and paraprofessionals could develop a plan to intermix targets during centers. Thus, instructional trials are distributed across time but within an activity. Like embedded and massed instruction, distributed instruction requires careful planning (e.g., when to intervene, adult support required to ensure a correct response), accurate data collection (e.g., reliability data collected by a second observer once a week), and comfort with procedures (e.g., fidelity data indicate adequate levels of accurate implementation) when determining when and how to promote target behaviors. Embedded instruction may be a compliment to massed instruction, in that behaviors learned during massed instructional trials could be targeted in unstructured or semi-structured activities in the classroom, promoting the generalization of behaviors.

Directedness

Another important consideration is whether instructional trials will occur during **child-directed** or **adult-directed** learning activities. Typical early childhood classrooms should include both of these types of activities. **Child-directed** activities are those in which children make decisions and choices about their own behaviors. Free play (indoors and outdoors) is a common child-directed activity. **Adult-directed** activities are those in which an adult leads a child or group of children and directs their behaviors. Many small and large group activities are adult-directed. Instructional sessions consisting of massed trials are necessarily adult-directed; trials embedded within or across activities can be inserted in child-directed or adult-directed activities. For example, trials intended to improve imitation of peer behaviors can be embedded during an adult-directed follow-the-leader game (Barton & Ledford, 2018) or during a child-directed sculpting activity (Sweeney, Barton, & Ledford, 2018).

Adult-led instruction is commonly associated with pre-planned trials and sessions where the adult provides an attending cue and obtains an attending response, presents the cue for a target behavior, shows the child how to be correct, and provides a consequence for child responding. Adult-led instructional trials can occur during child-directed or adult-directed activities. **Child-led instruction** commonly refers to the adult following the child's lead during play-based, "low structure situations," "responding to the child's focus of attention," and "employing naturally occurring antecedents and consequences" (Wolery & Hemmeter, 2011, p. 375). Child-led instruction can also occur during child-directed or adult-directed activities, but is commonly systematically planned for during child-directed activities.

Adult-led instructional trials utilize a relatively structured format, where clearly defined antecedent conditions and consequences are delivered and behaviors reinforced while teaching a variety of related or unrelated behaviors. In addition, with proper planning (e.g., multiple exemplars, functional behaviors, highlighting the critical features of a stimulus), adult-led instructional trials may also promote generalization, a critical aspect of learning (Wolery, 2012; Wolery, Ault, & Doyle, 1992). A child-led approach to instruction supports the belief that play is ultimately a child's form of work (or expected activity) (Wolery, 2006), and supports findings that enjoyable interactions related to play materials within the home, school, and community will likely contribute to a child's short- and long-term development (cf. Barton, 2016). Children can learn via adult- and child-led instruction in adult- and child-directed activities, necessitating a balance of each within early childhood settings.

Choosing Procedures and Procedural Variations

In many situations, there is more than one evidence-based practice that can be used to teach a specific behavior. Given this, what guidelines should be used to select just one? Although more specific information will be provided relevant to specific procedures in later chapters (e.g., when to choose progressive time delay versus constant time delay), some general guidelines are also warranted.

Research. When two evidence-based procedures can be used in a specific situation, one strategy for choosing which one to use is to look at the supporting research of each, to answer the question: Which strategy has been used more often, or more successfully, to teach a behavior similar to the one I want to teach and to teach children with similar characteristics? If available, you could also analyze any comparative research—for example, there are a number of comparative research studies regarding the relative effectiveness of different response prompting procedures or variations such as massed versus embedded trials (for a review, see Ledford et al., 2019). Oftentimes, comparative research that is directly applicable to your situation is unavailable; in these situations, you should place more emphasis on the characteristics of the children and adults who will be involved in the instruction, as described below.

Risk. When choosing procedures and variations (e.g., instructional arrangement), you should evaluate risk to the child in relation to the expected benefit. If two procedures or procedural variations are likely to yield similar benefits, the less risky procedure should be used. How might simple teaching procedures be risky? A few common risks include (a) isolation from peers, (b) slower learning which impacts growth opportunities and the ability to benefit from typical experiences, and (c) increased likelihood of errors, which can impact learning as well as child self-efficacy. Oftentimes, relative risks and benefits must be assessed—for example, teaching a child in a large group setting might result in slower learning, but might improve access to peer models.

Learning history and prerequisite behaviors. A child's learning history and the presence of critical learning behaviors may play a role in choosing a procedure or procedural variation. For example, some procedures require that a child waits for a prompt, inhibiting their own responding when they are not able to give a correct response, while other procedures do not (see Chapters 8 and 9). Similarly, some research has shown that once a child has experience with one systematic teaching procedure, they get better at using that procedure to learn subsequent information—a phenomenon called *learning to learn*. Thus, using an individual child's data to determine whether a specific procedure or procedural variation results in efficient learning is often the best predictor of what will result in learning in the future.

Implementer characteristics. Some teaching procedures are more complex than others—for example, progressive time delay requires the use of progressively longer intervals while constant time delay requires only one interval (see Chapter 8). Similarly, the system of least prompts requires the use of multiple prompt topographies while constant and progressive time delay requires only one (see Chapter 10). Some implementers may have more difficulty implementing complex procedures; for example, in one study, graduate students accurately performed progressive time delay following a training session but required additional coaching to use the system of least prompts with fidelity (Jones, 2018). Thus, when two procedures are likely to be similarly effective, using the most parsimonious procedure may be prudent.

Implementer preference. When given a choice, different implementers might prefer different procedures. Thus, when two procedures are likely to be equally effective and efficient, you might consider which the implementer prefers or which she is likely to implement with high fidelity.

Child preference. Similar to adult preference, data on child preferences suggest they are different across children and sometimes vary over time (Ledford, Chazin, Harbin, & Ward, 2017). Thus, providing access to two different interventions and asking the child to choose between them is one reasonable way to determine which procedure or procedural variation to use.

Research Abstract

Ledford, J. R., Chazin, K. T., Harbin, E. R., & Ward, S. E. (2017). Massed trials versus trials embedded into game play: Child outcomes and preference. *Topics in Early Childhood Special Education*, 37, 107–120.

In this single case design study, authors assessed whether children with and without disabilities learned discrete behaviors faster when trials were presented in massed formats or embedded into game play. During massed sessions, implementers first conducted several trials in which children were asked to name unknown stimuli such as letters. Then, the implementer played a board game with the child, with no trials included. During embedded sessions, implementers played a board game with the child, and some turns included opportunities for trials. For example, during a matching game, a letter would be affixed to some of the cards—when the child chose a card with an affixed letter, the implementer conducted a trial. Authors found that both massed and embedded instruction was effective for 11 of 12 children, and that about half of the children learned faster in each condition. Interestingly, children generally preferred the trial arrangement (i.e., massed or embedded instruction) from which they learned more quickly.

Summary

Learning is a multifaceted process comprised of four phases, some of which can be targeted simultaneously, but each of which require different considerations. Teaching is the process of attending to and arranging the environment to promote developmentally and culturally appropriate target behaviors that, when learned, lead to short- and long-term success for children. Identifying and understanding the basic foundations of learning and teaching allow us to better serve children who require supports. Analyzing the research base and child and implementer characteristics and preferences allows us to choose among available evidence-based practices.

Finnick decided to learn about recommended practices from DEC, NAEYC, and related organizations. He also read several published studies and systematic reviews to further evaluate which evidence-based practices he should use to target specific behaviors for children in his classroom. While familiarizing himself with these recommendations, he began establishing a relationship with his students and establishing instructional control, while assessing the needs of all students. Finnick identified specific behaviors and ideal times of the day where he could promote target behaviors to ensure each child learned the requirements of a behavior under typical conditions. Just like his students, Finnick is beginning to experience and be reinforced by his successes in teaching and, in turn, his students.

Related Resources

http://ectacenter.org/~pdfs/decrp/PGP_INS3_embedded_2018.pdf
https://ies.ed.gov/ncee/wwc/
www.naeyc.org
www.dec-sped.org

References

Barton, E. E., Bishop, C., & Snyder, P. (2014). High quality instruction through complete learning trials: Blending intentional teaching with embedded instruction. In K. Pretti-Frontczak, J. Grisham-Brown, & L. Sullivan (Eds.), *Young exceptional children monograph #16: Blending practices to strengthen quality early learning programs for ALL children* (pp. 73–96). Los Angeles, CA: DEC.

Barton, E. E. (2016). Critical issues and promising practices for teach play to young children with disabilities. In B. Reichow, B. A. Boyd, E. E. Barton, & S. L. Odom (Eds.), *Handbook of early childhood special education* (pp. 267–286). Switzerland: Springer International Publishing.

Barton, E. E., & Ledford, J. R. (2018). The effects of reinforcement on peer imitation in a small group play context. *Journal of Early Intervention, 40,* 69–86.

DEC (Division for Early Childhood of the Council for Exceptional Children). (2014). *DEC recommended practices in early intervention/early childhood special education.* Retrieved from: www.dec-sped.org/recommendedpractices.

DEC, NAEYC, & National Head Start Association. (2013). *Frameworks for response to intervention in early childhood: Description and implications.* Retrieved from https://divisionearlychildhood. egnyte.com.

Grisham-Brown, J., & Hemmeter, M. L. (2017). *Blended practices for teaching young children in inclusive settings* (2nd ed.). Baltimore, MD: Brookes.

Grisham-Brown, J., Schuster, J. W., Hemmeter, M. L., & Collins, B. C. (2000). Using an embedding strategy to teach preschoolers with significant disabilities. *Journal of Behavioral Education*, 10, 139–162.

Jones, S. K. (2018). *Relative effects of training on adult implementation of response prompting procedures.* Unpublished master's thesis. Nashville, TN: Vanderbilt University.

Ledford, J. R., Barton, E. E., Hardy, J. K., Elam, K., Seabolt, J., Shanks, M., Hemmeter, M. L., & Kaiser, A. (2016). What equivocal data from single case comparison studies reveal about evidence-based practices in early childhood special education. *Journal of Early Intervention*, 38, 79–91.

Ledford, J. R., Chazin, K. T., Harbin, E. R., & Ward, S. E. (2017). Massed trials versus trials embedded into game play: Child outcomes and preference. *Topics in Early Childhood Special Education*, 37, 107–120.

Ledford, J. R., Chazin, K. T., Gagnon, K., Lord, A., Turner, V. R., & Zimmerman, K. N. (2019). A systematic review of instructional comparisons in single case research (under review).

Sweeney, E., Barton, E. E., & Ledford, J. R. (2018). Using progressive time delay to increase levels of peer imitation during sculpting play. *Journal of Autism & Developmental Disorders.* doi: 10.1007/s10803-018-3638-2.

Venn, M. L., Wolery, M., Werts, M. G., Morris, A., DeCesare, L. D., & Cuffs, M. S. (1993). Embedding instruction in art activities to teach preschoolers with disabilities to imitate their peers. *Early Childhood Research Quarterly*, 8, 277–294.

Walker, G. (2008). Constant and progressive time delay procedures for teaching children with autism: A literature review. *Journal of Autism and Developmental Disorders*, 38, 261–275.

Wolery, M. (August 29, 2006). *Introduction to EI/ECSE and history of the field* [PowerPoint Presentation]. Nashville, TN: Vanderbilt University.

Wolery, M. (2012). Voices from the field. *Young Exceptional Children*, 15(4), 41–44.

Wolery, M., & Hemmeter, M. L. (2011). Classroom instruction: Background, assumptions, and challenges. *Journal of Early Intervention*, 33, 371–380.

Wolery, M., Anthony, L., Caldwell, N. K., Snyder, E. D., & Morgante, J. D. (2002). Embedding and distributing constant time delay in circle time and transitions *Topics in Early Childhood Special Education*, 22, 14–25.

Wolery, M., Ault, M. J., & Doyle, P. M. (1992). *Teaching students with moderate and severe disabilities: Use of response prompting strategies.* White Plains, NY: Longman.

5   Planning and Monitoring

Key Terms

Operational definitions	*Adult-paced instruction*	*Interobserver agreement*
Criterion statements	*Event and duration recording*	*Point-by-point agreement*
Measurement	*Partial interval recording*	*Gross agreement*
Free-operant condition	*Momentary time sampling*	*Procedural fidelity*

Chapter Objectives

After completing this chapter, readers should be able to:

- Understand the importance and value of planning for and monitoring fidelity of instructional programs and child outcomes.
- Develop feasible practices for collection of data.
- Describe multiple methods of measurement and estimation.
- Calculate reliability of data collected from two different observers.

Sipan recently graduated with his master's degree in interdisciplinary early childhood education and accepted a position as lead teacher at a local preschool program. As a first-year teacher, Sipan wants to carefully plan each moment of the school day and collect data to monitor student progress. He reads multiple textbooks and searches online for resources, but, ultimately, is unsure of how to balance all the responsibilities of running a classroom. Sipan plans a meeting with his administrator, Dr. O'Reilly, in hopes that she will guide him in the right direction.

The primary purpose of this chapter is to highlight how to plan and monitor instruction for multiple children during a variety of typically occurring activities (e.g., across the school day). Specifically, the chapter outlines procedures for the use of several different measurement systems, for counting or estimating child behavior for the purposes of progress monitoring. Recommendations for feasible and useful data collection are provided.

Introduction

Early childhood educators provide services to promote academic and social behaviors exhibited by children, regardless of exceptionality, but quality teaching and learning are only as meaningful as the tools and methods we use to plan for and document successes. Proper planning and monitoring are beneficial for children and educators alike—(1) children are likely to learn socially meaningful behaviors and (2) educators can determine if an intervention should continue (progress), be modified or replaced (lack of progress), or discontinued (the child acquired and generalized the target behavior). Operationally defining behaviors and selecting data collection systems are the first steps in documenting each child's progress over time. After specific behaviors have been identified and defined, educators must determine when, where, and how to teach each child across the day. Matrix planning is one option for planning how to meet the needs of all children and is a long-standing method used in early childhood settings; we discuss matrix planning in more detail in Chapter 14.

Planning and Monitoring Progress and Fidelity

Identifying individual and class-wide goals and objectives requires careful planning. Well-defined goals and objectives on a child's individualized education program (IEP) are an outcome of an interdisciplinary team reviewing assessment data, speaking with families about goals and priorities, and ensuring each stakeholder has an opportunity to provide feedback and recommendations. Assessment data and parent input are used to guide the IEP team in writing objectives that communicate (a) under what conditions a child should display a behavior (e.g., when presented with a sight word on a card during small group instruction), (b) what the behavior looks like in context, (c) the criterion for acceptable performance, and (d) an appropriate consequence when the target behavior occurs (e.g., preferred items; schedule of reinforcement). In contrast, developing well-defined goals and objectives for children with typical development usually involves input from fewer stakeholders. Although usually less formal than the IEP process, we recommend conducting age-appropriate assessments with all children and obtaining parent input on objectives for the school year. In addition, other classroom staff such as paraprofessionals should be involved in the planning process (Raver, 2004). Ultimately, well-crafted objectives communicate to all stakeholders the expectations for a child during the school year.

Operational definitions. Monitoring a child's acquisition of target behaviors requires educators to operationally define each target behavior. **Operational definitions** include three components—(1) a description of the target behavior (e.g., *socially appropriate play with peers* refers to the target child engaging in the same or similar activity as a peer who is within 0.30 meters), (2) examples of acceptable variations of the target behavior by context (e.g., rolling a ball back and forth with a peer; taking turns pouring sand through a sand wheel), and (3) non-examples that may be topographically similar to examples but not meet the full criteria for acceptability (e.g., proximal to peer, pouring sand through the same sand wheel, but engaging in stereotypy). Operational definitions can be based on observations of same-age peers with typical development, guidelines in published curricula, and input and feedback from families and related service providers. In addition, definitions can be based on dependent variables in published studies, especially those that included participants with similar characteristics to the target child. For example, a child's IEP includes an objective related to increasing age-appropriate activity on the playground; the child's teacher decides to measure *appropriate engagement*. First, she reviewed published studies that included children with similar characteristics to her student. After careful review, she selected a published study by Ledford, Lane, Shepley, and Kroll (2016) that measured multiple behaviors, such as physical activity and engagement on the playground. She decided to use the definition and transcribed it on her data sheet. She defined *appropriate engagement* as "appropriately playing with materials or peers or engaging in purposeful physical activity" and examples included "playing chase, playing with a bat to hit a ball, running toward the slide, imitating a peer," while non-examples included "walking in a repetitive sequence, wandering, [and] stereotypy" (Ledford et al., 2016, p. 166).

Criterion statements. Once target behaviors are identified and defined, criterion statements should be developed for each instructional objective. **Criterion statements** communicate to all involved individuals "how well a child must perform the skill" before it can be considered *mastered* (Wolery, 2004a, p. 538). Mastery is a relative term and dependent on the target behavior and context. For example, a child has an objective for independently requesting preferred items from adults during centers using various two-word combinations of nouns and verbs. It is unrealistic to expect a child to request preferred materials every time they are available during centers and, as such, the teacher and speech-language pathologist decide that the mastery criterion for this objective is when the child independently requests preferred items at least 50 percent of trials, compared to baseline-level responding, for three consecutive days across at least two adults. In contrast, the child is expected to independently request his lunch tray 90–100 percent of opportunities (taught only a few variations of appropriate requests for the lunch tray). Relatedly, targeting pre-academic behaviors, such as math facts or naming letters, involves a child recognizing the critical features of a stimulus (e.g., differentiating between the uppercase forms of A and H). An educator may select a mastery criterion of 88 percent unprompted correct responding (e.g., eight opportunities per session, allowing for one error) for a child who is learning to expressively identify multiple examples of the letters in her first name. The critical features of target stimuli are relatively stable and, as such, fewer errors are expected during instruction. Social communication targets, especially those that involve generalized forms of behaviors (e.g., *Subject + Verb + Noun* combinations during play-based activities) may require more flexibility than academic behaviors when selecting a mastery criterion. Finally, when targeting safety, the expectation is all related behaviors should occur with 100 percent accuracy (e.g., learning to cross the street when and only when the crosswalk sign is illuminated). Each of these examples highlights the importance of understanding the relationship between behavior and context and how each influences development of criterion statements.

Data Collection Systems

Measuring progress on objectives is key to determining if a child requires an intervention (baseline condition) and, if so, if he or she is responding to the intervention. **Measurement** is the process of objectively quantifying the occurrence or non-occurrence of a behavior by recording each instance of the behavior or estimating its occurrence (Cooper, Heron, & Heward, 2007; Ledford, Lane, & Gast, 2018; Wolery, Ault, & Doyle, 1992). First, educators must determine what dimension (or aspect) of a behavior they are interested in capturing during observations (Alberto & Troutman, 2012; Sulzer-Azaroff & Mayer, 1991). For example, an early childhood educator wants to promote conversation between peers during centers. Although an important skill, it requires further consideration before measuring the behavior in context. Is the teacher interested in how many times a child initiates an interaction with a peer or the number of exchanges during conversation (count), for how long children converse at a center or what percentage of time they spend talking with one another (duration), or how long it takes a child to respond to a peer's initiation (latency)? Answering such questions further specifies what should be measured and, in turn, how it should be measured. Additionally, the conditions under which a behavior will be measured warrant consideration. Measurement of some behaviors can occur under **free operant conditions**, meaning a child may display a behavior at any point during an observation. One example of this type of behavior would be spontaneous comments made to peers during centers; we would count these when they occur, which could happen at any time. Other behaviors should be measured given specific opportunities. One example of this type of behavior is correct responding to an adult question or correct responses to a peer request, which we refer to as **trial-based** behaviors. We would record responses only at specific times for these types of behaviors, generally following adult initiation of learning opportunity, such as asking a question.

Regardless of whether you are interested in free operant or trial-based behaviors, and whether you are interested in count, duration, or latency, measurement of targeted behaviors can occur using a variety of methods. Each involves (1) counting behavioral occurrences, (2) timing behavioral occurrences, (3) estimating counts, or (4) estimating time. Careful consideration of the appropriate measurement method is critical because the resulting data are used to make decisions about a child's progress, or lack thereof (cf. Ledford et al., 2018).

Event and duration recording. Event recording refers to counting each occurrence of a behavior during an observation or session, while duration recording refers to timing each occurrence. An event refers to a behavior with a clearly defined onset and offset (or a *beginning* and *end*). If interested in answering "How many times does the behavior occur?" then a count of behaviors is appropriate. In contrast, when answering, "For how long does the behavior occur?" then timing duration is appropriate.

Counting. A simple count of behaviors allows educators to measure how many times a behavior occurs per observation or session. A count is most commonly used to capture relatively brief behaviors (lasting 1 second or less), and can be used to measure discrete or chained behaviors. Additional options for using count are as follows:

- *Count with time stamps.* When counting a behavior under a free-operant condition, time stamps are recommended to increase the precision of measurement. For example, each instance of giving an item to a peer during a 5-minute observation is recorded, along with a time stamp of when the behavior occurred during the session. Electronic measurement, such as using an app to count occurrences, often automatically includes time stamps.
- *Window of time around onset and offset.* Attempting to count each instance of a high-rate behavior may provide an inaccurate representation of the true value of a behavior. For example, a child engages in challenging behaviors during whole group instruction, specifically using an open palm to smack her own legs; she typically engages in self-injury four to five times across a 1.5- to 2-second time period. In this example, the child is repeatedly displaying self-injury within a relatively short time period. Instead of attempting to count each occurrence, the operational definition should be modified and include a window of time for counting each bout of self-injurious behavior—onset refers to the first instance of self-injury and offset is recorded when two seconds or more elapse after the last occurrence of the target behavior.
- *Transform count to rate.* If a practitioner is interested in reporting the number of times a behavior occurred, the length of each session should be identical (e.g., 10-minute observations). If that is not possible, the data can be transformed to a rate measure (number of times the behavior occurred divided by the total time, in minutes). Rate is also an appropriate transformation for measuring fluency (number within a given time period; e.g., number of sight words read per minute).
- *Transform count to percentage.* When measuring occurrence during trial-based instruction, the target response is recorded for each trial and typically transformed to a percentage. A count can also be transformed to a percentage when there are an unequal number of opportunities for the child to respond across sessions.

Timing. Two options are available for measuring the duration of behaviors: (a) *total time* (or *total duration*) and (b) *time* or *duration per occurrence* (DPO). Total time yields the amount of time a child engaged in a target behavior during an observation. The duration of a behavior is recorded by starting a timer at the onset of the behavior and stopping a timer at the offset. This process is repeated until the end of the session; the total number of seconds the child engaged in the target behavior is recorded and graphed. DPO is procedurally similar, but involves additional steps. The duration of each instance of a behavior is recorded (onset and offset of a behavior equals one occurrence; e.g., behavior occurred for 30 seconds, then a second time for 25 seconds, and so on) and this process repeated for each subsequent occurrence. Thus, it is possible to report a count of each instance of the behavior (e.g., target behavior was observed ten times during a 20-minute session), the average duration per occurrence (add total duration of each occurrence and divide by the number of times the behavior occurred), and total duration (identical to *total time*); DPO is more informative than total time.

Estimations. When event and duration recording are not feasible, it is possible to *estimate* the number of times a behavior occurs or for how long it occurs. Contemporary guidelines for estimation systems indicate that partial-interval recording (PIR) and momentary time sampling (MTS) may be appropriate under specific conditions (whole interval recording *should not* be used); each system is prone to errors, which should be taken into consideration when deciding whether or not to use PIR or MTS.

When using each system,

1. An observation period is identified (e.g., 10 minutes during art).
2. The observation period is divided into intervals. In early childhood research, 5–10-second intervals are common in the literature (Lane & Ledford, 2014). For example, you might divide a 10-minute observation into 120 5-second intervals).
3. For each interval, behavioral occurrence is assessed (see specific rules below).
4. You can also designate a brief window of time (e.g., 5 seconds) following each interval as the time in which you record the behavior occurrence. This allows the observer time to record responses on the data sheet. For example, you might divide a 10-minute observation into 5-second intervals, with 5-second breaks for recording. This reduces the number of intervals from 120 to 60. This recording window is only necessary when there are concerns with accurately recording the target behavior. When using these systems, an interval timer is needed to ensure the length of intervals is held constant; these are typically freely available via applications for smart phones or other devices.

Partial-interval recording. When PIR is used, a behavior occurrence is recorded if a behavior occurs at any time during the interval. PIR may be appropriate for estimating how many times a behavior occurs during an observation. Each occurrence of a behavior should be scored once per interval (even if the target behavior occurred multiple times per interval) (Lane & Ledford, 2014). In addition, *onset* should be recorded in one interval and not across intervals. For example, when using 5-second intervals, a child begins displaying the target behavior at the 04.85-second mark of the third interval and the behavior continues until the 00.75-second mark of the fourth interval. The onset was at 4.85 seconds (third interval) and, as such, should only be recorded in that interval. PIR provides an *estimated count* of the target behavior and should be reported as such along the ordinate (or y-axis) of a graph. Because error associated with PIR is predictable, it is possible to correct error by using a Poisson-correction system (Ledford, Ayres, Lane, & Lam, 2015; Ledford et al., 2018; Yoder, Ledford, Harbison, & Tapp, 2018; http://tinyurl.com/Poisson-Correction). Once corrected, count each interval in which the behavior occurred and report the estimated count.

Momentary time sampling. MTS may be appropriate for estimating for how long a behavior occurs during an observation (Lane & Ledford, 2014). At the end of each interval, the observer looks at the child and records if the behavior is occurring or not occurring *at that moment only*. This process is repeated for each interval until the end of the observation. This system provides an *estimated duration* (or *percentage of intervals*) of the target behavior and should be reported as such along the ordinate (or y-axis) of a graph. Unlike PIR, error associated with MTS is random, meaning that MTS may overestimate or underestimate occurrences of a target behavior (Ledford et al., 2015; Ledford et al., 2018). At the end of the session, divide the number of occurrences by the total number of intervals and multiply by 100 to obtain an estimated duration. For example, if a behavior was occurring at the end of 30 intervals during an observation that lasted for 60 intervals, the estimate of behavior occurrence is 50 percent of the time (30 divided by 60, 50 percent of intervals).

Reliability and Training

We measure target behaviors in an effort to capture the true value of a behavior. To reduce risk of bias and control for human error, at least two people should collect data on target behaviors. For example, if a teacher was measuring the number of interactions a child initiated during a 30-minute free play activity, another adult (e.g., a paraprofessional) would record the same data, on the same child, at the same time. In research, this often occurs for a certain proportion of measurements (e.g., 25 percent of observations). In practice, it is optimal to collect these data intermittently, even if resources do not allow for frequent assessment.

The extent to which two people agree if a behavior occurred or did not is referred to as **interobserver agreement** (IOA). During adult-paced or trial-by-trial instruction, the implementer might record correct responding on a trial-by-trial basis while they are teaching. Simultaneously, a second person would observe and independently code the child's responses. Similarly, when using estimation systems or measuring behaviors under free operant conditions, a practitioner might be implementing a child-directed strategy and collecting data on child initiations, while another person simultaneously observes and records initiations. Optimally, observers should be situated in a manner that ensures neither can see what the other is coding.

Training. Before IOA data are collected, all adults should be trained on how to collect data with fidelity:

1. Review the operational definitions, data collection system, and corresponding data sheet.
2. Model how to collect data using a video example or during a live observation in the classroom.
3. Independently practice collecting data using a different video or during a second live observation.
4. Compare data and discuss discrepancies.
5. Repeat this process until independent observations yield a percentage agreement of 90 percent or higher.

At the end of each session, coded responses are compared to assess the extent to which both observers agreed a behavior occurred or did not occur. Disagreements indicate that observers are not making the same decisions about whether or not a behavior occurred. In research, when agreement is below 80 percent, data collection should cease and re-training should occur. In practice, it may mean that definitions should be clarified or additional training may be needed to improve accuracy or understanding of data collection rules. Agreement can be calculated using one of two overarching types of IOA—(1) point-by-point agreement (also known as trial-by-trial or interval-by-interval agreement) and (2) gross agreement.

Point-by-point agreement. Point-by-point agreement should be selected for trial-based instruction, interval recording, or when obtaining a count with time stamps.

- *Trial-based instruction.* Agreement is assessed by comparing codes for each trial (e.g., lead teacher recorded an unprompted correct response for the first trial and the secondary observer recorded the same response; trial-by-trial comparisons would continue for all remaining trials). The formula for calculating agreement is the number of agreements divided the number of agreements plus disagreements multiplied by 100, which yields a percentage of agreement for a session (see Figure 5.1 for an example).
- *Interval systems.* Similar to trial-based instruction, codes for each interval are compared to one another (e.g., both observers agreed that the behavior occurred during the first interval, did not occur during the second interval, and so on); the formula for calculating agreement is identical to trial-based instruction. Because interval-based systems may inflate the percentage of agreement, we recommend calculating occurrence agreement for low-rate behaviors (behavior occurs only a few times each session) and non-occurrence agreement for high-rate behaviors (behavior occurs multiple times each session).
  - Occurrence agreement. Identify intervals where at least one person said the behavior occurred. Count the number of intervals where both observers coded occurrence and divide that by the number of intervals with occurrence agreements plus occurrence disagreements and multiply by 100.
  - Non-occurrence agreement. Identify intervals where at least one person said the behavior *did not* occur. Count the number of intervals where both observers coded non-occurrence and divide that by the number of intervals with non-occurrence agreements plus non-occurrence disagreements and multiply by 100 (see Figure 5.2 for an example).
- *Count with time stamps.* Agreement is assessed by comparing each time a behavior occurred and its corresponding time stamp. Given the likelihood of human error and technical issues (e.g., app freezes), we recommend including a window of agreement. For example, a window of ±2 seconds can be used when measuring a behavior with a clearly defined onset and offset. Thus, if the lead teacher indicated the child displayed the target behavior at 01:15 and the paraprofessional indicated the behavior occurred at 01:17 it would be scored as an agreement. In contrast, if the lead teacher indicated the behavior occurred at 01:15 and the paraprofessional recorded 01:30, it is likely each potentially missed an occurrence of the behavior. The formula for calculating agreement is number of agreements within the window divided the number of agreements plus disagreements multiplied by 100 (see Figure 5.1 for an example).

Gross agreement. Gross agreement should be used when point-by-point agreement calculations are not possible. For example, if two observers are collecting data on the number of initiations during a 15-minute free play activity via tallying, it is not possible to assess whether each tally from one observer directly corresponds with a tally from the other observer. In this situation, you would just compare the number of tallies. Gross agreement is less precise than point-by-point agreement and is commonly used to assess agreement when measuring total count or total time (see Figure 5.3).

- *Total count.* Smaller count divided by the larger count multiplied by 100. For example, if one observer counted 4 initiations and the other counted 5, agreement would be calculated as (4/5)*100 percent or 80 percent.

- *Total time.* The same formula would be used for total time, with the smallest time recorded divided by the largest and multiplied by 100.

Frequency of Data Collection

"How often should I collect data?" or "How much data is *enough* data?" are common questions from pre-service professionals. These questions are more complicated than they may seem on the surface. First, a pre-intervention pattern of responding is established prior to introducing an intervention. Thus, a child's baseline level of responding should be measured and evaluated to ensure an intervention is needed. The general recommendation is to collect data on at least three separate occasions and, if data are relatively stable, introduce an intervention. If data are unstable, meaning there is variability or bounce in the data, additional observations are needed. This recommendation is rooted in baseline logic, meaning if an educator continued collecting child data under baseline conditions, he or she should expect the same pattern of responding to continue (cf. Ledford & Gast, 2018). Collection of baseline data allows practitioners to not only show that behaviors reached some desired level, but that behaviors were not at the desired level prior to implementation of the intervention, thus providing some evidence that the intervention implemented resulted in behavior change. Second, an intervention is introduced and responding is monitored to evaluate change over time. A previously established mastery criterion should drive this decision-making process. Thus, the question of *how often* and *how much* is directly related to the instructional objective, establishing a clear pattern of responding under a baseline condition, and demonstrating therapeutic improvements under an intervention condition. For example, some objectives may require relatively few intervention sessions to observe transfer of stimulus control and, as such, data should be collected multiple times per week; if data were collected once a week instructional time would likely be wasted because the child might have learned the behaviors but not have had a sufficient number of opportunities to demonstrate mastery. The frequency of data collection requires a "balance … between the demands of monitoring multiple goals [and objectives] and providing high-quality care and early intervention" (Wolery, 2004b, p. 552). To maximize instruction, each goal and related objectives should be prioritized. High-priority behaviors include keystone or pivotal behaviors (e.g., initiations, imitation; Wolery & Hemmeter, 2011) that, when learned, allow children the opportunity to experience new behavior–environment contingencies. In addition, priority should be given to pre-requisite behaviors (e.g., attend to adult and peers during small group instruction). Sample classroom data sheets are provided in Appendix 5.1.

Fidelity of Implementation

Procedural fidelity data allow educators to monitor the extent to which procedures are implemented as intended (Barton, Meadan-Kaplansky, & Ledford, 2018). Procedural fidelity is important when considering the impacts of an intervention: if an adult does not implement an intervention well, we would expect that child outcomes are impacted. For example, if a teacher was implementing a system of least prompts procedure, but she often provided extra prompts or task directions, a child's learning might be slowed. If we were unaware that fidelity to intervention procedures was low, we would not be able to connect the child learning outcomes with the teacher's behaviors.

The first step of assessing procedural fidelity is operationally defining each step of an instructional program, including baseline and intervention conditions. Baseline conditions may refer to *business-as-usual* in the classroom, but what that looks like in practice should be clearly defined for observers. For example, multiple children have an objective related to increasing the rate of social interactions during centers. The teacher plans to introduce visuals in the form of photographs and pictures of each child's preferences (e.g., television shows, toys, snacks) into the dramatic play center and measure if rate of interactions increase. The teacher is excited about her plan, but first wants to evaluate how children perform during baseline sessions. She operationally describes what typically occurs at the dramatic play center (free operant condition): (a) three children are assigned to the dramatic play center, (b) the timer is set for 10 minutes, (c) no additional adult supports are provided, with the exception of redirecting children back to the center, and (d) age-appropriate materials are available (materials are rotated bi-monthly in the center, with themes recorded on the data sheet). In this example, an observer would record the presence or absence of these steps on a data sheet (*yes* or *no*). A similar process would occur for defining expectations during adult-paced instruction (5 trials per child in a small group format): (a) teacher provides an attending cue to the target child, (b) teacher obtains an attending response, (c) teacher presents a word on an index card and asks, "What Word?" (d) teacher waits 5 seconds for a response and (e) provides reinforcement in the form of descriptive praise if the child is correct or (f) does not respond if the child is incorrect, (g) waiting 3 seconds before beginning the next trial. An observer would record occurrence or non-occurrence for each adult behavior by trial during the session. Whether under a free-operant condition or during adult-paced instruction, each of these steps would be monitored during baseline and intervention sessions; the only difference between baseline and intervention sessions is introduction of the intervention. Relatedly, the intervention would be operationalized and assessed across all conditions. The expectation is that the teacher would not provide a prompt in the dramatic play center or during small group instruction until a reliable pattern of responding is observed in the data. It is especially important to assess fidelity when multiple adults are responsible for providing instruction; for example, teachers should assess fidelity of instructional assistants or paraprofessionals, both for the purposes of guiding feedback provided to them (see Chapter 15) and to identify any differences among implementers. Guidelines for collecting procedural fidelity data are similar to those outlined in the *Reliability and Training* section for IOA. Like IOA, research guidelines suggest procedural fidelity data should be collected for *at least* 20 percent of sessions. The formula for calculating procedural fidelity is the number of observed behaviors divided by the number of planned behaviors multiplied by 100.

Research Abstract

Carroll, R. A., Kodak, T., & Fisher, W. W. (2013). An evaluation of programmed treatment-integrity errors during discrete-trial instruction. *Journal of Applied Behavior Analysis*, 46, 379–394.

In this single case design study, authors assessed whether children would learn as quickly if their instructors made systematic procedural fidelity errors. Participants included four preschool (4 years old) and two school-aged (6 and 9 years old) children with autism spectrum disorder. During the first comparison, instructors used constant time delay to teach discrete behaviors. During some sessions, implementers used the procedure correctly while during other sessions they made purposeful errors in order to test whether procedural errors impacted children's learning. All children learned faster when teachers conducted the trials with high fidelity. This suggests that professionals in early childhood need to conduct instructional procedures as intended to promote optimal outcomes for children.

Point-by-Point Agreement

UPC	Unprompted correct
UPE	Unprompted error
PC	Prompted correct
PE	Prompted error
NR	No response

Trial	Stimulus	Observer 1 Child Responses		Observer 2 Child Responses
1	1	UPC	✓	UPC
2	7	UPC	✓	UPC
3	3	PC	✓	PC
4	6	PC	✓	PC
5	5	PC	X	UPC
6	7	UPC	✓	UPC
7	5	UPC	✓	UPC
8	6	UPC	✓	UPC
9	1	PE	X	PC
10	3	PE	✓	PE

8 agreements / 8 agreements + 2 disagreements x 100=80%

Count with Time Stamps

Free Operant Condition
5-minute observation
Using 2-second window

Observer 1 Child Responses		Observer 2 Child Responses
0:30		0:31
0:45		0:46
-		1:15
1:25		1:25
2:44		
3:31		3:29
4:30		4:31

5 agreements within window / 5 agreements within window + 2 disagreements x 100 = 71.4%

Figure 5.1 Agreement Calculations.

Note: The top panel depicts how to calculate IOA for a trial-based session—a check mark indicates agreement and an X represents a disagreement. The bottom panel depicts IOA for an observational session when counting each occurrence and recording time stamps, using ±2 second window of agreement. Light fill indicates an agreement, and dark fill represents a disagreement.

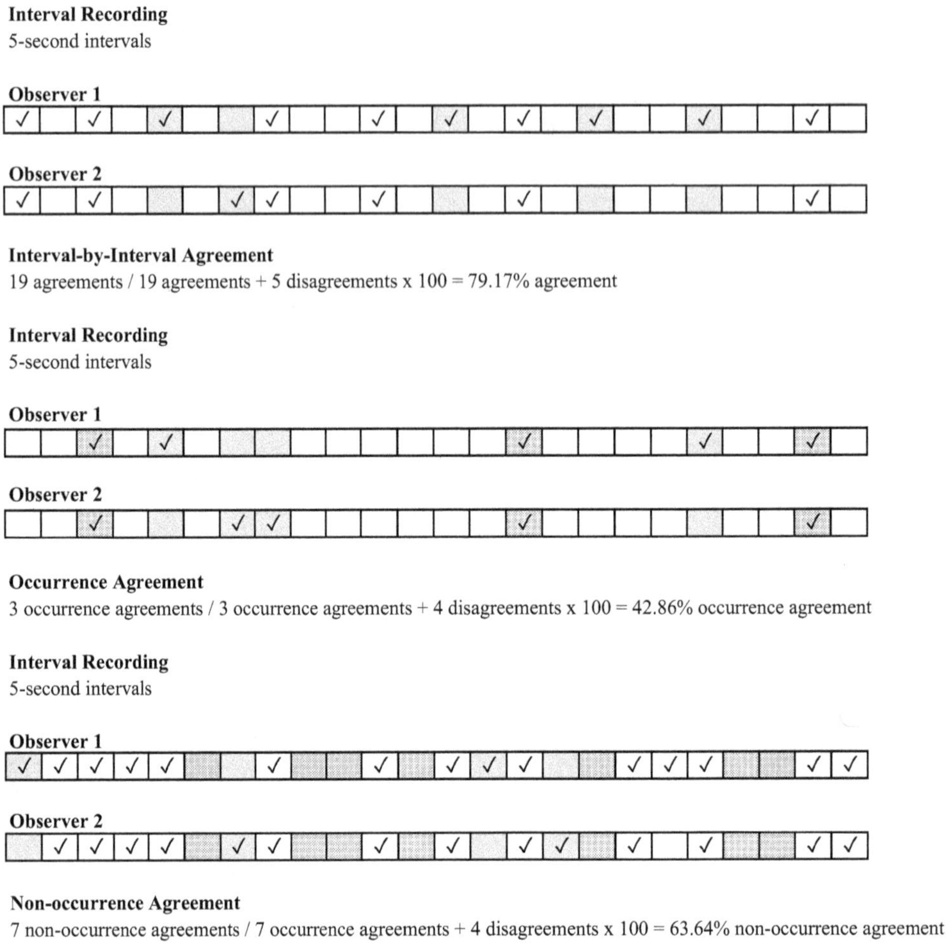

Interval Recording
5-second intervals

Observer 1

Observer 2

Interval-by-Interval Agreement
19 agreements / 19 agreements + 5 disagreements x 100 = 79.17% agreement

Interval Recording
5-second intervals

Observer 1

Observer 2

Occurrence Agreement
3 occurrence agreements / 3 occurrence agreements + 4 disagreements x 100 = 42.86% occurrence agreement

Interval Recording
5-second intervals

Observer 1

Observer 2

Non-occurrence Agreement
7 non-occurrence agreements / 7 occurrence agreements + 4 disagreements x 100 = 63.64% non-occurrence agreement

Figure 5.2 Agreement Calculations.

Note: Check marks indicate behavior occurrence as indicated by one observer. The first panel depicts point-by-point agreement using an interval-based system. Unfilled cells indicate agreements and filled cells indicate disagreements. The middle panel depicts occurrence agreement (relatively low-rate behavior); cells that indicate at least one person recorded the occurrence of a behavior are filled, with darker fill representing a disagreement (one person indicated occurrence) and light fill indicating an agreement (both people indicated occurrence). The bottom panel depicts non-occurrence agreement (relatively high-rate behavior); cells that indicate at least one person recorded the non-occurrence of a behavior are filled, with darker fill representing a disagreement (one person indicated non-occurrence) and light fill indicating an agreement (both people indicated non-occurrence).

Summary

Proper planning and monitoring are relatively complex processes for early childhood practitioners. We intervene on behaviors during typical activities, utilizing a variety of instructional approaches (embedded instruction, direct instruction), to promote learning in young children. Data are collected to monitor a child's progress on goals and object-ives, as well as guide us in modifying an intervention. Even the most well-trained student will likely encounter real-world challenges in the classroom (e.g., child displays severe and

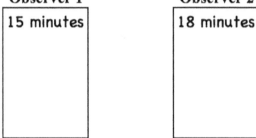

Gross Agreement
Total Count

Observer 1

lllll

Observer 2

llll

4 / 5 x 100=80%

Gross Agreement
Total Time

Observer 1

15 minutes

Observer 2

18 minutes

15 / 18 x 100 = 83.33%

Figure 5.3 Agreement Calculations.

Note: The top panel depicts a gross measure of agreement for the number of times a behavior occurred during an observation. The bottom panel depicts a gross measure of agreement for total time.

aggressive behavior directed at peers). The extent to which day-to-day challenges interfere with daily instructional responsibilities is lessened when educators spend time planning how to intervene on target behaviors, know how to identify and use appropriate data collection systems, monitor fidelity of implementation, and maximize instructional opportunities across the day.

Sipan is now in his third month as a lead teacher. Admittedly, he felt the first few weeks were nothing more than "putting out fires," addressing challenges as they arose (e.g., ensuring data accurately reflected each child's progress on goals and objectives). During this time period, Dr. O'Reilly scheduled daily meetings with Sipan. She encouraged Sipan to develop guidelines and expectations for all adults who worked in the classroom, including himself. Sipan began collaborating with paraprofessionals to develop an equitable schedule (e.g., rotation for diapering and toileting), provided training on how to collect data and implement procedures, and ensured everyone knew how to respond when unexpected issues arose. Today, Sipan still meets with Dr. O'Reilly, but only as needed. He better understands the complexities of running a classroom and recognizes the importance of carefully planning instruction and making data-based decisions related to each child's progress on goals and objectives.

References

Alberto, P. A., & Troutman, A. C. (2012). *Applied behavior analysis for teachers* (9th ed.). Upper Saddle River, NJ: Pearson.

Barton, E. E., Meadan-Kaplansky, H., & Ledford, J. R. (2018). Independent variables, fidelity, and social validity. J. R. Ledford & D. L. Gast (Eds.), *Single case research in behavioral sciences* (3rd ed.) (pp. 133–156). New York: Routledge.

Cooper, J. O., Heron, T. E., & Heward, W. L. (2007). *Applied behavior analysis* (2nd ed.). Columbus, OH: Pearson.

Lane, J. D., & Ledford, J. R. (2014). Using interval-based systems to measure behavior in early childhood special education and early intervention. *Topics in Early Childhood Special Education*, 34, 83–93.

Ledford, J. R., & Gast, D. L. (Eds.) (2018). *Single case research methodology: Applications in special education and behavioral sciences* (3rd ed.). New York: Routledge.

Ledford, J. R., Ayres, K., Lane, J. D., & Lam, M. F. (2015). Identifying issues and concerns with the use of interval-based systems in single case research: A pilot simulation study. *The Journal of Special Education*, 49, 104–117.

Ledford, J. R., Lane, J. D., & Gast, D. L. (2018). Dependent variables, measurement, and reliability. J. R. Ledford & D. L. Gast (Eds.), *Single case research in behavioral sciences* (3rd ed.) (pp. 97–131). New York: Routledge.

Ledford, J. R., Lane, J. D., Shepley, C., & Kroll, S. M. (2016). Using teacher-implemented playground interventions to increase engagement, social behaviors, and physical activity for young children with autism. *Focus on Autism and Other Developmental Disabilities*, 31, 163–173.

Raver, S. A. (2004). Monitoring child progress in early childhood special education settings. *Teaching Exceptional Children*, 36, 52–57.

Sulzer-Azaroff, B., & Mayer, G. R. (1991). *Behavior analysis for lasting change*. New York: Holt, Rinehart & Winston.

Wolery, M. (2004a). Using assessment information to plan intervention programs. In M. McLean, M. Wolery, & D. B. Bailey, Jr. (Eds.), *Assessing infants and preschoolers with special needs* (3rd ed.) (pp. 517–544). Upper Saddle River, NJ: Pearson.

Wolery, M. (2004b). Monitoring children's progress and intervention implementation. In M. McLean, M. Wolery, & D. B. Bailey, Jr. (Eds.), *Assessing infants and preschoolers with special needs* (3rd ed.) (pp. 545–584). Upper Saddle River, NJ: Pearson.

Wolery, M., & Hemmeter, M. L. (2011). Classroom instruction: Background, assumptions, and challenges. *Journal of Early Intervention*, 33, 371–380.

Wolery, M., Ault, M. J., & Doyle, P. M. (1992). *Teaching students with moderate and severe disabilities: Use of response prompting strategies*. White Plains, NY: Longman.

Yoder, P. J., Ledford, J. R., Harbison, A., & Tapp, J. (2018). Partial-interval estimation of count. *Journal of Early Intervention*, 40, 39–51.

Appendix 5.1

Sample School-Based Data Sheets

Date: _____
Location: _____
Instructor Initials: _____

Circle Each Code by Trial
+=unprompted correct, P+=prompted correct
UE=unprompted error, P-=prompted error
NR=no response

Sharing Items with Peers

Child Initials	Target	Data				
AB	Take shared item	+	+	+	+	+
		P+	P+	P+	P+	P+
		UE	UE	UE	UE	UE
		P-	P-	P-	P-	P-
		NR	NR	NR	NR	NR
ZB	Request a share	+	+	+	+	+
		P+	P+	P+	P+	P+
		UE	UE	UE	UE	UE
		P-	P-	P-	P-	P-
		NR	NR	NR	NR	NR
CG	Give 1 of multiple	+	+	+	+	+
		P+	P+	P+	P+	P+
		UE	UE	UE	UE	UE
		P-	P-	P-	P-	P-
		NR	NR	NR	NR	NR
AH	Request a share	+	+	+	+	+
		P+	P+	P+	P+	P+
		UE	UE	UE	UE	UE
		P-	P-	P-	P-	P-
		NR	NR	NR	NR	NR
EP	Take shared item	+	+	+	+	+
		P+	P+	P+	P+	P+
		UE	UE	UE	UE	UE
		P-	P-	P-	P-	P-
		NR	NR	NR	NR	NR
RT	Give 1 of multiple	+	+	+	+	+
		P+	P+	P+	P+	P+
		UE	UE	UE	UE	UE
		P-	P-	P-	P-	P-
		NR	NR	NR	NR	NR
AW	Request a share	+	+	+	+	+
		P+	P+	P+	P+	P+
		UE	UE	UE	UE	UE
		P-	P-	P-	P-	P-
		NR	NR	NR	NR	NR

Tolerate Denied Requests

Child Initials	Data				
EP	+	+	+	+	+
	P+	P+	P+	P+	P+
	UE	UE	UE	UE	UE
	P-	P-	P-	P-	P-
	NR	NR	NR	NR	NR
RT	+	+	+	+	+
	P+	P+	P+	P+	P+
	UE	UE	UE	UE	UE
	P-	P-	P-	P-	P-
	NR	NR	NR	NR	NR

Learning-to-Learn Behaviors
Respond to Attending Cue

Child Initials	Data				
AH	+	+	+	+	+
	P+	P+	P+	P+	P+
	UE	UE	UE	UE	UE
	P-	P-	P-	P-	P-
	NR	NR	NR	NR	NR
CG	+	+	+	+	+
	P+	P+	P+	P+	P+
	UE	UE	UE	UE	UE
	P-	P-	P-	P-	P-
	NR	NR	NR	NR	NR
AW	+	+	+	+	+
	P+	P+	P+	P+	P+
	UE	UE	UE	UE	UE
	P-	P-	P-	P-	P-
	NR	NR	NR	NR	NR

Ask to Join in Play
"Can I play?" Or "What are you playing"

Child Initials	Data				
AB	+	+	+	+	+
	P+	P+	P+	P+	P+
	UE	UE	UE	UE	UE
	P-	P-	P-	P-	P-
	NR	NR	NR	NR	NR
ZB	+	+	+	+	+
	P+	P+	P+	P+	P+
	UE	UE	UE	UE	UE
	P-	P-	P-	P-	P-
	NR	NR	NR	NR	NR
AH	+	+	+	+	+
	P+	P+	P+	P+	P+
	UE	UE	UE	UE	UE
	P-	P-	P-	P-	P-
	NR	NR	NR	NR	NR
AW	+	+	+	+	+
	P+	P+	P+	P+	P+
	UE	UE	UE	UE	UE
	P-	P-	P-	P-	P-
	NR	NR	NR	NR	NR

Number of initiations to peers
Tally during free play (2-minute sample)

Child Initials	Data
AB	
ZB	
CG	
AH	
EP	
RT	
AW	

Multiple Children Per Data Sheet

Data Sheet for CS
Date: _____
Location: _____
Instructor Initials: _____

Record the corresponding code in the correct box
(1 box=1 trial)
+=unprompted correct, P+=prompted correct
UE=unprompted error, P-=prompted error
NR=no response

Conversation with Peers
Q=Question, C=Comment
Record if an initiation or response, then tally number of
continuations

Q or C? (Circle)	Initiation?	Response?	Continuations (Tally)
Q C			
Q C			
Q C			
Q C			
Q C			
Q C			
Q C			
Q C			
Q C			
Q C			

Request Preferred Item from Peer
Record if spontaneous comments occur during observation
(tally marks)

Peer withholds item								
Spontaneous Comments								

Novel Imitation with Objects or Actions on Objects
Discriminative stimulus:
"Do this" or "Do what I'm doing" + model of action

Novel Imitation										

Discriminate mastered imitation targets
Discriminative stimulus:
"Do this" + model

Wave					Arms Up				
Pat Legs					Knock				
Pat Surface					Stomp Feet				

Independently Play at Center
Record activity and number of redirects to center
Target=5 minutes

Activity:	
Activity:	
Activity:	

Name Sight Words

Read				Jump			
Play				Crawl			
Eat				Drink			

Learning to Learn Behaviors
Small Group Instruction

Respond to Attending Cue						

Track Challenging Behavior
Record during whole- and small-group instruction

Whole Group Instruction

Physical Aggression	
Non-Compliance	
Self-Stimulatory Behavior	
Elopement (successes or attempts)	

Small Group Instruction

Physical Aggression	
Non-Compliance	
Self-Stimulatory Behavior	
Elopement (successes or attempts)	

Individual Data Sheet for a Child

6 Environmental Arrangement Strategies

Key Terms

Environmental arrangement	*Peer buddies*	*Physical environment*
Antecedent-based	*Peer models*	*Visual supports*
Social environment	*Peer confederates*	*Temporal environment*

Chapter Objectives

After completing this chapter, readers should be able to:

- Define environmental arrangement.
- Differentiate social, physical, and temporal components that comprise the environment.
- Provide strategies for arranging the social environment.
- Provide strategies for arranging the physical environment.
- Provide strategies for arranging the temporal environment.

Cory teaches children who are 3–5 years of age in a full-day inclusion classroom located in a rural town in the southeastern United States. She spends many hours before and after school setting up centers, but notices that oftentimes children with typical development play together, while children with autism spectrum disorder and those with intellectual disability play alone. She is unsure how to remediate this issue, but knows there are additional changes she can make in the environment and her own behavior to promote engagement and social communication between peers.

The primary purpose of this chapter is to describe the importance of environmental arrangement on effective teaching. Specific recommendations are provided for early childhood professionals on how to capitalize on the environment as a tool for promoting age-appropriate behaviors during typical activities, including peer-to-peer interactions.

Introduction

Understanding the relationship between a child's behavior and his or her immediate environment is critical to promoting socially meaningful behaviors. A child who is engaged and interactive is demonstrating that he or she has learned when and how to appropriately respond to a variety of stimuli across persons and activities. For example, a teacher notices that his student is having trouble choosing a center and offers the student a choice of the block center or dramatic play center; she selects the block center. When the student approaches the block center, she selects magnet tiles, constructs a tower, and begins to drop miniature items, like cars and balls, into the tower, narrating her play with exclamations and statements such as, "Whoa! Don't fall!" and "Whee! The car is diving into the water."

While building the tower, a peer approaches and sits beside her. Recognizing that her peer does not have any toys, but is interested in her play, she gives him a miniature car so he can join the activity. This simple example highlights the complexities of recognizing the subtle cues for contextually appropriate behaviors. Because of the student's successful experiences at the block center, she chose to engage in a play routine that previously led to pleasant consequences. In addition, she recognized that sharing a material with a peer allowed her to engage in shared play routine. Thus, the student responded to the antecedent conditions for engagement and interactions with a peer, which ultimately led to accessing preferred activities and social attention. Teaching children to respond to their environment is more likely to occur when adults attend to and modify the social, physical, and temporal aspects of the environment, such as planning meaningful activities, encouraging children to explore materials, and supporting peer-to-peer interactions.

Environmental modifications are fundamental to designing and implementing successful behavior change programs and lesson plans. To facilitate learning, adults may need to create (or embed) opportunities for children to learn when and how to display behaviors. Adults can arrange the environment to highlight the natural cues that indicate that a specific behavior should be produced and then they can show the child how to engage in the desirable behaviors. Following the behavior, the adult can provide contextually appropriate responses, including child-preferred social interactions, items, or activities.

Environmental Arrangement

Generally, we refer to environmental arrangement strategies as **antecedent-based** interventions; that is, these strategies involve changing the environment prior to expecting children to engage in a specific behavior. The EA strategies discussed in this chapter are generally intended to improve social behaviors and engagement; improving these behaviors and teaching children to engage in specific discrete skills (e.g., pre-academic behaviors) may require both environmental arrangement *and* systematic teaching. That is, effective environmental arrangement is a necessary but not sufficient condition for optimal child learning.

Social, Physical, and Temporal Environmental Arrangement Strategies

Social environmental arrangement. Inclusive settings are ideal for promoting peer-to-peer interactions and while some children will display prosocial behaviors with limited to no support from adults in such settings, some children will require support to learn when and how to interact with peers. While inclusive settings are a positive attribute that may contribute to increased opportunities for social interactions, inclusivity alone is often insufficient for promoting advanced, frequent, positive peer interactions. A number of adult- and peer-related strategies can be used to promote prosocial behaviors in young children.

1. **Friendship activities.** Common activities for young children can be modified to include opportunities for peer-to-peer interactions. Activities such as singing songs can be modified to include social behaviors like high-fives, hugs, and pats on the back or include opportunities to request a share or comment to a peer. For example, when planning a large group activity, the song "If you're happy and you know it" could be modified to include social actions ("If you're happy and you know it hug a friend") (e.g., Frea, Craig-Unkefer, Odom, & Johnson, 1999). Similarly, common activities such as morning meeting can be modified to include opportunities for children to share thoughts with a peer—this allows for not only increased peer interactions, but increased opportunities to respond when compared with alternative methods such as a teacher asking a single child to respond to a question.

2. **Divide materials among children.** Instead of providing all materials in a center, adults could divide materials among peers to promote requests for shares and social play. One option is to divide a larger set of materials (e.g., blocks) or divide pieces or parts of traditionally isolate toy sets or activities (e.g., puzzle pieces and puzzle board) among peers. Such arrangements may increase the rate of peer-to-peer interactions or create opportunities for adults to introduce relatively simple prompts for interactions (e.g., reminders to play together or share items) (Barton et al., 2016).

3. **Assign peer buddies.** Peer buddies are another relatively simple option for promoting social behaviors among children during free play activities (Morales & Ledford, 2016). Adults should pair children with typical social development with children who require supports to display social behaviors. Peer buddies may be assigned to children during an activity or across the day; this arrangement creates natural opportunities for social behaviors either through peer-to-peer interactions or observing peers' live models of socially appropriate behaviors during free play.

4. **Utilize peer models.** When planning instructional sessions (e.g., small group format at a center or table), children who typically display age-appropriate social behaviors can serve as peer models for children with social deficits or delays (Ledford & Wolery, 2015). Adults provide an opportunity for a peer to display a target behavior and subsequently provide reinforcement. Children in the group may be encouraged to attend to one another to increase the likelihood of observational learning (Ledford, Lane, Elam, & Wolery, 2012).

5. **Directly train peer confederates.** Some children with social deficits or delays may not respond or display variable responding to peers and, as such, it may be necessary to directly train peers to evoke target behaviors. A number of peer-training interventions are available in the literature, but the extent to which interventions are appropriate for improving target behaviors in young children varies within and across studies (Joseph, Strain, Olszewski, & Goldstein, 2016; Ledford, King, Harbin, & Zimmerman, 2018). Although outcomes vary, peer-training interventions commonly entail adults describing and modeling when and how to evoke target behaviors, role-playing with peers, and providing performance feedback following sessions (Pierce & Schreibman, 1995, 1997). In recent years, the *Stay-Play-Talk* intervention has received increased attention as a systematic approach to training peer confederates (see Appendix 6.1 for planning worksheet; Kohler, Greteman, Raschke, & Highnam, 2007; Ledford, Osborne, & Chazin, 2016). Peers are trained to stay near the target child, engage in the same or similar activities, and provide opportunities to practice target behaviors. Peers may require reminders and prompts to engage with the target child as well as external reinforcers (e.g., stickers) (Ledford et al., 2016). The procedures used to train peer confederates can be used with children with and without social deficits and delays. All children can be trained in small groups, which provides opportunities to practice target behaviors in context, as well as recognizes that interventions for improving social behaviors will likely benefit all children, regardless of risk status or diagnosis.

Research Abstract

Goldstein, H., English, K., Shafer, K., & Kaczmarek, L. (1997). Interaction among preschoolers with and without disabilities: Effects of across-the-day peer intervention. *Journal of Speech, Language, and Hearing Research, 40,* 33–48.

In this single case design study, eight preschoolers with developmental delays or Down syndrome were paired with eight preschoolers without disabilities. Researchers trained the preschoolers without disabilities to acknowledge and respond to unconventional communication behaviors such as unintelligible language. They then taught peers, in three separate lessons to *stay* near, *play* with, and *talk* to their buddy with disabilities. If peers used the *stay-play-talk* strategies, they received rewards. Researchers provided reminders to students to engage in these behaviors during free play activities. For all children, the number of interactions per 10-minute observation improved during intervention conditions. Outcomes of this study show that peer training, along with rewards and reminders, results in increased interactions between peers with and without disabilities.

Physical environmental arrangement. The physical arrangement of the classroom will directly impact when and how children interact with adults and with one another. In addition, ensuring all children can access materials and activities increases the likelihood of active engagement in age-appropriate activities.

1. **Carefully select materials.** A variety of age-appropriate materials should be available, including books, blocks, items to promote dramatic play (e.g., clothes, hats, props), play sets (e.g., miniature characters, house), and so on, with attention given to providing materials that promote diversity and inclusion (e.g., race, culture, exceptionality) (Division for Early Childhood of the Council for Exceptional Children [DEC], 2014). When possible, we recommend having duplicates of items, which can be used to promote imitation and parallel play. In addition, adding items that are unrelated to a play set or activity may promote early symbolic play behaviors (e.g., object substitution, which is using a pipe cleaner as a scarf or water hose for a fire truck).
2. **Physical arrangement.** The physical arrangement of items in a classroom can inhibit or facilitate engagement in activities and with peers. In general, furniture should be at age-appropriate heights (tables, chairs) and arranged in a manner that clearly indicates to children what will occur in that area. Avoid arranging tables in a manner that creates paths for children to run or chase one another (promote safety; e.g., all tables are placed in the middle of a room, creating an unplanned space for children to chase one another in the classroom) (DEC, 2014).
3. **Use visual supports.** Incorporating visual supports into a classroom provides children with static information about expectations in a given area or activity, as well as predictability across a day. We define **visual supports** as materials that assist children by helping children understand what they are expected to do.
   a. First, we recommend clearly labeling centers with corresponding text and visuals and displaying this information in an easily accessible manner (e.g., visual hanging above a center or visual posted outside a center).
   b. Second, the physical space of a classroom may limit the number of peers who can participate in a center. These high-traffic areas will need to be monitored to ensure all children have an opportunity to meaningfully engage in the center. When limiting the number of children who can be in a center at one time, we recommend including an additional visual support that represents an amount or number (e.g., two dots for two children where children place an item such as a clothespin on a dot). Limits should be carefully designed to ensure that all children have opportunities to engage in the center (e.g., two children do not monopolize

the center) and children know how to take turns at popular centers. Some centers might not need specific limits (e.g., the block center has a large rug around it and plenty of space for all children). However, if most children are requesting the same center, materials available in the remaining centers should be reviewed to ensure they are appealing and engaging.

c. Third, visuals may also be used to support peer-to-peer interactions. Including photographs or pictures of each child's family and interests (e.g., preferred children's book characters) may provide contextual supports for children who may be interested in peers, but unsure of what to say when initiating a conversation (Lane, Gast, Ledford, & Shepley, 2017; Winstead, Lane, Spriggs, & Allday, in press).

d. Fourth, incorporating visual schedules into a classroom is a relatively easy method for ensuring all children know what to expect across a day. We recommend incorporating a schedule for all children (layout of the day) and, when needed, an individualized schedule to support transitions for children who may be unfamiliar with the classroom schedule or those who display difficulty with exploring the classroom. Children need to practice following a visual schedule and receive reinforcement for attending to and complying with the schedule (e.g., Johnston, Nelson, Evans, & Palazolo, 2003; Meadan, Ostrosky, Triplett, Michna, & Fettig, 2011).

e. Finally, identify 3–5 classroom rules that highlight overarching (e.g., program-wide or school-wide) social expectations for all children and visually represent those in the classroom. Rules should be stated in a positive manner and explained to children, with observable and measurable actions modeled by adults, followed by role-playing with children. Reinforcement should be provided when target behaviors are observed in the classroom. Examples of possible rules for a classroom include "follow directions," "share," and "talk to friends." Consistently and frequently, adults should praise children who are following rules by explicitly stating both the specific, observable behavior (e.g., "You just *gave half your blocks to Natalia!*") and the rule that was followed ("Super job showing me you understand the rule *Be kind*").

Temporal environmental arrangement. An often-overlooked component of the environment is the temporal layout of a session or day. Providing adequate structure to a session or day assists with teaching children when and how to interact with same-age peers.

1. **Length of activities.** Typical preschool classrooms are likely to allow all children to participate in centers when and for how long they want. This approach is arguably more appropriate for young children who actively explore multiple centers and, as such, have multiple opportunities to learn contextually appropriate behaviors (e.g., construction task with a peer; sharing a straw hat with a peer when pretending to farm) with multiple peers. In contrast, children who typically stay in one center and engage in a singular task most school days will likely require additional supports to benefit from an inclusive setting. Thus, some children may benefit from being exposed to multiple centers for shorter bouts of time instead of one center for an extended period. That being said, the length of activities may need to be modified or varied based on the overarching goals for a child or multiple children (e.g., social communication improvements during gross motor activities). A good rule of thumb is that activities should last for as long as children will remain actively engaged, and no longer.

2. **Time of day.** Some children may be more likely to interact with peers and materials during certain times of the day. For example, a child who typically does not sleep well at night may be less likely to benefit from socially related instruction when arriving at school. This is not to say that opportunities for social behavior should be limited, but more so that planned instruction should be carefully considered in order to maximize outcomes for children. In contrast, young children may be more active in the morning and tired by the middle of the day or late afternoon. In this situation, adults should plan to capitalize on this time period of active engagement.

3. **Planning adequate opportunities.** Some children may display difficulties attending to the natural cues for behaviors and, as such, require multiple opportunities to learn when and how to display target behaviors. Multiple opportunities to practice a behavior may be considered "unnatural" or "atypical" for the environment, but, with proper planning, we argue that an increased number of opportunities to practice target behaviors will likely lead to a child displaying behaviors at an age-appropriate rate. Adaptability in adults is necessary when promoting key behaviors, such as those that are likely to promote access to previously unlearned contingencies or generalization. For example, a child with cognitive or language delays might benefit from consistent and frequent contrived opportunities to practice back-and-forth turn-taking during structured activities with a flexible peer and an adult, who can provide needed supports. After consistent contrived practice opportunities with support and feedback, the child may be more likely to become fluent in the skill so that he or she can use it during typical activities.

Potential challenges. Modifying the social, physical, or temporal environment may not be sufficient for addressing the needs of all children. That is, although environmental arrangement is critical when children are learning when and how to respond, systematic instruction and carefully planned consequences may be needed in addition to environmental arrangement. Such issues may arise when competing reinforcers for non-target behaviors are more readily available. This is likely occurring because a non-target behavior, or contextually inappropriate behavior, leads to a preferred outcome at a faster rate than a contextually appropriate behavior. For example, Jude and Jamie are paired together as peer buddies for the morning center rotation. Throughout the morning Jude has placed materials such as blocks on Jamie's head. Although Jamie continually tells Jude to "Stop" or "Leave me alone," Jude persists. Ms. Booker does not understand why this is happening since her goal when pairing children was to promote conversation around activities. In this scenario, there are two possible explanations for Jude's challenging behavior. First, Jude may know how to properly obtain a peer's attention (e.g., tap a peer on the shoulder, say their name), but, based on his previous experiences, peers do not always respond to his bids for attention. In contrast, peers almost always respond to his inappropriate behaviors, indicating that he can access attention at a relatively faster rate for inappropriate behavior compared to appropriate behaviors. Second, the child may not know how to obtain a peer's attention and relies on behaviors that, during past interactions, have led to such attention. Thus, a child may display challenging behaviors that indicate he or she has a performance deficit (*won't do*—competing reinforcers interfere with the child displaying socially appropriate behaviors) or a skill deficit (*can't do*— does not know when and how to display a behavior that leads to a preferred outcome), with both necessitating the introduction of systematic supports before improvements in target behaviors are observed.

Cory decided to rearrange the physical layout of the classroom and the classroom's schedule to ensure children had an adequate amount of opportunities to interact with one another. She then assigned peers with generalized social skills to serve as peer buddies for children with ASD. Following these changes, most children began displaying increased social communication with one another, with increases in responses and initiations. One child, Kirsten, continued to spend the majority of her time in the science center, where a game related to bugs was available. Cory decided to incorporate bug materials into her block and dramatic play centers, which were centers where most of the typically developing children spent a lot of time. Following this modification, Cory noticed that Kirsten began spending more time near her peers, making it easier for Cory to facilitate peer-to-peer interactions.

Related Resources

https://vkc.mc.vanderbilt.edu/ebip/environmental-arrangement/
www.dec-sped.org

References

Barton, E. E., Ledford, J. R., Lane, J. D., Decker, J., Germansky, S. E., Hemmeter, M. L., & Kaiser, A. (2016). The iterative use of single case research designs to advance the science of EI/ECSE. *Topics in Early Childhood Special Education*, 36, 4–14.

DEC (Division for Early Childhood of the Council for Exceptional Children (2014). DEC recommended practices in early intervention/early childhood special education. Retrieved from: www.dec-sped.org/recommendedpractices.

Frea, W., Craig-Unkefer, L., Odom, S. L., & Johnson, D. (1999). Differential effects of structured social integration and group friendship activities for prompting social interaction with peers. *Journal of Early Intervention*, 22, 230–242.

Johnston, S., Nelson, C., Evans, J., & Palazolo, J. (2003). The use of visual supports in teaching young children with autism spectrum disorder to initiate interactions. *Augmentative and Alternative Communication*, 19, 86–103.

Joseph, J. D., Strain, P., Olszewski, A., & Goldstein, H. (2016). A Consumer Reports-like review of the empirical literature specific to preschool children's peer-related social skills. In B. Reichow, B. A. Boyd, E. E. Barton, & S. L. Odom (Eds.), *Handbook of early childhood special education* (pp. 179–197). Switzerland: Springer International Publishing.

Kohler, F. W., Greteman, C., Raschke, D., & Highnam, C. (2007). Using a buddy skills package to increase the social interactions between a preschooler with autism and her peers. *Topics in Early Childhood Special Education*, 27, 155–163.

Lane, J. D., Gast, D. L., Ledford, J. R., & Shepley, C. (2017). Increasing social behaviors in young children with social-communication delays in a group arrangement in preschool. *Education and Treatment of Children*, 40, 115–144.

Ledford, J. R., & Wolery, M. (2015). Observational learning of academic and social behaviors during small group instruction. *Exceptional Children*, 81, 272–291.

Ledford, J. R., King, S., Harbin, E. R., & Zimmerman, K. N. (2018). Antecedent social skills interventions for individuals with ASD: What works, for whom, and under what conditions? *Focus on Autism and Other Developmental Disabilities*, 33, 3–13.

Ledford, J. R., Lane, J. D., Elam, K., & Wolery, M. (2012). Using response prompting procedures during small group instruction: Outcomes and procedural variations. *American Journal on Intellectual and Developmental Disabilities*, 117, 413–434.

Ledford, J. R., Osborne, K., & Chazin, K. T. (2016). Stay, play, talk procedures. In *Evidence-based instructional practices for young children with autism and other disabilities*. Retrieved from http://vkc.mc.vanderbilt.edu/ebip/stay-play-talk-procedures.

Meadan, H., Ostrosky, M. M., Triplett, B., Michna, A., & Fettig, A. (2011). Using visual supports with young children with autism spectrum disorder. *Teaching Exceptional Children*, 43, 28–35.

Morales, V. A., & Ledford, J. R. (2016). Peer training. In *Evidence-based instructional practices for young children with autism and other disabilities*. Retrieved from http://vkc.mc.vanderbilt.edu/ebip/peer-training.

Pierce, K., & Schreibman, L. (1995). Increasing complex social behaviors in children with autism: Effects of peer-implemented pivotal response training. *Journal of Applied Behavior Analysis, 28*, 285–295.

Pierce, K., & Schreibman, L. (1997). Multiple peer use of pivotal response training to increase social behaviors of classmates with autism: Results from trained and untrained peers. *Journal of Applied Behavior Analysis, 30*, 157–160.

Winstead, O., Lane, J. D., Spriggs, A. D., & Allday, R. A. (in press). Providing small group instruction to children with moderate to severe disabilities and same-age peers with typical development. *Journal of Early Intervention.*

Appendix 6.1

Stay-Play-Talk Planning Worksheet

Step	Question	Response
1	Which target students will participate in Stay, Play, Talk?	*Note: Target students should be imitative, understand simple language, and have lower social skills than their peers.*
2	Which confederate peers will participant in Stay, Play, Talk?	*Note: Confederate peers should exhibit age appropriate play and social skills, and also be highly compliant with teacher directions.*
3	Which children will be grouped together?	*Note: Pair each target child with 1–2 confederate peers, depending on attendance patterns of the peers. Consider shared interests and social history of the pair or trio.*
4	When will peer training occur?	
5	During which activities will Stay, Play, Talk occur?	*Note: Consider times during the day when children are naturally playing together (e.g., free play, centers, recess).*
6	Which prompting procedure will I use?	
7	What is my criterion for when prompts will be given (e.g, 1 minute without a peer interaction)?	
8	What is my prompt?	*Note: Visual prompts are typically used during Stay, Play, Talk.*
9	How often will Stay, Play, Talk occur?	*Note: A minimum of once daily is recommended.*
10	Who else might be present during a session?	*Note: Plan out who will implement, who will collect data, and the responsibilities of the rest of your teaching team.*
11	How will other children requesting to join a session be managed?	*Note: Consider ways for non-participants to be engaged elsewhere or develop rules about when they can join (e.g., after 10 min).*

From: Ledford, J. R., Osborne, K., & Chazin, K. T. (2016). Stay, play, talk procedures. In *Evidence-based instructional practices for young children with autism and other disabilities.* Retrieved from http://vkc.mc.vanderbilt.edu/ebip/stay-play-talk-procedures.

7 Child-Directed Strategies

Key Terms

Responsive interactions   Milieu teaching   Time delay
Child-directed strategies   Modeling   Incidental teaching
Mand-model   Expansions and recasts

Chapter Objectives

After completing this chapter, readers should be able to:

- Describe child-directed strategies and compare them to adult-directed strategies.
- Define responsive interactions and corresponding adult behaviors that serve as the foundation for instructional sessions.
- Describe environmental arrangement as strategies for promoting initiations and age-appropriate responses in children.
- Explain adult supports, including expansions and recasts, contingent imitation, modeling, open-ended questions, time delay, and related supports to promote target behaviors.
- Name possible child responses, suggested adult reactions to each, and how to trouble-shoot potential issues that may arise when implementing child-directed strategies.

Tabitha teaches in an inclusive preschool program and has experienced success promoting peer-to-peer interactions, pre-academic behaviors, and independence in many of her students. Although she has many positive experiences, she is unsure of how to promote social communication in her students who struggle to meaningfully share wants and interests. Tabitha schedules a meeting with Destinee, the school's speech-language pathologist, and Kieanna, the school's administrator, to discuss how to capitalize on her students' interests and how to promote social communication during play.

The purpose of this chapter is to describe the use of crucial child-directed strategies, including responsive interactions and other adult supports implemented during child-directed activities. Specific responsive interaction strategies are described, with applied examples of each; strategies are described as foundational adult behaviors likely to promote successful interactions during typical activities. Details and resources are provided to promote successful implementation of strategies in a variety of contexts and to proactively prevent potential problems and/or use data-based problem-solving when difficulties arise (e.g., insufficient improvements).

Introduction

Child-directed strategies are well suited for improving engagement with materials and for directly teaching children when and how to engage with others during typical activities. We refer to **child-directed strategies** as those that are used to promote engagement and social communication (initiations and responses) during typical activities or contrived activities that parallel a child's natural environment (i.e., play). Some might use a more restricted definition of the term to refer to instruction that can only occur once a child initiates engagement or an interaction; the adult introduces supports to expand on the child's initiation (Grisham-Brown & Hemmeter, 2017). Regardless of whether or not instruction begins when the child initiates, the use of the term "child-directed strategies" suggests that the materials and other contextual factors (e.g., activities, locations) are chosen or preferred by the child and he or she has some degree of control over the activity and teaching.

The extent to which child-directed instruction will succeed or fail is directly influenced by the quality of interactions between adults and children. A responsive adult behaves in a manner that communicates interest and attention to a child's actions and preferences. Relatedly, the responsivity of a child is also likely to influence the outcomes of instruction. **Responsive interactions** refer to an interaction style rooted in a transactional model for promoting social communication, recognizing that adults and children influence one another in regards to initiations and responsivity (Camarata & Yoder, 2002). For example, the adult's behaviors will influence how often the child responds and the child's behaviors will influence how often the adult initiates interactions. This bi-directional relationship requires careful attention when planning to promote behaviors during child-directed activities. Thus, before placing demands on a child, it is imperative to establish instructional control and reciprocity during interactions. This will increase the likelihood of effective and efficient instructional opportunities for socially meaningful behaviors during instruction. Throughout this chapter we highlight how to arrange the environment and intervene during age-appropriate activities, with attention given to the quality of interactions and what that looks like in practice.

Many of these strategies are commonly used in conjunction with environmental arrangement strategies, which are used to set up opportunities for the child to communicate wants and interests. In Chapter 6, we discussed arranging the social, physical, and temporal aspects of the environment; these broad strategies are commonly used as antecedent-based interventions for promoting engagement and peer-to-peer interactions. In this chapter we highlight how environmental arrangement may be utilized during child-directed instruction, an application of environmental arrangement that refers to arranging precise materials or interactions during a single, brief activity. Environmental arrangement is commonly incorporated into milieu teaching sessions. **Milieu teaching** procedures refer to instruction that occurs in a person's typical social environment (Snyder et al., 2015) and are most often used to promote early language acquisition in young children, including use of verbal and other communication modes. In contrast, adult-directed strategies typically refer to teacher-paced instruction that occurs during one-to-one or small group instructional arrangements. Adult-directed strategies can occur in the typical environment (e.g., can be embedded in play), but they are comprised of trials that are directed by adults, usually planned in an a priori fashion. We will discuss adult-directed strategies in Chapters 8–11.

Child-directed strategies may be used as stand-alone procedures or as part of a system of supports, within single activities and across the school day. Some procedures, such as modeling, are appropriate for a teaching behavior that is not yet known. These procedures assist a child in acquiring new skills. Other procedures, such as time delay, are appropriate for improving the use of a behavior the child can engage in, but does not do so at appropriate rates or in typical contexts (e.g., a child can say "car" but does not when a desired toy car is present but out of reach). Early childhood practitioners should use a balance of child- and adult-directed strategies to ensure children acquire key behaviors across domains (Wolery & Hemmeter, 2011). Thus, understanding and use of various teaching arrangements and strategies is warranted to ensure we, as professionals, are prepared to meet the needs of all children. Generally, substantial research support is available for the use of child-directed strategies to improve social communication skills and engagement, while substantial research support is available for the use of adult-directed strategies to improve pre-academic, academic, self-help, and play behaviors.

The remaining sections of this chapter will highlight a recommended foundation for interacting with all children and describe the process of embedding opportunities for social communication into play using child-directed strategies.

Target behaviors. Given the focus of child-directed strategies, we typically measure behaviors directly related to social communication and engagement. Measuring initiations, responses, and engagement during interactions allows for formative evaluation of progress over time. Initiations can be defined as "verbal or nonverbal attempts to communicate that are not preceded by a cue or prompt (i.e., occurred more than 5 seconds after a prompt)" (adapted from Lane, Ledford, Shepley, Mataras, Ayres, & Davis, 2016, p. 139). Responses to initiations can be defined as "any sounds emitted within 5 seconds of a cue or prompt, which includes a secondary indicator of meaning (e.g., child looks at an adult while vocalizing, reaches for an item, or engages in a 3-point gaze)" (adapted from Lane et al., 2016, p. 129). Engagement can be defined as actively manipulating items and meaningfully participating in activities. Given the broad nature of the term of engagement, we recommend assessing engagement against cognitive and social play taxonomies to better understand a child's typical item use and social play (cf. Barton, 2016) (see Figure 7.1 and Appendix 7.2 for descriptions of behaviors and a data sheet for measuring these behaviors; Barton & Wolery, 2010; Lifter, Sulzer-Azaroff, Anderson, & Cowdery, 1993; Ungerer & Sigman, 1981).

Responsive Interactions

Reciprocity during adult–child interactions is critical for ensuring long-term instructional success. The extent to which instruction will lead to robust improvements in socially meaningful behaviors is influenced by the responsivity of adults to children during interactions. Thus, the quality of shared attention between an adult and child influences the extent to which children will learn when and how to respond during interactions. Initially, some children may display limited interest in others, as well as limited interest in materials and activities. This can be challenging for well-intentioned parents and professionals who are attempting to build rapport with a child who has a limited repertoire of skills and interests. Reciprocity requires a back-and-forth exchange during interactions, but initial interactions may be one-sided with the adult struggling to engage the child. This can be especially problematic for professionals who begin placing demands on a child immediately after meeting them. It is important to take time to get to know the child, pair yourself with preferred items and activities, and begin to establish instructional control. These early interactions teach children that you will reliably provide social attention and tangible items following the occurrence of a socially appropriate behavior, which is the foundation of instruction within an antecedent-behavior-consequence paradigm. On the surface, planning how to interact with and respond to a child may seem like an ambiguous construct without observable and measurable behaviors to anchor such work in practice. While we recognize the subjectivity of a construct like relationships based on responsivity, we have an established literature that includes clearly defined actions an adult can engage in to promote responsive interactions. We define responsive interaction strategies as a collection of adult actions that indicate attention to, and interest in, a child's preferences, thoughts, communication, and actions on the environment (i.e., play). This attention and interest is likely to promote development of reciprocal exchanges and positive relationships between children and their caregivers (Hemmeter & Kaiser, 1990). A number of responsive interaction strategies can be used during interactions with children. We strongly recommend practicing these procedures and monitoring appropriate use during interactions. In addition, we recommend conducting a preference assessment to identify potential reinforcers likely to be of interest to children during sessions (see Chapter 3). Identifying this information a priori will be beneficial when planning instruction for a child. Responsive interaction strategies are largely based on early studies of the *Responsive Interaction Intervention* (e.g., Girolametto, 1988), incidental teaching (e.g., Hart & Risley, 1975), and the body of work from Kaiser and colleagues (enhanced milieu teaching [EMT]; e.g., Kaiser & Hampton, 2017; Kaiser & Woods, 2010) (procedures from these sources outlined below):

1. **Promoting Play and Engagement:**
   - Provide multiple sets of materials, including highly preferred items, for the child. Initially, including highly preferred items may assist with getting children to initiate play. Children who do not have access to varied and interesting materials are more likely to become unengaged or to engage in challenging behavior or stereotypy. For example, Anna sits at a table and begins engaging in repetitive motor movements with her fingers. The paraprofessional, Gladys, decides to roll a musical train back and forth across the table in an attempt to gain Anna's attention. After a few seconds Anna notices the train and begins to laugh and orient her gaze to Gladys.
   - Once a child initiates play, begin by imitating the child's appropriate actions on items within 1–3 seconds. This indicates to the child that you are attending to their actions, and promotes turn-taking. Children often attend to adults who imitate their actions.
   - In addition to imitating a child's actions on items, simultaneously narrate your actions on items using language the child can imitate (but do not require the child to imitate). This serves as input for the child without requiring a response, since the focus should be on engagement and communication.
   - Following imitation and narration, wait at least 5 seconds for the child to respond.
   - The goal of these actions is to establish turn-taking with the child, as well as potentially to establish routines with sets of materials. Establishing routines during age-appropriate activities allows predictability for the child and, once an intervention is introduced, focuses instruction on the child learning novel behaviors or expanding his or her current communicative repertoire.
   - Initially, children may not initiate to materials or may lose interest quickly. To address this issue consider the following: (a) remove an item that is interfering with more advanced forms of play (e.g., child is spinning the wheels of a miniature car); (b) introduce a novel item into the activity; (c) if the child is not engaged (*active avoidance* in the form of challenging behaviors; *passive avoidance* in the form of sitting or lying down), activate or manipulate a motivating item in the child's line of sight.

2. **Promoting Social Communication:**
   - Respond to all verbal attempts by the child to communicate with a thematically or contextually related verbalization within 1–3 seconds.
   - In addition, responses should be grammatically correct (semantically and syntactically appropriate) and at the target language level (length of communicative statement matches the child's expression and understanding) for the child.
   - If children use nonverbal modes of communication, adults should provide a language that matches the child's communicative intent. In this scenario, adults should provide language that describes orally what the child is communicating nonverbally.
   - Wait at least 5 seconds for the child to respond. If the child does not respond, do not provide a prompt (unless using a child-directed strategy) and continue the current activity, using the above strategies throughout an interaction.

The overarching goal when using responsive interaction strategies is to promote turn-taking and communication. The adult should respond immediately and contingently to a child's verbal and nonverbal communicative behavior. Also, we recommend monitoring and limiting the number of close-ended questions or prompts for specific information (e.g., What color is the bear? How many Lego do you have?) used when communicating with a child; such questions are likely to produce only "yes" or "no" responses and might interrupt the interaction or limit the child's engagement, which is counterproductive to expanding a child's social communication. Monitoring adult initiations and responses during interactions and practicing being responsive rather than directive are likely to help adults remember to use these responsive strategies during child-directed activities.

Environmental Arrangement within Child-Directed Activities

Initially focusing on building rapport with a child allows opportunities to assess spontaneous behaviors, as well as create opportunities to measure target behaviors using environmental arrangement strategies. We recommend using environmental arrangement strategies to identify a pre-intervention pattern of responding. That is, set up an opportunity for a child to communicate (either increasing the rate of responding or the complexity of communicative behaviors), wait approximately 5 seconds for a response, and then provide access to preferred items and activities, regardless of the extent to which the communication met instructional expectations. This will allow for formative evaluation of target behaviors under a baseline condition, which is necessary before introducing an intervention (see Appendix 7.1 for pre-intervention or probe condition data sheet). Common environmental arrangement strategies used during child-directed activities are as follows:

1. **Provide a choice:** Children who display difficulty engaging in activities and initiating interactions often benefit from a choice of materials or activities. Providing a choice introduces structure to an interaction, but allows the child to select materials or activities that are of interest to them, given the context. This strategy is primarily used to create opportunities for a child to request items from a field size of two or more items.

   Example: Braden is seated at the art table and expected to initiate to and begin a craft. Once seated, Braden begins to turn away from the table and look out the window. Braden's teacher, Ms. Booker, gains his attention and then offers a choice of crayons or stamps. Braden reaches for and says "stamps"; Ms. Booker provides stamps and paper and Braden begins to engage in the activity independently.

2. **Provide materials that require support:** Children may be interested in items that require assistance from another person (e.g., activating a wind-up toy; accessing an app on a mobile device). In this scenario, an adult or peer can initially demonstrate the function of the item, followed by allowing the child to attempt to use the item; this provides an opportunity for the child to request assistance and for the adult to model appropriate behaviors and engage in a responsive interaction with the child. Carefully monitor the child's responses and avoid using this strategy with children who are easily frustrated.

   Example: Ms. Booker gives Kirsten a basket of plastic wind-up animals while she is seated at the sensory table. Kirsten places a plastic animal in the water, but is distressed because the toy will not move. Ms. Booker gains Kirsten's attention, models how to use the toy, and then places it in the water. Kirsten unsuccessfully attempts to wind the toy and then gives the plastic frog to Ms. Booker and says, "frog." Ms. Booker expands her request with "Frog in water" and winds-up the toy and places it in the water.

3. **Maintain and control access to materials:** A commonly used strategy to promote requests is placing preferred items in view but out of reach of the child. The adult can arrange the environment by strategically placing items on shelves or cabinets. Relatedly, items may be situated near or behind another person. In this situation, the person is acting as a gatekeeper to the preferred items. Each scenario allows children to initiate requests for items that are inaccessible unless another person provides assistance. This can also be done with peers, during typical activities—giving one child a container full of markers can encourage her peers to initiate interactions with her to gain access to the markers, increasing the overall rate of peer interactions during the art activity.

   Example: In the dramatic play center, Gladys places three cause-effect toys on shelves to encourage children to engage in the center and request preferred items. Atticus chooses to play with a few of the plastic kitchen utensils and plates in the center. Gladys helps Atticus plan a picnic for his peers and a few stuffed animals. Gladys uses this opportunity to activate a stuffed dog on a shelf; the dog barks when patted. Atticus notices the sound, reaches toward the dog, and shifts his gaze between the dog and Gladys. Gladys says "dog!" and gives the dog to Atticus who continues the picnic with his new stuffed pet.

4. **Introduce unexpected situations into play:** Introducing novelty in the form of an unexpected change in routine or activity may promote requests and comments about a situation. Examples include providing an inadequate amount of a key item for an activity (giving a child a pinch of Play-Doh), sabotaging an activity by providing all but a few of the items needed to complete or meaningfully participate in an activity (child initiates to a painting activity but cannot find paintbrushes), and adults or peers engaging in unexpected actions with items (the teacher places a doll's hat on top of his own head).

   Example: Antonio takes Ms. Booker by the hand and guides her to sit and play with baby dolls on the floor. Ms. Booker taught Antonio a routine of feeding, cleaning, and putting the babies to sleep. In an effort to introduce variability into this particular play routine, Ms. Booker places a blanket on the doll's head. Antonio laughs and comments, "That's silly," and the two begin playing a game of peek-a-boo with the doll.

5. **Promote appropriate protests:** Oftentimes there is a focus on promoting prosocial behaviors in children, with less attention given to providing opportunities for children to appropriately indicate displeasure or disagree with another person (e.g., "Please

don't take it"). Promoting appropriate protests allows children to learn when and how to use negatives to communicate, instead of engaging challenging behaviors likely to impede long-term social success. These types of appropriate protests allow children to effectively self-advocate when needed.

Example: Lee prefers to build towers using cardboard blocks and will oftentimes yell at peers who ask to knock over the towers before he has completed his "work." Ms. Booker decides to address this issue by first asking Lee if she can knock over the tower and immediately providing a verbal model of an appropriate protest ("Not now. I'm still building"). Through repeated exposure and practice, Lee begins to use the phrase independently with peers.

Arranging the environment may support initiations and age-appropriate responses, as well as exploration of materials and learning more advanced forms of play. Initially, professionals may focus on an adult–child teaching paradigm, with the adult promoting social communication during typical activities. Some children may display limited interest in peers (ignoring or seemingly unaware of peers), while other children may be interested in peers but require supports to engage near or with peers in the same or similar activities. Once children are reliably proximal to peers, promoting initiations and responses with peers will likely be a goal of instruction. Relatedly, an overarching goal for a child may be to select a preferred material at a center, followed by more advanced forms of play, such as using miniature objects as intended and eventually using those objects for non-literal purposes (cf. Barton, 2016).

Interventions for Social Communication

Responsive interactions between adults and children serve as the foundation for implementing structured supports to promote social communication in children. These strategies should be used in conjunction with environmental arrangement strategies.

Expansions and recasts. Expansions and recasts typically fall under the umbrella of responsive interaction strategies, but can be used as stand-alone strategies for promoting social communication. In addition, expansions and recasts are also commonly recommended when implementing milieu teaching procedures (Woods, Kashinath, & Goldstein, 2004). Expansions refer to restating a child's verbalization and adding 1–2 meaningful words to it, but not requiring the child to imitate the additional words (e.g., a child says "car" and the adult expands "I'm pushing the car!"). Expansions provide the child with additional language models that he or she could use under similar conditions in the future. Expansions typically include models for appropriate morphological markers and introduce novel vocabulary and its associated meaning within a syntactically appropriate structure (Roberts & Kaiser, 2011). Expansions can be thought of as a form of "future teaching," where a child is exposed to new information without the expectation for an immediate response. The goal of such exposure is that a child will begin using this information during future interactions or increase the relative ease at which the child learns those target behaviors during later sessions. In addition, children may initiate or imitate a word or phrase, but omit a sound (issue related to phonology) or display syntactical issues (sentence structure) that impede the functionality of a word or phrase in conversation. In this scenario, an adult should recast the word or phrase, repeating the word or phrase and stressing omitted sounds or using an appropriate syntactic structure, as a form of teaching or correcting a child's verbalization.

Contingent imitation. Imitation is a foundational skill that allows others to learn contextually appropriate skills by observing others. Imitation is considered a behavioral cusp, in that learning to imitate others allows a child to access, or experience, new contingencies that

Social Play

Behavior	Definition
Unoccupied	Child observes social and physical environment; lack of action on items.
Solitary	Child engages in independent play; actively manipulates items, but items differ from peers' items.
Onlooker	Child observes social and physical environment; early conversation between peers may emerge during these observations.
Parallel	Child engages in independent play; actively manipulates items and items are similar to peers; early conversation likely between peers.
Associative	Child engages in independent play with same items as peers; children are proximal to one another; conversation between peers related to items and actions on items.
Cooperative	Child engages in goal-oriented play with peers; varied conversation topics and related actions on items.

Cognitive Play

Behavior	Definition
Sensorimotor	Child interest in items is limited to sensory exploration (e.g., block in mouth; cause-effect; knock over a peer's stacked blocks).
Relational play	Child actively manipulates like items, typically engaging in construction tasks (e.g., stacking blocks) with items (lacks pretense).
Functional play	Child's literal use of items (e.g., drink from cup; eat with fork).
Functional play with pretense	Child's non-literal use of items (e.g., "drink" from empty cup; wipe doll's face with napkin).
Symbolic play	
Object substitution	Child's non-literal use of items, with behaviors that indicate child is using item as if it were another item (e.g., block is an airplane; stacked blocks are an apartment building).
Imagining absent objects	Child engages in motor behaviors that indicate (e.g., mime actions- lack of accompanying verbalization) an absent item is present (e.g., "driving a car" by moving hands back and forth while seated on a chair).
Assigning absent attributes	Child describes contextually-related characteristics of self, peers, and related items during play-based activities (e.g., while engaging in a mealtime play scheme, child indicates her peer is angry because the family dog stole his snack).
Social pretend play	Child displays flexibility in play routines by intermixing various types of cognitive play behaviors during interactions with peers.

Source: Modified from Barton, 2016.

Figure 7.1 Social and Cognitive Play Taxonomies.

were previously unavailable to him or her (Cooper, Heron, & Heward, 2007). Contingently imitating a child's behavior is a commonly used, stand-alone strategy when targeting early social communication and play behaviors but, like expansions and recasts, is commonly referred to as a responsive interaction strategy. When implementing contingent imitation, an adult imitates a child's appropriate behaviors, which is meant to serve as a reinforcer for the child's actions (i.e., indicating to the child the action was appropriate for the context) (Ingersoll & Gergans, 2007). In addition, as a responsive interaction strategy, it promotes turn-taking during play-based activities and conversation (Gazdag & Warren, 2000).

Modeling. Modeling is the procedure by which most typically developing children learn new words. This procedure, like other milieu teaching procedures, is contingent on the child's interest and initiations to items and activities (Snyder et al., 2015). An opportunity begins when an adult arranges the environment and waits for the child to initiate. As soon as the child expresses interest in an item or activity, the adult immediately provides a full verbal model of the target behavior and waits approximately 5 seconds for the child to imitate the verbal model. The time period of 5 seconds was selected based on previously published literature, but can be modified based on the child's needs (requires additional time to respond) or other contextual needs. If a child imitates the target behavior, he or she receives access to a preferred item or activity; approximations of a target behavior are accepted. In addition, the adult should expand on or recast the child's verbalization. If a child does not respond or displays unrelated behavior, this process should be repeated once more. If the child does not display the target behavior, but continues to persist in his or her attempts to obtain an item or activity, the adult should reinforce the communicative behavior (see Appendix 7.3 and 7.4).

Open-ended questions or statements. Children who reliably imitate others' verbal behavior may have an established vocabulary but not reliably respond to others during interactions. One approach to promote increased responsivity is to ask open-ended questions (e.g., "What are you playing?") or provide directives in the form of statements (e.g., "Tell me about your giraffe.") during an activity. The mand-model procedure is a commonly used milieu teaching procedure designed to promote responsiveness during conversation (Rogers-Warren & Warren, 1980; Warren, McQuarter, & Rogers-Warren, 1984). In addition, this procedure is also appropriate for targeting specific words or phrases in which a child needs additional support to learn to use in context. The mand-model procedure typically involves an adult interrupting a child's play or, when a child is transitioning between activities, providing a mand (statement or a non-yes or no question) and waiting approximately 5 seconds for the child to respond. Like the modeling procedure, if the child does not respond or displays a non-target behavior, the adult would provide a full verbal model of the target behavior and wait 5 seconds. If the child imitates the target behavior, he or she receives access to a preferred item or activity and the adult should expand on or recast the child's verbalization. If the goal of a session is to increase a child describing his or her play (e.g., use a present progressive form of a verb) or if a child's response is expected or known (e.g., child is playing with blocks), the adult should use a model prompt, with the goal of the child imitating the adult's verbal model. If a child's response is unknown, as in the adult is unaware of the child's potential response, the adult could ask another open-ended question that includes additional supporting information in the form of choices, such as "Do you want the red car or the blue car?" or "Should we play with blocks or dolls?" If a child initiates to an item or activity, but does not use the target word or phrase following the prompt, the adult should reinforce the child with access to the item or the continuation of an activity (see Appendix 7.5).

Time delay. Time delay is a milieu teaching procedure that was originally used to promote independent requests during routine activities (i.e., child requesting a lunch tray in the cafeteria; Halle, Marshall, & Spradlin,1979). To begin a session, an individual uses an environmental arrangement strategy and waits for the child to respond to the cue for the target behavior (Halle et al., 1981). If the child does not respond within this time period or displays a non-target behavior, the adult provides a verbal model of the target behavior and, like the modeling procedure, waits a specified interval for the child to imitate the verbal model. Responses to the child's behavior are procedurally identical to the modeling procedure. Time delay is typically considered a less intrusive procedure than modeling and the mand-model procedure because, with the exception of the environmental arrangement, no additional supports are provided during the initial interval for a response. The delay allows the child time to provide the target response independently. Thus, when deciding to use time delay to promote independent requests, in general, or when targeting specific words or phrases, time delay is well suited for a child who is imitative and responsive, but does not readily use social communication independently (see Appendix 7.6). This time delay procedure is similar to, but distinct from, constant and progressive time delay procedures discussed in the next chapter.

Incidental teaching. Incidental teaching is one of the earliest examples of milieu teaching procedures, originally used by Hart and Risley (1968) with young children with disabilities in a preschool classroom. The primary purpose of incidental teaching is expanding a child's current repertoire of requesting phrases by encouraging the use of elaborated forms of requests (Hart & Risley, 1975). Thus, when selecting an incidental teaching procedure, a child should be imitative and independently request preferred items and activities. When using this procedure, an adult arranges the environment and waits for the child to initiate an elaborated form of a request. If the child displays the target behavior, the adult provides positive attention, reinforces the child with access to an item or activity, and expands on the request. If a child does not display the elaborated form of a request, the adult decides to use the modeling, mand-model, or time delay procedure and then waits a specified time period (e.g., 5 seconds) for the child to respond. If the child does not respond, the adult may provide an additional model prompt or use the mand-model procedure and wait for a response (e.g., 5 seconds). If the child displays the target behavior, the adult provides positive attention, reinforces the child with access to an item or activity, and expands on the request. As mentioned with other milieu procedures, if the child does not display the target behavior, but continues to persist in his or her attempts to obtain an item or activity, the adult should reinforce the communicative behavior (see Appendix 7.7).

Modifications to naturalistic procedures. When targeting social communication in children who are traditionally minimally verbal, such as children with autism spectrum disorder or intellectual disability, a modified version of these naturalistic procedures may be beneficial for improving early forms of requests and comments (e.g., Lane, Shepley, & Lieberman-Betz, 2016). In previously published studies, researchers have utilized a 0-second prompt delay during sessions prior to introducing time delay procedures, but did not indicate how long prompt delay sessions were used before introducing a prompt delay (cf. Lane, Lieberman-Betz, & Gast, 2016). Implementing 0-second prompt delay sessions provides children with models of target vocabulary, establishing the relationship between the cue for a target behavior and access to that item or activity, following imitation of another person's model prompt. It may not be necessary for children to learn to imitate each specific vocabulary target, instead it may be more important to establish imitation of communicative behaviors during responsive interactions (respond to model prompts at least 50 percent of sessions; Lane, Shepley, Sartini, & Hogue, in press). Once children demonstrate they can imitate a verbal model, individuals may introduce a 5-second prompt delay. Thus, it may be necessary to initially begin sessions using a 0-second prompt delay to expose children to target behaviors, followed by 5-second prompt delay intervals within a responsive adult–child format. Relatedly, some studies used time delay with children with ASD, and provided up to two verbal models for target behaviors, instead of one (e.g., Lane et al., 2016) (see Appendices 7.8 and 7.9). Also, it may be beneficial to include visual supports (e.g., picture cards) or alternative and augmentative modes of communication. Such supports provide additional, static input for the child during play and related activities (e.g., Kaiser & Wright, 2013; Kaiser, Nietfeld, & Roberts, 2010; Kasari et al., 2014).

Research Abstract

Lane, J. D., Shepley, C., & Lieberman-Betz, R. (2016). Promoting expressive language in young children with or at-risk for autism spectrum disorder in a preschool classroom. *Journal of Autism and Developmental Disorders*, 46, 3216–3231.

In this single case design study, four young children with, or at-risk for, autism spectrum disorder (ages: 4 and 5 years) were taught to request preferred items and activities during centers. The classroom teacher rotated preferred materials within sessions to promote engagement and intervention sessions included a modified version of time delay, with the teacher providing up to two verbal models of target words and phrases (if a participant did not display the target response during play). Three participants acquired the target behaviors and displayed at least some increases in non-target behaviors, including expanded requests and spontaneous comments. One participant required modifications to ensure he remained engaged in activities and requested preferred items: (a) environmental modifications—sessions alternated between adult- (fewer materials) and child-paced (centers) instructional formats and (b) instructional modifications—during adult-paced instruction the adult embedded questions asking the child to label the item (ensured child had exposure to the correct labels for items). Outcomes from this study suggested that young children with autism spectrum disorder may benefit from naturalistic instruction, although some may require modifications, including response prompts and instruction on how to appropriately play with materials.

Measurement and Responses to Child Behaviors

Child-directed strategies can be used on an ongoing basis, with adults adapting instructional targets and selecting procedures based on each child's need and subsequent progress. Although these procedures are flexible and appropriate methods for interacting with and improving a wide variety of behaviors in children, when implementing child-directed strategies it is important to have clearly stated objectives that include a mastery criterion. When targeting broad forms of behaviors (e.g., increasing independent use of action + object combinations) or generalized tendencies (e.g., initiations with peers), a less stringent mastery criterion may be ideal (50–80 percent above baseline levels). When targeting specific instructional targets (e.g., "ball in [tower]," "[want to] eat my snack"), a more stringent criterion should be selected (75–80 percent of opportunities) (see Appendix 7.10 for a data sheet that allows for intermixing instructional procedures). The variability in mastery criteria for social communication and engagement recognizes that individuals do not necessarily have to engage in a target behavior each time an opportunity arises. Thus, we recommend identifying a mastery criterion that is stringent, but appropriate given the target behaviors.

Five types of responses are possible when implementing child-directed strategies. In the following examples, we refer to a 5-second prompt delay, meaning a child is allowed 5 seconds to respond to an initial cue or prompt for a behavior; additional prompt delay intervals are possible (e.g., 3 seconds, 4 seconds, 6 seconds). In addition, consistency is important when selecting a prompt delay interval. For example, if a 4-second prompt delay is used during baseline sessions, that same delay should be used during intervention sessions. Also, general guidelines for responding to child behaviors are provided, with specific responses dependent on each procedure.

1. **Unprompted corrects:** Unprompted correct responding refers to a child independently displaying a target behavior within 5 seconds of the initial cue (or antecedent) for the behavior. When a child displays an unprompted correct response: (a) provide positive attention, (b) recast (if an approximation) or expand on (e.g., social communication—add one to two meaningful words) the target behavior, and (c) provide access to the reinforcer (e.g., preferred item, continuation of activity).

2. **Unprompted error:** Unprompted error responding refers to a child displaying a behavior, other than the target behavior, within 5 seconds of the initial cue (or antecedent) for the behavior. If a child displays continued interest in an item or activity (persists in attempting to obtain an item or activity using a non-target behavior), reinforce the communicative behavior by providing and labeling the item or activity.

3. **Prompted corrects:** Prompted correct responding refers to a child imitating an adult's verbal model within 5 seconds. When a child displays a prompted correct response— (a) provide positive attention, (b) recast (if an approximation) or expand on (e.g., social communication—add one to two meaningful words) the target behavior, and (c) provide access to the reinforcer (e.g., preferred item, continuation of activity).

4. **Prompted incorrect:** Prompted incorrect responding refers to a child displaying a behavior, other than the target behavior, within 5 seconds of an adult's verbal model. If a child displays continued interest in an item or activity (persists in attempting to obtain an item or activity using a non-target behavior), reinforce the communicative behavior by providing and labeling the item or activity.

5. **No response:** No response refers to absence of a behavior within 5 seconds following the initial cue (or antecedent) for the behavior or following an adult's verbal model of a target behavior. If a child has lost interest in an item or activity (oriented away from the adult or item; engaged with item or self-stimulatory behavior), end the trial, and plan an additional opportunity to evoke the target behavior at a later time or wait for the child to independently initiate to an item or activity.

6. **Spontaneity:** Spontaneous behaviors are separate from unprompted correct responding and refer to a child displaying or using an approximation of a target behavior independent of an adult's planned opportunity. Procedurally, you should respond to spontaneous behaviors like an unprompted or prompted correct response. Monitor this behavior across instructional sessions and, when possible, during relatively brief free-operant observations to assess generalization.

Event recording should be used when measuring target behavior or spontaneity. Event recording will yield a count of target behaviors, which can be reported as *count per session* (equal observation periods; e.g., 10 minutes) or converted to a measure of *rate per minute* (unequal observation periods; e.g., 10 minutes, 5 minutes, 8 minutes). In addition, if a planned number of opportunities are provided each session, responses can be converted to a percentage. Estimation systems are inappropriate for obtaining a count of target behaviors and, as such, we do not recommend such systems when measuring social communication and related discrete behaviors (Lane & Ledford, 2014; Ledford, Lane, & Gast, 2018; Ledford, Ayres, Lane, & Lam, 2015). Engagement can be measured by recording and coding the type of play behaviors a child displays during a set time period (provides a count and description of types of play), timing the duration of engagement in an activity (provides a time-based measure of behavior), or using momentary time sampling to estimate the percentage of intervals that a child is engaged.

Additional considerations. Prior to introducing an intervention, it is important to establish a pre-intervention pattern of responding (or baseline condition) (*unprompted correct,* *unprompted incorrect*, or *no response*) and, following introduction of an intervention, continue to monitor the same target behavior over time (*unprompted correct*, *unprompted incorrect*, *prompted correct*, *prompted incorrect*, or *no response*). Collecting data across sessions (or opportunities) and conditions allows for formative evaluation of progress, as well as assists with determining if a modification to the intervention is necessary. Relatedly, the literature supports accepting approximations for target behaviors. Although accepting approximations may lead to delayed responding in target behaviors (cf. Schreibman et al., 2015), it ensures that all communicative behaviors are reinforced and not punished, which is especially important for vulnerable populations who may have a limited repertoire of communicative behaviors. As children learn new skills and expand their vocabularies, it may be appropriate to reinforce behaviors that more closely match the terminal forms of an instructional target (e.g., say "car" instead of dropping a beginning, medial, or ending sound). We recommend closely collaborating with a speech-language pathologist for decisions related to articulation.

Troubleshooting Sessions

Although each of the child-directed strategies discussed in this chapter have research to support their use with young children, issues may arise that require modifications or additions to procedures. The best way to determine if modifications or additions are necessary is to collect data on a session-by-session basis, and collect procedural fidelity data and interobserver agreement.

1. **Adult behaviors.** First, it is critical that an adult have a child's attention during instruction. It may be necessary to include general and specific attending cues and obtain a corresponding response from the child. This ensures a child is aware of changes in the environment and, in turn, likely to contact contingencies for target behaviors. Attending cues may only be necessary when beginning instruction or one to two times at the beginning of each session. If a child is not attending, then is not possible to determine if an intervention is ineffective due to the procedures or because the child is not fully aware of the contingencies that have been put in place during these activities. Second, if procedures are not implemented as designed, it is not possible to determine if an intervention is effective or ineffective. Thus, it is important to practice procedures prior to implementing them with a child and ensure each planned step of an intervention is implemented as designed. Third, prior to beginning an intervention, a data collection system and observable and measurable definitions of target behaviors should be established. Over time, a person's definition of a target behavior may begin to slowly shift away from the original definition, meaning that a person is no longer collecting data on the target behavior. Another person should collect procedural fidelity and interobserver agreement data for at least 20 percent of sessions in each condition, with at least 80 percent agreement for each. This will assist in determining if a child's lack of progress is related to procedural issues or data collection. If each of these are evaluated and at adequate levels, patterns of responding should be evaluated to determine if modifications or additions to procedures are necessary.

2. **Prompt dependency.** A child may become reliant on an adult's prompt, such as a full verbal model, only displaying the target behavior when shown how to be correct. If this pattern of responding is observed over time, the child is likely prompt dependent, indicating that the child is not necessarily learning when to display the target behavior. That is, the child is responding to the prompt and not the natural cue for the target

behavior. If prompt dependency is suspected, a differential reinforcement procedure should be considered. A person differentially reinforces unprompted and prompted correct responses by varying the amount of reinforcement provided for each type of response. For example, following an unprompted correct response (e.g., child says, "play blocks") a child receives positive attention and a handful of blocks. In contrast, following a prompted correct response, the child receives positive attention and one block. Relatedly, previous studies have found that some children may display delayed increases in independent use of target behaviors. Thus, it may be necessary to wait before implementing differential reinforcement procedures to allow the child time to learn to respond independently. Also, children who are transitioning from a modeling procedure to less intrusive procedures (e.g., time delay) may display delays in unprompted correct responses due to being reinforced for prompted correct responses for an extended period.

3. **No response or errors.** A child may not respond or may display a high rate of errors before or after a prompt is provided. If a child does not respond or displays an unprompted incorrect response, a more helpful prompt should be provided (e.g., full verbal model). If the child does not respond to the prompt or makes an error following the prompt (prompted incorrect response), a number of options are available to remediate this issue. Wolery and colleagues (1992) highlighted the following considerations:

   a. **Provide the prompt a second time:** As stated in the *Potential modifications* section, some children may require a second opportunity to display a target behavior. That is, if a child does not respond to a model prompt, a second model prompt should be provided. Being aware of a child's previous pattern of responding during similar intervention conditions will assist with making this decision. In addition, comparing a child's characteristics (e.g., present levels of performance; social communication capabilities) to those of participants in published studies (descriptions, inclusion and exclusion criteria) can also assist with making this decision.

   b. **Select a different prompt:** A child may not reliably respond to one type of prompt for a target behavior and, as such, may require additional information to know how to be correct. For example, a child with ASD may not reliably imitate an adult's full verbal model, but consistently respond when a pictorial prompt is paired with a full verbal model. Thus, some children may require a different type of prompt or a combination of prompts before increases in target behaviors are observed.

   c. **Provide a hierarchy of prompts:** Least-to-most prompting hierarchies allow a child to self-select the amount of support he or she needs to display a target behavior. Prior to beginning sessions, the adult should arrange prompts from least to most intrusive and restrictive, with the most intrusive prompt provided as the last prompt in the hierarchy. Following an opportunity for an independent response (e.g., 5 seconds), the initial prompt in the hierarchy is delivered followed by an opportunity to respond to the prompt. If the child makes an error or does not respond, the process is repeated until the most intrusive prompt is introduced.

   d. **Modify the target behavior:** Some behaviors may be developmentally inappropriate or not functional for a child and, as such, target behavior should be revisited and modified. We recommend becoming familiar with typical patterns of development (e.g., age at which a child is likely to use a certain morphological marker) and collaborating with other professionals when identifying instructional targets. In addition, children may begin to display challenging behaviors because, due to the requirements of a target behavior (e.g., physically unable to display a target behavior), they cannot access reinforcement and may attempt to escape the non-preferred instructional situation.

e. **Do not reinforce challenging behaviors:** Some children may display challenging behaviors during instruction due to a learning history that includes attention for inappropriate behaviors or escape from non-preferred activities or people. For example, a child may not respond to a verbal prompt because under previous conditions the adult spent more time reprimanding him for not responding than providing positive attention for appropriate behaviors. The function of a challenging behavior will likely vary from child to child and, as such, a functional behavior assessment may be necessary to identify why the challenging behavior occurs and appropriate methods to reduce the challenging behavior during future sessions.

Summary

Child-directed strategies are preferred when targeting engagement and social communication in young children. Child-directed strategies capitalize on the natural contingencies for behaviors that are present in a child's immediate environment, highlighting the sometimes subtle cues for those behaviors while incorporating a child's interests and preferences into instruction to ensure learning and maintenance of behaviors occur. Teaching when and where a child will use a behavior increases the likelihood of generalization, as well as promoting long-term academic and social success.

After her meeting, Tabitha has a better understanding of how to interact with her students in a manner that recognizes each child's interests and supports their engagement. She individualizes instruction for each student, creating opportunities for social communication during play-based activities. Some students who initially displayed low engagement responded to environmental arrangement strategies and required fewer prompts and engaged in more appropriate interactions with materials and peers throughout the school year.

References

Barton, E. E. (2016). Critical issues and promising practices for teach play to young children with disabilities. In B. Reichow, B. A. Boyd, E. E. Barton, & S. L. Odom (Eds.), *Handbook of early childhood special education* (pp. 267–286). Switzerland: Springer International Publishing.

Barton, E. E., & Wolery, M. (2010). Training teachers to promote pretend play in young children with disabilities. *Exceptional Children, 77,* 85–106.

Camarata, S., & Yoder, P. (2002). Language transactions during development and intervention: Theoretical implications for developmental neuroscience. *International Journal of Developmental Neuroscience, 20,* 459–465.

Cooper, J. O., Heron, T. E., & Heward, W. L. (2007). *Applied behavior analysis* (2nd ed.). Upper Saddle River, NJ: Merrill/Prentice Hall.

Gazdag, G., & Warren, S. F. (2000). Effects of adult contingent imitation on development of young children's vocal imitation. *Journal of Early Intervention, 23,* 24–35.

Girolametto, L. E. (1988). Improving the social-conversational skills of developmentally delayed children: An intervention study. *Journal of Speech and Hearing Disorders, 53,* 156–167.

Grisham-Brown, J., & Hemmeter, M. L. (2017). *Blended practices for teaching young children in inclusive settings* (2nd ed.). Baltimore, MD: Brookes.

Halle, J. W., Baer, D. M., & Spradlin, J. E. (1981). Teachers' generalized use of delay as a stimulus control procedure to increase language use in handicapped children. *Journal of Applied Behavior Analysis, 14,* 389–409.

Halle, J. W., Marshall, A. M., & Spradlin, J. E. (1979). Time delay: A technique to increase language use and facilitate generalization in retarded children. *Journal of Applied Behavior Analysis*, 12, 431–440.

Hart, B. M., & Risley, T. R. (1968). Establishing use of descriptive adjectives in the spontaneous speech of disadvantaged preschool children. *Journal of Applied Behavior Analysis*, 2, 109–120.

Hart, B. M., & Risley, T. R. (1975). Incidental teaching of language in preschool. *Journal of Applied Behavior Analysis*, 8, 411–420.

Hemmeter, M. L., & Kaiser, A. P. (1990). Environmental influences on children's language: A model and case study. *Education and Treatment of Children*, 13, 331–346.

Ingersoll, B., & Gergans, S. (2007). The effect of a parent-implemented imitation intervention on spontaneous imitation skills in young children with autism. *Research in Developmental Disabilities*, 28, 163–175.

Kaiser, A. P., & Hampton, L. H. (2017). Enhanced milieu teaching. In R. J. McCauley, M. E. Fey, & R. B. Gillam (Eds.), *Treatment of language disorders in children* (2nd ed.) (pp. 87–119). Baltimore, MD: Brookes.

Kaiser, A. P., & Woods, J. (2010). Kid Talk Tactics Project: Training manual. Retrieved from https://vkc.mc.vanderbilt.edu/kidtalk.

Kaiser, A. P., & Wright, C. A. (2013). Enhanced milieu teaching: Incorporating AAC into naturalistic teaching with young children and their partners. *Perspectives on Augmentative and Alternative Communication*, 22, 37–50.

Kaiser, A. P., Nietfeld, J. P., & Roberts, M. Y. (2010). Applying evidence-based practices to support communication with children who have autism spectrum disorders [Monograph]. *Young Exceptional Children*, 12, 39–53.

Kasari, C., Kaiser, A. P., Goods, K., Nietfeld, J., Mathy, J., Landa, R., Murphy, S., & Almirall, D. (2014). Communication interventions for minimally verbal children with autism: Sequential multiple assignment randomized trial. *Journal of the American Academy of Child & Adolescent Psychiatry*, 56, 635–646.

Lane, J. D., & Ledford, J. R. (2014). Using interval-based systems to measure behavior in early childhood special education and early intervention. *Topics in Early Childhood Special Education*, 34, 83–93.

Lane, J. D., Ledford, J. R., Shepley, C., Mataras, T. K., Ayres, K. M., & Davis, A. B. (2016). A brief coaching intervention for teaching naturalistic strategies to parents. *Journal of Early Intervention*, 38, 135–150.

Lane, J. D., Lieberman-Betz, R., & Gast, D. L. (2016). An analysis of naturalistic interventions for increasing spontaneous expressive language in children with autism spectrum disorder. *The Journal of Special Education*, 50, 49–61.

Lane, J. D., Shepley, C., & Lieberman-Betz, R. (2016). Promoting expressive language in young children with or at-risk for autism spectrum disorder in a preschool classroom. *Journal of Autism and Developmental Disorders*, 46, 3216–3231.

Lane, J. D., Shepley, C., Sartini, E., & Hogue, A. (forthcoming). *Promoting engagement and expressive communication in children with autism spectrum disorder and intellectual disability in the classroom* (under review).

Ledford, J. R., Ayres, K., Lane, J. D., & Lam, M. F. (2015). Identifying issues and concerns with the use of interval-based systems in single case research: A pilot simulation study. *The Journal of Special Education*, 49, 104–117.

Ledford, J. R., Lane, J. D., & Gast, D. L. (2018). Dependent variables, measurement, and reliability. J. R. Ledford & D. L. Gast (Eds.), *Single case research in behavioral sciences* (3rd ed.). New York: Routledge.

Lifter, K., Sulzer-Azaroff, B., Anderson, S., & Cowdery, G. E. (1993). Teaching play activities to preschool children with disabilities: The importance of developmental considerations. *Journal of Early Intervention*, 17, 139–159.

Roberts, M. Y., & Kaiser, A. P. (2011). The effectiveness of parent-implemented language interventions: A meta-analysis. *American Journal of Speech-Language Pathology*, 20, 180–199.

Rogers-Warren, A., & Warren, S. F. (1980). Mands for verbalization: Facilitating the display of newly trained language in children. *Behavior Modification*, 4, 361–382.

Schreibman, L., Dawson, G., Stahmer, A. C., Landa, R., Rogers, S. J., McGee, G. G., ... Halladay, A. (2015). Naturalistic developmental behavioral interventions: Empirically validated treatments for autism spectrum disorder. *Journal of Autism and Developmental Disorders*, 45, 2411–2428.

Snyder, P. A., Rakap, S., Hemmeter, M. L., McLaughlin, T. W., Sandall, S., & McLean, M. E. (2015). Naturalistic instructional approaches in early learning: A systematic review. *Journal of Early Intervention*, 37, 69–97.

Ungerer, J., & Sigman, M. (1981). Symbolic play and language comprehension on autistic, mentally retarded, and normal children. *Developmental Psychology*, 20, 293–302.

Warren, S. F., McQuarter, R. J., & Rogers-Warren, A. K. (1984). The effects of teacher mands and models on the speech of unresponsive language-delayed children. *Journal of Speech and Hearing Research*, 51, 43–52.

Wolery, M., & Hemmeter, M. L. (2011). Classroom instruction: Background, assumptions, and challenges. *Journal of Early Intervention*, 33, 371–380.

Wolery, M., Ault, M. L., & Doyle, P. M. (1992). *Teaching students with moderate to severe disabilities: Use of response prompting strategies*. New York: Longman.

Woods, J., Kashinath, S., & Goldstein, H. (2004). Effects of embedding caregiver-implemented teaching strategies in daily routines on children's communication outcomes. *Journal of Early Intervention*, 26, 175–193.

Appendix 7.1

Pre-Intervention Sessions
Fidelity of Implementation and Data Collection Form

Child: _____ Date: _____   Session #: _____   Instructor: _____   Setting: _____

Time at Start of Session: _____ Time at End of Session: _____

Target Behavior(s): _____

EAS=Environmental Arrangement Strategy

#	Adult Used EAS	Waited 5-s for child to respond	*Child Used Target Behavior (Circle)*		Reinforcement		
					Adult reinforced approximations	Adult Provided Positive Attention	Adult Used Recast or Expanded Target Language
-	√	√	Yes	No	√	√	√
1			Yes	No			
2			Yes	No			
3			Yes	No			
4			Yes	No			
5			Yes	No			
6			Yes	No			
7			Yes	No			
8			Yes	No			
Spontaneous target language		Tally:					

Summary of Data	
% unprompted target responses	
# spontaneous target requests	
% Procedural Fidelity	
% Reliability	

Appendix 7.2

Assessment of Play Behaviors

Child: _____ Date: _____   Observation #: _____   Observer: _____   Setting: _____

Time at Start of Session: _____ Time at End of Session: _____

Cognitive Play Codes	Social Play Codes
Sensorimotor (SR)	Unoccupied (UN)
Relational (RE)	Solitary (SO)
Functional (FX)	Onlooker (ON)
Functional with pretense (FP)	Parallel (PA)
Object substitution (OS)	Associative (AS)
Imagining absent objects (IO)	Cooperative (CO)
Assigning absent attributes (IA)	

Directions: Provide age-appropriate materials and activities and observe the child's actions on objects. The observation can occur when the target child is present (alone) or when peers are present. Assess both, as each one provides differing information. Record the items manipulated during the observation and note number of times item was selected and approximate length of engagement. For each occasion, code the type of cognitive play observed. In addition, code the social component of play. Write a summary at the end of the observation.

Item Selected	Approximate Length of Engagement	Action on Object	Type of Cognitive Play	Type of Social Play

Summary of Observation:

Appendix 7.3

Sample Intervention Session Form
Fidelity of Implementation and Data Collection Form

Child: Braden   Date: 12/30   Session #: 4   Instructor: JL   Setting: Free Play

Time at Start of Session: 10:04 am Time at End of Session: 10:15am

Target Behavior(s): Imitate protoverbs during play (in, on) and verbs (stack, build)

*White rows refer to adult behaviors and gray, child behaviors

Model Procedure (Imitating Language)
Data Coding Key: P+=prompted correct; P−=prompted incorrect; NR=no response

	1	2	3	4
Arranged Environment	√	√	√	√
Child Initiated	√	√	√	√
Provided Model Prompt	√	√	√	√
Waited 5-s for Response	√	√	√	√
Child Imitated Response	P+	-	-	P+
Reinforced Approximation	√	-	-	√
Provided Positive Attention	√	-	-	√
Used Recast Strategy or Expanded Target Language	√	-	-	√
Child Provided an Incorrect Response		P−	P−	
Provided Model Prompt (Second Time)		√	√	
Waited 5-s for Response		√	√	
Child Imitated Response (Second Model)		P+	P+	
Reinforced Approximation		√	√	
Provided Positive Attention		√	√	
Used Recast Strategy or Expanded Target Language		√	√	
Child Lost Interest and Adult Ended Trial				

Spontaneous target language	Tally: ||||

Summary of Data	
% prompted correct target responses	50% (following first model), 50% (following second model)
# spontaneous target language	4
% Procedural Fidelity	100% correct implementation of procedures
% Reliability	100% agreement with instructor

Appendix 7.4

Intervention Sessions
Fidelity of Implementation and Data Collection Form

Child: _____ Date: _____   Session #: _____   Instructor: _____   Setting: _____

Time at Start of Session: _____ Time at End of Session: _____

Target Behavior(s): _____

Model Procedure (Imitating Language)
Data Coding Key: P+=prompted correct; P−=prompted incorrect; NR=no response

	1	2	3	4
Arranged Environment				
Child Initiated				
Provided Model Prompt				
Waited 5-s for Response				
Child Imitated Response				
Reinforced Approximation				
Provided Positive Attention				
Used Recast Strategy or Expanded Target Language				
Child Provided an Incorrect Response				
Provided Model Prompt (Second Time)				
Waited 5-s for Response				
Child Imitated Response (Second Model)				
Reinforced Approximation				
Provided Positive Attention				
Used Recast Strategy or Expanded Target Language				
Child Lost Interest and Adult Ended Trial				

Spontaneous target language	Tally:

Summary of Data	
% prompted correct target responses	
# spontaneous target language	
% Procedural Fidelity	
% Reliability	

Appendix 7.5

Intervention Sessions
Fidelity of Implementation and Data Collection Form

Child: _____ Date: _____ Session #: _____ Instructor: _____ Setting: _____

Time at Start of Session: _____ Time at End of Session: _____

Target Behavior(s): _____

Mand-Model Procedure (Responding to Adult's Vocal Behavior)
Data Coding Key: +=unprompted correct; −=unprompted incorrect; P+=prompted correct; P−=prompted incorrect; NR=no response

	1	2	3	4
Approached and Interrupted (Ongoing Activity, Next Turn, Next Activity)				
Adult Provided a Mand				
Waited 5-s for Response				
Child Provided Independent Response at Target Language Level				
Reinforced Approximation (Continuation, Turn, Began Next Activity)				
Provided Positive Attention				
Used Recast or Expanded Target Language				
Child Provided an Incorrect Response				
Provided Model Prompt				
Waited 5-s for Response				
Child Imitated Response				
Reinforced Approximation (Continuation, Turn, Began Next Activity)				
Provided Positive Attention				
Used Recast or Expanded Target Language				
Child Lost Interest and Adult Ended Trial				

Spontaneous target language	Tally:

Summary of Data	
% unprompted correct target responses	
# spontaneous target language	
% Procedural Fidelity	
% Reliability	

Appendix 7.6

Intervention Sessions
Fidelity of Implementation and Data Collection Form

Child: _____ Date: _____   Session #: _____   Instructor: _____   Setting: _____

Time at Start of Session: _____ Time at End of Session: _____

Target Behavior(s): _____

Time Delay (Promoting Spontaneous Language)
Data Coding Key: +=unprompted correct; −=unprompted incorrect; P+=prompted correct; P−=prompted incorrect; NR=no response

	1	2	3	4
Established Attention & Withheld Assistance/Pause in Routine				
Looked at Child Expectantly				
Waited Specified Time Delay (Note Delay: _____ seconds)				
Child Initiated Correct Response				
Reinforced Approximation with Natural Consequence				
Provided Positive Attention				
Used Recast or Expanded Target Language				
Child Provided an Incorrect Response				
Provided Model Prompt				
Waited Specified Time Delay (Note Delay: _____ seconds)				
Child Imitated Response				
Reinforced Approximation with Natural Consequence				
Provided Positive Attention				
Used Recast or Expanded Target Language				
Child Lost Interest and Adult Ended Trial				

Spontaneous target language	Tally:

Summary of Data	
% unprompted correct target responses	
# spontaneous target language	
% Procedural Fidelity	
% Reliability	

Appendix 7.7

Intervention Sessions
Fidelity of Implementation and Data Collection Form

Child: _____ Date: _____ Session #: _____ Instructor: _____ Setting: _____

Time at Start of Session: _____ Time at End of Session: _____

Target Behavior(s): _____

Incidental Teaching (Expanding Spontaneous Language)
Data Coding Key: +=unprompted correct; −=unprompted incorrect; P+=prompted correct; P− =prompted incorrect;
NR=no response

	1	2	3	4
Engaged Child & Used Environmental Arrangement Strategy				
Child Initiated Vocally or Non-Vocally (Non-Target Language)				
Used a Milieu Procedure (Note Procedure: ____)				
Waited Specified Time Delay (Note Delay: ____ seconds)				
Child Responded Independently (Mand, TD) or Imitated Response (Model)				
Reinforced Approximation				
Provided Positive Attention				
Used Recast or Expanded Target Language				
Child Provided an Incorrect Response				
Provided a Controlling Prompt (Note Prompt: ____)				
Waited Specified Time Delay (Note Delay: ____ seconds)				
Child Displayed the Target Language				
Reinforced Approximation				
Provided Positive Attention				
Used Recast or Expanded Target Language				
Child Lost Interest and Adult Ended Trial				

1st. Model, mand, time delay
2nd. Mand (repeated or asked for more information), model

Spontaneous target language	Tally:

Summary of Data	
% unprompted correct target responses	
# spontaneous target language	
% Procedural Fidelity	
% Reliability	

Appendix 7.8

Intervention Sessions
Fidelity of Implementation and Data Collection Form

Child: _____ Date: _____   Session #: _____   Instructor: _____   Setting: _____

Time at Start of Session: _____ Time at End of Session: _____

Target Behavior(s): _____

Modified NLI Procedure: ASD and ID (Promoting Early Social Communication)
0-s Delay Trials
Data Coding Key: +=unprompted correct; −=unprompted incorrect; P+=prompted correct; P−=prompted incorrect; NR=no response

	1	2	3	4
Engaged Child in Routine Activity				
Used Environmental Arrangement Strategy and Looked Expectantly at Child				
Child Initiated (Non-Target Language)				
Immediately Provided a Model Prompt (0-s delay)				
Waited 5-s for Response				
Child Imitated Response				
Reinforced Approximation				
Provided Positive Attention				
Used Recast or Expanded Target Language				
Child Provided an Incorrect Response				
Provided Model Prompt (Second Time)				
Waited 5-s for Response				
Child Imitated Response (Second Model)				
Reinforced Approximation				
Provided Positive Attention				
Used Recast or Expanded Target Language				
Child Lost Interest and Adult Ended Trial				

Spontaneous target language	Tally:

Summary of Data	
% unprompted correct target responses	
# spontaneous target language	
% Procedural Fidelity	
% Reliability	

Appendix 7.9

Intervention Sessions
Fidelity of Implementation and Data Collection Form

Child: _____ Date: _____   Session #: _____   Instructor: _____   Setting: _____

Time at Start of Session: _____ Time at End of Session: _____

Target Behavior(s): _____

Modified NLI Procedure: ASD and ID (Promoting Early Social Communication)
5-s Delay Trials
Data Coding Key: +=unprompted correct; −=unprompted incorrect; P+=prompted correct; P−=prompted incorrect; NR=no response

	1	2	3	4
Engaged Child in Routine Activity				
Used Environmental Arrangement Strategy and Looked Expectantly at Child				
Child Initiated (Non-Target Language)				
Waited 5-s for Response				
Child Provided Target Language				
Reinforced Approximation				
Provided Positive Attention				
Used Recast or Expanded Target Language				
Child Provided an Incorrect Response				
Provided Model Prompt				
Waited 5-s for Response				
Child Imitated Response				
Reinforced Approximation				
Provided Positive Attention				
Used Recast or Expanded Target Language				
Child Provided an Incorrect Response				
Provided Model Prompt (Second Time)				
Waited 5-s for Response				
Child Imitated Response				
Reinforced Approximation				
Provided Positive Attention				
Used Recast or Expanded Target Language				
Child Lost Interest and Adult Ended Trial				

Spontaneous target language	Tally:

Summary of Data	
% unprompted correct target responses	
# spontaneous target language	
% Procedural Fidelity	
% Reliability	

Appendix 7.10

Intermix of Milieu Procedures
Fidelity of Implementation and Data Collection Form

Child: _____ Date: _____ Session #: _____ Instructor: _____ Setting: _____
Time at Start of Session: _____ Time at End of Session: _____
Target Behavior(s): _____

Data Coding Key: +=unprompted correct; −=unprompted incorrect; P+=prompted correct; P−=prompted incorrect; NR=no response. *Milieu Procedure Key*: M=Modeling, MM=Mand-Model, TD=Time Delay, IT=Incidental Teaching, **EAS**=Environmental Arrangement Strategy

#	Adult Used EAS	Waited 5-s for child to respond	Milieu Procedure	Child Behavior	Child Response	Reinforcement		
						Adult reinforced approximations	Adult Provided Positive Attention	Adult Used Recast or Expanded Target Language
-	√	√	M	Protoverb: *In*	P+	√	√	√
1								
2								
3								
4								
5								
6								
7								
8								
Spontaneous target language	Tally:							

Summary of Data	
% unprompted correct responses	
# spontaneous target language	
% Procedural Fidelity	
% Reliability	

8 Introduction to Prompting Procedures and Time Delay

Key Terms

Controlling prompts	*Non-controlling prompts*	*Response prompts*
Stimulus prompts	*Response prompting procedures*	*Single prompt procedures*
Hierarchical prompt procedures	*Discriminative stimulus*	*Pre-prompt delay interval*
Post-prompt delay interval	*Errorless learning*	*0-second trial*
Delay trial	*Unprompted correct*	*Unprompted error*
Prompted correct	*Prompted error*	*Wait training*
Differentiated reinforcement		

Chapter Objectives

After completing this chapter, readers should be able to:

- Name the characteristics of systematic prompting procedures.
- Describe the differences between controlling and non-controlling prompts.
- Outline the procedural steps for CTD and PTD procedures.
- Describe the difference between CTD and PTD procedures.
- Explain child and implementer characteristics that might influence the choice to use PTD versus CTD.
- Explain commonly encountered problems when CTD and PTD procedures are used, and identify potential solutions.

Amal provides children with ample opportunities to learn basic literacy skills; for example, she provides interesting and developmentally appropriate books, reads often with children during free choice centers, and plans engaging small group reading activities. Despite these opportunities, Amal identifies three children in her class who are transitioning to kindergarten soon who do not demonstrate that basic letter knowledge. Amal is concerned but is unsure about whether direct instruction is warranted, given that they do appropriately participate in child- and teacher-led literacy activities, and are still relatively young.

Chapters 6 and 7 primarily focused on teacher behaviors that occurred prior to an activity (e.g., arranging the environment) or in the context of child-directed learning trials. The following chapters will focus on adult-directed strategies for teaching children specific behaviors—these adult-directed trials can occur during child-led play activities or adult-led activities, which will be discussed in greater depth in Chapter 12. The primary purpose of this chapter is to define and describe the use of systematic response prompt procedures in general, and to explain the rationale, procedures, and outcomes for two specific strategies—constant time delay (CTD) and progressive time delay (PTD). The procedures described in this chapter are directly related to many of the Division for Early Childhood Recommended Practices in the area of Instruction (INS3-INS7, INS10).

Categorizing Prompts

Controlling versus Non-Controlling Prompts

Prompting, or providing assistance for correct responding, is an essential teaching strategy. Prompts can be categorized according to various dimensions. For example, they can be characterized by the amount of assistance provided: **controlling prompts** ensure correct responding (adult shows the child how to be correct) and **non-controlling prompts** increase the likelihood of correct responding, but do not ensure a correct response. This characterization is individual in nature; a controlling prompt for one child may not reliably result in correct responding for another. For example, a teacher might model handwashing for a child who reliably imitates the actions of others; this physical model might serve as a controlling prompt. For a child who does not yet reliably imitate the actions of others, this would be ineffective (i.e., not a controlling prompt).

Categorizing Prompts by Topography

Prompts can also be categorized according to topography (i.e., what the prompt looks like). Common topographies are described below, along with examples and prerequisite behaviors. Children must demonstrate these prerequisite behaviors to benefit from the use of the specific topography as a controlling prompt.

- **Vocal (verbal) model:** Consists of the prompter saying a targeted vocal response.
  - **Example:** Following the presentation of a discriminative stimulus that is red in color, the teacher asks what color it is, and provides the verbal model "Red."
  - **Prerequisite behaviors:** Verbal imitation (i.e., the child reliably responds to "say ___ " by repeating the word).
- **Vocal (verbal) hint:** Consists of the prompter providing more information to the child via verbalization.
  - **Example:** Following the presentation of a discriminative stimulus that is red in color, the teacher asks what color it is, and provides the verbal hint "It starts with 'r'."
  - **Prerequisite behaviors:** Adequate receptive language (i.e., the child can use the extra information provided in the prompt).
- **Picture prompt:** Consists of the prompter providing more information to the child via a photograph, line-drawing, or other two-dimensional representation.
  - **Example:** Following the discriminative stimulus of leaving the stall area of the bathroom, a teacher shows the child a photograph of the sink to indicate the student should go to that area to begin handwashing.
  - **Prerequisite behaviors:** Object–picture correspondence (i.e., the child can match a photograph with a corresponding object)
- **Physical model:** Consists of the prompter engaging in the targeted response when it is a physical movement.
  - **Example:** Following the discriminative stimulus of leaving the stall area of the bathroom, a teacher turns on the water in a sink adjacent to the one the child should use and looks expectantly at the child.
  - **Prerequisite behaviors:** Motor imitation (i.e., the child reliably responds to "do this" by doing what that person was doing).

- **Gesture:** Consists of the prompter using a conventional motoric action to indicate desirable behaviors.
  - **Example:** Following the discriminative stimulus of leaving the stall area of the bathroom, a teacher points to the faucet to prompt the child who should turn it.
  - **Prerequisite behaviors:** Typical responses to conventional gestures (i.e., the child reliably engages in a routine behavior when an adult points toward a related item such as sitting when an adult points to a chair).
- **Full physical guidance:** Consists of a prompter moving a child's body such that he or she is engaging in the targeted behavior.
  - **Example:** Following the discriminative stimulus of having soap on hands during handwashing, a teacher puts his hands on the outside of the child's hands and rubs the child's hands together.
  - **Prerequisite behaviors:** Child does not engage in problem behavior contingent on touch.
- **Partial physical guidance:** This prompt consists of a prompter moving a child's body such that he or she begins performing part of the targeted behavior.
  - **Example:** Following the discriminative stimulus of having soap on hands during handwashing, a teacher puts his hands on the outside of the child's hands and places the hands together, but does not assist the child in rubbing his hands together.
  - **Prerequisite behaviors:** Child does not engage in problem behavior contingent on touch.

Research Abstract

Kodak, T., Fuchtman, R, & Paden, A. (2012). A comparison of intraverbal training procedures for children with autism. *Journal of Applied Behavior Analysis*, 45, 155–160.

   In this single case design study, two children with autism spectrum disorders (ages: 4 & 5 years) were taught to answer questions using a progressive time delay procedure. The instructor divided questions into two sets and used one set in each of two variations of the condition—they taught one set using a verbal model as a controlling prompt and taught the other set using a picture of the answer as a controlling prompt. One participant only learned to answer questions independently when a verbal model was used as the controlling prompt; the other participant learned approximately equally well with both prompt types. Outcomes from this study suggest that selection of prompt topographies should be individualized.

Response versus Stimulus Prompts

Finally, prompts can be characterized by the nature of the assistance: **response prompts** are social behaviors (i.e., instructor behaviors) designed to provide assistance for performing the response—all of the prompts described above are response prompts. **Stimulus prompts** involve changing a stimulus to increase the likelihood of correct responding. Table 8.1 provides examples of common stimulus prompts and response prompts. Although we will refer to the prompting procedures described in the next several chapters as "response prompting procedures," in some cases, it might be possible to include stimulus prompts rather than response prompts in the context of these procedures.

Table 8.1 Sample Stimulus and Response Prompts

Situation	Stimulus Prompt	Response Prompt
Solomon is a 4-year-old boy with ASD who does not yet identify his peers, in person or via photos. His teacher provides three photographs, and asks "Which one is [name]?"	Teacher reduces the field from 3 to 2, by removing one incorrect stimulus.	Teacher points to the correct response.
Angel is a 5-year-old typically developing girl. She can identify her photo as well as photos of her peers, but does not yet identify her own or others' written names.	Teacher makes a "matching board," on which Angel can match a photo of each peer to the identical photo when they arrive at school. The photo that is matched also includes each peer's written name. Over time, the teacher makes the child's photograph less salient and the written name more salient (e.g., blurring the photo, and making the font larger), until the child can match the written name to the photo.	Teacher makes a "matching board," on which Angel can match a photo of each peer to their written name when they arrive at school. She initially provides the written name along with a verbal prompt ("This says Charlie") to assist Angel in matching the written name with the photo.

Response Prompting Procedures

The first important point regarding the procedures discussed in this chapter is that **response prompting procedures** are different from *prompts* (assistance provided for engaging in a target behavior), because they are operationalized practices that involve the planned provision *and* systematic removal of prompts over time. Use of prompts without systematic rules for their provision and removal is not an evidence-based practice—however, several different response prompting procedures have been identified as evidence-based (Browder, Ahlgrim-Delzell, Spooner, Mims, & Baker, 2009; Walker, 2008; Wong et al., 2015). In this chapter, we will discuss two related response prompting procedures, constant time delay (CTD), and progressive time delay (PTD). CTD and PTD are **single prompt procedures**—that is, they involve the use of a single prompt topography. In Chapters 10 and 11, **hierarchical prompt procedures** are discussed—these procedures use different prompt topographies within or across sessions. When response prompting procedures are used, children can engage in correct responses and errors, and can engage in those behaviors before or after prompts are provided. Thus, there are four total potential responses: unprompted correct responses (UPC), unprompted error responses (UPE), prompted correct responses (PC), and prompted error responses (PE). These responses are further described in the *Data Collection* section later in this chapter.

Constant Time Delay (CTD)

CTD was first assessed for use in the late 1970s and early 1980s, for teaching discrete and chained behaviors to individuals with significant disabilities (see Snell & Gast, 1981;

Wolery & Gast, 1984). It was developed as a less complex procedural variation of a previously developed procedure, PTD (discussed at length later in the chapter). Much of the early work on CTD was conducted by Mark Wolery and David Gast at the University of Kentucky (Bennett, Gast, Wolery, & Schuster, 1986; Godby, Gast, & Wolery, 1987; Johnson, 1977; Kleinert & Gast, 1982) although many studies have been conducted in the nearly 40 years since then—a simple Google Scholar search for "constant time delay" produces almost 15,000 results.

The components of a trial for CTD include: (1) provision of the discriminative stimulus, (2) a pre-prompt response interval, (3) provision of a controlling prompt, (4) a post-prompt response interval, and (5) response consequences. When CTD is used, the prompt is removed by delaying it in time. That is, prompts are initially provided immediately after the discriminative stimulus and are later provided after a delay. When children are capable of responding correctly (e.g., when they have learned the behaviors), they are likely to respond before the prompt (during the pre-prompt response interval) because it results in faster reinforcement. This reduces the likelihood that children will continue to wait for assistance once they are capable of responding independently, sometimes referred to as "prompt dependence."

Prior to conducting CTD instruction, you should identify the discriminative stimulus, the duration of your response intervals, the controlling prompt, and the consequences for each type of response. You should also ensure children have applicable prerequisite skills (see Table 8.3). You should also determine the **mastery criterion**, which will govern when you will discontinue instruction. The mastery criterion tends to include an accuracy benchmark (e.g., 90 percent unprompted correct responding) and a standard regarding how often it occurred (e.g., over three consecutive sessions). Given previous research, we suggest a mastery criterion of 100 percent responding over at least three consecutive days, as some researchers have used a less stringent criterion and maintained behavior change did not occur (Ledford & Wolery, 2013; 90 percent average across three consecutive days).

- **Discriminative Stimulus:** This refers to situations in which you would expect the child to engage in the behavior of interest. For some, such as pre-academic behaviors, the discriminative stimulus is often a teacher question ("What letter is this?"). For other behaviors, the discriminative stimulus may be a previous child behavior (e.g., one discriminative stimulus for beginning handwashing by walking to the sink is exiting the bathroom stall after toileting) or a typically occurring or contrived event (e.g., a peer request).
- **Pre-Prompt Response Interval:** As noted below, there are two different pre-prompt response intervals when CTD is used. The first is a 0-second interval. The other, a delay interval, should be selected individually, and should be based on the typical amount of time it takes a child to respond. For example, it is common for most children to respond to known questions within just a few seconds; so, for answering discrete questions such as "What is this?," you might choose a pre-prompt response interval of 3 seconds. For some children, such as those who tend to respond more slowly or to have motor delays that impact responding, a longer delay may be needed. In research studies, prompts of 3–5 seconds are common, but delays of 10 seconds or more have been used (see Table 8.2).
- **Controlling Prompt:** This should be selected individually, based on the type of assistance that is likely to lead to correct responding. For example, for vocal behaviors such as answering a question, a verbal model is often selected as the controlling prompt. For motoric behaviors such as selecting an item from an array, the controlling

prompt might be a gesture (e.g., pointing to the correct item) or a physical prompt (e.g., moving the child's hand to the correct item). Generally, when multiple prompts are under consideration, you should choose a prompt that is likely to result in correct responding (i.e., is controlling) *and* that is the least restrictive.

- **Post-Prompt Response Interval:** Generally, the post-prompt response interval is the same duration as the "delay" interval for the pre-prompt response, and should be chosen based on individual child response times. *Unlike the pre-prompt response interval, the post-prompt response interval stays the same across all sessions.*
- **Response Consequences:** Prior to using CTD, you should decide what consequences will occur when the child responds correctly or incorrectly.
  - **Reinforce Correct Responses:** Generally, the same identified reinforcer is provided contingent on prompted *and* unprompted responses. That is, the child receives the same reward regardless of whether they needed help to engage in the correct response.
  - **Remind the Child to Wait:** Often, instructors choose to remind a child to wait if they respond incorrectly prior to the prompt—a UPE response (e.g., error during the pre-prompt response interval). This can be provided as a verbal reminder ("Remember to wait if you don't know the answer") or as a gesture (put finger to lips). Following the wait reminder, the instructor can either provide the correct response (e.g., "Red") or end the trial.
  - **Ignore or Correct Errors:** When a child engages in an incorrect response after the prompt, researchers have typically ignored this error and ended the trial. For example, if a child says "green" after you have provided the verbal model "blue," you would not respond verbally. Alternatively, you could say "No, that's blue." The benefit to ignoring is that you will not inadvertently reinforce incorrect responses with verbal attention; the benefit to error correction is that the child is provided information that may influence their learning.

Initial Instructional Sessions: 0-second Trials

During initial instructional sessions for all behaviors, 0-second trials will be used. These trials are identical to delay trials except that the pre-prompt interval duration is 0 seconds.

Table 8.2 Sample 0-Second and Delay Trials

Component	Sample Trial A	Sample Trial B
Discriminative Stimulus	Teacher question: "What color?" along with the provision of a red train.	Peer request for a toy: "Can I have that one?" while pointing to a toy in the child's possession.
Pre-Prompt Response Interval	0 seconds (no wait time)	Teacher waits 3 seconds for child to respond
Controlling Prompt	"Red"	Teacher points to visual with two options—"When I'm done" or "Sure."
Post-Prompt Response Interval	Teacher waits 3 seconds for child to respond	Teacher waits 3 seconds for child to respond
Child Behavior	*Child says "Red"*	*Child says "When I'm done"*
Response Consequences	Teacher says "That train is red!" and gives it to the child.	Teacher gives a thumbs up and puts a token on a class-wide chart, and peer says "OK"

That is, the discriminative stimulus is presented, and is *immediately* followed by provision of the controlling prompt. The flow chart below (Figure 8.1) depicts the steps of a single 0-second trial; Figure 8.2 depicts a trial corresponding with Sample Trial B.

The purpose of 0-second trials is to pair the discriminative stimulus with a prompt that already produces correct responding, with the eventual goal of removing the prompt such that the discriminative stimulus alone will produce correct responding. The use of the immediate prompt produces **errorless learning,** which means that the child is provided opportunities to learn new information without making any errors due to guessing. You should use 0-second trials for at least one session during which all responses are prompted corrects (e.g., no errors). This suggests that the child can correctly respond given the controlling prompt. For young children and learners without a long history of direct instruction, you might choose to conduct as many as two to four sessions using 0-second trials, with 100 percent PC responding.

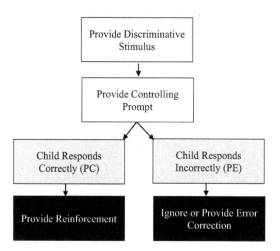

Figure 8.1 Steps for a 0-Second CTD Trial.

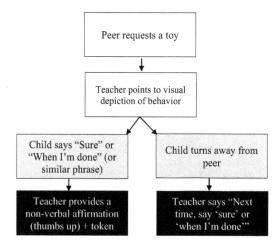

Figure 8.2 Sample 0-Second CTD Trial.

Later Instructional Sessions: Delay Trials

Following sessions in which 0-second trials are used, all remaining sessions should include **delay trials.** These trials are identical to 0-second trials except that the pre-prompt interval duration is more than 0 seconds (commonly 3–5 seconds). That is, the discriminative stimulus is presented, and is followed by a waiting period prior to the delivery of the controlling prompt. Figure 8.3 depicts a trial corresponding with a 3-second delay trial (Sample Trial A) and Figure 8.4 depicts an example.

The purpose of delay trials is to allow the child an opportunity to respond in the presence of the discriminative stimulus alone. However, the prompt is always available to ensure correct responding. You should use delay trials for all remaining sessions unless the child does not consistently produce primarily PC and UPC responses. If this occurs for multiple sessions, you may decide to conduct additional 0-second trials to allow the child more time to learn the behaviors without the need to wait for a prompt. Alternatively, you can conduct **wait training** prior to the initiation of instruction (as described by Ledford & Wolery, 2013); wait training procedures are described later in the chapter.

Note that even after the child consistently responds to the discriminative stimulus with unprompted corrects, the prompt is *always* available. For example, if a child responds with 100 percent unprompted correct responding one day, but waits on the first trial the following day, you should respond by providing the controlling prompt. This teaches children that the instructor will always provide help when it is needed. Delay trials only end when the specified mastery criterion is met.

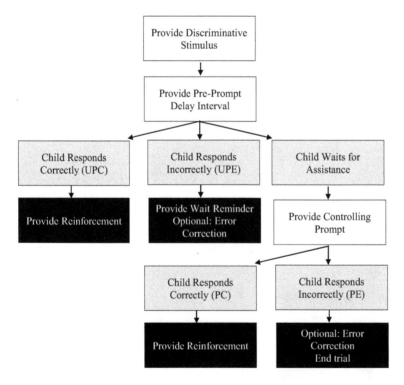

Figure 8.3 Steps for a Delay Trial Using CTD.

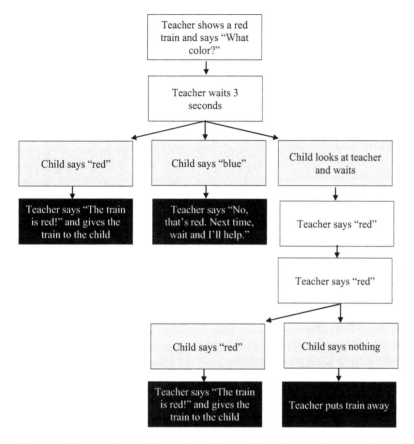

Figure 8.4 Sample Delay Trial with a 3-Second Pre-Prompt Response Interval.

Table 8.3 Child Prerequisite Skills for Constant Time Delay

Category	Description
Reinforcer	The instructor has identified one or more preferred items or activities as a potential reinforcer
Prompt	The instructor has confirmed which specific prompts control responding (e.g., what instructor behaviors are necessary to ensure correct responding) for the targeted behaviors.
Waiting	The instructor has confirmed that when the child does not know the answer, he or she can wait for assistance rather than "guessing" and potentially providing an incorrect response.

Research Abstract

Appelman, M., Vail, C. O., & Lieberman-Betz, R. G. (2014). The effects of constant time delay and instructive feedback on the acquisition of English and Spanish sight words. *Journal of Early Intervention, 36,* 131–148.

In this single case design study, kindergarten boys with mild delays (three White, one African-American) were taught to read English sight words using constant time delay. All children learned to read targeted words, which were taught in three sequential sets. Moreover, all children demonstrated "learning to learn"—that is, they learned the later sets faster than the initial set. This phenomenon is common in systematic instruction, suggesting that children get better (more efficient) at learning when professionals use ongoing, systematic instruction. When students responded with the correct word, the instructor confirmed their response and then told the child the Spanish translation (e.g., when a child read "yes," the instructor told the child that "si" was "yes" in Spanish)—a procedure called instructive feedback (see Chapter 12). Children learned to read all of the taught words and more than half of the Spanish translations.

Progressive Time Delay (PTD)

PTD was established as an effective procedure for the transfer of stimulus control in the 1970s, using stimulus prompts, rather than response prompts (Touchette, 1971). The use of PTD with response prompts was quickly adopted (Striefel, Bryan, & Aikins, 1974), and nearly all subsequent research with PTD has been conducted with response prompts. It is less commonly referred to as "progressive prompt delay"—we will use the more common term *time delay* given the historical use, although we note that the progressive nature of PTD is truly delaying the *prompt* in time, rather than delaying time itself.

The only difference between CTD and PTD procedures is that PTD includes multiple post-prompt interval durations. Both procedures involve use of 0-second trials and prompt delay trials, where a terminal delay is identified a priori. For example, both CTD and PTD could be used to teach sight words to Child A and Child B, with a 3-second terminal delay identified for both children. For CTD sessions, two types of trials would occur with Child A—0-second trials and 3-second delay trials. For PTD sessions, there might be four possible types of trials for Child B: 0-second trials plus three types of delay trials—1-second, 2-second, and 3-second trials (e.g., Ledford, Chazin, Harbin & Ward, 2017). The stepwise change between sessions is typically 1 second (e.g., 0-, 1-, 2-, and 3-second trials) or 2 seconds (e.g., 0-, 2-, and 4-second trials; e.g., Sweeney, Barton, & Ledford, 2018); the criterion for increasing the pre-prompt interval is usually 100 percent correct responding (prompted plus unprompted correct responding; Ledford et al., 2017). Note that most children will engage in primarily prompted correct responding during early sessions—this is acceptable, and expected. Increasing prompt delays are never contingent on unprompted responses alone.

Some studies have also included rules for moving to a lower pre-prompt interval (e.g., moving from a 2-second back to a 1-second interval)—generally, this has been done when students have engaged in a criterion number of unprompted error responses (i.e., the child is not waiting for the prompt; see Shepley, Lane, & Shepley, 2016 for an example). Table 8.4 shows data from 12 instructional sessions, including the delay for each session. For these hypothetical data, the criterion for increasing the pre-prompt delay interval was two sessions with at least 90 percent correct responding (prompted plus unprompted) and the criterion for decreasing the pre-prompt delay interval was one session with at least 25 percent unprompted errors. The terminal pre-prompt delay was 3 seconds, and the mastery criterion for ending instruction was two consecutive days with 100 percent unprompted correct responding.

Table 8.4 Hypothetical Data and Decision-making for PTD Procedures

Session	Pre-Prompt Delay	PC	UPC	PE	UPE	Rationale for Delay Change
1	0 sec	100	0	0	0	100% correct = 1st day of criterion met at 0-second delay
2	0 sec	100	0	0	0	100% correct = 2nd day met, increase from 0-second to 1-second delay
3	1 sec	100	0	0	0	100% correct = 1st day of criterion met at 1-second delay
4	1 sec	80	20	0	0	100% correct = 2nd day of criterion met at 1-second delay, increase from 1-second to 2-second delay
5	2 sec	50	20	0	30	25% unprompted correct responses = criterion met for decreasing delay from 2 to 1 second
6	1 sec	50	50	0	0	100% correct = 1st day of criterion met at 1-second delay
7	1 sec	30	70	0	0	100% correct = 2nd day of criterion met at 1-second delay, increase from 1-second to 2-second delay
8	2 sec	30	60	0	10	90% correct = 1st day of criterion met at 2-second delay
9	2 sec	30	70	0	0	100% correct = 2nd day of criterion met at 2-second delay, increase from 2-second to 3-second delay
10	3 sec	10	90	0	0	100% correct = 1st day of criterion met at 3-second delay
11	3 sec	0	100	0	0	100% correct = 2nd day of criterion met at 3-second delay, remain at 3-second delay because 3 seconds is terminal delay
12	3 sec	0	100	0	0	100% correct = final mastery criterion met

Data Collection for CTD and PTD

Data collection for CTD and PTD procedures are similar. During initial 0-second trials—for each opportunity to respond—teachers should identify whether the response was:

1. **Prompted Correct (PC):** The child provided the correct answer, within the designated response interval *following* the teacher prompt.
   - **Example:** *The teacher says "What color is this? Blue" and the child says "Blue" one second later.*

2. **Prompted Error (PE):** The child provides an erroneous answer, or does not respond within the designated response interval *following* the teacher prompt.
   - **Example:** *The teacher says "What color is this? Blue" and the child says "Green" one second later.*
   - **Example:** *The teacher says "What color is this? Blue" And the child gives no response within the next 3 seconds, which was the designated response interval.*

During later sessions, when a progressive or constant delay is used, there are two additional potential responses:

3. **Unprompted Correct (UPC):** The child provided the correct answer, within the designated response interval *prior to* the teacher prompt.
   - **Example:** *During a 2-second delay trial, the teacher says "What color is this?" and the child says "Blue" one second later.*
4. **Unprompted Error (UPE):** The child provides an erroneous answer *prior to* the teacher prompt.
   - **Example:** *During a 2-second delay trial, the teacher provides a blue stimulus and says "What color is this?" and the child says "Green" one second later.*

Some researchers have identified a fifth potential response category—termed a "non-response" or "no response" (e.g., Appelman, Vail, & Lieberman-Betz, 2014). To make data collection as parsimonious as possible, we prefer to identify a non-response following a prompt as an error (e.g., if you provide a prompt, and the child does not respond, we consider that an error).

Analyzing Data

Before instruction commences, you should collect baseline data—that is, you should confirm that the child is unable to perform the behavior independently without instruction. If the child is not able to respond correctly during baseline conditions, you should proceed with instruction.

   Following each instructional session, the instructor should calculate the percentage of responses that are UPCs, PCs, UPEs, and PEs by dividing the number of each type of response by the total number of trials. For example, given nine unprompted correct responses in one session, and a single prompted correct response, the percentages would yield the following: 90% UPC, 10% PC, 0% UPE, 0% PE. Ideally, the instructor would also graph at least the UPC and PC responses, so that expected changes in those responses could be evaluated over time.

Expected Data Patterns

When PTD and CTD are used, during initial sessions (0-second pre-prompt delay; the prompt is always provided), we anticipate mostly prompted correct responses. Following introduction of delay trials, we expect unprompted correct responses to increase while prompted correct responses decrease. Throughout instruction, we expect prompted and unprompted errors to remain at relatively low levels (e.g., 0–10 percent of trials). Figure 8.5 shows two common data patterns. The top panel shows an immediate and gradual increase in unprompted corrects and a corresponding decrease in prompted corrects over time.

Ambiguous Responses

Sometimes, children engage in responses that are difficult to categorize. Our suggestion is to decide, before instruction begins, how to categorize each ambiguous response. We

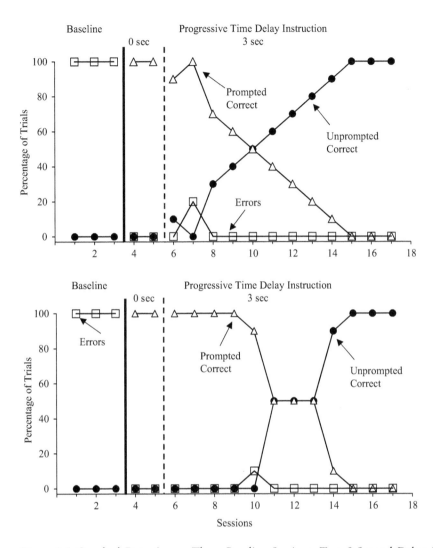

Figure 8.5 Graphed Data Across Three Baseline Sessions, Two 0-Second Delay Sessions, and 12 Instructional Sessions.

Note: The top panel shows small, incremental changes over time in unprompted correct responding (one common data pattern) and the bottom panel shows an extended period with no change, followed by rapid changes in unprompted correct responding. Prompted and unprompted errors are combined in one data path—errors are high during baseline conditions and consistently low during instruction.

provide suggestions for how to treat each of these responses, but you should note that the critical thing is to (a) identify how you will categorize these responses (i.e., as PC, UPC, PE, or UPE), (b) consistently provide consequences consistent with that categorization, and (c) consistently record data according to that categorization. Three examples of common ambiguous responses are described below.

Echolalia. Some young children, especially those with autism spectrum disorder or language delays, may engage in echolalia—repeating what someone else says. Thus, when a teacher says "What color?" in the context of a 2-second delay trial, a child may be likely to respond with "What color?" Because imitating others is an important skill (see Chapter 2), we suggest treating echolalia as a non-response (i.e., ignoring it), rather than as an erroneous response. Thus, when the child repeats a task direction, complete the trial as if he or she had said nothing (i.e., after the given response interval, provide the controlling prompt).

Self-corrects. Some young children, especially those who tend to engage in impulsive behaviors, may respond incorrectly within the given response interval, and then immediately provide the correct response. You may choose to record these responses as correct responses or as errors. Generally, we prefer to record errors and provide consequences as such, because students may learn that they can guess an answer, and change their response based on subtle teacher behaviors (i.e., self-correcting until the teacher smiles). However, in some cases, you may decide to treat immediate self-corrects as correct responses.

Simultaneous responses. Sometimes, the teacher provides the controlling prompt at the same time as the child gives his or her response. This is obviously a correct response, but is not clearly *prompted* or *unprompted*. Given that both responses are typically reinforced, the conservative data collection decision is to identify these responses as prompted corrects.

Determining Whether to Use CTD or PTD

Only one experimental study has been done comparing the use of CTD and PTD to teach discrete behaviors; the results were ambiguous—suggesting that both procedures worked equally well for teaching discrete behaviors to individuals with disabilities. CTD and PTD have also been used to teach children without disabilities (cf. Ledford et al., 2017). They have been widely used in self-contained classrooms for young children (e.g., Lane, Gast, Shepley, & Ledford, 2015; Lane, Gast, Ledford, & Shepley, 2017; Shepley et al., 2016), inclusive early childhood settings (e.g., Ledford et al., 2017; Ledford & Wolery, 2013), and other community settings (e.g., Rogers, Hemmeter, & Wolery, 2010). Many studies with PTD and CTD have been conducted with classroom teachers and other practitioners, thus both procedures have been shown to be effective in typical contexts with typical implementers. Thus, the decisions regarding *which* procedure to use should largely be made based on individual child and implementer characteristics. We outline below several common characteristics that may lead to a choice of using one procedure over the other.

Impulsive versus Cautious Learners

Young children are generally less skilled at inhibiting responding than older children and adults. Moreover, they have often been reinforced for "guessing" answers when they are not sure of a correct response. Thus, some young learners may benefit from the use of PTD, which allows children to have more experience with prompted correct responding before accessing a long pre-prompt response interval (i.e., the terminal delay). Children who have impulsive behaviors outside of instruction might be especially good candidates for PTD as compared to CTD.

Inexperienced versus Seasoned Learners

Many young children in early childhood programs have not had any experience with systematic instruction. Thus, they have not yet learned prerequisite skills such as waiting when they are unable to answer correctly. These children may benefit from the use of PTD as compared to CTD because of the gradual increase in delay interval. A child who has "learned to learn" from a time delay procedure like PTD may then be able to generalize those learning behaviors to CTD.

Learners who are Tolerant versus Intolerant of Errors

Some learners are highly intolerant of errors—that is, when they make a mistake, they become upset, engage in problem behaviors, or become less interested in instruction. Because learners do not have to immediately wait for the terminal delay in PTD, errors may be less likely (especially for learners who are impulsive or inexperienced). Thus, these learners may engage in fewer error responses and thus have better outcomes when PTD is used instead of CTD.

Novice versus Expert Instructors

PTD was initially developed as a clinical procedure—not for use in classrooms. CTD was developed to simplify procedures for teachers. CTD requires the use of two types of trials: 0-second trials and trials with a terminal delay (e.g., 4-second trials). PTD requires the use of more types. For example, a PTD procedure may include 0-second, 1-second, 2-second, 3-second, and 4-second trials. Providing these trial types with high fidelity may be difficult for novice instructors or in more complex arrangements such as group instruction with four children (as compared to individual instruction). Thus, CTD may be a more appropriate procedure if the instructor is inexperienced or if their supervisor (e.g., consulting special education teacher, classroom coach) has less time to provide coaching and feedback.

Amal decides to conduct systematic instruction to teach children specific behaviors related to the letters in their names, using a PTD procedure. For one child, she embeds progressive time delay trials into book reading, a preferred activity. For another, she conducts a brief 2–3 minute session after he completes his arrival routine each day. One child is progressing well, but the other continues to wait for the prompt, even though Amal suspects he could answer correctly independently. Amal decides to search in the research literature to determine whether this problem has been encountered by others, and what their solutions were.

Considerations for Instruction

When CTD and PTD procedures are used, children generally transition from making all PCs to making all UPCs, with few or no UPEs or PEs. Some children, however, require modification to initially developed CTD and PTD procedures to improve the speed of acquisition. Three common problems associated with instructional responding are discussed below—none are specific to CTD and PTD procedures but are applicable across prompting procedures in general.

Improving Attention to Stimuli

To ensure adequate attention to stimuli, some children require extra cues. As described above, the adult should ensure children attend *prior* to providing the task direction or other discriminative stimulus. This means that the adult should *not* provide multiple task directions until the child attends, but should *first* ensure attending, and then give a single task direction. Some children will attend to stimuli without the use of any cues—when a teacher presents a photograph, for example, some children will look at the photograph and respond to a related teacher directive. If a learner does not do this, there are several types of *attending cues* that can be used, as discussed in Chapter 4.

Preventing UPE Responding

In previous research studies, some children have engaged in an initially high percentage of unprompted errors when the implementer proceeds from initial 0-second trials to the terminal delay (e.g., 5-second trials). These children "guess" an incorrect answer rather than waiting for the assistance (prompt) that would help them achieve correct responding. The easiest way to avoid this problem is to establish that a child is able to wait for an answer when they are not able to independently respond correctly before using PTD and CTD procedures. For example, if you are considering using a time delay procedure, you could assess this by telling a child "I'm going to show you some pictures, and you won't know what some of them are. If you don't know, just look at me, and I'll tell you the right answer." If the child is able to wait in this context, they are unlikely to engage in UPE responding during PTD or CTD instruction. If they do not wait in this context, they are likely to need *wait training* to ensure optimal learning from PTD or CTD.

Wait training is an instructional procedure used to teach children to differentiate their responses based on whether the stimulus presented is known or unknown. For example, if a child can correctly name colors *red* and *green* but not *yellow* or *blue*, we want them to say "red" or "green" during the applicable trials, but we want them to wait for a prompt during *yellow* and *blue* trials. The procedural steps for wait training are:

1. Identify at least one stimulus for which the child can give an unprompted correct response.
2. Identify several stimuli for which the child cannot yet give an unprompted correct response. You may use stimuli not usually encountered by young children, such as Greek letters, or nonsense stimuli. You need a sufficient number of these such that the child does not learn them during wait training.
3. Intermix the known and unknown stimuli and prepare a data collection form.
4. Provide a contingency review. For example, you might say: "Today, I have some pictures you know and some that are new. If you know the answer, tell me. When you don't know, wait [put finger to lips while saying wait]."
5. Conduct trials.
   a. For *known* stimuli, provide the task direction (e.g., "What is this?") and wait for the child to respond. Provide reinforcement for UPCs. If the child responds incorrectly, re-evaluate whether the stimuli are known.
   b. For *unknown* stimuli, provide the task direction (e.g., "What is this?") and immediately provide a cue that the child should wait (e.g., put your finger over your lips, hold your hand out, say "shhh"). Initially, ensure the child waits for a very small interval (e.g., half a second), then provide the prompt and reinforce PC responding. Across sessions, increase the interval gradually (e.g., half a second, 1 second, 1.5 seconds, 2 seconds, 2.5 seconds) until you have reached whatever terminal delay you will use in PTD or CTD instruction. When a child successfully waits for that interval for unknown stimuli, while successfully providing UPCs for known stimuli, he or she has established appropriate waiting behaviors.

Preventing PE Responding

Most children engage in little to no PE responding. When PE responding occurs, usually one of two problems is present: inadequate reinforcement or unmatched prompts.

As outlined in Chapter 3, reinforcement is the cornerstone of learning new skills. Thus, failure to learn can often be attributed to lack of appropriate reinforcement. Often, teachers bemoan a child's failure to learn a specific skill, and when asked, report that the only reward available for doing so is teacher attention (e.g., "good job!"). As described in Chapter 3, social praise may not serve as an effective reinforcer for most children. Thus, reward selection should be individualized—what is valuable enough to a child that they are willing to "work" for it? Optimally, you should conduct a preference assessment prior to using CTD or PTD, as described in Chapter 3. For a child whose preferences vary (e.g., prefers candy but only when sessions are far-removed from meal and snack times), or for children who prefer varied reinforcers (e.g., chooses different reinforcers each day), a mini pre-session preference assessment may be needed. When these are used, the child is provided a choice of potential reinforcers immediately prior to the session, and they choose which reinforcer they will work toward earning for that session only. For example, if an MSWO preference assessment suggests three highly preferred items of six tested items, you might provide the child a choice of those three items before every session. This ensures the child receives a preferred reward following correct responding, and thus is motivated to reduce errors.

As identified earlier, PTD and CTD procedures require the use of a controlling prompt—that is, a prompt that ensures correct responding when given. Sometimes controlling prompts are difficult to identify. For example, it is possible that you think a child will respond to a gesture prompt to choose a correct photograph from a field of three, so you begin 0-second trials by saying "Give me the [stimulus name]" and immediately follow that direction by pointing to the correct stimulus. However, the child consistently responds instead by picking whatever image is on his right (referred to as "side bias"). This suggests that your prompt (the gesture) is not, in fact, controlling his behavior. In this case, you might select a different prompt topography, such as partial or full physical prompting, to ensure correct responding and prevent errors.

Reducing Prolonged PC Responding

The purpose of delay trials is to allow children to answer independently once they have learned the correct behavior. Most children will begin to respond prior to the prompt because that reduces the latency to reinforcement (e.g., they can get access to the reinforcer faster). Some children, however, continue to wait for the prompt, which results in guaranteed access to the reinforcer. This is generally not problematic, as children have widely varying learning speeds—for example, some children have acquired targeted discrete skills using these procedures in as few as two to three delay sessions (e.g., Ledford et al., 2017; Wolery, Anthony, Caldwell, Snyder, & Morgante, 2002), while others have learned similar skills in as many as 60 sessions (Ledford & Wolery, 2013). In addition, it is common for children who initially make errors to revert back to waiting for the prompt to ensure access to reinforcement. However, if you believe that the child may be able to answer independently, you can assess this and then provide differentiated reinforcement for unprompted responses.

Assessment. To determine whether a child is able to answer independently, you can conduct a probe session. You should indicate to the child, optimally through multiple means, that this session is different from the typical instructional context. For example, you might conduct this session in a different location, at a different time of day, and you might say at the onset of the session "Today, I'm not going to help you with any answers. I want you to guess if you aren't sure. Okay?" You can intersperse known stimuli with the instructional stimuli to ensure the child is independently responding to known items. If the child responds correctly to stimuli during this probe, you can start differentiated reinforcement. If the child responds incorrectly, you should continue conducting 0-second trials.

Differentiated reinforcement. In some studies, researchers have provided **differentiated reinforcement** for children who have continued to wait for a prompt following extended instruction; that is, they get more, or more highly valued, reinforcers for engaging in unprompted compared to prompted correct responding (e.g., Wolery, Werts, Snyder, & Caldwell, 1994). During sessions with differentiated reinforcement, you should indicate to the child that they will receive different rewards for prompted and unprompted correct responses. For example, you might say "Today, you will get a token if you get the answer right. If you say the right answer *before me*, you get *two* tokens!" It is likely better to add an extra reward rather than taking one away. For example, if you provided a verbal praise plus a token prior to differentiated reinforcement, you should offer something above and beyond that for unprompted correct responses during differentiated reinforcement, rather than reducing the reinforcement available for prompted correct responses (e.g., praise only). Once the student reaches the mastery criterion, you can remove the additional reinforcement and provide the originally planned reinforcement for both prompted and unprompted correct responses.

Conclusion

CTD and PTD procedures are well-researched procedures that are evidence-based for teaching discrete behaviors to young children with and without disabilities. They are useful and efficient procedures for establishing a transfer of stimulus control, but require that children are able to wait for a prompt when they cannot answer independently. We suggest their use for children who can wait for a prompt, for teaching a variety of discrete behaviors.

After a few weeks of PTD instruction, including providing differentiated reinforcement for one child for unprompted versus prompted responding, both children have learned all of their targeted behaviors, and have started to use these skills during typically occurring classroom activities. Moreover, having learned these behaviors has resulted in the children becoming more excited about acquiring other new literacy skills—they learned some non-targeted letter sounds during book reading one day, which had never previously happened. Amal is excited that the brief, systematic instructional trials resulted in relatively large learning improvements in their literacy skills.

Data Collection Forms

https://vkc.mc.vanderbilt.edu/ebip/wp-content/uploads/2016/05/PTD_Small-Group-Instruction_Data-Sheet.pdf

https://vkc.mc.vanderbilt.edu/ebip/wp-content/uploads/2016/05/PTD_Data-Sheet_Chained-Skills.pdf

Related Resources

https://vkc.mc.vanderbilt.edu/ebip/progressive-time-delay/
https://iris.peabody.vanderbilt.edu/module/asd2/cresource/q1/p03/
http://afirm.fpg.unc.edu/time-delay

References

Appelman, M., Vail, C. O., & Lieberman-Betz, R. G. (2014). The effects of constant time delay and instructive feedback on the acquisition of English and Spanish sight words. *Journal of Early Intervention*, 36, 131–148.

Bennett, D., Gast, D. L., Wolery, M., & Schuster, J. (1986). Time delay and system of least prompts: A comparison in teaching manual sign production. *Education and Training of the Mentally Retarded*, 21, 117–129.

Browder, D., Ahlgrim-Delzell, L., Spooner, F., Mims, P. J., & Baker, J. N. (2009). Using time delay to teach literacy to students with severe developmental disabilities. *Exceptional Children*, 75, 343–364.

Godby, S., Gast, D. L., & Wolery, M. (1987). A comparison of time delay and system of least prompts in teaching object identification. *Research in Developmental Disabilities*, 8, 283–305.

Johnson, C. (1977). Errorless learning in a multihandicapped adolescent. *Education and Treatment of Children*, 1, 25–33.

Kleinert, H. L., & Gast, D. L. (1982). Teaching a multihandicapped adult manual signs using a constant time delay procedure. *Journal of the Association of the Severely Handicapped*, 6, 25–32.

Lane, J. D., Gast, D. L., Ledford, J. R., & Shepley, C. (2017). Increasing social behaviors in young children with social-communication delays in a group arrangement in preschool. *Education and Treatment of Children*, 40, 115–144.

Lane, J. D., Gast, D. L., Shepley, C., & Ledford, J. R. (2015). Including social opportunities during small group instruction of preschool children with social-communication delays. *Journal of Early Intervention*, 37, 3–22.

Ledford, J. R., & Wolery, M. (2013). Peer modeling of academic and social behaviors during small-group direct instruction. *Exceptional Children*, 79, 439–458.

Ledford, J. R., Chazin, K. T., Harbin, E. R., & Ward, S. E. (2017). Massed trials versus trial embedded into game play: Child outcomes and preference. *Topics in Early Childhood Special Education*, 37, 107–120.

Rogers, L., Hemmeter, M. L., & Wolery, M. (2010). Using a constant time delay procedure to teach foundational swimming skills to children with autism. *Topics in Early Childhood Special Education*, 30, 102–111.

Shepley, C., Lane, J. D., & Shepley, S. B. (2016). Teaching young children with social-communication delays to label actions using videos and language expansion models: A pilot study. *Focus on Autism and Other Developmental Disabilities*, 31, 243–253.

Snell, M. E., & Gast, D. L. (1981). Applying time delay procedures to the instruction of the severely handicapped. *Journal of the Association for the Severely Handicapped*, 6, 3–14.

Striefel, S., Bryan, K. S., & Aikins, D. A. (1974). Transfer of stimulus control from motor to verbal stimuli. *Journal of Applied Behavior Analysis*, 7, 123–135.

Sweeney, E., Barton, E. E., & Ledford, J. R. (2018). Using progressive time delay to increase levels of peer imitation during sculpting play. *Journal of Autism and Developmental Disorders*. Advance online publication.

Touchette, P. E. (1971). Transfer of stimulus control: Measuring the moment of transfer. *Journal of the Experimental Analysis of Behavior*, 3, 347–354.

Walker, G. (2008). Constant and progressive time delay procedures for teaching children with autism: A literature review. *Journal of Autism and Developmental Disorders*, 38, 261–275.

Wolery, M., & Gast, D. L. (1984). Effective and efficient procedures for the transfer of stimulus control. *Topics in Early Childhood Special Education*, 4, 52–77.

Wolery, M., Anthony, L., Caldwell, N. K., Snyder, E. D., & Morgante, J. D. (2002). Embedding and distributing constant time delay in circle time and transitions. *Topics in Early Childhood Special Education, 22*, 14–25.

Wolery, M., Werts, M. G., Snyder, E. D., & Caldwell, N. K. (1994). Efficacy of constant time delay implemented by peer tutors in general education classrooms. *Journal of Behavioral Education, 4*, 415–436.

Wong, C., Odom, S. L., Hume, K. A., Cox, A. W., Fettig, A., Kucharczyk, S., ... & Schultz, T. R. (2015). Evidence-based practices for children, youth, and young adults with autism spectrum disorder: A comprehensive review. *Journal of Autism and Developmental Disorders, 45*, 1951–1966.

9 Other Single Prompt Strategies

Key Terms

Simultaneous prompting	*Instructional session*	*Probe session*
Pre-prompt response interval	*Controlling prompt*	*Post-prompt response interval*
Errorless learning	*No-no prompting*	*Model-lead-test*

Chapter Objectives

- Name the similarities and differences between simultaneous prompting and time delay strategies.
- Outline the procedural steps for simultaneous prompting procedures.
- Describe when you would and would not use simultaneous prompting instead of a time delay strategy.
- Explain commonly encountered problems when simultaneous procedures are used, and identify potential solutions.
- Outline the procedural steps for no-no prompting and describe why we do not suggest its use at this time.
- Outline the procedural steps for model-lead-test strategies and describe under what conditions we suggest its use.

Gale is trying to decide which systematic procedure to use to teach Fatima, a 3-year-old with cognitive and language delays, to request preferred items using her personal augmentative/alternative communication (AAC) device. Currently, Gale models language often on the device, and Fatima inconsistently presses buttons but does not use it to request preferred items without assistance. Gale has read about progressive and constant time delay, but Fatima does not currently wait for a prompt when she doesn't know an answer, and Gale is not sure that Fatima will quickly develop these behaviors. Because requesting is a critical skill, Gale wants to start right away, but she isn't sure where to start.

Progressive and constant time delay procedures are the most well-researched single prompt strategies. However, there are several other single prompt strategies with varying amounts of research support. The primary purpose of this chapter is to define and describe the use of these single prompt procedures, and to explain the rationale, procedures, and outcomes of these strategies. Specifically, we will describe simultaneous prompting procedures, no-no prompting procedures, and model-lead-test procedures. The procedures described in this chapter are directly related to many of the Division for Early Childhood Recommended Practices in the area of Instruction (INS3-INS7, INS10).

Simultaneous Prompting Procedure

Simultaneous prompting procedures were established after time delay prompting procedures (cf. Wolery & Gast, 1984), and were initially described as "antecedent prompt and test" procedures by Wolery, Ault, and Doyle (1992). Beginning in the early 1990s, several studies were published showing that simultaneous prompting could be used to teach young children to engage in targeted discrete behaviors (Gibson & Schuster, 1992; Schuster & Griffin, 1993; Wolery, Holcombe, Werts, & Cipolloni, 1993). Compared with CTD and PTD, a larger proportion of studies assessing the effects of simultaneous prompting procedures have included older children with disabilities rather than young children with and without disabilities.

Unlike time delay procedures, simultaneous prompting requires *two types of sessions*. These sessions are **instructional sessions**, during which you will apply the prompting procedures, and **probe sessions**, during which you will test the child's ability to respond independently. No prompts are provided during probe sessions. Because waiting is not a prerequisite skill for the use of simultaneous prompting (see Table 9.1), some children who might not readily benefit from time delay strategies may learn well from simultaneous prompting procedures.

The components of an instructional trial for simultaneous prompting include: (1) provision of the discriminative stimulus, (2) provision of a controlling prompt, (3) a post-prompt response interval, and (4) response consequences. Note that there is never a pre-prompt interval. That is, you always immediately follow the presentation of the discriminative stimulus with the provision of a prompt. Because we never give children the opportunity to respond independently during instructional sessions, probe sessions are needed to assess transfer of stimulus control. Thus, rather than conducting delay trials *during instruction*, which give children the opportunity to either answer independently or wait for the prompt, we instead conduct different sessions altogether. Procedurally, probe sessions are similar to baseline—that is, no intervention is present. These sessions allow us to determine when to discontinue instruction.

Prior to conducting simultaneous prompting procedures, you should decide on the discriminative stimulus to be used, the duration of your response interval, the controlling prompt, and the consequences for each type of response. You should also determine the mastery criterion for probe sessions, which will govern when you will discontinue instruction. Mastery criteria tend to include an accuracy benchmark (e.g., 90 percent unprompted correct responding) and a standard regarding how often it occurred (e.g., over three consecutive sessions). Given previous research, we suggest a mastery criterion of 100 percent responding over at least three consecutive days, as some researchers have used a less stringent criterion and maintained behavior change did not occur (Ledford & Wolery, 2013; 90 percent average across three consecutive days).

- **Discriminative Stimulus:** As with CTD and PTD, this refers to situations in which you would expect the child to engage in the behavior of interest (e.g., teacher presentation of a letter with the question "What letter is this?"; a peer request).
- **Pre-Prompt Response Interval:** The pre-prompt response interval is *not present for simultaneous prompting sessions*. Alternatively, you might conceptualize this delay as always being 0 seconds for simultaneous prompting (i.e., similar to initial PTD/CTD sessions).
- **Controlling Prompt:** As with CTD/PTD, this should be selected individually, based on the type of assistance that is likely to lead to correct responding (see Chapter 8 for a list of topographies). As a reminder, when multiple prompts are under consideration,

Table 9.1 Child Prerequisite Skills for Simultaneous Prompting

Category	Description
Reinforcer	The instructor has identified one or more preferred items or activities as a potential reinforcer.
Prompt	The instructor has confirmed which specific prompts control responding (e.g., what instructor behaviors are necessary to ensure correct responding) for the targeted behaviors.
Waiting	There are no prerequisite behaviors related to waiting.
Incorrect Responding	Because the prompt is not available during probe sessions, children should not have a history of engaging in challenging behavior following incorrect responses.

you should choose a prompt that is likely to result in correct responding (i.e., is controlling) *and* that is the least restrictive.

- **Post-Prompt Response Interval:** This interval should be chosen based on individual child response times and should remain the same across instructional sessions.
- **Response Consequences (Instructional Sessions):** Prior to using simultaneous prompting, you should decide what consequences will occur when the child responds correctly or incorrectly.
  - **Reinforce Correct Responses:** Because the prompt will always be provided immediately, only prompted correct responses are possible. These responses should be reinforced.
  - **Ignore or Correct Errors:** Similar to CTD and PTD, errors after the prompt (the only type of error possible during instructional sessions) are generally either ignored (instructor ends the trial) or error correction is provided.
- **Response Consequences (Probe Sessions):** Consistent with the instructional procedures, you should reinforce correct responses and either ignore or provide error correction for incorrect responses. During probe sessions, no prompts occur, so all responses are unprompted.

Instructional Sessions

During all instructional sessions for all behaviors, 0-second trials will be used. That is, the discriminative stimulus is presented, and is *immediately* followed by provision of the controlling prompt. The flow chart below (Figure 9.1) depicts the steps of a single 0-second trial; Figure 9.2 depicts a sample trial. The purpose of 0-second trials is to pair the discriminative stimulus with a prompt that already produces correct responding, with the eventual goal of removing the prompt such that the discriminative stimulus alone will produce correct responding. The use of the immediate prompt produces **errorless learning**, as described for CTD and PTD procedures in the previous chapter. During instructional sessions, the only possible responses are prompted corrects (PCs) and prompted errors (PEs).

Probe Sessions

The purpose of probe sessions is to allow the child to respond in the presence of the discriminative stimulus alone, if they are able to do so. For simultaneous prompting, data during instructional sessions nearly always include 100 percent prompted correct responding. Thus,

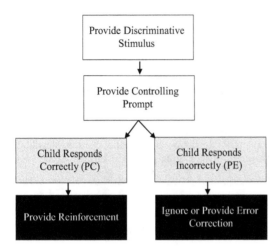

Figure 9.1 Steps for an Instructional Trial.

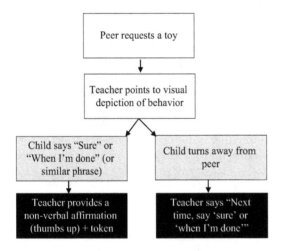

Figure 9.2 Sample Instructional Trial.

the data collected during probe sessions are those on which we make mastery decisions (i.e., the data that tell us whether the child is learning). During probe sessions, prompts are not present. Thus, the only possible responses are unprompted corrects (UPCs) and unprompted errors (UPEs). Figure 9. 3 shows the steps for a probe trial and Figure 9.4 shows a sample trial. Table 9.2 highlights differences between instructional and probe trials.

Data Collection for Simultaneous Prompting

Data collection for simultaneous prompting procedures are similar to those of time delay procedures, but only two of four responses are possible during instruction, while only the other two are possible during probe sessions. During instruction, potential responses are:

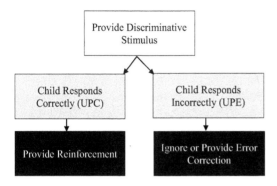

Figure 9.3 Steps for a Probe Trial.

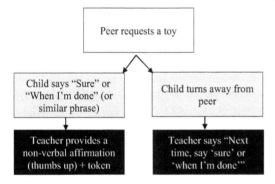

Figure 9.4 Sample Sequence for a Probe Trial.

Table 9.2 Sample Instructional and Probe Trials

Component	Instructional Trial	Probe Trial
Discriminative Stimulus	Child exits bathroom stall	Child exits bathroom stall
Controlling Prompt	Point to sink	NA
Response Interval	3 seconds	3 seconds
Child Behavior	*Walks to sink (prompted correct)*	*Walks away from sink (unprompted error)*
Response Consequences	Verbal praise, provide immediate controlling prompt for next step	Provides error correction by physically prompting child to walk to sink; starts response interval for next step

1. **Prompted Correct (PC):** The child provided the correct answer, within the designated response interval *following* the teacher prompt.
   - ***Example:*** *During a game, the teacher says "It's your turn" and immediately prompts the child to pick up a playing card by pointing to the deck. The child picks up the card.*

2. **Prompted Error (PE):** The child provides an erroneous answer, or does not respond within the designated response interval *following* the teacher prompt.
   - **Example:** *During a game, the teacher says "It's your turn" and immediately prompts the child to pick up a playing card by pointing to the deck. The child puts one of his cards on the deck, rather than picking one up.*
   - **Example:** *During a game, the teacher says "It's your turn" and immediately prompts the child to pick up a playing card by pointing to the deck. The child gives no response within the next 3 seconds, which was the designated response interval.*

During probe sessions, no prompts are provided. Thus, the potential responses are:

3. **Unprompted Correct (UPC):** The child provided the correct answer, within the designated response interval.
   - **Example:** *During a game, the teacher says "It's your turn" and waits 3 seconds. The child picks up a card from the deck.*
4. **Unprompted Error (UPE):** The child provides an erroneous answer.
   - **Example:** *During a game, the teacher says "It's your turn" and waits 3 seconds. The child engages in stereotypy for the duration of the response interval.*

Analyzing Data

Before instruction commences, you should collect data in several consecutive probe sessions; this serves as your baseline measurement to confirm the child is not able to independently perform the skills prior to instruction. If the child is not able to respond correctly during probe sessions, you should proceed with instruction. See Table 9.3 for

Table 9.3 Sample Sequence of Instructional and Probe Sessions

Session	PC	PE	UPC	UPE	Decision
1 (Instruction 1)	10	90			PCs lower than expected; collect more instructional data to determine whether a different controlling prompt or reinforcer is needed
2 (Instruction 2)	10	90			PCs continue to be lower than expected; change controlling prompt or reinforcer
3 (Probe 1)			0	100	0% UPC; continue instruction
4 (Instruction 3)	100	0			PCs high; continue instruction
5 (Instruction 4)	100	0			PCs high; continue instruction
6 (Probe 2)			40	60	UPCs increasing but not at criterion; continue instruction
7 (Instruction 5)	100	0			PCs high; continue instruction
8 (Instruction 6)	100	0			PCs high; continue instruction
9 (Probe 3)			80	20	UPCs increasing but not at criterion; continue instruction
10 (Instruction 7)	100	0			PCs high; continue instruction
11 (Instruction 8)	100	0			PCs high; continue instruction
12 (Probe 4)			100	0	100% UPC; first day at criterion; continue instruction
13 (Instruction 9)	100	0			PCs high; continue instruction
14 (Instruction 10)	100	0			PCs high; continue instruction
15 (Probe 5)			100	0	Mastery criterion met; discontinue instruction

a sample sequence of instructional and probe sessions, along with the corresponding instructional decisions.

Following each probe session, the instructor should calculate the percentage of UPC and UPE responses by dividing the number of each type by the total number of trials and multiply by 100. For example, given ten trials and four UPCs, the calculation for the percentage of UPCs is 40 percent; that means the percentage of UPEs must be 60 percent, since those are the only two response options. Because these numbers are calculable from each other, you can choose to only graph UPCs.

Following each instructional session, the instructor should review responding. When an appropriate controlling prompt is selected and effective reinforcers are used, PC responding should always be at or near 100 percent. High percentages of prompted errors suggest the need to modify instruction (see the *Common Problems* section later in the chapter).

Expected Data Patterns

When simultaneous prompting is implemented, we expect all instructional sessions to lead to 100 percent correct responding. Note the bottom left panel in Figure 9.5, which shows initially moderate levels of PCs (70 percent); the dashed line denotes a change in provided reinforcers leading to an immediate change to 100 percent PC responding.

During probe sessions, UPCs may initially remain at low levels, but should increase over time. Figure 9.5 shows two common data patterns. The top right panel shows an immediate and rapid increase in responding and the bottom right panel shows a delayed and more gradual increase.

Research Abstract

Sewell, T. J., Collins, B. C., Hemmeter, M. L., & Schuster, J. W. (1998). Using simultaneous prompting within an activity-based format to teach dressing skills to preschoolers with developmental delays. *Journal of Early Intervention*, 21, 132–145.

In this single case design study, two young children with developmental delays were taught three different dressing skills each, in the context of a multiple probe across behaviors design. Instructors used distributed trials, teaching the behaviors at typically occurring opportunities throughout the day (e.g., putting on a jacket prior to going outside). Both children learned how to independently engage in the dressing skills, and maintained the skills following intervention completion. Results of this study suggest simultaneous prompting can be used systematically in the context of typical classroom activities.

Ambiguous Responses

Echolalia, self-corrects, and simultaneous responding are possible in instructional sessions; self-corrects are also possible during probe sessions. These responses can be dealt with in the same way as discussed in Chapter 8.

Determining Whether to Use Simultaneous Prompting or a Time Delay Procedure

Few experimental comparisons have been conducted comparing time delay procedures to simultaneous prompting for teaching discrete behaviors. In all of these comparisons (Head, Collins, Schuster, & Ault, 2011; Schuster, Griffen, & Wolery, 1992; Swain, Lane,

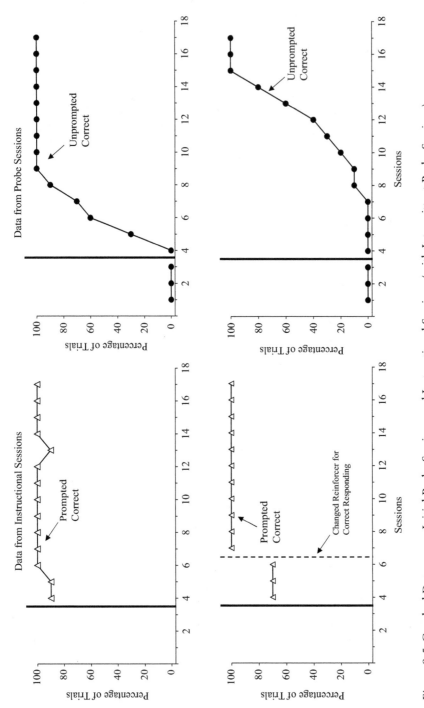

Figure 9.5 Graphed Data across Initial Probe Sessions and Instructional Sessions (with Intermittent Probe Sessions).

Note: The top panel shows immediate and rapid behavior change; the bottom panel shows data with a delayed and graduate trend to criterion. Note that only two responses are possible in each condition; thus, the percentage of error responses can be calculated by subtracting the percentage of correct responses from 100 percent.

& Gast, 2015; Tekin & Kircaali-Iftar, 2002), results were either undifferentiated (e.g., children learned at the same speed with both procedures) or mixed (i.e., some children learned faster with one procedure and some learned faster with another or a child learned better with simultaneous prompting for one comparison and learned better with time delay for the second comparison). Thus, as is always recommended, practitioners should select the instructional procedure that best fits the relevant individuals and contexts (Ledford et al., 2016; see Chapter 4 for more information about choosing between interventions). We outline below several common characteristics that may lead to a choice of using one procedure over the other.

Impulsive versus Cautious Learners

Very impulsive learners, who are unlikely to quickly learn to wait (see information about Wait Training in Chapter 8), may benefit from the use of simultaneous prompting because this procedure does not require that the child learn to wait.

Learners who are Tolerant versus Intolerant of Errors

Some learners are highly intolerant of errors—that is, when they make a mistake, they become upset, engage in problem behaviors, or become less interested in instruction. Simultaneous prompting procedures rarely result in erroneous responding during intervention sessions if an appropriate controlling prompt is identified. However, probe sessions often include high percentages of errors, and no prompts are available to assist the child to respond correctly. For example, the bottom left panel shows hypothetical data in which a child responds incorrectly to more than half of opportunities during probe sessions for nine consecutive sessions.

Instructor Preference

It is difficult to determine whether time delay or simultaneous prompting procedures are more complex. Simultaneous prompting requires utilization of two different sessions—instructional sessions and probe sessions—and time delay procedures require only one. However, time delay requires the use of at least two different pre-prompt delay intervals across sessions (0-second trials and delay trials). Some practitioners may find it easier to identify two times during the day when the two separate session types can be implemented; others may find it easier to use different time delays.

Gale decides to use a simultaneous prompting procedure to teach Fatima to request preferred items. She will teach in the context of a contrived turn-taking game with the teacher. Gale will give Fatima time to play with the preferred item, and then will say "In 5 seconds it will be my turn—five, four, three, two, one—my turn." She will hold out her hand to retrieve the item. She decides to use the controlling prompt of pointing to a picture of the item of Fatima's AAC device as soon as she removes the item (a physical model) because Fatima reliably imitates an adult who models on her device.

Considerations for Instruction

Determining Ratio of Instructional to Probe Sessions

An important consideration for the use of simultaneous prompting is that the prompt is available to the child during only some sessions (i.e., instructional sessions, but not probe sessions). Some children might find it frustrating to be tested often, without assistance. Instructors can choose more intermittent assessment (e.g., one probe session for every fourth instructional session) or more frequent assessment (e.g., one probe session for every instructional session). Probe sessions can be very brief (e.g., 1 minute), but even brief sessions that result in high rates of incorrect responding may be disliked by some children. The benefit of less frequent probe sessions is that children are exposed to fewer sessions in which they may be unsuccessful (i.e., give a large percentage of unprompted error responses). The benefit of more frequent probe sessions is that you can identify immediately when a child has acquired the target behavior. Reichow & Wolery (2009) found that fewer errors were emitted by children during initial probe sessions when intermittent probes were conducted; they suggest using intermittent probe sessions during initial instruction, particularly for children who are likely to engage in problem behavior contingent on errors.

Providing Children with Information about Session Type

Regardless of the frequency of probe sessions, children should be able to differentiate when they will receive assistance versus not (i.e., whether they are participating in an instructional or probe session). Instructors can facilitate this with either verbal descriptions ("Now we're going to do some [learning/testing], where I [give you help/see what you know without any help]") or other cues (e.g., instructional sessions occur at one table during morning centers, probe sessions occur on the floor during nap).

Preventing PE Responding

Most children engage in little to no PE responding. When PE responding occurs, usually one of two problems is present: inadequate reinforcement or unmatched prompts. The procedures for addressing this issue, outlined below, are exactly the same as those described for CTD and PTD in Chapter 8.

Failure to learn can often be attributed to a lack of appropriate reinforcement. When simultaneous prompting is used, reward selection should be individualized—that is, what is valuable enough to a child that they are willing to "work" for it. Optimally, you should conduct a preference assessment prior to using simultaneous prompting, as described in Chapter 3. For a child whose preferences vary (e.g., prefers candy but only when sessions are far-removed from meal and snack times), or for children who prefer varied reinforcers (e.g., chooses different reinforcers each day), a mini pre-session preference assessment may be needed. When these are used, the child is provided a choice of potential reinforcers immediately prior to the session, and they choose which reinforcer they will work toward earning for that session only. For example, if an MSWO preference assessment suggests three highly preferred items of six tested items, you might provide the child a choice of those three items before every session. This ensures the child receives a preferred reward following correct responding, and thus is motivated to reduce errors.

As identified earlier, simultaneous prompting procedures require the use of a controlling prompt during all instructional sessions—that is, a prompt that ensures correct responding when given. Sometimes controlling prompts are difficult to identify. For example, it is possible that you think a child will respond to a gesture prompt to identify the correct photograph from a field of three, so you begin 0-second trials by saying "Give me the [stimulus name]" and immediately follow that direction by pointing to the correct stimulus. However, the child consistently responds instead by picking whatever image is on his right (referred to as "side bias"). This suggests that your prompt (the gesture) is not, in fact, controlling his behavior. In this case, you might select a different prompt topography, such as partial or full physical prompting, to ensure correct responding and prevent errors.

Reducing Prolonged UPE Responding

The purpose of probe trials is to allow children to answer independently once they have learned the correct behavior. Most children will begin to respond correctly during probe trials because it allows for access to reinforcement (if an appropriate reinforcer has been identified; see above). Some children, however, exhibit prolonged unprompted error responding. Children have widely varying learning speeds—for example, some children have acquired targeted discrete skills using these procedures in as few as three instructional sessions (e.g., Reichow & Wolery, 2009), while others have learned similar skills in up to 60 sessions (Fetko, Schuster, Harley, & Collins, 1999; Parrot, Schuster, Collins, & Gassaway, 2000).

Switch to CTD or PTD instructional sessions. Some children may have difficulty understanding that the prompted response from instructional sessions can be used during probe sessions. In this case, the delay and subsequent prompt that occurs *during instructional sessions* might be useful for these children. The change from simultaneous prompting to CTD or PTD is a simple one; treat initial simultaneous prompting sessions as extended 0-second sessions and begin conducting delay sessions according to the rules of either CTD or PTD. Because there is always a chance to engage in unprompted responses during instructional sessions when CTD and PTD are used, probe sessions can be discontinued.

Use a prompt/test procedure following error correction. Another option is to change the probe session by altering consequences for unprompted errors. One way to do this is by providing the correct answer (e.g., "No, that's red") and then immediately repeating the discriminative stimulus ("What is it?" while presenting a red car). This allows the child to answer correctly following the discriminative stimulus rather than the prompt; a history of doing this may make it more likely that he or she attends to the discriminative stimulus-response relationship. This procedure will be used less often as unprompted correct responses become more frequent, and eventually will not be used at all as the child achieves mastery levels (i.e., 100 percent unprompted correct responding).

Conclusion

The simultaneous prompting procedure is well researched, although much of the research has been conducted with older children with disabilities. It is a useful and efficient procedure for establishing a transfer of stimulus control, and does not require that children are able to wait for a prompt when they cannot answer independently. We suggest its use for children who cannot yet wait for a prompt, for teaching a variety of discrete behaviors.

Other Single Prompt Procedures

No-No Prompting (NNP)

No-no prompting mirrors some teachers' typical practices—that is, they provide an opportunity for a child to answer correctly, then give them another opportunity to try contingent on an error, and finally provide a controlling prompt. It might look something like this:

Teacher: *Malik, what color is this?*
Malik: *Green!*
Teacher: *No, try again. It's ...*
Malik: *Purple!*
Teacher: *No, it's ...*
Malik: *Red!*
Teacher: *No, it's yellow.*
Malik: *Yellow.*
Teacher: *Great! Here you go (hands Malik yellow car).*

As you can see, given the example above, the "no-no" part of the procedure's name comes from the fact that the instructor provides two **no statements** before providing any assistance. These statements indicate to the child that their answer was incorrect and that they should try again. Although NNP might mirror some practitioners' normal practices, the research base on NNP is quite small. The first identified study using NNP was published in 2010 (Leaf, Sheldon, & Sherman, 2010), and only one identified study (to date) was conducted by a separate research group (Fentress & Lerman, 2012). However, NNP has components of both trial-and-error and error correction procedures (Gast, 2011), which have been more widely studied. Unfortunately, research suggests that these procedures are not as efficient as errorless learning procedures such as time delay, simultaneous prompting, and the system of least prompts.

The components of an instructional trial for NNP include: (1) provision of the discriminative stimulus, (2) pre-prompt response interval, (3) no statement, if error, (4), another pre-prompt response interval, (5) no statement, if error, (6) a third pre-prompt response interval, (7) controlling prompt if error, (8) post-prompt response interval, and (9) response consequences. Note that there are three pre-prompt intervals. That is, a child has three opportunities to give the correct answer prior to the prompt.

There are several conceptual concerns with no-no prompting, in addition to the relatively small evidence base. The first is that it may lead to a considerable number of errors compared to other procedures (Fentress & Lerman, 2012). This could also lead to a pattern of learned errors—if a child is repeatedly reinforced, for example, for saying "green" and then "red" when "red" is the target response, he or she may continue to make that error. In addition, no-no prompting naturally includes a thinner schedule of reinforcement for child responses—that is, a child may need to make as many as four responses before being provided with reinforcement. This may impact the rapidity of learning. Although there is some evidence to suggest that NNP does not result in protracted learning times compared to other prompting procedures (Fentress & Lerman, 2012), the trials themselves may be needlessly long at the beginning of instruction. For example, when compared with simultaneous prompting, an NNP trial consists of three extra pre-prompt response intervals and two extra no statements. Although this may only consist of an extra few seconds per trial, over a session, and even a school year, these changes may add up to result in considerable instructional inefficiency. From an ethical standpoint, if you have evidence (e.g., baseline data) that suggests that a child cannot independently perform a behavior, it may not be desirable to continue to allow them to fail for multiple opportunities before providing them with assistance. Thus, in general, we do not suggest the use of NNP, unless future research elucidates additional benefits for doing so.

Model-Lead-Test (M-L-T)

Like the time delay procedures, the research base for M-L-T procedures is relatively well developed, with the first published references for the procedure in the early 1980s (i.e.,

Table 9.4 Within-Session and Across-Session M-L-T

Components	Within-Session M-L-T	Across-Session M-L-T
Model	Trials 1–5	Sessions 1–2
Lead	Trials 6–10	Sessions 3–10
Test	Trials 11–15	Sessions 11–15

Carnine, Kameenui, & Maggs, 1982). It has been assessed in research studies much less frequently than the time delay procedures, although use of M-L-T has increased recently (e.g., Browder et al., 2018; Knight, Creech-Galloway, Karl, & Collins, 2018; Knight, Smith, Spooner, & Browder, 2012). M-L-T includes the use of three trial types: *model* trials, *lead* trials, and *test* trials.

M-L-T is different than other procedures in that it is primarily a structure for ordering trials, rather than a specified procedure. One way in which M-L-T procedures have varied is that different trial types have been temporally distributed in different ways. Two variations are shown in Table 9.4 above within-session M-L-T (see Knight et al., 2012), and across-session M-L-T (see Browder et al., 2018). In addition, the *lead* trials have been conducted somewhat differently across studies—for example, Knight and colleagues (2012) conducted *lead* trials using a procedure similar to simultaneous prompting or time delay 0-second instructional trials. That is, they modeled the correct response, and the child repeated the model. Browder and colleagues, however, conducted *lead* trials by using a hierarchy of prompts (see Chapter 10).

The *model* trials are not similar to components of other procedures discussed thus far (i.e., time delay, simultaneous prompting, NNP). During these trials, the instructor models correct responding without requiring a child response. For example, if a practitioner was teaching a child to name colors using five miniature cars, she might model for trials 1–5 by saying "It's my turn," and then picking up each car and naming the color ("This is green, this is blue …"). Then, she would conduct *lead* trials. These trials are similar to instructional trials conducted with other procedures. That is, they do require a response from the child, but assistance from the instructor is provided. So, the instructor might say "You say it with me. This is green" (discriminative stimulus and controlling prompt). Then, the instructor would provide a response interval for the child to repeat the color. During *test* trials, the instructor might say something like "Now it's your turn" and then point to each car without naming the color. *Test* trials are similar to simultaneous prompting probe trials.

Like simultaneous prompting, M-L-T procedures do not require the child wait. Like time delay procedures, M-L-T does not require separate sessions, although conducting separate probe sessions after a child demonstrates mastery during *test* trials is warranted, to ensure the child can independently perform the behavior without the initial model and lead trials. Variations of the M-L-T procedures, including only *lead* and *test* trials, have been shown in two studies to be superior to simultaneous prompting in terms of the speed of learning (Celik & Vuran, 2014; Singleton, Schuster, Morse, & Collins, 1999). Because there is limited comparative research, it is not clear to what extent M-L-T performs similarly to other procedures (time delay, system of least prompts), but it may be that M-L-T is particularly well suited to teach relational information (e.g., opposite concepts), as this type of behavior has been taught often with M-L-T (e.g., Celik & Vuran, 2014; Knight et al., 2012).

For three weeks, Gale conducts short daily sessions during which she uses simultaneous prompting, using a physical model as the controlling prompt, to teach Fatima to request a preferred item. She conducts probe sessions twice per week. During the sixth probe session, at the end of the third week, Fatima independently requests preferred items on 100 percent of opportunities. Gale decides to expand her teaching by adding a peer confederate to the simultaneous prompting sessions—the peer, Kaedrianna, serves the role previously played by the teacher, while Gale provides support and feedback, as needed. After a few more weeks, Fatima is consistently and frequently using her device to make requests of adults and other children—and her parents have reported that she has generalized this skill to home.

Related Resources

https://csesa.fpg.unc.edu/resources/ebp-briefs/prompting
https://vkc.mc.vanderbilt.edu/ebip/other-procedures/

References

Browder, D. M., Spooner, F., Lo, Y. Y., Saunders, A. F., Root, J. R., Ley Davis, L., & Brosh, C. R. (2018). Teaching students with moderate intellectual disability to solve word problems. *The Journal of Special Education*, 51, 222–235.

Carnine, D., Kameenui, E., & Maggs, A. (1982). Components of analytic assistance: Statement saying, concept training, and strategy training. *The Journal of Educational Research*, 75, 374–377.

Celik, S., & Vuran, S. (2014). Comparison of direct instruction and simultaneous prompting procedure on teaching concepts to individuals with intellectual disability. *Education and Training in Autism and Developmental Disabilities*, 49, 127–144.

Fentress, G. M., & Lerman, D. C. (2012). A comparison of two prompting procedures for teaching basic skills to children with autism. *Research in Autism Spectrum Disorders*, 6, 1083–1090.

Fetko, K. S., Schuster, J. W., Harley, D. A., & Collins, B. C. (1999). Using simultaneous prompting to teach a chained vocational task to young adults with severe intellectual disabilities. *Education and Training in Mental Retardation and Developmental Disabilities*, 34, 318–329.

Gast, D. L. (2011). A rejoinder to Leaf: What constitutes efficient, applied, and trial and error. *Evidence-Based Communication Assessment and Intervention*, 5, 234–238.

Gibson, A. N., & Schuster, J. W. (1992). The use of simultaneous prompting for teaching expressive word identification to preschool children. *Topics in Early Childhood Special Education*, 12, 247–267.

Head, K. D., Collins, B. C., Schuster, J. W., & Ault, M. J. (2011). A comparison of simultaneous prompting and constant time delay procedures in teaching state capitals. *Journal of Behavioral Education*, 20, 182–202. doi: 10.1007/s10864-011-9127-8.

Knight, V. F., Creech-Galloway, C. E., Karl, J. M., & Collins, B. C. (2018). Evaluating supported e-text to teach science to high school students with moderate intellectual disability. *Focus on Autism and other Developmental Disabilities*, 33, 227–236.

Knight, V. F., Smith, B. R., Spooner, F., & Browder, D. (2012). Using explicit instruction to teach science descriptors to students with autism spectrum disorders. *Journal of Autism and Developmental Disorders*, 42, 378–389.

Leaf, J. B., Sheldon, J. B., & Sherman, J. A. (2010). Comparison of simultaneous prompting and no-no prompting in two-choice discrimination learning with children with autism. *Journal of Applied Behavior Analysis*, 43, 215–228.

Ledford, J. R., & Wolery, M. (2013). Peer modeling of academic and social behaviors during small group instruction. *Exceptional Children*, 79, 439–458.

Ledford, J. R., Barton, E. E., Hardy, J. K., Elam, K., Seabolt, J., Shanks, M., Hemmeter, M. L., & Kaiser, A. (2016). What equivocal data from single case comparison studies reveal about evidence-based practices in early childhood special education. *Journal of Early Intervention*, 38, 79–91.

Parrot, K. A., Schuster, J. W., Collins, B. C., & Gassaway, L. J. (2000). Simultaneous prompting and instructive feedback when teaching chained tasks. *Journal of Behavioral Education*, 10, 3–19.

Reichow, B., & Wolery, M. (2009). Comparison of everyday and every-fourth-day probe sessions with the simultaneous prompting procedures. *Topics in Early Childhood Special Education*, 29, 79–89.

Schuster, J. W., & Griffen, A. K. (1993). Teaching a chained task with a simultaneous prompting procedure. *Journal of Behavioral Education*, 3, 299–315.

Schuster, J. W., Griffen, B. S., & Wolery, M. (1992). Comparison of simultaneous prompting and constant time delay procedures in teaching sight words to elementary students with moderate mental retardation. *Journal of Behavioral Education*, 2, 303–325.

Singleton, D. K., Schuster, J. W., Morse, T. E., & Collins, B. C. (1999). A comparison of antecedent prompt and test and simultaneous prompting procedures in teaching grocery words to adolescents with mental retardation *Education and Training in Mental Retardation and Developmental Disabilities*, 34, 182–199.

Swain, R., Lane, J. D., & Gast, D. L. (2015). Comparison of constant time delay and simultaneous prompting procedures: Teaching functional sight words to students with intellectual disabilities and autism spectrum disorder. *Journal of Behavioral Education*, 24, 210–229.

Tekin, E., & Kircaali-Iftar, G. (2002). Comparison of the effectiveness and efficiency of two response prompting procedures delivered by sibling tutors. *Education and Training in Mental Retardation and Developmental Disabilities*, 37, 283–299.

Wolery, M., & Gast. D. L. (1984). Effective and efficient procedures for the transfer of stimulus control. *Topics in Early Childhood Special Education*, 4, 52–77.

Wolery, M., Ault, M. J., & Doyle, P. M. (1992). *Teaching students with moderate to severe disabilities. Use of response prompting strategies.* New York: Longman.

Wolery, M., Holcombe, A., Werts, M. G., & Cipolloni, R. M. (1993). Effects of simultaneous prompting and instructive feedback. *Early Education and Development*, 4, 20–31.

10 Introduction to Prompting Hierarchies and the System of Least Prompts

Key Terms

Controlling prompts
Hierarchical procedures
Prompted error
Prompted correct

Non-controlling prompts
System of least prompts
Unprompted correct

Single prompt procedures
Discriminative stimulus
Unprompted error

Chapter Objectives

After completing this chapter, readers should be able to:

- Outline procedural steps when using the system of least prompts.
- Define "non-controlling" prompts and describe why you might use them.
- Explain potential procedural variations and prompting hierarchies used in the SLP.
- List the types of child responses, and suggested adult reactions to each.
- Describe possible problems when SLP is used, and identify potential solutions for each.

Stacey is the lead teacher in an inclusive preschool classroom for 4-year-olds. She recently reworked her classroom's daily schedule to reduce the number of transitions and ensure there are ample opportunities throughout the day for children to engage in object play. Most of her children independently engage in complex object play including social pretend play at the dramatic play and blocks centers. However, she has noticed two children with disabilities, Cory and Kamala, rarely engage in object play and spend a good portion of free play times engaged with the same toys using repetitive actions with those toys. As a result, these children rarely interact with their peers during free play and there are limited opportunities to embed learning related to other skills.

Chapters 8 and 9 defined and described the use of systematic response prompt procedures (e.g., CTD, PTD, simultaneous prompting); these procedures involve the use of a single prompt topography—a **controlling prompt**. Strategies discussed in this chapter will also use **non-controlling** prompts—those that provide assistance to the child, but do not guarantee correct responding. This chapter will describe a second set of systematic prompting procedures that are different than the **single prompt procedures** discussed previously—**hierarchical procedures**, which are also referred to as *multiple prompt strategies*. Specifically, procedural details will be provided for the **system of least prompts (SLP)**, the most commonly used hierarchical strategy. In addition, procedural variations will be highlighted. Sufficient detail and resources will be provided to allow readers to successfully implement procedures in a variety of contexts and to proactively prevent potential problems and use data-based problem-solving when difficulties arise (e.g., insufficient improvements, problem behavior).

What is the System of Least Prompts?

SLP is a response prompting procedure in which the implementer initially gives the child an opportunity to respond independently to the **discriminative stimulus.** If the child does not respond accurately without prompts and after a pre-specified wait interval, the implementer provides a non-controlling prompt, also referred to as an intermediate prompt. If the child does not respond accurately with the non-controlling prompt, the implementer provides either a more intrusive prompt or the controlling prompt depending on the pre-determined levels of the prompt hierarchy. When using SLP, the prompts are considered self-fading, meaning that the child learns how to learn—as the child learns to perform a skill correctly, more intrusive prompts are not needed. As such, the child self-selects the level of support required and independent responding, or responding with the less intrusive prompts, indicates the child is learning the target.

SLP is a popular, commonly used prompting procedure. Its popularity is perhaps due to its flexibility or perceived ease of use. SLP might be perceived as unsystematically giving children assistance when they need it or when they are incorrect. However, SLP is systematic and structured. The prevalence and popularity of SLP has been documented by multiple researchers (Fisher, Kodak, & Moore, 2007; Shepley, Lane, & Ault, 2018), although evidence regarding its relative efficacy and efficiency when compared with other procedures has been limited (Wolery & Hemmeter, 2011). For example, SLP was found to be less efficient than CTD or PTD (Ault, Wolery, Doyle, & Gast, 1989; Schuster, Morse, Ault, Crawford, & Wolery, 1998; Walker, 2008). Shepley and colleagues (2018) conducted a systematic review of the research on SLP and found it to be evidence-based for chained target behaviors and for learners ages 13 and above and recommended single-prompt strategies when targeting academics and related behaviors. However, they noted there were multiple studies with young children that included SLP as part of a treatment package that provided relatively strong evidence of effectiveness (e.g., play behaviors). Multiple researchers have demonstrated the efficacy of SLP for teaching a range of skills (e.g., object play—Barton et al., 2016; purchasing skills—Cihak & Grim, 2008; requesting help—Taber et al., 2003; conversation skills—Filla, Wolery, & Anthony, 1999).

As with all response prompting procedures, the goal of the SLP is to transfer stimulus control from the implementer delivering the prompts to the typically occurring stimulus (e.g., environmental, temporal, or socially mediated discriminative stimuli; Wolery, Ault, & Doyle, 1992). When using the SLP procedure the implementer establishes a prompt hierarchy with a minimum of two prompt levels—one of which is the controlling prompt—and a target stimulus. The implementer delivers the target discriminative stimulus (e.g., task direction; see Chapter 8 for information regarding discriminative stimulus), gives the child an opportunity to respond, and then delivers the prompt hierarchy from least to more intrusive or helpful. If the child responds correctly, the implementer provides the reinforcement, whereas if the child responds incorrectly, the implementer delivers the next, more intrusive prompt. The SLP procedure is also commonly referred to as a 'least to most' prompt hierarchy, increasing assistance, or a three-prompt procedure. These names accurately refer to the prompting hierarchy that is pre-determined, delivered from less to more assistive, and often, but not always, includes three prompt levels (independent, non-controlling or less intrusive prompt, and controlling prompt).

The components of a trial for SLP include: (1) provision of the discriminative stimulus, (2) a pre-prompt response interval, (3) intermediate or non-controlling prompt(s), (4) a post-prompt response interval, (5) controlling prompt, (6) a post-prompt response interval, and (7) response consequences. Prompts are delivered in a pre-determined hierarchy of increasing assistance. That is, the first prompt level—delivered after the discriminative stimulus and opportunity to respond independently—provides minimal assistance (e.g., a visual, a choice) and the final level provides complete assistance or the controlling prompt. More prompt levels can be added as needed based on the child's learning history or performance. For example, the first prompt level might use visual, the next level might provide more assistance with a gesture or model prompt, and the controlling prompt level—the final level—provides complete assistance with a full physical prompt. Table 10.1 illustrates two sample trials. Trial A is designed to increase the frequency of object play and the discriminative stimulus is the presence of toys and the statement, "Let's play!" Trial B is designed to teach a child to wash their hands.

SLP is particularly useful for teaching behaviors with multiple correct responses such as play, social skills, and communication skills and has been used more often for teaching these behaviors than other response prompting procedures (e.g., PTD, CTD; Barton, 2016; Filla et al., 1999). There are some variations of SLP in which the task direction is repeated at each level of the hierarchy. However, initial comparison studies have shown that repeating the task direction is not more effective than not repeating the task direction (Humphreys, Polick, Howk, Thaxton, & Ivancic, 2013), and not having to repeat the task direction might be more feasible. Likewise, West and Billingsley (2005) found that when using SLP, pairing verbal prompts with other prompts was not more effective and was less efficient than using a prompt sequence devoid of verbal prompts. Thus, we recommend avoiding use of repeated verbal prompts or task directions.

Table 10.1 Sample SLP Trial Sequences

Hierarchy Component	Example Trial A	Hierarchy Component	Example Trial B
Discriminative Stimulus/Task Direction	"Lets play!" and toys	Discriminative Stimulus/Task Direction	Transition in from the playground and visual
Wait Response Interval	*10 seconds*	*Wait Response Interval*	*5 seconds*
Intermediate Prompt	[secures attention] Verbal and Physical Model: "My car is going fast!"	**First Intermediate Prompt**	[secures attention] Gesture: Points to sink
		Wait Response Interval	*5 seconds*
		Second Intermediate Prompt	Physically guides child to sink.
Wait Response Interval	*5 seconds*	*Wait Response Interval*	*5 seconds*
Controlling Prompt	Full Physical and Verbal: "Look how fast your car is!" and while using hand over hand assistance to have the child move their car	**Controlling Prompt**	Physically guides child to turn on water and wash hands
Child Behavior Response Consequences	Child plays with car "Wow! Your car is fast!" and deliver an edible reinforcer	Child Behavior Response Consequences	Child washes hands "You washed your hands! You can get your lunch now"

Prompt Types

Chapter 8 outlines specific prompt topographical categories. Two different types of prompts are used when implementing SLP. Non-controlling and controlling prompts are always individually determined for each child and each behavior. A controlling prompt for one child may not reliably result in correct responding for other children. For example, physical models of toy play might function as a controlling prompt for children who reliably imitate adult actions. However, model prompts would not serve as a controlling prompt for children who do not yet imitate others. Likewise, full physical prompting might function as a controlling prompt for the transition from outdoor play to lunch time, but some children might resist full physical prompting. In this case, partial physical guidance or verbal and visual supports might reliably result in the child transitioning from outdoor play to lunch time. Likewise, for an individual child, a full physical prompt might be necessary to control transition behavior, but a physical model might serve as a controlling prompt for responding to a teacher-led trial in which the teacher requests that the child select the correct letter.

SLP trials typically use two prompt levels (see Example A in Table 10.1) or three prompt levels (see Example B in Table 10.1) although as many as four levels can be used. However, trials with four levels might be overly long, less efficient, and result in unnecessary delays in mastery. Types of prompts should be selected based on the child's learning history and the target behaviors. For example, full physical assistance might be a controlling prompt for some children whereas for other children a model and verbal prompt might function as a controlling prompt. Barton (2015), for instance, used model plus verbal prompts to teach play without a verbal alone prompt, given the likelihood that children with delays in play have delays in receptive language and might not be responsive to a verbal prompt alone, which is supported by other researchers (West & Billingsley, 2005). Given these procedures, more intrusive prompts are only delivered if children need them; the learner selects the level of prompting needed. When children are capable of responding independently and correctly (e.g., when they have learned the behaviors), they are likely to respond before more intrusive prompts are provided (e.g., the controlling prompt), because it results in faster reinforcement. This reduces the likelihood that children will continue to wait for more assistance once they are capable of responding independently and might prevent prolonged prompted correct responding. New trials begin immediately after the delivery of the reinforcement, which occurs after prompted or independent correct responding from the child. When using SLP procedures, trials stay exactly the same for every trial in each session throughout instruction. That is, SLP is different than time delay strategies because there is no change from one trial type to another (e.g., 0-second trials to 3-second trials) and is different than simultaneous prompting because there is only one type of session (i.e., no probe sessions). Table 10.2 provides examples of SLP prompt levels. Figure 10.1 depicts a trial corresponding with Sample Trial A from Table 10.1.

Table 10.2 Sample SLP Prompt Levels

Level	Prompts		
Target Stimulus	Independent	Independent	Independent
1	Model	Visual and Choice	Visual Cue
2	Full Physical	Gesture	Verbal Hint
3		Physical Model	Verbal Rule
4			Verbal Model

Potential Child Responses and Adult Reactions

As with most response prompting procedures, there are five total potential responses: unprompted correct responses (UPC), unprompted error responses (UPE), prompted correct responses (PC), prompted error responses (PE), and no responses (NR). UPC responses occur after the target stimulus without adult assistance. PC responses occur after a prompt and it is often helpful to monitor the level of support the child requires. For single-prompt strategies, PC refers to correct responding in the presence of the controlling prompt—for SLP and other hierarchical procedures, additional information is needed to determine whether PC is a correct response in the presence of intermediate or controlling prompts. Over time, we expect the child to start to respond to the less intrusive prompt level and need the controlling prompt level less often. For example, when teaching play using a verbal task direction, model prompt at the intermediate level, and full physical prompt at the controlling level, you might need to use the controlling prompt often during the first several sessions, but eventually the child should respond to the model prompt. However, if this does not occur, the prompts or reinforcers might need to be modified to facilitate independent responding. Tracking the PCs at a specific level allows you to make decisions regarding instruction to ensure efficient and effective learning. Both UPC and PC should be immediately reinforced. UPE and PE occur after the target stimulus or any of the prompt levels, respectively, and should be followed by the next level prompt. NR also are followed by the next level prompt. As described in Chapter 8, for ease of data collection we recommend categorizing NR as equivalent to a PE.

Planning Instruction Using SLP

Prior to conducting SLP instruction, you should decide on the discriminative stimulus to be used, the duration of your response intervals, the types of intermediate and controlling prompts to be used, and the consequences for each type of response. You should also determine the **mastery criterion**, which will govern when you will discontinue instruction. The mastery criterion tends to include a rate, count, or accuracy benchmark (e.g., ten unprompted correct responses, 90 percent unprompted correct responding) and a standard regarding how often it occurred (e.g., over three consecutive sessions).

- **Discriminative Stimulus:** This identifies the stimulus under which you want children to respond independently. For chained behaviors, the discriminative stimulus might be a verbal task direction (e.g., "Your turn to wash hands!") or the typical environmental antecedent (e.g., transition into the classroom). For discrete behaviors, the discriminative stimulus might be a verbal task direction (e.g., "Do this") or a verbal and stimulus prompt (e.g., "Let's play!" with toys present).
- **Pre- and Post Prompt Response Intervals:** The wait interval should be selected based on the target behavior and the child's typical response time. The wait interval should be carefully determined to give the child a sufficient amount of time to perform the target behavior independently or respond to the prompt. Depending on the context and the target, longer wait intervals might be acceptable. In some cases, the pre-prompt response interval might be longer to allow the child more time to independently respond. However, the wait intervals should typically be the same after each prompt level. For example, when teaching play, you might extend the initial wait interval to give the child some time to explore the toys. You also want to ensure the child has limited opportunities for error.
- **Intermediate Prompts:** Intermediate prompts should be selected based on their level of assistance, likelihood of leading to correct responding, and feasibility given the

context and the target behavior. Intermediate prompts generally give the child some help in performing the target behavior, but do not ensure a correct response.

- **Controlling Prompts:** The controlling prompts are described in Chapter 8. These should be selected individually, based on the child's learning history. Generally, you should choose a prompt that is likely to result in correct responding (i.e., is controlling) *and* that is the least restrictive. In some cases, a controlling prompt test should be conducted prior to starting instruction to ensure you have identified a controlling prompt. It is worth noting again that controlling prompts are child-specific.
- **Consequences:** Prior to using SLP, you should decide what consequences will occur when the child responds correctly or incorrectly.
  - **Reinforce Correct Responses:** Importantly, the identified reinforcer is provided contingent on prompted *and* unprompted responses. This way the child is reinforced regardless of whether they needed help.
  - **Ignore or Correct Errors:** Using the SLP, the implementer always provides the correct response, thus error correction is not needed. If no responses or an error occurs after intermediate prompts, the implementer simply provides the next level prompt. Incorrect responses after the controlling prompt are typically ignored, which ensures the implementer does not inadvertently reinforce incorrect responses with attention.

Procedural Variations of the SLP

Several researchers have used SLP in combination with other procedures. For example, when teaching play, researchers have used contingent imitation and verbal mapping in combination with the SLP to successfully increase play; contingent imitation and verbal mapping might be important in this context to establish a play interaction. SLP also has been used in combination with functional communication training, video modeling intervention packages, and comprehensive social skill trainings (e.g., Shepley et al., 2018; van der Meer & Rispoli, 2010). Although the efficacy of SLP is difficult to discern when embedded within an intervention package, Shepley and colleagues noted the use of SLP in combination with other treatment was promising given several studies had moderate to strong evidence. Also, as with other procedures, SLP has been delivered in embedded trials or distributed trials in addition to massed trial formats (see Chapter 14 for more information regarding planning instruction across the day).

Research Abstract

Barton, E. E. (2015). Teaching generalized pretend play and related behaviors to young children with disabilities. *Exceptional Children*, 81, 489–506.

  In this single case design study, the author used an intervention package including the system of least prompts, contingent imitation, and descriptive comments to teach four children with disabilities to increase their pretend play and play-related behaviors. The children who were recruited were chosen because they had individualized goals related to play. The author used evidence-based coaching practices (see Chapter 15) to train the classroom teachers to implement the intervention package—including the use of the system of least prompts. Some adaptations to the system of least prompts procedures were made for two of the participants, including changing the controlling prompts and reinforcement in response to their data patterns. All children demonstrated increases in all target play behaviors, generalized to a free play context, and maintained increases in target play behaviors when the intervention was withdrawn, indicating the system of least prompts was effective for teaching play.

Determining When to Use SLP

Decisions regarding which procedures to use should largely be made based on individual child and implementer characteristics and the target behaviors. In their review of SLP, Shepley and colleagues found SLP to be particularly effective for teaching chained behaviors for students older than 13. There was insufficient evidence to support its use for other types of target behaviors or with younger learners. There is a burgeoning body of evidence supporting the use of SLP to teach target skills such as play and leisure skills, conversational skills, and transitions (Barton, 2015; Filla et al., 1999; Shepley et al., 2018). However, several studies have shown that CTD or PTD often produce more efficient learning than SLP when teaching discrete target behaviors to learners with a range of characteristics. SLP's popularity might indicate that it is perceived as more feasible and easier to implement than other response prompting procedures, which might improve fidelity of use. Thus, decisions about using SLP should consider efficiency of learning and the implementer preferences.

Stacey decides the children, Cory and Kamala, need systematic instruction to increase their frequency and complexity of object play. For Kamala, who rarely engages with the toys at all, she decides to try using the system of least prompts with three levels—Let's Play as the task direction, a choice of toys as the intermediate prompt, and full physical assistance for the controlling prompt. She plans to conduct brief 5-minute sessions each day to engage her with the toys. For Cory, who mostly interacts with the blocks by lining them up by size or color, she decides to use the system of least prompts to teach him to engage in more varied behaviors. She uses three levels including—Let's Play as the task direction, a verbal and model prompt, and full physical assistance for the controlling prompt. She plans to conduct 5-minute sessions twice per day during free play.

Considerations for Instruction

When SLP is used, children should quickly transition from making all PCs to making all UPCs, with few or no UPEs or PEs. Some children, however, require modifications to initially developed SLP procedures to improve the speed of acquisition. These considerations are similar for most response prompting procedures (see Chapters 8 and 9); however, there are specific considerations for SLP. Adaptations might need to be made to the prompts, response intervals, or reinforcement.

Prompt Adaptations

One change that could be made when using SLP is refinements to the prompt levels. For example, say you are teaching a child to imitate his peers' play behaviors using three prompt levels: a verbal task direction, a visual prompt, and full physical prompting, but the child has repeated UPEs. You might change the visual prompt to a visual with a verbal prompt or a physical model to make the prompt more salient. Also, depending on the context and the target behaviors, children might be guessing the incorrect answer rather than waiting for the assistance (prompt) that would help them achieve correct responding. In these cases, wait training might be useful (see Chapter 8). If the child is not attending to the task direction/target stimuli or prompts, you might need to change the task direction or use more salient stimuli and prompts. If excessive PC or PE occurs, the prompt types might be inappropriate for the target behavior and should be adapted. When prolonged PC occurs, you might consider adding a clear contingency review prior to instructional

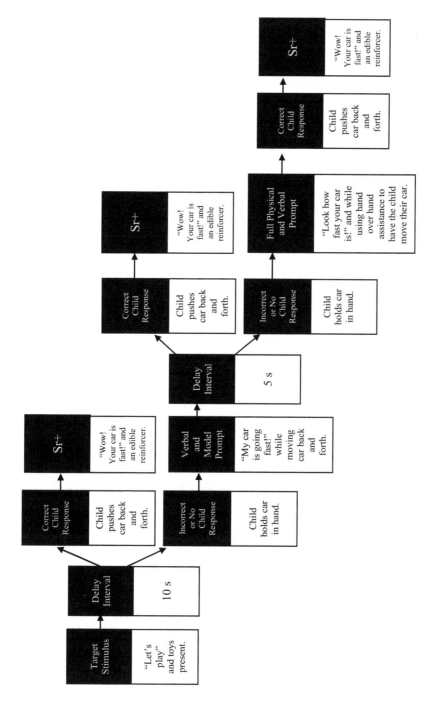

Figure 10.1 Procedural Steps for the System of Least Prompts Procedure.

sessions (along with reinforcement changes described below). Some children might be resistant to controlling prompts using hand over hand assistance. In these cases, other, less intrusive controlling prompts should be used to improve efficiency of learning.

Wait Training

If children consistently respond without waiting for the prompt level that provides enough assistance for them to be correct, you may need to use wait training to teach them to wait (see Chapter 8). You also might consider reducing the response intervals to increase engagement, or extending response intervals to give the child more time to consider the prompts and respond.

Reinforcement

Adaptations to reinforcement should be considered in cases with prolonged PC or PE, or excessive problem behaviors. Also, reinforcement should be continually reviewed to ensure learning is efficient and effective.

Research Abstract

Filla, A., Wolery, M., & Anthony, L. (1999). Promoting children's conversations during play with adult prompts. *Journal of Early Intervention*, 22, 93–108.

In this single case design study, the authors trained classroom teachers to use an intervention package, including the system of least prompts and environmental arrangement, with nine young children with and without disabilities to teach them to use play-related conversations in triads. Each triad included one child with disabilities and two peers. The environmental arrangement consisted of a theme box of toys and restricted play space. Children were given a choice between two theme boxes (e.g., school, party, bakery, cookout) before each session and told to play in a specific area of the inclusive classroom. Rates of conversation did not change with the use of environmental arrangements only. When teachers introduced the system of least prompts—which consisted of three levels: general, direct, and model prompts—rates of conversation increased to levels higher than previous experimental conditions for two of the three triads. The authors monitored and graphed the frequency and levels of prompts used across sessions, which showed they used fewer model and direct prompts over the course of the intervention as the children mastered the target skills.

Data Collection for SLP

Data collection for SLP procedures are similar to procedures described in Chapters 8 and 9. Teachers identify whether the response was: PC, UPC, PE, or UPE. Baseline sessions should be conducted to confirm that the child needs instruction and to establish the child's current functional repertoire within the instructional context. Following each session, data should be recorded, graphed, and analyzed. Data patterns should be carefully monitored to ensure the child is making adequate progress or to make decisions about changes to the instructional procedures. When SLP is used, the child initially might have few to no UPC and high levels of PC. After several sessions, we expect levels of UPC to increase and eventually exceed levels of PC. Figure 10.2 provides two sets of hypothetical graphed data when using SLP. The top panel shows a gradual increase in UPC preceded by initially high

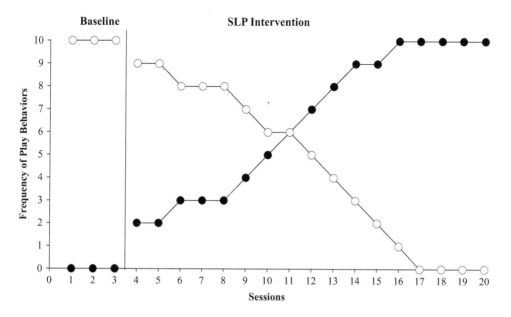

Figure 10.2a Teaching Play Using SLP.

Note: This graph depicts a gradual increase in UPC preceded by initially high rates of PC for play behaviors. Closed circles are unprompted play (UPC) and open circles are prompted play (PC). UPE and PE are not graphed.

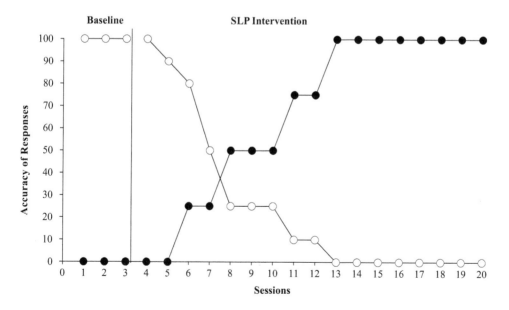

Figure 10.2b Teaching Social Skills Using SLP.

Note: This graph depicts a gradual increase in percentage accuracy of UPC preceded by initially high levels of PC for target discrete social responses. Closed circles are unprompted responses (UPC) and open circles are prompted responses (PC). UPE and PE are not graphed.

rates of PC for a rate-based target behavior. The lower panel shows immediate increase correct (UPC) for accuracy-based target behavior. Several resources are provided at the end of this chapter with links to forms that can be used to collect data when using SLP.

Conclusion

SLP is a popular instructional procedure with burgeoning evidence for its use. It is particularly useful for teaching play or social behaviors. However, it is often less efficient than PTD or CTD, particularly for discrete skills. SLP should be carefully planned and implemented with specific prompts and levels determined, based on the child's learning history, the target behaviors, and the context. The flexibility of SLP has likely led to its popularity despite comparison studies showing that PTD or CTD might be more efficient. When using SLP, child progress should be carefully monitored and instructional adaptations should be made as needed to ensure efficient learning.

After a few days of instruction, Stacey notices that Cory is resisting the full physical prompting. She changes the controlling prompt to modeling with a verbal prompt and Cory's rate of unprompted play increases during her daily sessions. After a few weeks she notices that Cory has started engaging with new toys outside of the instructional sessions. Kamala quickly started engaging in unprompted play during the instructional sessions. Stacey was excited about their progress and planned to change their individual goals to focus on more complex play types.

Additional Resources

https://vkc.mc.vanderbilt.edu/ebip/system-of-least-prompts/
https://vkc.mc.vanderbilt.edu/ebip/data-sheets/

References

Ault, M. J., Wolery, M., Doyle, P. M., & Gast, D. L. (1989). Review of comparative studies in instruction of students with moderate and severe handicaps. *Exceptional Children*, 55, 346–356.

Barton, E. E. (2015). Teaching generalized pretend play and related behaviors to young children with disabilities. *Exceptional Children*, 81, 489–506.

Barton, E. E. (2016). Critical issues and promising practices for teach play to young children with disabilities. In B. Reichow, B. A. Boyd, E. E. Barton, & S. L. Odom (Eds.), *Handbook of early childhood special education* (pp. 267–286). Switzerland: Springer International Publishing.

Cihak, D. F., & Grim, J. (2008). Teaching students with autism spectrum disorder and moderate intellectual disabilities to use counting-on strategies to enhance independent purchasing skills. *Research in Autism Spectrum Disorders*, 2, 716–727.

Filla, A., Wolery, M., & Anthony, L. (1999). Promoting children's conversations during play with adult prompts. *Journal of Early Intervention*, 22, 93–108.

Fisher, W. W., Kodak, T., & Moore, J. W. (2007). Embedding an identity-matching task within a prompting hierarchy to facilitate acquisition of conditional discriminations in children with autism. *Journal of Applied Behavior Analysis*, 40, 489–499.

Humphreys, T., Polick, A. S., Howk, L. L., Thaxton, J. R., & Ivancic, A. P. (2013). An evaluation of repeating the discriminative stimulus when using least-to-most prompting to teach intraverbal behavior to children with autism. *Journal of Applied Behavior Analysis*, 46, 534–538.

Schuster, J. W., Morse, T. E., Ault, M. J., Crawford, M. R., & Wolery, M. (1998). Constant time delay with chained tasks: A review of the literature. *Education and Treatment of Children*, 74–106.

Shepley, C., Lane, J. D., & Ault, M. J. (2018). A review and critical examination of the system of least prompts. *Remedial and Special Education*. doi: 10.1177/0741932517751213.

Taber, T. A., Alberto, P. A., Seltzer, A., & Hughes, M. (2003). Obtaining assistance when lost in the community using cell phones. *Research & Practice in Severe Disabilities*, 28, 105–116.

Van der Meer, L. A., & Rispoli, M. (2010). Communication interventions involving speech-generating devices for children with autism: A review of the literature. *Developmental Neurorehabilitation*, 13, 294–306.

Walker, G. (2008). Constant and progressive time delay procedures for teaching children with autism: A literature review. *Journal of Autism and Developmental Disorders*, 38, 261–275.

West, E. A., & Billingsley, F. (2005). Improving the system of least prompts: A comparison of procedural variations. *Education and Training in Developmental Disabilities*, 131–144.

Wolery, M., & Hemmeter, M. L. (2011). Classroom instruction: Background, assumptions, and challenges. *Journal of Early Intervention*, 33, 371–380.

Wolery, M., Ault, M. J., & Doyle, P. M. (1992). *Teaching students with moderate to severe disabilities: Use of response prompting strategies*. New York: Longman.

11 Other Prompting Procedures and Determining which Procedure to Use

Key Terms

Most-to-least prompts   Graduated guidance

Chapter Objectives

After completing this chapter, readers should be able to:

- Outline procedural steps when using most-to-least prompting and graduated guidance.
- Explain procedural variations when using most-to-least prompting and graduated guidance.
- List the types of child responses, and suggested adult reactions to each.
- Explain similarities and differences among system of least prompts, most-to-least prompting, and graduated guidance.
- Describe possible problems when multiple prompt strategies are used, and identify potential solutions for each.
- Discuss strengths and weaknesses of all previously discussed strategies (CTD, PTD, SP, SLP, MTL, and graduated guidance).

Mazie teaches children who are 3–5 years of age in a full-day, inclusive classroom. She has taught her students to transition across activities and routines independently using small group transitions and some peer-mediated instruction. She had a new student, Joseph, start in her class last week and Joseph has not successfully transitioned through any routines. She has tried several stimulus prompts (e.g., visuals, timers), but has not been successful. She knows there are other procedures she can use and spends time talking to her colleagues and doing her own research to see what might work to teach Joseph to independently transition, as appropriate, across the day.

Chapters 8 and 9 defined and described the use of systematic response prompt procedures (e.g., CTD, PTD, simultaneous prompting). Chapter 10 provided procedural details for the system of least prompts (SLP) procedure, the most commonly used hierarchical strategy. The purpose of this chapter is to describe two other hierarchical prompting procedures—most-to-least prompts and graduated guidance.

Most-to-least Prompting

Most-to-least prompting (MTL) is a hierarchal teaching strategy that uses different levels of prompts to facilitate learning. As with the SLP, when using MTL, prompts are arranged in order of their intrusiveness or the amount of help they provide. When using SLP you start with the *least* intrusive prompt (see Chapter 10). Conversely, when using MTL, you

Table 11.1 Sample MTL Trial Sequence for a 3-Level Hierarchy

Hierarchy Component	Sessions at Level 1	Sessions at Level 2	Sessions at Level 3
Discriminative Stimulus/Task Direction	"Time to line up!" and ring the bell		
Prompt	**Controlling Prompt** Immediately provide full physical assistance to guide the child to the door and in line with her peers	**Intermediate Prompt** Provide a gesture prompt and immediately point to the door	**Independent Level** Deliver the task direction only and no additional prompts
	Decreasing Level of Assistance ⟶		
Child Behavior	Child lines up at the door		
Response Consequences	"Thanks for lining up with your friends, Maddie! You can go outside and play!"		

begin with the *most* intrusive prompt (i.e., the controlling prompt) and systematically fade prompts to provide less assistance until the child has mastered the skill. A skill is considered mastered when the prompts are removed completely and the child uses the skill independently and consistently.

As with SLP, at least two levels of prompts are identified. One prompt level should consistently result in the target response—the controlling prompt. The additional prompt level(s) should be less intrusive and provide decreasing amounts of assistance. The final prompt level should provide minimal assistance. When using MTL, one level of prompt is used across trials within a session. In other words, prompts are changed across rather than within sessions. Prompts are systematically changed across sessions from the most intrusive to the least intrusive. This is an important distinction from SLP in which different levels of prompts can be used within a session depending on the child's responses. Prompts are always identified based on the child's current repertoire and learning history and should be feasible and relevant given the target responses.

When using MTL, prompts are delivered systematically, gradually removing more intrusive prompts and replacing them with less intrusive ones. The MTL procedure is designed to provide progressively less assistance as the child learns the skills (Meadan, Ostrosky, Santos, & Snodgrass, 2013). Prompt changes can occur at pre-determined intervals or as the child begins responding without the prompts. However, it is difficult to assess skill mastery prior to changing prompts, thus making decisions regarding when to remove more intrusive prompts difficult. For example, successful completion of a routine given full physical prompts does not necessarily correspond with a likelihood that the child will subsequently successfully complete the routine with gesture prompts. There is limited empirical guidance regarding replacing more intrusive prompts with less intrusive ones when using MTL. Although MTL has been shown to be effective for teaching new skills to children, research has demonstrated that CTD, PTD, or SLP might be more efficient and produce fewer errors than MTL when teaching, for example, play or leisure skills (Libby, Weiss, Bancroft, & Ahearn, 2008; Miller & Test, 1989).

Table 11.1 outlines the procedural steps for using MTL with three levels and illustrates example MTL trials for teaching a child to line up at the door during the transition to the playground. Table 11.2 provides examples of MTL prompt levels. See Chapter 8 for a comprehensive discussion of prompt types.

Table 11.2 Sample MTL Prompt Levels

Level/Session Type	Prompts		
Task Direction			
1	Gesture and Visual	Verbal and Model	Full Physical
2	Independent	Verbal	Model and Verbal
3		Independent	Verbal and Gesture
4			Independent

Potential Child Responses and Adult Reactions

When using MTL there are four total potential responses: unprompted correct responses (UPC), unprompted error responses (UPE), prompted correct responses (PC), prompted error responses (PE). The first several sessions are likely to consist of mostly PC responses. UPC responses occur after the discriminative stimulus without adult assistance. PC responses occur after a prompt. Both UPC and PC should be immediately reinforced. UPE and PE occur after the discriminative stimulus or any of the prompt levels, respectively. You can ignore errors, provide wait reminders (UPE), or provide the planned prompt level for the instructional session (UPE) or next-intrusive prompt (PE) contingent on errors.

Planning Instruction Using MTL

Prior to conducting MTL instruction, you should decide on the task direction/discriminative stimulus to be used, the types of intermediate and controlling prompt to be used, and the consequences for each type of response. You should also determine criteria for changing prompt levels and the **mastery criterion**.

- **Discriminative Stimulus:** This refers to the task direction and identifies the stimulus under which you want children to respond independently.
- **Prompt Levels:** Prompts should be selected based on their level of assistance, likelihood of leading to correct responding, and feasibility given the context and the target behavior.
  - *Controlling prompts:* The controlling prompts are described in Chapter 8. The controlling prompt should always—or most of the time—result in the target behavior.
  - *Intermediate prompts:* Intermediate prompts provide some assistance, but less assistance than the controlling prompt.
- **Consequences:** Prior to using MTL, you should decide what consequences will occur when the child responds correctly or incorrectly.
  - **Reinforce Correct Responses:** The identified reinforcer is provided contingent on prompted *and* unprompted responses.
  - **Ignore or Correct Errors:** If the child gives no responses, or errors occur during sessions with the controlling prompt, a new controlling prompt should be selected. If no responses or errors occur during sessions with an intermediate prompt you might return to an earlier level of prompting (i.e., one that provided more assistance).

The components of a trial for MTL include: (1) provision of the discriminative stimulus, (2) prompt (with more intrusive prompts provided in early sessions and less intrusive prompts provided in later sessions), and (3) response consequences. The same level of prompt is delivered throughout one session. The trial steps within the first sessions are:

1. Secure the child's attention
2. Deliver the task direction
3. Use the level 1 prompt (most assistance, controlling prompt)
4. Deliver reinforcement
5. Record data

All trials within one session use the same prompt types (i.e., level). After several sessions, as the child starts to use the skill without prompting, or based on a predetermined number of sessions, use the next, less intrusive prompt type (i.e., level). The trial steps within the next sessions are:

1. Secure the child's attention
2. Deliver the task direction
3. Use the level 2 prompt (less assistance than the controlling prompt)
4. Deliver reinforcement
5. Record data

After several sessions, depending on the planned levels, you might test the child's mastery of the skill. The trial steps are:

1. Secure the child's attention
2. Deliver the task direction
3. Do not deliver any prompts, and observe the child
4. Deliver reinforcement
5. Record data

If the child responds consistently, accurately, and independently (or meets the mastery criterion), she has mastered the skill. If the child does not consistently or accurately respond at this level return to a previous prompt level and repeat the steps.

Research Abstract

Davenport, L. A., & Johnston, S. S. (2015). Using most-to-least prompting and contingent consequences to teach numeracy in inclusive early childhood classrooms. *Topics in Early Childhood Special Education*, 34, 250–261.

In this single case design study, the authors used an MTL prompting procedure to teach numeracy and math skills to three children with disabilities in an inclusive early childhood classroom. The target skills were receptive identification (i.e., pointing to) number symbols and shapes. The most-to-least prompting procedure used a verbal task direction and progressed from a full physical prompt (i.e., hand over hand) to partial physical prompt (i.e., moving the participant's elbow toward the target) to no prompt after the task direction. The authors established a criterion for moving to the next prompt level, which was four out of five opportunities correct for three consecutive sessions. Specific praise was provided for all correct responses, and errors were verbally corrected and followed by the next higher prompt in the hierarchy until the child emitted the correct response. All three children learned their target numbers or shapes and accuracy was maintained over time after the intervention concluded.

Procedural Variations of the MTL

MTL has been used to teach a variety of skills, many of which involve motor responses. MTL can be used to teach discrete or chained skills. When using chained skills, you should identify the mastery criterion for each step before fading to a less intrusive prompt. When teaching chained skills, you might reduce intrusiveness for one step at a time, starting at the beginning (forward chaining) or end (backward chaining) of the chain—when using these variations, you would continue prompting non-targeted steps of the chain with the most intrusive prompt. Most often, you would use total task chaining—that is, you would switch from more intrusive to less intrusive prompts at the same time for all steps in the chain.

Mazie reviews several websites known to reliably present evidence-based practices, the journal associated with the professional organization she belongs to, and the textbooks she saved from her graduate program. She decides to try a most-to-least prompting procedure to teach Joseph to transition independently. She decides this might be effective given Joseph has not responded to less intrusive prompts such as visuals or peer models. She decides to start with the transition from small groups to the playground, given Joseph often requests to go outside and this transition occurs at least twice per day. She creates an instruction plan including prompt levels, reinforcement, and criterion for changing prompt levels and determining mastery; she also creates data collection sheets. She plans to use full physical prompting for at least six transitions; verbal plus visual plus gesture prompts for at least six transitions; and verbal plus visual prompts for six transitions. She also plans to measure generalization across other routines across the days.

Graduated Guidance

Graduated guidance (GG) is a prompting strategy that uses physical prompting only. GG is useful for teaching skills that need physical assistance. The research on GG is robust and supports teaching chained motor behaviors. For example, GG has been useful for teaching handwashing, toileting, transitioning, and writing. GG is not useful for teaching discrete or verbal behaviors (see Chapters 8–10). GG is similar to SLP in that you adjust the level of prompting within a session based on the child's responses. You use the amount of physical assistance needed to help the child complete the target behavior and, during each session, you make in-the-moment decisions to gradually fade the level of assistance. GG differs from other response prompting procedures because you have to make in-the-moment judgments about the type and amount of prompting needed to ensure the child performs the skill. GG requires considerable skills by the implementer, given the need for instantaneous judgments and decisions.

When using GG, the level of physical assistance provided is gradually faded within and across sessions. Initially, the child might need more intrusive assistance (e.g., full physical assistance to wash hands), but, over time, within and across sessions, the child might need less intrusive assistance (e.g., gentle touch on the wrist to start washing hands). As the child learns the skill and physical prompts are faded, you should continue to monitor and even shadow the child's behaviors and provide more assistance as needed. See Table 11.3 for a list of procedural steps for GG.

Joseph has been doing well with the MTL procedure and met the mastery criterion in nine days for the transition from small groups to the playground. He also started to generalize to other transitions and is independently transitioning from handwashing to lunch each day. However, he does not yet independently complete the handwashing routine right after coming in from the playground. Mazie remembers reading about the graduated guidance procedure when she was looking up procedures to help with his transitioning. Joseph has

Table 11.3 Procedural Steps for Using GG

Discriminative Stimulus/Task Direction	"Wash your hands before lunch"			
Physical Prompt Types	Immediately provide full physical assistance to guide the child to the sink to complete all steps for washing hands	Immediately provide full physical assistance to guide the child to the sink, but lightly guide the child's hands to turn on the water and complete the remaining steps	Immediately lightly guide the child's body to the sink. Guide the child's elbows toward the faucet to turn on the water and complete the remaining steps	Independence Shadow the child (stand behind the child) and be prepared to provide physical assistance as needed

Fading Prompts Within the Session

→

Child Behavior Response Consequences	Child washes hands "Your hands are so clean! You can sit down for lunch with your friends!"

been responsive to physical prompting so she decides to try graduated guidance to teach Joseph to independently wash his hands. She identifies several different levels of physical prompting, reinforcers, and the mastery criterion, and creates data collection sheets.

Potential Child Responses and Adult Reactions

When using GG, you must closely monitor the child's attention, behavior, and movements and immediately respond with more or less assistance. If the child begins to make an error, immediately provide more assistance. Also, all prompted and unprompted behaviors within and across steps of the chained task should be reinforced, but different types of reinforcement can be provided for completing individual steps or the entire task. For example, you might provide verbal praise for each step, and a preferred toy for completing all the steps.

Planning Instruction Using GG

When using GG, you should identify the discriminative stimulus (e.g., cue/task direction), the types of physical prompting you might use, and the consequences for all responses. You should also determine the **mastery criterion**.

- **Discriminative Stimulus:** This refers to the cue and identifies the stimulus under which you want children to respond independently.
- **Physical prompt levels:** Physical prompts should be selected based on their level of assistance, likelihood of leading to correct responding, and feasibility given the context and the target behavior. Typically, GG starts with full physical assistance for completing all steps. However, this will vary based on the child's current repertoire and the tasks. See Table 11.4 for sample GG prompt levels for one behavior.

Table 11.4 Example GG Prompt Levels

Skill	Using Visual Schedule	Handwashing	Toileting
	Deliver the Task Direction		
	Full Physical		
	Guide the child's body to the wall with the schedule and her hands to remove the appropriate cards	Guide the child's body to the sink, guide hands to turn on the faucet, and guide hands under the water. Shadow hands for remaining steps	Guide the child to the bathroom and provide a physical prompt to pull down her pants and sit on the toilet. Gently guide the child's hands to pull up pants, and walk to the sink
	Guide the child's body to the wall with the schedule and guide her elbow toward the schedule	Guide the child's body toward the sink, touch elbows and guide toward the faucet. Shadow hands for remaining steps	Guide the child to the bathroom and gently move her hands to pull down her pants and sit on the toilet. Gently guide the child's elbows as she pulls up her pants and shadow the child while she walks to the sink
	Gently guide the child's body to the wall with the schedule		Guide the child to the bathroom and shadow through the remaining steps
	Independent		
	Monitor the child's behaviors and provide assistance as needed		
Reinforcement	Reinforce the child for each step (e.g., verbal praise)		

Decreasing assistance →

- **Consequences:** Prior to using GG, you should decide what consequences to provide for completing each step and the entire task. PE and UPE will always result in increased physical assistance.

GG trials include: (1) provision of the discriminative stimulus, (2) physical prompts (with more intrusive prompts provided when needed, based on moment-to-moment instructor decisions), and (3) response consequences. Different levels of assistance are provided throughout one session; thus, decisions need to be made in the moment. The steps might include:

1. Secure the child's attention
2. Deliver the task direction
3. Provide full physical assistance for all steps within the task
4. Deliver reinforcement for each step and at task completion
5. Record data.

Within or after several sessions, as the child starts to use the skill, prompts might be faded. The trial steps might be:

1. Secure the child's attention
2. Deliver the task direction
3. Provide full physical assistance for the first step and less assistance for the remaining steps
4. Deliver reinforcement for each step and at task completion
5. Record data.

Note, however, that the steps listed above are not pre-planned—instead, they are based on a child's behaviors within the session (i.e., more success on the initial step and less success for remaining steps). After several more sessions, you might test the child's mastery of the skill. The trial steps are:

1. Secure the child's attention
2. Deliver the task direction
3. Do not deliver any physical prompts, but stand close to the child and be prepared to provide assistance if needed
4. Deliver reinforcement
5. Record data.

If the child responds consistently, accurately, and independently (or meets the mastery criterion), she has mastered the skill.

Research Abstract

Brodhead, M. T., Higbee, T. S., Pollard, J. A., Akers, J. S., & Gerencser, K. R. (2014). The use of linked activity schedules to teach children with autism to play hide-and-seek. *Journal of Applied Behavior Analysis, 47*, 645–650.

The authors designed an intervention using linked activity schedules, graduated guidance, and edible reinforcements to teach children to play a social game (i.e., hide and seek). Six children with autism who had mastered the use of individual activity schedules were grouped into dyads. Each child had their own binder with activity schedules for playing hide and seek, which were linked to their partner's activity schedule. The authors used a graduate guidance procedure with verbal prompting to teach the children to use the linked activity schedules. Baseline levels of performance were at zero for all children. All children met the mastery criterion within eight to ten intervention sessions, which was maintained during a resequencing condition when the hider and seeker locations were randomly determined; however, levels of responding returned to baseline levels when the schedules were removed.

Table 11.5 Comparison of SLP, MTL, and GG

	SLP	MTL	GG
Prompt Hierarchy	Least to most assistance	Most to least assistance	Least-to-most assistance
Types of Prompts	Any	Any	Physical
Skills	Most empirical support for using SLP with play and social skills	A range of skills, particularly skills that are brand new to the child's repertoire	Chained tasks that require physical assistance
Ease of Implementation	Requires making decisions within a session regarding prompts	Same prompt type delivered across a session. Required making decisions about prompt types between sessions	Requires making decisions within a session regarding prompts/level of assistance
Within Session Decisions	The type of prompt to use and when to deliver reinforcement	When to deliver reinforcement	The type of prompt/ level of assistance to use and when to deliver reinforcement
Across Session Decisions	If the mastery criterion has been achieved	When to use a different level of prompting and if the mastery criterion has been achieved	If the mastery criterion has been achieved
Flexibility	Types of prompts, prompt hierarchy, response intervals, and reinforcement are individually determined		
Efficiency of Learning	Not as efficient as PTD/CTD for discrete behaviors	Not as efficient as PTD/ CTD for discrete behaviors or SLP for play behaviors	
Context	Can be embedded or distributed during one-to-one instruction. Used during child and adult-directed activities	Can be embedded into small groups and one-to-one instruction. Used during adult-directed activities	Can be embedded, massed, or distributed during one-to-one instruction. Used during child and adult-directed activities

Comparing the System of Least Prompts, Most-to-Least Prompting, and Graduated Guidance

The prompt hierarchy strategies described in this chapter and Chapter 10 share many similarities. Table 11.5 provides an overview and comparison of these prompting procedures. The information can be used to make instructional decisions regarding which strategy to use for specific skills and contexts.

Mazie uses graduated guidance for several days during handwashing with Joseph. She also coaches her assistant in using graduate guidance with other children in the class who also are struggling with independent handwashing using a checklist and performance feedback. Joseph slowly started completing steps independently. After two weeks with slower than expected acquisition of the steps, Mazie decides to review the reinforcement, which currently includes verbal praise for each step and being able to sit at the lunch table. She adds two new reinforcers: a sticker and being able to pick his own chair at the table, which should result in rapid acquisition of the skill. She is thrilled to have two new strategies in her instructional tool box and looks forward to continuing to use both as her children learn new skills.

Additional Resources

https://vkc.mc.vanderbilt.edu/ebip/graduated-guidance/
https://autismpdc.fpg.unc.edu/sites/autismpdc.fpg.unc.edu/files/prompting-steps-GG-
    prep.pdf

References

Libby, M. E., Weiss, J. S., Bancroft, S., & Ahearn, W. H. (2008). A comparison of most-to-least and least-to-most prompting on the acquisition of solitary play skills. *Behavior Analysis in Practice*, 1, 37–43.

Meadan, H., Ostrosky, M. M., Santos, R. M., & Snodgrass, M. R. (2013). How can I help? Prompting procedures to support children's learning. *Young Exceptional Children*, 16, 31–39.

Miller, U. C., & Test, D. W. (1989). A comparison of constant time delay and most-to-least prompting in teaching laundry skills to students with moderate retardation. *Education and Training in Mental Retardation*, 4, 363–370.

12 Procedural Variations for Increasing Learning

Key Terms

Instructive feedback　　　　*Expansions*　　　　　*Novel instructive feedback*
Parallel instructive feedback　*Observational learning*　*Small group instruction*
Target stimulus　　　　　　*Non-target stimulus*

Chapter Objectives

After completing this chapter, readers should be able to:

- Identify instructive feedback as a procedure with the potential for improving learning outcomes, and explain procedures for using instructive feedback.
- Describe how to use small groups instruction.
- Name several important benefits of teaching children in small groups.
- Describe how teachers can improve observational learning for children who do not exhibit high rates under typical contexts.

Elizabeth is a lead classroom teacher in an inclusive classroom in a western state. She and her co-teacher, Sharice, have been struggling with designing the classroom schedule this year to ensure all children have sufficient supports. They have three children with IEPs in their classroom, three other children who are being evaluated, and eight children with typical development. They also are using a new, state-required curriculum and recently attended a three-day workshop on using the curriculum. They know they need to find more time in the day to provide systematic instruction to several children in the class including most of the children with IEPs.

Introduction

A primary goal of instruction should be to use the most effective practices related to improvements in socially valid outcomes. However, in some cases, two or more procedures might be equally effective (i.e., result in behavior change), but one might result in more efficient learning. Thus, the efficiency of instruction also should be considered when selecting teaching practices. Wolery, Ault, and Doyle (1992) conceptualized efficiency as: rapidity of learning (i.e., number of trials or total duration), generalization, emergence of relationships, broader learning, and future learning. Essentially, efficiency considers instructional efficacy and compares learning across procedures. For example, SLP might be effective for teaching a discrete skill, but PTD is equally as effective and in less time and with fewer trials (Bennett, Gast, Wolery, & Schuster, 1986). When selecting an instructional procedure, teachers should consider efficacy and efficiency. Likewise, when designing an instructional program, teachers should design instruction to facilitate efficient learning (e.g., facilitating generalization, broader learning, future learning). Increasing the efficiency of learning ensures the child learns more in less time and has a broader functional repertoire. The use of instructive feedback and observational learning, particularly in small group instructional contexts, has been found to increase the efficiency of learning for children with disabilities (Ledford, Lane, Elam, & Wolery, 2012) and will be described in the next section. Instructive feedback and observational learning provide increased learning opportunities for children with little added instructional or planning time.

Instructive Feedback

Instructive feedback (IF) is an instructional adaptation in which the teacher adds additional, incidental information—non-target stimuli—to an instructional trial. The child is not required to respond to the extra stimuli and they are not reinforced if they do respond. There are no programmed consequences for these non-target stimuli; the information is simply added to the instruction (i.e., trials). Children often acquire target and non-target stimuli, which results in more effective and efficient learning. For example, if a child is learning to name shapes (e.g., triangle, square, rectangle), the teacher might use PTD and add information regarding the beginning sound to the consequence. The trial might look like this:

Teacher: *"What shape is this?" while pointing to a picture of a square*
Teacher: *Waits the appropriate interval (e.g., 4 seconds).*
Child: *(In less than 4 seconds) "Square!"*
Teacher: *"That is right. This is a square. Square starts with the /ssss/ sound," and delivers the reinforcement.*
Child: *Repeats the /ssss/ sound, and is not reinforced.*

Instructive feedback can be provided verbally or visually. Generally, three variations of instructive feedback are used: (1) *expansions* and (2) *novel* and *(3) parallel instructive feedback* (Reichow & Reichow, 2012). **Expansions** refer to instructive feedback where the target stimulus and corresponding behavior are different than the instructive feedback stimulus and behavior, but are conceptually related. For example, you might teach a child to identify letter sounds (target stimuli) and provide instructive feedback regarding the letter name (non-target stimuli).

Teacher: *"Which letter makes the /ssss/ sound?"*
Child: *Points to the letter S.*
Teacher: *"That is right /ssss/. This is the letter S." Delivers the reinforcement.*

Novel instructive feedback is conceptually different from the target stimuli and has different responses. For example, you might teach a child to identify letter sounds (target stimuli) and provide instructive feedback on addition facts (non-target stimuli).

Teacher: *"Which letter makes the /ssss/ sound?"*
Child: *Points to the letter S.*
Teacher: *"That is right /ssss/. One plus one equals two!" Delivers the reinforcement.*

Parallel instructive feedback is conceptually different from the target stimuli but has the same responses (e.g., teach a child to identify addition facts [target stimuli] and provide instructive feedback regarding other numbers with the same result [non-target stimuli]). For example, in one study, young children were taught to read sight words that appeared on commonly occurring community signs (e.g., restroom) and were shown a graphic that depicted the sign as instructive feedback. When researchers probed whether children had learned the instructive feedback, they requested the children label the graphic signs, which required the same response as labeling the sight word (Ledford, Gast, Luscre, & Ayres, 2008).

Teacher: "What is one plus three?"
Child: "Four!"
Teacher: "That is right, four! Two plus two also equals four!" Delivers the
    reinforcement.

Importantly, instructive feedback is typically provided for every trial regardless of the child's response. The previous examples highlight how to provide instructive feedback when the child produces the correct response. The following examples illustrate how you might provide instructive feedback when the child makes an error. A trial might look like this:

Teacher: "What shape is this?" while pointing to a picture of a square.
Child: No response.
Teacher: Waits the appropriate interval (e.g., 4 seconds).
Teacher: "Square! Square starts with the /ssss/ sound. Say, square."
Child: "Square."
Teacher: Provides reinforcement.

Instructive feedback also can be provided during the antecedent or task direction. In the following example, the teacher names the color during the task direction:

Teacher: "What is the name of this <u>red</u> shape?" while pointing to a picture of a red
    square.
Child: No response.
Teacher: Waits the appropriate interval (e.g., 4 seconds).
Teacher: "Square."
Child: "Square."
Teacher: Provides reinforcement.

Across these examples, instruction is programmed such that the child learns non-target stimuli that are not directly taught and for which there are no programmed consequences. The research on elementary and high school students with disabilities indicates instructive feedback can be programmed during antecedent or consequence events for students with a range of disabilities, a variety of targets, and across contexts (e.g., Gast, Wolery, Morris, Doyle, & Meyer, 1990; Wolery et al., 1991). The research on using instructive feedback with younger children (e.g., preschool, kindergarten) with disabilities also suggests it can be effective for increasing the efficiency of instruction and should be used (Lane, Gast, Shepley, & Ledford, 2015; Ledford et al., 2008; Reichow & Wolery, 2011), but additional research is needed examining contexts under which it is most efficient and effective.

Research Abstract

Reichow, B., & Wolery, M. (2011). Comparison of progressive prompt delay with and without instructive feedback. *Journal of Applied Behavior Analysis*, 44, 327–340.

   In this single case research design, the authors taught academic skills (e.g., sight words, naming pictures) to four children with disabilities using a progressive time delay procedure with and without instructive feedback. The authors compared efficiency of learning in conditions with and without instructive feedback. During instructive feedback conditions, the research presented the instructive feedback stimulus and provided a verbal model after delivering reinforcement for all unprompted and prompted correct responses, but not for errors. The researcher did not wait for the participant to respond to the instructive feedback and provided no reinforcers for responding to the instructive feedback stimulus. All children learned target responses and instructive feedback targets. The authors concluded that the use of progressive time delay with instructive feedback was about twice as efficient as progressive time delay without instructive feedback, in terms of the number of skills learned relative to the instructional time.

Observational Learning

Observational learning is the acquisition of behaviors demonstrated by others (Bandura, 1977). Children and adults use observational learning to acquire a wide range of behaviors. For example, when faced with a new procedure for proceeding through an airport security line, most adults would efficiently learn what behaviors they should engage in by watching other adults who proceeded through the line prior to them. In early childhood settings, children who are taught different behaviors during small group instructional contexts might learn the behaviors taught to their peers. For example, if one child is taught to name shapes and another is taught to name colors, each child might learn to name both shapes and colors. Observational learning can be programmed across a variety of contexts and for a range of skills. However, observational learning requires that (a) children are imitative, (b) there are opportunities to observe peers performing and getting reinforced for the target skills, and (c) children attend to the task direction and peer behaviors (Wolery et al., 1992). Teachers can improve observational learning opportunities by ensuring children have generalized imitation skills; providing multiple and varied opportunities to attend to their peers across activities, transitions, and routines; and increasing the saliency of behaviors that should be imitated. Observational learning is particularly important in early childhood settings, as children can learn how to play, communicate, and engage in increasingly complex social interactions. Children might be more likely to imitate the behaviors of their peers—engage in observational learning—when they also observe their peers access reinforcement. Small group instructional arrangements are particularly useful for increasing observational learning (Ledford et al., 2012), which will be described in the next section.

Small Group Instructional Opportunities

Small group instruction involves using systematic prompting procedures in groups of two to four children. Small group instruction involves the use of intentional, specific instructional procedures to teach targeted skills (Ledford et al., 2012) and is not the same as grouping children for center activities or during transitions or routines. In their review of small group instruction, Ledford and colleagues (2012) identified small group instruction as an evidence-based practice for teaching discrete skills, such as reading words or answering questions, to children with disabilities. They found almost all participants learned non-target skills or skills directly taught to their peers and many learned all or most of the behaviors taught to their peers. Small groups have been used to teach a variety of academic and social behaviors to young children with and without disabilities (Lane et al., 2015; Lane, Gast, Ledford, & Shepley, 2017; Ledford & Wehby, 2015; Urlacher, Wolery, & Ledford, 2016). Small groups also have been used to teach young children to play board games (Barton et al., 2018) and imitate their peers' pretend play behaviors (Barton & Ledford, 2018).

Small groups can include children with and without disabilities, children of different ages, and children with different stimuli and instructional targets. Children who cannot yet imitate should be taught to imitate prior to engaging in small group instruction. Critical components of small group instructional opportunities include attending cues, target stimuli for each child, instructive feedback for each child, programmed opportunities for observational learning, and reinforcement. The attending cues should be child-specific and ensure the child attends to her cues and her peers' cues; this facilitates learning of other children's targets. Target stimuli also should be child-specific and based on individual or curricular goals. Instructive feedback should be programmed to ensure children acquire non-target stimuli. Opportunities for observational learning should be systematically programmed to ensure children learn their targets and their peers' targets. Both the provision of instructive feedback and observational learning opportunities improve the efficiency of instruction by increasing the number of behaviors learned without adding substantial time to instructional sessions.

Small group instructional arrangements have several advantages over one-to-one or large group instruction. Teaching in small groups might be more feasible and efficient for teachers than one-to-one instruction. Small groups allow teachers an opportunity to provide instruction to more than one child at a time, while ensuring children learn target skills. Children also learn more skills than they would in a one-to-one context, given the increased opportunities for observational learning of peers' targets. Also, small groups provide opportunities for positive social interactions and potentially learning specific social skills (Ledford & Wolery, 2013, 2015). When engaged in small groups, children also learn other important skills including how to wait for a turn, respond to delayed reinforcement, and attend to peers' instruction, which might make future learning more efficient. When adequately facilitated, children also might learn other important social skills such as their peers' names, preferences, and interests, which might increase social interactions and lead to ongoing friendships.

Elizabeth and Sharice had included two specific small group instructional contexts into the morning, which allowed them to address several of the individual and curricular goals. However, they quickly realized the groups were too large and likely needed more than just two small groups. They set up a planning meeting with the speech language pathologist, Sherrod. They met and planned how they might revise the schedule and the small groups. They discussed what was working within the small groups, which included that the children were learning some of their peers' targets and had more structured opportunities to interact with each other. This was especially important for two of the children with ASD who actively avoided their peers and rarely had positive social interactions. They redesigned the day to include several small groups with no more than two or three children They also convinced Sherrod to conduct small groups focused on language, communication, and speech in their classroom with the children on her caseload rather than pulling them out.

Research Abstract

Ledford, J. R., & Wolery, M. (2015). Observational learning of academic and social behaviors during small-group direct instruction. *Exceptional Children*, 81, 272–291.

   In this single case research design, the authors taught children with disabilities and their peers academic and social behaviors using progressive time delay and observational learning in small groups—one child with a disability and two peers. All children learned all target academic behaviors when progressive time delay was implemented in small groups. Also, children with and without disabilities learned some of their peers' academic targets, which demonstrates the efficacy of observational learning for academic skills. Peers were taught to share the tokens they received for correct responses, and children with disabilities learned to share by observing their peers' sharing behaviors. Reinforcement adaptations for sharing behaviors were needed for two children with disabilities.

Planning and Conducting Small Group Instruction

When planning and conducting small group instruction the following should be considered (see Figure 12.1 for a small group instruction procedural checklist). First, the *number of children* within the group should be determined based on their ages, the specific targets, and the context. The group composition should depend on the children's experiences with learning in groups and the larger classroom composition. The groups should be designed to ensure that efficient learning can occur within the small group and that effective instruction and supervision is feasible for the remaining children in the classroom. Second, the *target skills* for each child should be identified. Target skills should be determined based on individual and classroom goals. Children with little experience in small groups might have targets related to learning from group instruction. Otherwise, children can be taught similar or completely different skills. Importantly, at least two targets should be identified per student (i.e., intermixed trials, Ledford et al., 2012). Third, the *instructional procedures* should be identified. For example, for a small group including children who do not yet wait for a prompt, a professional might choose to use simultaneous prompting. The instructional procedures should be systematic, effective, and efficient for teaching the target skills. The child's learning history should be considered when determining the number of trials per child and per session, the order of trial presentation (i.e., the child should be able to predict when it is her turn), and the mastery criterion. Teachers should present as many trials as possible within a brief period of time. Fourth, *learning opportunities* per trial or skill should be identified for each child. This includes opportunities for observational and incidental learning (i.e., instructive feedback). These should be specifically planned and implemented as intended. Fifth, the *attending cues* should be identified for each child. Generally, individual attending cues should be used to evoke the children's attention to the target stimulus. Group attending cues (e.g., "Everyone, look at me!") indicate to all children they should attend to the target stimulus, ensuring all children are engaged, which, in turn, will likely facilitate observational learning. General attending cues are meant to draw the child's attention to the stimulus, but not to relevant features, and do not require a response other than orienting to the teacher and stimuli, whereas, specific attending cues draw the child's attention to the stimulus and relevant features and require a response. Specific attending cues might be more likely to facilitate observational learning than general attending cues (Ledford et al., 2012). Sixth, *reinforcement* should be

Table 12.1 Components of PTD Trials for Two Children Taught in a Small Group

Component	Michelle	Joe
Target Stimulus	Color names	Letter sounds
Non-target stimulus	Object labels	Letter identification
Discriminative Stimulus	Teacher question: "What color?" while holding a green ball	Teacher question: "What sound?
Pre-Prompt Response Interval	0 seconds (no wait time)	0 seconds (no wait time)
Controlling Prompt	"Green"	"/bb/"
Post-Prompt Response Interval	Teacher waits 3 seconds for child to respond	Teacher waits 3 seconds for child to respond
Child Behavior	*Child says "Green"*	*Child says "/bb/"*
Response Consequences (including instructive feedback)	Teacher says "The ball is green! Show Joe the green ball!" and gives it to the child while pointing to Joe	Teacher says "B sounds like / bb/." And gives the child two tokens. "You can share a token with Michelle!"

identified per child. Effective reinforcers should be identified based on child characteristics, feasibility within a small group context (e.g., tokens to earn time on an iPad might be more feasible than giving the child time on an iPad during small group instruction), and specific to the prompting procedures used. The consequences for student responses might include social praise alone or praise paired with a secondary (e.g., a token) tangible, or edible reinforcers. Group reinforcement contingencies also can be used within small group contexts (see Chapter 3). Reinforcement can be used to facilitate social interactions across children by teaching children to hand tokens to each other and passing out tokens to the group. Seventh, a plan for collecting data and *monitoring child progress* on all target and non-target stimuli should be identified.

Several different types of prompting procedures and instructive feedback can be implemented within small group settings. Table 12.1 illustrates how to use instructive feedback with PTD in a small group setting with two children with different targets.

Research Abstract

Barton, E. E., Pokorski, E. A., Sweeney, E. M., Velez, M., Gossett, S., Qiu, J., Flaherty, C., & Domingo, M. (2018). An empirical examination of effective practices for teaching board game play to young children. *Journal of Positive Behavior Interventions, 20,* 138–148.

The authors used an intervention package including peer modeling, the system of least prompts, and a visual schedule within small groups to teach children with or at-risk for disabilities to play three board games with their peers. Prior to starting the study, the authors used verbal and model prompts and behavior-specific praise to teach the peers to (a) play each game and (b) use specific strategies to be a good friend during the game. The system of least prompts hierarchy included a verbal task direction, "Let's play!", a gestural and verbal prompt (i.e., pointed to the visual schedule and said, "What's next?"), and model and verbal prompt as the controlling prompt. However, the controlling prompt was changed to a full physical (hand-over-hand prompt) for two participants. All children demonstrated increases in all target board game play behaviors when the intervention was introduced, generalized to a different board game, and maintained increases in target play behaviors when the intervention was withdrawn, indicating the system of least prompts was effective for teaching board game play in small groups.

Table 12.2 and Figure 12.1 illustrate how to use instructive feedback with SLP in a small group setting with two children with play targets.

Conclusion

There is robust evidence in support of using instructive feedback and small group instruction to teach academic behaviors and facilitate observational and incidental learning. Thus, small group instructional contexts should be used more often and to teach more target behaviors than one-to-one learning formats, especially when children are pulled out from their typical classroom environment. Small groups also afford multiple opportunities for facilitating and learning social skills, making them important instructional tools for early childhood contexts.

The small groups were working well. Initially, Elizabeth and Sharice had to teach some of the children how to engage and learn in small groups using peers as models. The children quickly began learning their targets as well as many of their peers' targets. Teachers also programmed specific opportunities for social interactions and found that several of the children generalized these social skills to other contexts and peers. After a few weeks they shared with parents at the fall parent–teacher conferences that children were learning many new skills and that their small group instruction was efficient and effective. Sherrod also started using more small groups in classrooms across the school rather than pulling children out of their classrooms.

Table 12.2 Components of SLP Trials for Two Children Taught in a Small Group

Component	Christine	Ford
Target Stimulus	Pretend play	Pretend play
Non-target stimulus	Play sequences	Verbalizations related to play
Task Direction	"Let's play!"	"Let's play!"
Response Interval	10 seconds	10 seconds
Intermediate Prompt	Teacher models feeding a baby and says, "My baby is hungry!"	Teacher models stacking blocks to make a tower and says, "My tower is tall!"
Response Interval	5 seconds	5 seconds
Controlling Prompt	Teacher uses full physical prompting and has the child feed a baby and says, "Your baby is hungry!"	Teacher uses full physical prompting to make a tower and says, "My tower is tall!"
Child Behavior	*Child feeds the baby the bottle*	*Child stacks the blocks*
Response Consequences (including instructive feedback)	Teacher says "Your baby was hungry. Now you can rock her!" while rocking the baby.	Teacher says "Your tower is tall too! Tall tower!"

Procedural Fidelity Checklist: Teaching Board Game Play in Small Groups

Date:	Session:	Peer:
Game:	Implementer:	PF:

Greet students	Yes No NA	Model a turn (game play priming)	Yes No NA
Game set up correctly with all materials	Yes No NA	End session after game over / timer goes off	Yes No NA
Start timer after saying "Let's play!"	Yes No NA	Session between 5 and 15 minutes	Yes No NA
Review game-specific rules	Yes No NA	Thank children for playing	Yes No NA
Review 4 steps on visual schedule	Yes No NA		

Turn	SLP				Teacher Behaviors			
	Step 1*	Step 2*	Step 3*	Step 4*	Turn Praise	Prosocial Praise	Narration	Reinforcement
1								
2								
3								
4								
5								
6								
7								
8								
9								
10								
11								
12								
13								
14								
15								

*Mark **C** (correct) or **IN** (incorrect) for implementation of SLP for each turn for child (mark correct if child completed independently and no SLP was required)
NOTE: 1 turn is equivalent to each child taking his/her turn

Figure 12.1 Example Procedural Checklist for Using SLP and Small Group Instruction to Teach Board Game Play.

Resources

Data collection sheets: https://vkc.mc.vanderbilt.edu/ebip/data-sheets/

References

Bandura, A. (1977). *Social learning theory*. Englewood Cliffs, NJ: Prentice-Hall.

Barton, E. E., & Ledford, J. R. (2018). The effects of reinforcement on peer imitation in a small group play context. *Journal of Early Intervention, 40,* 69–86.

Barton, E. E., Pokorski, E. A., Sweeney, E. M., Velez, M., Gossett, S., Qiu, J., O'Flaherty, C., & Domingo, M. (2018). An empirical examination of effective practices for teaching board game play to young children. *Journal of Positive Behavior Interventions, 20,* 138–148.

Bennett, D. L., Gast, D. L., Wolery, M., & Schuster, J. W. (1986). Time delay and system of least prompts: A comparison in teaching manual sign production. *Education and Training of the Mentally Retarded, 21,* 117–139.

Gast, D. L., Wolery, M., Morris, L. L., Doyle, P. M., & Meyer, S. (1990). Teaching sight word reading in a group instructional arrangement using constant time delay. *Exceptionality: A Special Education Journal, 1,* 81–96.

Lane, J. D., Gast, D. L., Ledford, J. R., & Shepley, C. (2017). Increasing social behaviors in young children with social-communication delays in a group arrangement in preschool. *Education and Treatment of Children, 40,* 115–144.

Lane, J. D., Gast, D. L., Shepley, C., & Ledford, J. R. (2015). Including social opportunities during small group instruction of preschool children with social-communicating delays. *Journal of Early Intervention, 37,* 3–22.

Ledford, J. R., & Wehby, J. H. (2015). Teaching children with autism in small groups with students who are at-risk for academic problems: Effects on academic and social behaviors. *Journal of Autism and Developmental Disorders, 45,* 1624–1635.

Ledford, J. R., & Wolery, M. (2013). Peer modeling of academic and social behaviors during small-group direct instruction. *Exceptional Children, 79*(4), 439–458.

Ledford, J. R., & Wolery, M. (2015). Observational learning of academic and social behaviors during small-group direct instruction. *Exceptional Children, 81,* 272–291.

Ledford, J. R., Gast, D. L., Luscre, D., & Ayres, K. M. (2008). Observational and incidental learning by children with autism during small group instruction. *Journal of Autism and Developmental Disorders, 38,* 86–103.

Ledford, J. R., Lane, J. D., Elam, K. L., & Wolery, M. (2012). Using response-prompting procedures during small-group direct instruction: Outcomes and procedural variations. *American Journal on Intellectual and Developmental Disabilities, 117,* 413–434.

Reichow, B., & Reichow, T. (2012). Evidence-based strategies for teaching children with autism spectrum disorders. In E. E. Barton & E. Harn (Eds.), *Teaching young children with autism* (pp. 127–149). Thousand Oaks, CA: Corwin & National Association for School Psychologists.

Reichow, B., & Wolery, M. (2011). Comparison of progressive prompt delay with and without instructive feedback. *Journal of Applied Behavior Analysis, 44*(2), 327–340.

Urlacher, S., Wolery, M., & Ledford, J. R. (2016). Peer modeling of commenting during small group direct instruction for academic behaviors. *Journal of Early Intervention, 38,* 24–40.

Wolery, M., Ault, M. J., & Doyle, P. M. (1992). *Teaching students with moderate and severe disabilities: Use of response prompting strategies.* White Plains, NY: Longman.

Wolery, M., Doyle, P. M., Ault, M. J., Gast, D. L., Meyer, S., & Stinson, D. (1991). Effects of presenting incidental information in consequent events on future learning. *Journal of Behavioral Education, 1*(1), 79–104.

13 Behavior Reduction Strategies

Key Terms

Challenging behavior   *Elopement*   *Disruption*
Aggression   *Property destruction*   *Self-injury*
Non-compliance   *Pyramid model*   *Contingent*
Immediate   *Satiation*   *Deprivation*
Low-probability behaviors   *High-probability behaviors*   *Premack principle*
Differential reinforcement

Chapter Objectives

After completing this chapter, readers should be able to:

- Define and give examples of several different challenging behavior topographies.
- Describe several strategies designed to prevent challenging behavior.
- Explain why functions of behavior are important.
- Provide a rationale for the use of functional behavior assessment and intervention.

Jamilah, a teaching assistant in a preschool classroom at a local childcare center, has just been transferred to a new classroom due to recent staff turnover. After her first day, she is exhausted! Although the children in this classroom are similar in age to those in her previous classroom, she feels that children in this classroom require more teaching support to engage in successful peer interactions, have more challenging behavior, and complete fewer routines independently. As she discusses the classroom differences with her co-worker, Serah, she begins to realize that many differences she attributed to the children may actually reflect differences in teaching practices. The lead classroom teacher, a first-year teacher who is new to the school, has requested feedback from Jamilah, so she begins a list of strategies she's seen other teachers use to promote engagement and independence and prevent and respond to challenging behavior.

Although the focus of this text is to provide information regarding the teaching of new behaviors, good teachers use effective instruction while also providing the supports necessary to minimize the occurrence of challenging behaviors. Effective instruction, including instruction of social and emotional skills, is one of the primary ways by which teachers can reduce challenging behaviors. The purpose of this chapter is to describe some strategies for preventing challenging behavior and responding to those behaviors when they do occur.

Challenging Behavior in Early Childhood Contexts

A significant minority of children in early childhood settings engage in **challenging behavior**; these behaviors can be defined as actions taken by children with the potential to cause harm or disrupt the engagement or learning of self or others. In addition, you might also consider challenging behavior in a school context to include any actions taken by children that are not aligned with classroom rules or expectations. Challenging behavior negatively impacts academic development for up to one-quarter of children (Conroy, Brown, & Olive, 2008; Qi & Kaiser, 2003); early intervention to prevent and reduce challenging behavior is crucial because engaging in less challenging behavior predicts academic success (Brennan, Shaw, Dishion, & Wilson, 2012). Unfortunately, responses to challenging behavior in early childhood settings often include suspension and expulsion rather than teaching and remediation, particularly for children with disabilities and children of color (U.S. DOE, 2014, 2016). As a matter of fact, preschool children are three times more likely to be suspended or expelled than school-age students. (Gilliam, 2005). Suspending and expelling children based on challenging behavior reduces their access to effective instruction, peer interactions, and opportunities to learn to engage in adaptive responses that are likely to replace challenging behaviors.

It is important to note that behaviors identified as appropriate for some time periods of early childhood are considered inappropriate (or challenging) in others. Similarly, many behaviors identified as challenging in one context are perfectly appropriate in others. For example, young children learn that crying results in feeding and diaper changes—in these contexts, crying is adaptive because it communicates to caregivers a need. As children develop more sophisticated communicative repertoires, crying becomes more inefficient than speaking (e.g., child can say "crackers," which leads to a greater likelihood of receiving the specific preferred item). Similarly, grabbing an item from a peer is an adaptive behavior for a young toddler, as it leads to access to interesting materials. As children develop, they learn that another consequence for grabbing items is that peers may cry or attempt to retrieve the toy. Given the first example, many children learn to request items and activities using words rather than crying, given a sufficient number of verbal models, but without systematic instruction. However, most children require some explicit instruction to learn to ask for a turn rather than taking a toy. Similarly, some behaviors are adaptive in some situations but not others. Children who speak loudly and run on the playground are likely to gain benefits of physical activity and have successful social interactions; when they engage in these behaviors in the classroom, it may disrupt learning. These examples exemplify two important points: (1) challenging behavior often begins as an adaptive and developmentally appropriate response to environmental conditions, and (2) teaching alternative behaviors is an important component of reducing challenging behaviors. Table 13.1 includes a list of common challenging behaviors seen in early childhood contexts.

Class-Wide and Individualized Supports

All educators should use preventative strategies, or universal instructional strategies; these are recommended practices that result in the development of nurturing relationships and supportive environments for all children. All children should have access to high-quality instruction and supports—without access to this level of supports, it is not possible to evaluate whether children may require more individualized services to promote socially meaningful behaviors. Common examples of universal instructional strategies include responsive interactions, predictable and engaging routines and activities, and use of appropriate instructional strategies throughout the school day. Some children may need additional supports to learn socially appropriate behaviors, such as social interactions with peers and age-appropriate responses to changes in the environment. Common examples include explicit social skills instructions for children who have delays in social development, and modifications of classroom activities, materials, or expectations. Finally, children who

Table 13.1 Common Types of Challenging Behaviors in Early Childhood Contexts

Behavior Type	Topographies/Definitions	Example
Elopement	Leaving a designated area without permission	Running from mother in parking lot Attempting to leave classroom while teachers lead large group activity
Disruption	Actions that reduce the ability of others to engage in activities	Loudly calling out during large group activities Throwing stuffed animals at peers while they are engaging in block building
Aggression	Activities that physically harm others, or have the potential to harm others	Hitting a teacher who said "clean up" Biting a peer who takes a toy Pushing a peer who does not leave an area after a request
Property Destruction	Actions that cause damage to materials	Ripping up art work that belongs to peers Throwing toys that results in breakage
Self-Injury	Actions that physically harm self, or have the potential to harm self	Biting own hand when excited Hitting head against table when preferred items are removed
Non-compliance	Actions following a command that are different than those instructed	Continuing to play with toys following an instruction to "put toys on shelves" Running to the opposite side of the playground when a teacher says it is time to go inside Child remains seated when the teacher asks the child to leave the table and go to circle time

engage in persistent challenging behavior will likely require an individualized intervention to learn socially meaningful behaviors and, as such, a functional behavior assessment should be conducted to develop an individualized behavior intervention plan. Table 13.2 includes scenarios that could indicate a need for individualized supports.

Preventative and Related Instructional Strategies

A number of preventative procedures and related strategies can be implemented within a session or across the day. These procedures and strategies highlight the importance of focusing attention primarily on adaptive and prosocial behaviors and less on challenging behaviors. Challenging behaviors are exactly as described, *challenging*, and require specialized attention, but focusing solely on challenging behaviors requires reactivity to stressful situations—leaving little to no time for instruction. Oftentimes, professionals might address challenging behaviors *in the moment* with the goal of promoting safety of the child, peers, and other adults and, following an occurrence, may want to reason with the child, indicate why what the child did was wrong, and so forth. Such approaches are rarely useful for addressing challenging behaviors, especially in those with the most significant need. Using preventative procedures and strategies assists with establishing and capitalizing on teachable moments throughout the day.

Plan and Teach Classroom Routines

One of the most important strategies for preventing challenging behavior in early childhood contexts is to carefully plan and teach classroom routines. Although early childhood

Table 13.2 Scenarios Indicating Need for Individualized Supports

Tier	Child	Concern	Solution
1	Jasmine	**Age:** 2.5 years **Challenging Behavior:** Peer aggression **Contexts:** When a peer is engaged with a preferred material or another child tries to take her materials	Jasmine's teacher realizes she has not explicitly modeled and prompted use of alternative strategies to gain access to preferred materials. She begins to do so during small group and center activities; she also encourages parallel play with toys while she is nearby. Jasmine begins to request toys and has started imitating peer play and interacting with other children more often.
2	Tom	**Age:** 4.5 years **Challenging Behavior:** Disruption (calling out, touching peers or their materials) **Contexts:** Large group activities	Tom's teacher has observed that he has more difficulty than his peers understanding appropriate and inappropriate social initiations. She decides to provide explicit instruction to Tom and two peers to teach them to initiate appropriately. Tom begins to use the appropriate strategies during large group activities and during free play indoors and on the playground.
3	Sarah	**Age:** 3 years **Challenging Behavior:** Elopement **Contexts:** Throughout the day	Sarah's teachers have had ongoing concerns regarding her elopement from the classroom for several months. Sarah attempts to leave the classroom unless she is playing with blocks, eating a snack, or within arm's-length of an adult. Sarah's teachers have tried several preventative strategies and have taught her to request opportunities to leave the room. However, Sarah continues to leave the classroom frequently. After conducting a functional behavior assessment, adults in her classroom begin to provide non-contingent positive attention on a frequent schedule and provide instruction to teach Sarah more complex social initiation behaviors, including requesting attention from adults and peers and commenting on her play. In the past week, Sarah has only attempted to leave the classroom one time.

classrooms commonly include multiple routines in the daily schedule (e.g., arrival, circle time, toileting, centers, mealtimes), children may be unaware how to complete behaviors that comprise routines. Thus, unclear expectations during routines may inadvertently lead to challenging behaviors. For example, during small group instruction children typically sit on a carpet in the book center, facing the teacher, followed by reinforcer selection, and waiting for a turn. A child new to the classroom is likely unfamiliar with these steps and, as such, may engage in behaviors to escape or avoid the unfamiliar activity, engage in behaviors to gain teacher or peer attention, etc. Teachers need to plan time in the daily schedule to establish and teach routines by modeling and clearly explaining expectations, providing supports until the child can complete the routine independently (e.g., prompts) or introducing supports that can remain in place throughout the day (e.g., visual activity schedule). The beginning of a school year may feel too busy to add in substantial amounts of teaching regarding expectations; however, investing time in teaching routines will decrease challenging behaviors and maximize instructional opportunities throughout the school year. Planning throughout the school day is discussed in detail in Chapter 14, but it is worth mentioning here that planning and teaching routines assist in prevention of challenging behavior in several ways: (1) It increases independence and reduces wait time for children—when children know what to do and when to do it, engagement increases. (2) It allows for professionals to plan the temporal order of activities, to ensure children get adequate access to physical activity. (3) It allows professionals to know, for each portion of the day, what their roles and responsibilities are; this can result in less time spent establishing roles in the moment and more time available to interact with children.

Establish Clear Contingencies

Promoting socially appropriate behaviors is directly related to the extent to which reinforcers are delivered immediately following each occurrence of a target behavior. When promoting socially appropriate behaviors, **contingent** (i.e., provided when behavior occurs) and **immediate** (i.e., provided in close temporal proximity) delivery of reinforcers is of paramount importance. This communicates to the child the relationship between the *antecedent* (under this condition), *behavior* (display this target behavior), and *consequence* (a pleasant consequence will follow) (Cooper, Heron, & Heward, 2007; Sulzer-Azaroff & Mayer, 1991; Umbreit, Ferro, Liaupsin, & Lane, 2007). Following this simple protocol will establish clear and context-specific expectations for all children. Additional considerations related to reinforcement procedures warrant attention.

Satiation and deprivation. Satiation refers to the extent to which a reinforcer temporarily loses its value as indicated by a decrease in a target behavior. In contrast, a child is in a state of **deprivation** when he or she has not had access to a reinforcer for a certain amount of time (e.g., Cooper et al., 2007). Changes in the immediate environment cue the child that a reinforcer is available, meaning the child *could* display a behavior and *would* likely receive access to a reinforcer. If a child is motivated for a reinforcer, the value of the reinforcer is increased and the child is likely to display behaviors that lead to accessing the reinforcer (state of deprivation). In contrast, if a child lacks motivation for a reinforcer (e.g., child had uninterrupted access to tablet games prior to small group instruction), the value of the reinforcer is lessened and the child is less likely to display behaviors that lead to accessing the reinforcer (state of satiation; e.g., child likely won't select the tablet from the reinforcer menu during small group instruction) (Cooper et al., 2007). The extent to which satiation and deprivation influence responding is dependent on each child and requires consideration when planning instruction. To reduce satiation, restrict certain reinforcers to specific activities (e.g., tablet is only available during small group instruction), provide access to varied reinforcers, provide small amounts of a reinforcer (e.g., if using edibles, providing one small piece of a cookie instead of multiple cookies), and rotate reinforcer options across sessions.

Momentum and the Premack principle. Children are less likely to engage in some behaviors compared to others (e.g., less likely to greet peers, but more likely to imitate the actions of others). Behaviors children are unlikely to engage in are referred to as **low-probability** behaviors, while those that children are more likely to engage in are referred to as **high-probability** behaviors. One method for promoting increases in low-probability behaviors is to build **behavioral momentum** by asking a child to engage in a series of high-probability behaviors (e.g., "Touch your nose," "Clap your hands," "Say, 'ball' ") immediately followed by a low-probability request ("Say, 'hi' "). High-probability requests may target behaviors that are topographically similar (e.g., task directions that produce a verbal response when targeting a low-probability verbal behavior) or dissimilar (e.g., task directions that produce a motor or verbal response when targeting low-probability verbal behavior) to the target behavior; this can vary and is dependent on the child. Some research has shown that children are more likely to engage in low-probability behaviors when requests to engage in those behaviors are followed by repeated requests for high-probability behaviors (Esch & Fryling, 2013) or to do so more quickly (Wehby & Hollohan, 2000). In addition to the high-probability requests, children may require additional supports to engage in the low-probability behavior (e.g., prompt). A reinforcer should be provided immediately following completion of the low-probability behavior (Umbreit et al., 2007). In contrast to behavioral momentum, the **Premack principle** asserts that access to a highly preferred activity will serve as a reinforcer for completing less-preferred actions or activities (Umbreit et al., 2007) Procedurally, when utilizing the Premack principle in practice, the contingency is clearly defined and the child receives access to an activity reinforcer. Both the Premack principle and the use of behavioral momentum rely on the effectiveness of reinforcement to increase desirable behaviors. Thus, the use of these strategies is essential for increasing adaptive and prosocial behaviors, and thus reducing the likelihood of challenging behavior. Table 13.3 shows applied examples of behavioral momentum and the Premack principle.

Non-contingent reinforcement. NCR refers to providing reinforcement on an interval-based schedule, while inappropriate behaviors are placed on extinction (Lane, 2006). For example, a student who typically engages in property disruption (e.g., tearing papers, breaking crayons) to obtain teacher attention might be provided with high-quality teacher attention at a high rate—more often than the student engages in the challenging behavior. This allows the child to gain access to high-quality and high-frequency reinforcement. To improve feasibility, that rate is slowly changed over time to match typical contingencies. For example, teacher attention may be provided every 5 minutes (unless property disruption was occurring at that moment). As the child is successful (decreased occurrences of property disruption), the interval is increased, with attention eventually provided every 10 minutes or on the average of every 10 minutes, which a teacher might find easier to implement. To determine how frequently NCR should be provided, first measure inter-response times (IRT)—time the duration between the offset of the challenging behavior and the onset of the next occurrence. Measure IRTs until a relatively clear IRT is established (e.g., shortest IRT is typically 15 minutes between occurrences). Begin the NCR procedure by setting a timer for the shortest IRT and provide the reinforcer at the end of the interval (Alberto & Troutman, 2012; Umbreit et al., 2007). Although it is sometimes important to systematically plan specific instances of NCR, all children should have frequent access to preferred interactions and materials, not contingent on their own behavior. One example of this is a classroom with a high rate of positive teacher attention and frequent opportunities to engage in interesting activities.

Offer Choices

One relatively simple method for promoting socially appropriate behaviors is offering choices throughout the day, especially during activities that may be difficult for some children. If there are activities the child must do, but the order is unimportant, let the child choose which activity he or she does first (e.g., Geiger, Carr, & LeBlanc, 2010). Similarly, if a child is expected to rotate through four different centers, he or she could select the order. When completing an activity is not optional (e.g., handwashing prior to lunch), you might consider giving a child a choice regarding timing (e.g., "Would you like to wash your

Table 13.3 Scenarios: Use of Behavioral Momentum and the Premack Principle

Context	Behavioral Momentum	Premack Principle
Payton, a 4-year-old child who often refuses to leave the playground	Near the end of outdoor activities, a preferred adult plays Simon Says with Payton. She gives several fun requests (e.g., do 3 frog jumps, give me a super high five) (high-probability behaviors) and then provides a request for Payton to go to an assigned "line up" area (low-probability behavior). If he does not independently do so, she provides immediate prompts to follow through.	Payton especially enjoys helping the teacher set up for lunch. She arranges the schedule such that lunch set-up occurs during the last few minutes of playground time; Payton is provided with rules and reminders that he can assist with lunch set-up if and only if he lines up within 30 seconds of the teacher direction (with 30 seconds depicted with a visual timer). He complies with the request to line up (low-probability behavior) because he gets contingent access to a preferred activity (reinforcer).
Parker, a 3-year-old child who often requires multiple reminders to clean up toys prior to large group activities	Immediately prior to the teacher cue "clean up," the paraprofessional in Parker's classroom sits with him and tells him to make silly faces by imitating her ("Do this!"). After three silly faces, she tells him to "clean up." If he does not do so, she provides immediate prompts to follow through.	Parker's teacher plans to start large group activities as soon as two peers are ready, rather than waiting until all children have come to the carpet. Before the clean up cue, she reminds Parker that she will start singing as soon as some children are ready, and that he must clean up two toys before he can join them. He cleans up more readily (low-probability behavior) because he gets faster access to high-quality teacher attention (reinforcer).

hands now or in two minutes?") or materials (e.g., "Would you like to use the stepstool or your tip toes?). Some children demonstrate lower engagement or high-frequency problem behaviors during unstructured activities such as free choice. Providing structured choices during these activities may help the child organize his or her activities. For example, you might say "It's time for centers! Would you like to go to the blocks center or house-keeping?" During teacher-directed activities, choice can be utilized by offering a choice of reinforcers prior to beginning individual or small group instruction (e.g., reinforcer menu of visuals depicting options of reinforcers).

Token Systems

A long-standing method for promoting socially appropriate behaviors is using a **token system,** or token economy, within activities or across the day. Tokens are items (of little value to children and relatively easy to administer; e.g., 2.54 cm x 2.54 cm laminated paper with a photo of a preferred character; stickers) that do not have value beyond serving as a placeholder for accessing preferred items, or backup reinforcers, after the child has earned a set number of tokens (e.g., earned 5 tokens during small group instruction; earned 10 tokens during centers) or providing an opportunity to "cash in" tokens after a set time period (e.g., at the end of centers). Some children will require frequent opportunities to earn tokens (e.g., access reinforcers every 30 minutes) while others may be content to trade in tokens for backup reinforcers once a week; this is dependent on each child's individual needs and can be modified as the child is successful.

Overarching considerations for token systems (cf. Alberto & Troutman, 2012):

1. Identify tokens.
2. Identify backup reinforcers.
3. Identify a target behavior (e.g., sharing items during centers) or generalized forms of a behavior (e.g., social communication) for which tokens will be dispensed. Tokens may be administered for each occurrence of a behavior (e.g., each discrete behavior during small group instruction) or for a response duration (e.g., receive a token for being engaged with materials for 5 minutes during play-based activities).
4. Plan the token delivery, noting that more frequent delivery of tokens and reinforcers should occur during initial learning opportunities.
5. Dispense tokens contingently and immediately following each instance of the target behavior or at the end of an interval, with a plan to thin the schedule of reinforcement; children should understand why they are receiving a token (provide descriptive praise).
6. Avoid using response cost—taking tokens away when inappropriate behaviors occur. If this method is used, children should begin with a bank of tokens—children can only lose so many tokens before this method is ineffective (e.g., child lost 5 tokens on his token board within the first 30 minutes of school and now there are no more tokens on his board).

For young children or those with moderate to severe disabilities, a token system where a child can earn a set number of tokens, which in turn provides an opportunity for the child to select a preferred item or activity from a reinforcer menu, may be more feasible than a system where reinforcers cost variable amounts and children must "cash in" based on those values.

Contracts

Contracting is a relatively simple procedure where a contingency is established by the adult and a child for purposes of promoting socially appropriate behaviors in children who display performance deficits, meaning the child *can* display the behavior but typically does not (often related to insufficient reinforcement within the environment). Contracts can be used in conjunction with a token system (e.g., child must earn 10 tokens to access the reinforcer; the adult completes or honors the contract by providing the reinforcer). A contract communicates the expectations for the child and adult, including the target behavior (number of occurrences, response duration) and reinforcement (delivered immediately; amount and time with the reinforcer). Contracts can be written using text or visual depictions of contingencies, oftentimes created in a linear manner (e.g., first, then, then; condition, behavioral expectations, consequence) (Cooper et al., 2007). Contracts can take many forms, but, regardless of form, should be fair, easily understood, and focus on the child's successes (Alberton & Troutman, 2012). For example, a professional might develop a contract with a child by determining that the child gets one minute of iPad play at the end of the day for every time he follows a teacher direction to transition to a new area or activity. Because young children have more limited verbal and cognitive skills when compared with older children, these agreements should be developed with simple and easy-to-understand rules, and should be accompanied by visual representations and as-needed verbal reminders. A first-then board is an example of a simple contract.

Differential Reinforcement

Differential reinforcement has a long-standing history in the literature. All differential reinforcement (DR) procedures include reinforcement and extinction procedures; reinforcement involves presentation of a pleasant consequence following the occurrence of a socially appropriate behavior, while extinction involves withholding reinforcement for a previously reinforced behavior or when a behavior occurs beyond acceptable levels (Umbreit et al., 2007). There are four types of DR procedures: (1) **differential reinforcement of incompatible (DRI)** or (2) **alternative behaviors (DRA)**, (3) **differential reinforcement of low-rate behaviors (DRL)**, and (4) **differential reinforcement of other behaviors (DRO)**. DRI and DRA involve reinforcing socially appropriate behaviors that are incompatible (e.g., child can be *in seat* or *out of seat*, but not both at the same time) or alternative to a challenging or non-preferred behavior. Practically and procedurally, DRI and DRA procedures are similar and, as such, will be grouped together in the following section. DRL and DRO are behavior reduction strategies that involve reinforcing the presence of a behavior at a socially appropriate rate (DRL; e.g., child continually asks questions during whole group activity; asking questions is socially appropriate, but needs to occur at a reduced rate in context) or reinforcing absence of a behavior while all *other* behaviors are essentially reinforced (DRO) (Cooper et al., 2007; Chazin & Ledford, 2016; Alberto & Troutman, 2012).

DRI/DRA. To use this procedure, professionals should identify a socially appropriate incompatible or alternative behavior and reinforce each instance of the target behavior (e.g., continuous schedule of reinforcement) or the target response duration (e.g., engaged in play activity for 5 minutes), with a plan to thin the schedule of reinforcement (e.g., fixed ratio schedule) and increase the interval (e.g., 10 minutes), as the child is successful (Chazin & Ledford, 2016). All occurrences of the socially inappropriate behavior should be put on extinction, unless there are safety issues that require immediate attention (provide minimal attention and redirect, as needed) (e.g., Wilder, Harris, Reagan, & Rasey, 2007). The DRI/DRA procedure typically leads to gradual changes in the target behavior. **Shaping** is a procedure with a rich history in the published literature for establishing alternative behaviors that are not yet in a child's repertoire. First, a terminal behavior should be selected. For example, you might want a child to request a turn rather than grabbing toys from a peer, but saying "Is it my turn now?" Once the target behavior is selected, begin by reinforcing approximations of the terminal behavior (Alberto & Troutman, 2012). Initially, it may be necessary to reinforce a far approximation of the terminal behavior that is already in the child's repertoire, followed by increasing topographical expectations over time. That is, approximations become more and more topographically similar to the terminal behavior until the child's behavior looks like the terminal behavior. For example, you might first reinforce the child holding out their hand rather than grabbing, then require the child to hold out their hand and say "my turn," and then complete the terminal target behavior of saying "Is it my turn now?" When using this procedure, systematic prompting procedures can be used to ensure the behaviors occur. Responses may be inconsistent, especially when initially increasing expectations (Umbreit et al., 2007).

DRL. To use this procedure, professionals should identify an appropriate rate at which a behavior can occur within a set time period (e.g., "You can ask two questions during circle time"; the teacher sets the timer for 10 minutes) or duration for a target behavior (e.g., "You need to try on your own for two minutes. When the timer goes off I will help you."), and communicate the expectation to the child (use clear verbal statements and visual supports, as needed). If the child meets the desired level of the target behavior within the allotted time, provide a reinforcer (Lattal & Neef, 1996). Expectations should be modified over time, as the child is successful, and until the target behavior occurs at a similar rate as same-age peers. If the child does not meet the target amount or duration, the timer should be reset and, with minimal attention, communicate to the child "we are going to try again" (avoid reprimands or focusing on lack of success during that interval) (Alberto & Troutman, 2012; Sulzer-Azaroff & Mayer, 1991). The DRL procedure typically leads to gradual changes in the target behavior.

DRO. DRO is traditionally reserved for the most challenging behaviors, such as self-injury or aggression (e.g., Mazaleski, Iwata, & Vollmer, 1993). Like NCR, first measure IRT (duration measure of the offset of the target behavior and the onset of the next behavior) and measure multiple times (e.g., Roane & DeRosa, 2014). Begin the DRO procedure by setting a timer for the shortest IRT and provide a powerful reinforcer (can be related or unrelated to the current activity) at the end of the interval—only if there were zero occurrences of the challenging behavior during the interval. It should be noted the child may display other challenging behaviors during the interval, but, as long as the target challenging behavior did not occur, all other challenging behavior should be ignored, within reason (Cooper et al., 2007). The rationale for this approach is that the target challenging behavior is so severe that it requires focused attention; other behaviors can be addressed later. If the child displays the target challenging behavior during the interval, the timer should be reset. If this issue continues, the length of the interval should be adjusted to a smaller interval (e.g., 15 minutes to 10 minutes; based on observations/data), with expectations increased over time (e.g., increased interval size). The DRO procedure typically leads to relatively rapid reduction in challenging behaviors, but the extent to which this occurs is mediated by the strength of identified reinforcers (Alberto & Troutman, 2012).

Functional Behavior Assessment and Intervention

Sometimes, challenging behavior is consistent or significant enough that individualized assessment followed by related intervention is required. Functional behavior assessment (FBA) is a process for gathering information about the child's challenging behaviors to maximize the effectiveness behavior intervention plans (BIPs). To date, the strongest evidence for addressing severe challenging behavior involves the use of FBAs to design individualized, function-based interventions (FBIs; Dunlap & Kern, 2018). FBAs can include a variety of indirect and direct assessments (e.g., interviews, questionnaires, direct observations, experimental analysis) to generate or confirm when and why a child engages in challenging behavior (Horner & Carr, 1997). FBI, Positive Behavioral Interventions and Supports, and the Pyramid Model for Promoting Social Emotional Competence and Addressing Challenging Behavior framework are complementary approaches to addressing challenging behaviors and promoting social emotional competence in young children, and have strong evidence to support their efficacy in early childhood settings (Conroy, Dunlap, Clarke, & Alter, 2005; Hemmeter, Snyder, Fox, & Algina, 2016; Dunlap & Fox, 2011; Dunlap, Lee, Joseph, & Strain, 2015).

The primary assumption underlying FBA is the understanding that the challenging behavior is serving a specific function for the individual (e.g., gaining attention, escaping a demand, getting access to a tangible item or activity). There are two overarching functions of behavior—including challenging behavior—*obtaining* or *avoiding/escaping*. FBA is a systematic process for understanding the challenging behavior and the environmental factors or events that might occasion (or precede) (i.e., antecedents) and maintain (or follow) (i.e., consequences) the challenging behavior to identify the purpose or function of the challenging behavior.

Extensive research has shown that FBIs are an effective approach for reducing challenging behaviors and increasing socially meaningful behaviors in early childhood classrooms (Reeves, Umbreit, Ferro, & Liaupsin, 2013; Wood, Ferro, Umbreit, & Liaupsin, 2011). FBIs are a result of a collaborative, assessment-based approach to developing effective, individualized interventions for those with challenging behaviors (Lucyshyn, Horner, Dunlap, Albin, & Ben, 2007). Studies that compared FBIs to interventions that are not function-based have noted distinct benefits from FBIs (Ingram, Lewis-Palmer, & Sugai, 2005).

Functional Behavior Assessment Process

Defining the Challenging Behavior

There are six major components in the FBA process. The *first component* of the FBA is describing the target child's challenging behavior(s). This includes operationalizing the form (i.e., what the behavior looks like), and documenting the frequency/rate, duration, and the intensity of this challenging behavior. It is important to be specific and precise when defining the challenging behavior. Imprecise or vague definitions of a challenging behavior might lead to differing perceptions about when the challenging behavior is most and least likely to occur, which will negatively impact the FBI. For example, "*Ronald is non-compliant and aggressive*" might seem to clearly describe the challenging behavior to one person, but can mean something completely different across people and situation. A better example might be, "*When provided with a verbal prompt to complete a non-preferred or difficult task, Ronald is unlikely to comply. When the verbal prompt is repeated and an adult provides a physical prompt, Ronald physical aggresses. He will kick with both feet, scratch, and hit with an open hand—to resist the adult's physical prompt.*" It is critical to operationally define the challenging behavior so that you know what to measure. However, FBAs are used to address the function of the challenging behavior (i.e., why the behavior is occurring or the purpose of the challenging behavior) and identify conditions that maintain the behavior—rather than the exact form of the behavior. The FBA process with young children typically involves both indirect and direct measures of the challenging behavior(s) and its contexts (Wood, Blair, & Ferro, 2009); these will be described in the next sections.

Indirect Assessments

The *second component* is indirect assessments. The primary caregivers—parents and teachers—and other professionals working with the child should be interviewed to gather information from adults who are caring for the child and present when the challenging behavior occurs. The interviews provide information regarding the adults' perception of the challenging behaviors and when they are most and least likely to occur. Interviews should be conducted with at least two different adults who are present when the challenging behavior is likely to occur. Family members should always be included in the process and interviewed if possible, even if the challenging behaviors only occur at school. Family members can provide information regarding things that are happening that might impact the child's behaviors at school (e.g., lack of sleep, health issues, new medications) and environmental factors that make the challenging behavior more or less likely to occur. These interviews can be informal, although several structured interviews exist that are recommended for use with young children.

Functional Assessment Interview Form (FAIF; O'Neill et al., 2015) is a structured interview designed to gather information about the form of the challenging behavior, antecedents and consequences to the challenging behavior (i.e., what is likely to occur right before and right after the challenging behavior), contexts under which the challenging behavior is most and least likely to occur, possible functions of the challenging behavior, the child's functional communication repertoire, and the child's preferences. The National Center for Pyramid Model Innovations (www.challengingbehavior.com) created an adapted version of the FAIF for young children: *Functional Assessment Interview Form-Young Children* (FAIF-YC). The FAIF-YC and the FAIF include the same components and the FAIF-YC includes specific sections related to the young child's play and communication skills.

Checklists and behavior rating scales are other indirect assessment tools that can be used to supplement information gathered from interviews and observations. The *Functional Assessment Screening Tool* (FAST; Iwata & DeLeon, 2005) also is an indirect functional assessment tool. The FAST is a checklist designed to gather information regarding potential maintaining consequence(s) (i.e., function) of the challenging behavior and is completed by a classroom teacher or behavior analyst. The *Motivational Assessment Scale* (Durand & Crimmins, 1992) is a checklist designed to gather information regarding contexts under which the challenging behavior is most likely to occur. Both the FAST and the MAS are checklists and can be completed directly by the respondent or in an interview format. For example, the behavior analyst might use both the FAFI-YC and the MAS in a semi-structured interview with a child's teachers and parents.

Direct Observations

The *third component* includes direct assessments and observations. Direct observations are a critically important component of the FBA; they provide objective information about the behavior and conditions under which it occurs. Teacher, parents, and other professionals who are present when the challenging behavior occurs can complete direct observations. These can be done informally, although the observations should always record what occurred immediately prior to the challenging behavior, the challenging behavior that occurred, and what occurred immediately after the challenging behavior. Observations should be conducted when the challenging behavior is most likely to occur, which can be determined through the interviews. However, it also might be useful to complete a routines or activity analysis to identify contexts or antecedents that increase the likelihood of the challenging behavior. Figures 13.1 and 13.2 provide examples of antecedent, routine, and activity checklists (Dunlap, Wilson, Strain, & Lee, 2013).

The antecedent analysis (Figure 13.1) can be used to identify specific antecedents or contexts that make the challenging behavior more or less likely to occur. The routines and activity analysis checklists provide information regarding the routines or activities, respectively, during which the challenging behavior is most and least likely to occur. In Figure 13.1 the teachers recorded the child's sleep duration the night before, which adult brought the child to school, and the child's challenging behavior (tantrums at arrival). A quick summary of the results suggests that on mornings when the child has slept fewer than 10 hours *and* the babysitter brings her to school, she is more likely to have a tantrum that lasts longer than 20 minutes. This will be important information to use in designing the BIP.

In Figure 13.2 the teachers recorded the child's challenging behavior during each daily routine. A quick summary of the results suggests that the child is most likely to engage in physical aggression during large group times and most likely to engage in non-compliance during large group times, transitions to large group, and center times. The child is least likely to engage in challenging behaviors during mealtimes and when outside. This will be important information to use in designing the BIP.

Date	Sleep Duration for previous night**	Mom or babysitter brought to school	Duration of crying during arrival transition	Summary
10/15	10	Mom	0 minutes	Slept well, mom brought to school, no crying
10/16	6	Mom	5 minutes	Slept poorly, mom brought to school, minimal crying
10/17	6	Babysitter	35 minutes	*Slept poorly, babysitter brought to school, excessive crying*
10/18	11	Mom	0 minutes	Slept well, mom brought to school, no crying
10/19	8	Mom	3 minutes	Slept poorly, mom brought to school, minimal crying
10/22	11	Babysitter	4 minutes	Slept well, babysitter brought to school, minimal crying
10/23	11	Mom	0 minutes	Slept well, mom brought to school, no crying
10/24	7	Babysitter	37 minutes	*Slept poorly, babysitter brought to school, excessive crying*
10/25	7	Babysitter	41 minutes	*Slept poorly, babysitter brought to school, excessive crying*
10/26	8	Babysitter	29 minutes	*Slept poorly, babysitter brought to school, excessive crying*

**Reported by parent or babysitter

Figure 13. 1 Antecedent Analysis.

Date : Time	Routine	Physical Aggression (tally)	Non-compliance (tally)
8:30	Arrival/Cubby	--	--
8:35	Morning Free Play	/	/
9:00	Morning Snack	--	--
9:30	Centers	--	/////
10:10	Transition to Large group	--	///
10:15	Large Group	/////	////
10:30	Outside	--	--
11:30	Lunch	--	--
12:00	Quiet Cot Time	--	--
1:15	Centers	--	/////
1:55	Transition to Large group	--	///
2:00	Large Group	///	///
2:15	Outside	--	--
3:00	Dismissal	--	--

Figure 13.2 Routine and Activity Analysis.

When the team has identified times during the day when the challenging behavior is most likely to occur, continuous Antecedent-Behavior-Consequence (A-B-C) observations should be conducted to identify the exact conditions under which challenging behavior is most likely to occur and the potential maintaining consequences for the challenging behaviors. Two general types of A-B-C observations can be conducted—general or specific.

Date/Time	Antecedent	Behavior	Consequence
10.15.2018/ 10:30 am	*Ms. Natalya verbally and physically prompted Jim to clean up the blocks.*	*Jim kept playing with the blocks, ignored the verbal prompt, and hit Ms. Natalya with the blocks >5 times when she physically prompted him.*	*Ms. Natalya put the blocks away herself, while Jim continued to play with a few of the blocks.*
10.15.2018/ 2:30 pm	*Ms. Natalya verbally and physically prompted Jim to line up to go inside.*	*Jim kept swinging and ignored her verbal prompt. When she attempted to physical prompt him to get off the swing and line up, he kicked her three times.*	*She moved away from Jim and he continued to swing.*

Figure 13.3 Example A-B-C Observation Form.

General A-B-C observations include descriptively recording what happens right before the challenging behavior, the challenging behavior, and what happens right after the challenging behavior (see Figure 13.3).

In Figure 13.3, the observer records exactly what happens before and after the challenging behavior. When using this type of A-B-C form, the observer has to be careful to record exactly what happens without judgment. Individualized forms also can be developed and used to conduct continuous A-B-C recording. Forms can be developed based on the child's challenging behavior and when it is most likely to occur, which might be more feasible and provide more objective information. Appendices 13.1, 13.2a, 13.2b, and 13.3 are examples of structured A-B-C forms created for individual children. These structured forms can be used to document exactly what is happening before and after the challenging behavior. They might make continuous A-B-C recording more feasible for classroom teachers to complete during the day and make summarizing information for a BIP easier. Relatedly, successful training and experience with structured forms may improve later use of narrative formats (Lerman, Hovanetz, Strobel, & Tetreault, 2009).

Experimental Analyses

The *fourth component* is the use of experimental analysis of functions of the challenging behaviors—functional analyses. This includes testing contexts in which the challenging behavior is most likely to occur. These are used less frequently in early childhood contexts because they require evoking the challenging behavior, which requires high level behavioral expertise and careful consideration of safety precautions. However, functional analyses directly test environmental variables that might be maintaining the challenging behaviors. They are considered more precise than A-B-C assessments as they test causal relations between environmental variables and challenging behaviors. Function-based assessment and intervention, including experimental functional analyses, when appropriate, are considered to be gold standard tertiary supports for problem behaviors (Dunlap & Fox, 2011).

Functional analysis (FA) involves the manipulation of environmental variables to assess consequent events that maintain challenging behaviors (Iwata, Dorsey, Slifer, Bauman, & Richman, 1982). Traditional FAs are conducted in the context of multi-element single case research designs by which the frequency or duration of challenging behaviors across different environmental conditions are compared. These conditions are designed to temporarily increase challenging behavior. Specific functions—obtaining or avoiding/escaping—are tested and compared across different conditions: tangible, attention, escape demands, and control (play). A robust literature supports the use of functional analysis to identify maintaining consequences of challenging behaviors. FAs provide a quantitative direct observation and test of the function of challenging behaviors. They confirm information obtained during the descriptive FBA components and help to isolate the specific environmental variables that are likely to be maintaining the challenging behaviors.

In most cases, the results will show clear differentiation of one or two conditions. That is, if challenging behavior occurs only during the attention condition, the challenging behavior is likely maintained by adult attention and the BIP should be developed to address this (see Figure 13.4). However, in some cases, the challenging behavior might occur during both the attention and demand conditions in which case the challenging behavior is likely maintained by both adult attention and escaping demands, and the BIP will have to address both functions. Where there is not clear differentiation in the results, or challenging behavior occurs across conditions at similar rates, the challenging behavior might be automatically rather than socially or environmentally mediated. Automatically maintained behaviors can present in many different forms (e.g., aggression, self-injurious behaviors), what makes them automatically maintained is the fact that environmental consequences do not impact them. Although the specific conditions tested during FA are based on the descriptive data collected, the following conditions listed in Table 13.4 are often included.

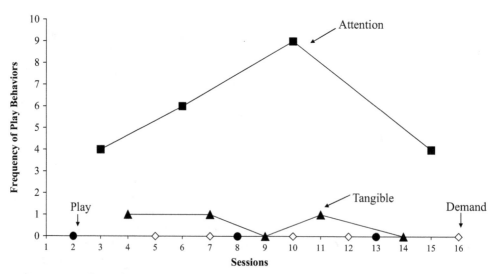

Figure 13.4 Traditional FA Graph.

Note: This graph depicts the results of a traditional FA conducted in a multi-element single case research design. The closed squares are from the attention condition. Closed triangles are from the tangible condition. Closed circles are from the play (control condition). Open diamonds are from the demand condition.

Table 13.4 Common FA Conditions for Young Children

Condition	Description	Purpose	Consequence for Challenging Behavior
Play	There are no demands and continuous adult attention	Typically used as a control condition	No consequence
Tangible	There are no demands, preferred items are withheld	Used to test if access to tangibles (e.g., toys, iPad) is maintaining the challenging behavior	Access to tangible items (Preferred items should be identified prior to conducting the FA and used during this condition)
Attention	There are no demands, adult attention is withheld. The child can play with moderately preferred items	Used to test if access to adult attention is maintaining the challenging behavior	Adult attention (Adult attention can be in the form of a redirection, "Sit in your chair and put your arms on the table" and should mimic what typically occurs)
Demand	Demands are provided at regular intervals	Used to test if delaying or avoid demands are maintaining the challenging behavior	The demand is temporarily removed

The *trial-based FA* (TFA) was developed as a less resource-demanding assessment to determine the function of problem behavior, and has been shown to be nearly as effective as the traditional FA (Bloom, Iwata, Fritz, Roscoe, & Carreau, 2011). TFAs can be completed during regular activities in typical settings (Lambert, Bloom, Kunnavatana, Collins, & Clay, 2013; LaRue, Lenard, Weiss, Bamond, Palmieri, & Kelley, 2010). Also, TFAs are typically latency-based, which means children have only a single opportunity to engage in challenging behavior per trial segment (Bloom, Lambert, Dayton, & Samaha, 2013). This reduces the duration of time children engage in challenging behavior, which is particularly useful for children with severe challenging behavior (Bloom et al., 2011; LaRue et al., 2010). TFAs have been conducted in early childhood settings by early childhood practitioners (Lambert, Bloom, & Irvin, 2012; Rispoli, Burke, Hatton, Ninci, Zaini, & Sanchez, 2015). TFA procedures consist of a series of probes, which can be embedded into ongoing classroom activities. Each trial includes a brief (e.g., 1 or 2 minute) segment during which a specific contingency for the challenging behavior is established (test), followed by a segment during which the reinforcer is available continuously (control). Segments are terminated if and when challenging behavior occurs. For example, during demand trials, tasks are presented during the test segment and terminated if challenging behavior occurs, whereas no tasks are presented during the control segment. Likewise, during attention trials, the child might be provided with a moderately preferred toy, and no adult attention during the test segment. When challenging behavior occurs, the adult provides attention, and the test segment ends. During the control segment, the child is given the same moderately preferred toy, and continuous adult attention.

Structural analysis (SA) is similar to FA except that it is used to test antecedent events that might increase the likelihood of the challenging behavior. SAs involve the manipulation of environmental stimuli to assess antecedent events that occasion aberrant responses

(Wheeler, Carter, Mayton, & Thomas, 2002). They have been used to test the likelihood of challenging behavior across choice versus no choice conditions (Dunlap, Kern-Dunlap, Clarke & Robbins, 1991), teacher versus student choice conditions (Vaughn & Horner, 1997), and different types of tasks (Butler & Luiselli, 2007).

FA and SA have several advantages over descriptive FBA. Specifically, they can demonstrate a causal relation and predict maintaining variables, can be conducted in a short time, and might improve staff understanding of maintaining reinforcers. However, they also require the supervision of a trained behavior analyst, and can be difficult to conduct in early childhood environments. Given they also temporarily evoke the challenging behavior, early childhood staff and parents might be resistant to using them. In addition, there a number of variations of FAs, and each should be considered when developing procedures for FA.

Hypothesis Statements

The *fifth component* is generating hypothesis statements regarding the challenging behavior. The hypothesis statement is a "best guess" about the function of the behavior or why the behavior is occurring (i.e., to obtain or to escape/avoid; Crone, Hawken, & Horner, 2015; Dunlap et al., 2015). In general, the function of the challenging behavior is determined by summarizing information regarding the typical antecedents and consequences of the challenging behaviors and examining the outcomes of the experimental analyses, if conducted. The hypothesis statement is used to design an intervention (FBI) directly matched to the function of challenging behavior, and often focuses on teaching and reinforcing appropriate behaviors that serve the same function as the challenging behavior. The goal of the hypothesis statement is to identify specific, concrete circumstances under which the challenging behavior is likely to occur. The format is usually: Context, challenging behavior, and consequence. The following are example hypothesis statements.

> **Example Hypothesis #1:** John engages in physical aggression and non-compliance during large group activities and transitions inside from the outdoor playground. When this occurs during large group activities, the teachers ask John to leave the large group activity. When this occurs during the transition inside, the teacher repeatedly tells John to line up, which delays the transition inside. This indicates that John engages in physical aggression and non-compliance to avoid large group activities and delay the transition inside.

> **Example Hypothesis #2:** Across the day, Margot engages in self-injurious behavior (i.e., banging head against hard surfaces or using hands to hit head with a closed fist) and excessive crying in the absence of adult attention. When she is provided adult attention or a preferred toy, she stops engaging in SIB and crying. This indicates that Margot engages in self-injurious behaviors and excessive crying to access adult attention and preferred toys.

Behavior Intervention Plan

The *sixth component* is creating the BIP, which will include prevention practices, practices to teach replacement skills, and new responses to the challenging behaviors that make the challenging behavior ineffective, inefficient, and irrelevant. The BIP should outline the specific function-based intervention practices teachers should use to address the target child's challenging behavior while teaching replacement skills. Effective BIPs include intentional, systematic practices for preventing challenging behaviors *and* teaching the child new skills or promoting skills in the child's repertoire that he or she can do but typically does not display (based on the results of the FBA). The BIP should include three types of strategies: prevention strategies to make the challenging behavior less likely to occur, strategies to teach replacement skills, and new responses to the challenging behavior to make the challenging behavior ineffective.

Prevention strategies. Prevention strategies (discussed previously in this chapter) should be used across the day to make events and interactions that might occasion the challenging behavior easier for the child to manage. For example, for escape-maintained (i.e., to avoid demands) challenging behaviors, you might modify the expectations, review the contingency, provide choices or preferred activities after a more difficult or non-preferred activity, teach the child when they can request a break, and use visual supports to review when the child has access to reinforcers. For challenging behaviors that are maintained by access to adult attention or tangible items, you might give the child non-contingent reinforcement in the form of teacher attention throughout the day on a regular schedule, provide regular and predictable access to adult attention or the preferred tangible items, and use visual supports to review when the child has access to adult attention or preferred tangibles.

Teaching replacement skills. The BIP also should include specific strategies for teaching the child a new socially and developmentally appropriate skill that (a) replaces the challenging behavior and (b) serves the same function as the challenging behavior. Some children may display what is known as a performance deficit, meaning they have a socially and developmentally appropriate behavior in their repertoire, but require additional modifications to the environment (e.g., dense schedule reinforcement for replacement behavior) to promote increased use of the behavior under the same conditions as the challenging behavior. Regardless of type, the replacement skill should be more effective and efficient than the challenging behavior in regards to accessing reinforcement and should be based on the child's current repertoire.

One of the most common strategies for promoting replacement skills is **functional communication training** (FCT). FCT is a procedure to teach children how to appropriately access reinforcers and simultaneously reduce socially inappropriate behaviors (Cooper et al., 2007). Children are taught to request attention from an adult or peer, a break from an activity, leave an activity early, etc. The targeted behaviors serve the same function as the socially inappropriate behaviors (e.g., teach child to request a break instead of throwing materials, which previously led to a break). Initially, the adult should arrange an opportunity for the child to display the socially appropriate behavior (antecedent that typically cues the challenging behavior) and immediately prompt the child to display the target behavior. For example, a teacher might encounter a child who uses visuals to communicate and understands conventional gestures but who also engages in screaming and crying behaviors when presented with difficult tasks. In this case, the adult could present a difficult task and immediately gesture to the visual that indicates, "Help." Then, the adult would immediately provide the child with assistance completing a difficult or non-preferred task) (Braithwaite & Richdale, 2000). The adult can then delay the prompt in time, as well as increase expectations (e.g., provided a break following each request, followed by a break after 2 minutes, 5 minutes, until reaching 10 minutes) until the child's behavior is similar to same-age peers in the same context.

New responses. New responses to the challenging behavior ensure that the challenging behavior is not maintained and the new skill is learned. Adults should respond to the challenging behavior in a way that makes the challenging behavior ineffective. In other words,

Table 13.5 Examples of New Responses to Challenging Behaviors

Response	Function Addressed	Description
Avoid providing attention	Attention*	Provide minimal to no attention to the challenging behavior, while ensuring the child's safety
Provide an immediate, clear redirection	Demand	Provide a clear redirection stating exactly what the child should or might do. State the redirection only one time with minimal attention
Reinforce the nearest child who is engaging in the appropriate behaviour	Attention	Provide attention and behavior-specific praise to children engaged in the appropriate behaviors
Attend to the other child	Attention, Tangible	If the challenging behavior was physical aggression, provide immediate attention to the child who was hurt. The challenging behavior was taking a toy from a peer, give the preferred tangible back to the peer

*This strategy should be used for all challenging behavior to avoid establishing attention as a secondary reinforcer.

the challenging behavior should no longer serve the same function and is put on extinction. Table 13.5 provides some examples of new ways to respond to challenging behaviors when working with young children.

Implementing and Monitoring the Behavior Intervention Plan

The *seventh component* is implementing and monitoring the BIP. Chapter 5 provides specific strategies for monitoring behavior change over time. Successful BIP are comprehensive and implemented with fidelity across settings and adults. Chapters 15 and 16 provide specific strategies for coaching others to implement the BIP. The BIP will require coordinated and consistent support from all adults in the child's life. The BIP should be implemented consistently for several days before changes to the BIP are made. Changes might be needed as the child learns more complex skills, as the environment changes, or if new challenging behaviors emerge.

Conclusion

Given appropriate supports and effective instruction, some young children are still likely to engage in challenging behavior. These behaviors are not unexpected, but may make it more difficult for teachers to focus on engaging in positive interactions and effective instruction with children. Professionals should consider the extent to which universal preventative practices have been implemented, and should consider more intensive supports when needed.

After the first week of work, Jamilah brings a list of strategies to her regularly scheduled planning time with the lead classroom teacher. Jamilah, along with her previous lead teacher, wrote down several strategies that they used to prevent challenging behavior, including: (1) using and teaching routines, (2) providing frequent positive feedback to children engaging in appropriate behavior, and (3) carefully scheduling outdoor activities such that children had a sufficient amount of physical activity. She also shared with her new teacher their strategy of providing minimal attention to minor behavioral infractions and only giving a command when they were willing and available to follow through. Jamilah's new lead teacher is very receptive to these ideas, and they draft a policy that ensures adults in the classroom are applying the newly planned preventative and consequence-based strategies. Over the next few weeks, Jamilah's data collection suggests that the number of instances of challenging behavior is consistently decreasing.

References

Alberto, P. A., & Troutman, A. C. (2012). *Applied behavior analysis for teachers* (9th ed.). Upper Saddle River, NJ: Pearson.

Bloom, S. E., Iwata, B. A., Fritz, J. N., Roscoe, E. M., & Carreau, A. B. (2011). Classroom application of a trial-based functional analysis. *Journal of Applied Behavior Analysis*, 44, 19–31.

Bloom, S. E., Lambert, J. M., Dayton, E., & Samaha, A. L. (2013). Teacher-conducted trial-based functional analyses as the basis for intervention. *Journal of Applied Behavior Analysis*, 46, 208–218.

Braithwaite, K. L., & Richdale, A. L. (2000). Functional communication training to replace challenging behaviors across two behavioral outcomes. *Behavioral Interventions*, 15, 21–36.

Brennan, L. M., Shaw, D. S., Dishion, T. J., & Wilson, M. (2012). Longitudinal predictors of school-age academic achievement: Unique contributions of toddler-age aggression, oppositionality, inattention, and hyperactivity. *Journal of Abnormal Child Psychology*, 40, 1289–1300.

Butler, L. R., & Luiselli, J. K. (2007). Escape-maintained problem behavior in a child with autism: Antecedent functional analysis and intervention evaluation of noncontingent escape and instructional fading. *Journal of Positive Behavior Interventions*, 9, 195–202.

Chazin, K. T., & Ledford, J. R. (2016). Differential reinforcement. In *Evidence-based instructional practices for young children with autism and other disabilities*. Retrieved from http://vkc.mc.vanderbilt.edu/ebip/differential-reinforcement.

Conroy, M. A., Brown, W. H., & Olive, M. L. (2008). Social competence interventions for young children with challenging behavior. In W. H. Brown, S. L. Odom, & S. R. McConnell (Eds.), *Social competence of young children: Risk, disability, and intervention* (pp. 205–232). Baltimore, MD: Brookes.

Conroy, M. A., Dunlap, G., Clarke, S., & Alter, P. J. (2005). A descriptive analysis of positive behavioral intervention research with young children with challenging behavior. *Topics in Early Childhood Special Education*, 25, 157–166.

Cooper, J. O., Heron, T. E., & Heward, W. L. (2007). *Applied behavior analysis* (2nd ed.). Columbus, OH: Pearson.

Crone, D. A., Hawken, L. S., & Horner, R. H. (2015). *Building positive behavior support systems in schools: Functional behavioral assessment*. New York: Guilford Publications.

Dunlap, G., & Kern, L. (2018). Perspectives on functional (behavioral) assessment. *Behavioral Disorders*, 43, 316–321.

Dunlap, G., Lee, J. K., Joseph, J. D., & Strain, P. (2015). A model for increasing the fidelity and effectiveness of interventions for challenging behaviors: Prevent–teach–reinforce for young children. *Infants & Young Children*, 28, 3–17.

Dunlap, G., Wilson, K., Strain, P. S., & Lee, J. K. (2013). *Prevent-teach-reinforce for young children: The early childhood model of individualized positive behavior support*. Baltimore, MD: Brookes.Durand, V. M., & Crimmins, D. B. (1992). *The Motivation Assessment Scale (MAS) administration guide*. Topeka, KS: Monaco and Associates.

Dunlap, G., & Fox, L. (2011). Function-based interventions for children with challenging behavior. *Journal of Early Intervention*, 33, 333–343.

Dunlap, G., Kern-Dunlap, L., Clarke, S., & Robbins, F. R. (1991). Functional assessment, curricular revision, and severe behavior problems. *Journal of Applied Behavior Analysis*, 24, 387–397.

Esch, K., & Fryling, M. J. (2013). A comparison of two variations of the high-probability instructional sequence with a child with autism. *Education and Treatment of Children*, 36, 61–72.

Geiger, K. B., Carr, J. E., & LeBlanc, L. A. (2010). Function-based treatments for escape-maintained problem behavior: A treatment-selection model for practicing behavior analysts. *Behavior Analysis in Practice*, 3, 22–32.

Gilliam, W. S. (2005). *Prekindergarteners left behind: Expulsion rates in state prekindergarten systems*. New Haven, CT: Yale University Child Study Center.

Hemmeter, M. L., Snyder, P., Fox, L., & Algina, J. (2016). The efficacy of the Pyramid Model: Effects on teachers, classrooms and children. *Topics in Early Childhood Special Education*, 36, 133–146.

Horner, R. H., & Carr, E. G. (1997). Behavioral support for students with severe disabilities: Functional assessment and comprehensive intervention. *The Journal of Special Education*, 31, 84–104.

Ingram, K., Lewis-Palmer, T., & Sugai, G. (2005). Function-based intervention planning: Comparing the effectiveness of FBA function-based and non—function-based intervention plans. *Journal of Positive Behavior Interventions*, 7, 224–236.

Iwata, B., & DeLeon, I. (2005). *The functional analysis screening tool*. Gainesville, FL: The Florida Center on Self-Injury, University of Florida.

Iwata, B. A., Dorsey, M. F., Slifer, K. J., Bauman, K. E., & Richman, G. S. (1982). Toward a functional analysis of self-injury. *Analysis and Intervention in Developmental Disabilities*, 2(1), 3–20.

Lambert, J. M., Bloom, S. E., Irvin, J. (2012). Trial-based functional analysis and functional communication training in an early childhood setting. *Journal of Applied Behavior Analysis*, 45, 579–584.

Lambert, J. M., Bloom, S. E., Kunnavatana, S. S., Collins, S. D., & Clay, C. J. (2013). Training residential staff to conduct trial-based functional analyses. *Journal of Applied Behavior Analysis*, 46, 296–300.

Lane, K. (2006). *Increasing behavior Part II: Implementing reinforcement effective group and peer reinforcement plans*. Unpublished presentation. SPED 3210. Vanderbilt University.

LaRue, R. H., Lenard, K., Weiss, M. J., Bamond, M., Palmieri, M., Kelley, M. E. (2010). Comparison of traditional and trial-based methodologies for conducting functional analyses. *Research in Developmental Disabilities*, 31, 480–487.

Lattal, K. A., & Neef, N. A. (1996). Recent reinforcement-schedule research and applied behavior analysis. *Journal of Applied Behavior Analysis*, 29, 213–230.

Lerman, D. C., Hovanetz, A., Strobel, M., & Tetreault, A. (2009). Accuracy of teacher-collected descriptive analysis data: A comparison of narrative and structured recording formats. *Journal of Behavioral Education*, 18, 157–172.

Lucyshyn, J. M., Albin, R. W., Horner, R. H., Mann, J. C., Mann, J. A., & Wadsworth, G. (2007). Family implementation of positive behavior support for a child with autism: Longitudinal, single-case, experimental, and descriptive replication and extension. *Journal of Positive Behavior Interventions*, 9, 131–150.

Mazaleski, J. L., Iwata, B. A., & Vollmer, T. R. (1993). Analysis of the reinforcement and extinction components in DRO contingencies with self-injury. *Journal of Applied Behavior Analysis*, 26, 143–156.

O'Neill, R. E., Albin, R. W., Storey, K., Horner, R. H., & Sprague, J. R. (2015). *Functional assessment and program development*. Ontario: Nelson Education.

Qi, C. H., & Kaiser, A. P. (2003). Behavior problems of preschool children from low-income families: Review of the literature. *Topics in Early Childhood Special Education*, 23, 188–216.

Reeves, L. M., Umbreit, J., Ferro, J. B., & Liaupsin, C. J. (2013). Function-based intervention to support the inclusion of students with autism. *Education and Training in Autism and Developmental Disabilities*, 48, 379–391.

Rispoli, M., Burke, M., Hatton, H., Ninci, J., Zaini, S., Sanchez, L. (2015). Training Head Start teachers to conduct trial-based functional analysis of challenging behavior. *Journal of Positive Behavior Interventions*, 17, 1–10.

Roane, H. S., & DeRosa, N. M. (2014). Reduction of emergent dropping behavior during treatment of elopement. *Journal of Applied Behavior Analysis*, 47, 633–638.

Sulzer-Azaroff, B., & Mayer, G. R. (1991). *Behavior analysis for lasting change*. New York: Holt, Rinehart & Winston.

Umbreit, J., Ferro, J., Liaupsin, C., & Lane, K. (2007). *Functional behavioral assessment and function-based intervention: An effective practical approach*. Upper Saddle River, NJ: Prentice-Hall.

U.S. Department of Education Office for Civil Rights. (2014, March). Civil Rights Data Collection: Data Snapshot (School Discipline). Retrieved from www2.ed.gov/about/offices/list/ocr/whatsnew.html#2014

U.S. Department of Education Office for Civil Rights (2016). Data Snapshot: Early Childhood Education. Retrieved from www2.ed.gov/about/offices/list/ocr/docs/crdc-early-learning- snapshot.pdf.

Vaughn, B. J., & Horner, R. H. (1997). Identifying instructional tasks that occasion problem behaviors and assessing the effects of student versus teacher choice among these tasks. *Journal of Applied Behavior Analysis*, 30, 299–312.

Wehby, J. H., & Hollahan, M. S. (2000). Effects of high-probability requests on the latency to initiate academic tasks. *Journal of Applied Behavior Analysis*, 33, 259–262.

Wheeler, J. J., Carter, S. L., Mayton, M. R., & Thomas, R. A. (2002). Structural analysis of instructional variables and their effects on task-engagement and self-aggression. *Education and Training in Mental Retardation and Developmental Disabilities*, 37, 391–398.

Wilder, D. A., Harris, C., Reagan, R., & Rasey, A. (2007). Functional analysis and treatment of noncompliance by preschool children. *Journal of Applied Behavior Analysis*, 40, 173–177.

Wood, B. K., Ferro, J. B., Umbreit, J., & Liaupsin, C. J. (2011). Addressing the challenging behavior of young children through systematic function-based intervention. *Topics in Early Childhood Special Education*, 30, 221–232.

Wood, B. K., Blair, K. S., & Ferro, J. B. (2009). Young children with challenging behavior: Function-based assessment and intervention. *Topics in Early Childhood Special Education*, 29, 68–78.

Appendix 13.1

Structured A-B-C for a child with pica

ABC Data Sheet

Directions: Complete each column following an occurrence of disruptive behavior with the date, time and your initials. In the antecedent column, record the location, people he's interacting with, and check/specify what was happening prior to the behavior. Next, tell us more about the behavior by circling or describing the behavior that occurred and making notes about special circumstances and length/severity. When the behavior has stopped for 30 seconds, the episode is considered complete and data for the subsequent instance should be taken in the next row of boxes. Complete the consequence column by indicating what happened immediately following the behavior.

Target Behavior: Pica is defined as bringing any inedible object into contact with the mouth which breaks the plane of the lips. Objects or substances included may be later taken out of mouth or swallowed. This does not include food during meal times or the "chewy."

Date & Initials	Antecedent (what happened before)	Behavior Description (child's actions)	Behavior Notes (length, severity, comments)	Consequence (what happened immediately after)	Additional Comments

Date:
 	
Time:
 	
Initials:
	Location:
	
	Interacting with: Teacher Peer Other
	☐ **Desired item/activity**: *requested withheld taken*
	  specify
	☐ **Transition**: from _____ to _____
	☐ **Diverting your Attention**: looking/walking away talking to someone else *specify*
	☐ **Directions Given**: *specify*
	☐ **Other**: *specify*
		Pica
		
		Object/Substance:
		_____
				☐ **Escape From**: *directions/task setting social interaction transition*
				☐ **Tangible/Activity**: *given taken-away*
				  specify
				☐ **Attention**: *verbal physical proximity none*
				☐ **Other** *specify* _____	

Date:
 	
Time:
 	
Initials:
	Location:
	
	Interacting with: Teacher Peer Other
	☐ **Desired item/activity**: *requested withheld taken*
	  specify
	☐ **Transition**: from _____ to _____
	☐ **Diverting your Attention**: looking/walking away talking to someone else *specify*
	☐ **Directions Given**: *specify*
	☐ **Other**: *specify*
		Pica
		
		Object/Substance:
		_____
				☐ **Escape From**: *directions/task setting social interaction transition*
				☐ **Tangible/Activity**: *given taken-away*
				  specify
				☐ **Attention**: *verbal physical proximity none*
				☐ **Other** *specify* _____	

Date:
 	
Time:
 	
Initials:
	Location:
	
	Interacting with: Teacher Peer Other
	☐ **Desired item/activity**: *requested withheld taken*
	  specify
	☐ **Transition**: from _____ to _____
	☐ **Diverting your Attention**: looking/walking away talking to someone else *specify*
	☐ **Directions Given**: *specify*
	☐ **Other**: *specify*
		Pica
		
		Object/Substance:
		_____
				☐ **Escape From**: *directions/task setting social interaction transition*
				☐ **Tangible/Activity**: *given taken-away*
				  specify
				☐ **Attention**: *verbal physical proximity none*
				☐ **Other** *specify* _____	

Appendix 13.2a and b

Structured A-B-C for a child with multiple challenging behaviors

ABC Data Collection

Student: *P. T.*　　　　　　　　Date:　　　　　Observer:
　　　　　　　　　　　　　　　　Time:

Behavior 1: Non-compliance refers to not following established classroom procedures (e.g., remaining on dot during circle time) or not
Behavior 2: Aggressive behavior refers to intentional, forceful hitting, kicking, or throwing of objects directed at the body of an adult or peer
Behavior 3: Property destruction refers to intentionally knocking over or throwing objects, or forcefully hitting or kicking objects with his body

Occurrence	Time/ Activity	Adult Present	Task demand or prompt	Non-preferred activity	No access to preferred	Receiving attention	Receiving little/no	Provoked by peer	Transition	Other	Behavior	Work removed/ delayed	Accessed preferred	Reprimand or redirect	Peer attention	Ignored	Other
						Antecedent *What happened before the behavior?*					Behavior				Consequence *What happened after the behavior?*		
Behavior 1 Totals			0	0	0	0	0	0	0	0	0	0	0	0	0	0	0
Behavior 2 Totals			0	0	0	0	0	0	0	0	0	0	0	0	0	0	0
Behavior 3 Totals			0	0	0	0	0	0	0	0	0	0	0	0	0	0	0

Using the information above, what is your best guess as to why the behavior occurs?

When this occurs... (list triggers)	Student displays this... (name problem behavior)	In order to.. (select all that apply)	
		Access/Get	Avoid/Escape
		Access/Get	Avoid/Escape
		Access/Get	Avoid/Escape

Notes:

Appendix 13.3

Structured A-B-C for a child with multiple challenging behaviors across several activities

Date	Time	Antecedent	Behavior	Consequence
		□Choice □Redirection □New Task □Routine □Peer prompt □Told "no" □Instruction/Directive □Other _____	□Physical Aggression □Property Destruction □Non-compliance □Other _____	□Adult Attention □Peer Attention □Redirection □Changed Activity □Removed Demand □Physical Prompt □Quiet Area □Other _____
		□Choice □Redirection □New Task □Routine □Peer prompt □Told "no" □Instruction/Directive □Other _____	□Physical Aggression □Property Destruction □Non-compliance □Other _____	□Adult Attention □Peer Attention □Redirection □Changed Activity □Removed Demand □Physical Prompt □Quiet Area □Other _____
		□Choice □Redirection □New Task □Routine □Peer prompt □Told "no" □Instruction/Directive □Other _____	□Physical Aggression □Property Destruction □Non-compliance □Other _____	□Adult Attention □Peer Attention □Redirection □Changed Activity □Removed Demand □Physical Prompt □Quiet Area □Other _____
		□Choice □Redirection □New Task □Routine □Peer prompt □Told "no" □Instruction/Directive □Other _____	□Physical Aggression □Property Destruction □Non-compliance □Other _____	□Adult Attention □Peer Attention □Redirection □Changed Activity □Removed Demand □Physical Prompt □Quiet Area □Other _____

14 Teaching throughout the School Day

Key Terms

Routines   *Activities*   *Transitions*
Universal   *Targeted*   *Individualized*
Objective-by-strategy matrix   *Objective-by-activity matrix*   *Activity-by-instructor matrix*

Chapter Objectives

After completing this chapter, readers should be able to:

- Identify important components of a young child's day.
- Plan instruction across typical routines, activities, and transitions.
- Develop a developmentally appropriate classroom schedule that maximizes learning opportunities and appropriately utilizes adult resources.

Jessie is an experienced preschool teacher who was recently moved to open a new classroom in a local public elementary school. She has carefully planned her schedule using a system she has used many times before. She has included typical routines and activities and minimized the number of transitions. However, this year she is in a new school and has little information about the students who will be in her class. She anticipates that she will have to make a few adjustments. She has ten children with typical development and eight children with IEPs. She reviews the IEP goals, and makes a draft classroom schedule with a plan for when to teach each IEP goal. However, she is concerned about making sure children have sufficient learning opportunities across the day. She also knows how important it will be to teach children the schedule during the first few weeks of school to facilitate their independence with the routines, activities, and transitions.

This chapter will provide guidance on the use of previously discussed methods using a comprehensive plan focused on teaching across contexts (e.g., across routines, activities, and transitions throughout the day) that includes developmentally appropriate activities and explicit teaching of classroom expectations. This chapter will include practical suggestions for each common context (e.g., circle time), including typical difficulties and suggested solutions.

Rationale for Teaching Across Multiple Routines, Activities, and Transitions

Young children acquire new skills in many different ways, but we know they learn best when instruction is systematic, engaging, and developmentally appropriate, when sufficient numbers of learning trials are delivered, and when generalization and maintenance are intentionally facilitated. Further, experts in early childhood (NAEYC, 2009) and early childhood special education (DEC, 2014) support embedding instruction into ongoing contexts to teach a range of skills (Wolery & Hemmeter, 2011). In fact, Wolery and Hemmeter (2011) described teaching as the "act of organizing and manipulating environmental structures, entities, and events (including adult behavior) ..." (p. 372). Typical contexts in early childhood are routines, activities, and transitions. Intentionally planning and designing the school day such that sufficient learning opportunities are provided is essential to ensure children make adequate progress.

Teaching across multiple contexts is important for four primary reasons. First, planning to provide systematic instruction for specific goals across more than one context might be important for ensuring all children receive a sufficient number of learning opportunities. Planning is critical here as without systematic planning, teachers are less likely to recognize when to teach, what to teach, or how to teach. Second, providing opportunities for children to learn or practice new skills in typical contexts might be important for facilitating skill fluency or maintenance. Third, teaching across the day is more efficient and promotes observational learning, especially when teachers use multiple small group activities. Further, teaching across the day and during multiple activities (e.g., small groups, circle time, transitions) gives all children opportunities to gain from the learning opportunities of their peers (Daugherty, Grisham-Brown, & Hemmeter, 2001). Finally, and perhaps most importantly, teaching across the day promotes generalized skill use. A child has not truly mastered a skill until s/he uses the skill spontaneously, across a variety of people, activities and materials.

Classroom Schedules

Children need time each day to play, read, eat, interact with their peers, and engage with their environments. A good early childhood classroom schedule should be intentionally designed to ensure there is a mix of types of activities, few transitions, and multiple opportunities for social interactions. Further, the school day should be predictable and flexible. Predictability helps children know what to expect and how to be successful. However, it also will be important to be flexible and make changes to the schedule as children's needs change or if an activity or routine is not working well. In this chapter we will refer to the schedule as the big picture or the main activities to be completed each day. The contexts are the specific steps or parts of the day that occur regularly; these are *routines*, *activities*, and *transitions*. Although these terms are often used interchangeably, **routines** are daily activities that typically occur in the same order, at approximately the same time and in the same manner. They often involve caring for basic needs and have a clear beginning and ending. **Activities** are planned events during which the primary goals and materials change. In early childhood settings, **transitions** are (1) when children and adults move from one area to another or (2) the time between discontinuing one activity or routine and beginning a new activity or routine. Transitions can occur for individual children, in small groups, or in large groups. *Routines*, *activities*, and *transitions* should be predictable and scheduled, while also being inherently flexible, allowing for planned (e.g., field trips, special visitors) or unanticipated (e.g., fire drills, thunderstorms) changes.

Setting up the Schedule

The schedule will need to be taught directly. The schedule should consist of blocks of times for specific activities and a routine sequence. The daily schedule should be repetitive and help children learn the classroom expectations and predict the daily routines. Creating a predictable environment increases the likelihood that children are engaged, attentive, and expectant learners. That is, they are ready to learn and practice new skills. When designing the schedule consider the following factors:

1. *Is there a* **balance** *of activities that differ in types of expectations and locations?*

Classroom schedules should include a balance of activities that differ in the amount of movement required or expected (e.g., listening to stories, music and movement, lining up to go outside), noise level, learning expectations (e.g., child or teacher led activities), and locations (e.g., indoor, outdoor, at tables, on the floor). Scheduling quiet activities after highly active activities might not be appropriate as it will likely take children longer to decrease their activity levels and calm down (Alger, 1984). Likewise, activities that require a child's sustained attention (e.g., story time) should occur immediately after quiet, calm activities to support their attention to the task and reduce the transition times. Large and small group activities should be carefully planned such that both occur during the day, but that more time is spent in small group activities. Large group activities that require sustained attention to distal stimuli (e.g., circle time, story time) should last fewer than about 10–15 minutes to avoid disengagement. Small groups should be used throughout the day as they provide ideal opportunities for embedding a range of child goals. Additionally, small and large group activities should be scheduled to minimize transition time and maximize child engagement.

Finally, current recommendations indicate that children need 60 minutes of MVPA per day, although multiple studies indicate that young children do not get the recommended amount in early childhood settings (Pate et al., 2015; Tandon, Saelens, & Christakis, 2015). Thus, this should be a priority for early childhood programs. Physical activity can occur during one long, morning session prior to lunch or in two shorter sessions scheduled across the day. There is some research that suggests antecedent exercise might facilitate engagement, reduce challenging behaviors, and/or increase the likelihood of healthier mealtime choices (Luke, Vail, & Ayres, 2014; Neely, Rispoli, Gerow, & Ninci, 2015; Price & Just, 2015). For these reasons, highly exertive activities should be carefully planned such that they occur before more demanding activities or preceding meals.

2. *Where are the* **adults** *and how many are available?*

The schedule should be designed in consideration of the available adults. Activities during which children will require more support should be scheduled when more adults are available (e.g., bathroom, handwashing before meals, meals or snack set-up). Further, all adults should have a specific role, task, or zone during each activity (Casey & McWilliam, 2005). Adult roles should be predetermined to ensure children are not waiting for activities to be set up and down time is minimized. In classrooms with just two adults, one adult can be setting up or prepping for the next activity while the other adult is leading the current activity. When more adults are available, each adult should have a specific role. If an extra teacher or therapist will be present during a specific time each day, s/he might be able to run a small group activity or work with a specific child. Setting up the schedule with assigned adult roles ensures materials are in place and ready for children. This minimizes transition times and increases engagement and independence. Further, having specific adults lead activities ensures that s/he can devote his/her full attention to the activity, support children's engagement, and deliver planned instruction. See sections later in this chapter that describe the use of matrices to plan adult roles across the day.

3. *When are children most likely to be* **engaged and attentive?**

The schedule should be designed to maximize participation, engagement, and attention. Routines are the least flexible of contexts, given that they often have to occur at set times (e.g., you have to wash hands before mealtimes, toileting has to occur twice per morning). However, teachers can arrange the activities and transitions to support engagement and participation during routines. When possible, transitions should occur in small groups such that adults can support increasing independence for all children and reduce wait time. For example, when transitioning into the classroom from the playground before mealtimes, if there are two teachers, one can transition half the children into the classroom for handwashing while the other stays on the playground. If possible, one teacher can leave the playground ahead of time and get lunch or a snack ready to reduce wait time further. If not, children can read quietly after washing hands while waiting for lunch to be ready. The careful planning and scheduling of transitions and routines ensures children are engaged and attentive. Likewise, activities should be planned to maximize child engagement. Developmentally appropriate child directed and small group activities should be used as often as possible. Regularly rotating activities including centers and toys can be an effective means to increase engagement. Teachers should collect data to determine which activities are the most engaging and those activities that offer numerous opportunities to teach multiple goals.

4. *How many* **different activities** *should be available?*

The types and variety of activities available to children should be developmentally appropriate. For example, infants and toddlers will need fewer centers with fewer activities. As toddlers learn the classroom routine and expectations of centers, teachers can expand the number and types of centers. For preschoolers, the number of activities (i.e., centers) should be designed based on the number of children in their classroom as well as the goals and needs of the children within the class. The number and types of centers should change as their interests and skills evolve. Introducing new activities or centers based on children's interests can be effective for increasing engagement. On the other hand, having too many activities or center options might reduce children's sustained engagement in any one center—if this is the case, professionals can offer fewer centers at any one time, but regularly rotate toys such that novel materials are available more often. Careful consideration and regular assessment should be used to ensure that the number of activities or centers support the engagement of all children.

5. *What* **skills** *need to be embedded across the day and are there sufficient opportunities to do so?*

Intentional planning means making evidence-based decisions about what to teach, where to teach, and when to teach. Further, these decisions must include the selection of the best method(s) to teach the targeted skill and how often the skill should be taught. Teachers should prioritize individual goals and group-wide goals that are socially and ecologically valid; this includes both IEP goals *and* other goals that all children need to learn. Each goal should have more than one assigned intervention strategy and most will be addressed across contexts. Remember that the naturally changing contexts within the school day often provide opportunities for the teaching, reteaching and practice of multiple goals (i.e., different routines, activities, and transitions).

*6. Is the **duration** of each activity sufficient for facilitating learning?*

The duration of each activity should be sufficient for facilitating learning and engagement. For example, center time or free play should be of a sufficient duration to facilitate sustained engagement—it should be long enough to ensure children can be engaged in meaningful and increasingly complex activities but not too long such that children become bored or unengaged. Additionally, children should have enough time to become involved in different centers, change their activity choice within a center (depending on center structure), and engage with different peers. For example, children should have enough time to allow for multiple play schemes in dramatic play or with blocks. The duration and order of routines might need to change as children learn and develop. For example, the duration of circle time might increase slowly as children learn to sit and listen to a story. Snack time might have to be adapted as children learn to eat snacks with their peers.

*7. Is there an appropriate mix of **social and independent** activities?*

To maximize learning and engagement, the majority of activities should be small group or child-directed. Children learn as they interact with the physical and social environment. There should be intentional opportunities for children to interact with each other *and* the classroom materials. Plan to teach objectives that involve peer-related social skills between children with and without special needs in social activities. In fact, **all children** should have **multiple** positive interactions with peers across activities, routines, and transitions; children will require varying levels of support depending on their social competence. There should be intentional, sufficient, and supportive interactions between children with and without disabilities. However, children must also be given the opportunity to learn to independently engage with the classroom environment, including a variety of toys and materials. Importantly, independent activities can occur in small group contexts (e.g., a small group art activity with independent projects) or in centers with multiple children (e.g., puzzle table). The schedule should be carefully planned to ensure each child has an appropriate amount of exposure to both types of activities. Regular assessment and refinement of one's own planning is crucial and will indicate success when children are making adequate progress on their goals.

*8. Are the schedule expectations **developmentally appropriate**?*

Developmentally appropriate practices refer to the understanding of children's current functional repertoires and designing the environment to include intentional opportunities for the children to demonstrate independent skill use (i.e., goals they have mastered and maintained and generalized), as well as acquire new skills (i.e., brand new skills), practice new skills (i.e., skills they have acquired and are becoming more fluent with), and generalize the use of new skills (i.e., using new skills across activities, routines, materials, or people; use related but non-target behaviors under the same or similar antecedent conditions). Developmentally appropriate does not mean simplifying things—it means ensuring children have sufficient learning opportunities that facilitate their engagement and learning. Classroom schedules should be carefully planned to ensure children are not bored (e.g., spending all day using mastered skills) or overly challenged (e.g., spending all day acquiring new skills without opportunities to generalize skills or practice mastered skills). Children that learn and play in a developmentally appropriate environment are provided with planned opportunities where they can successfully demonstrate previously learned skills and acquire and practice new skills.

Jessie uses the first two weeks of school to teach children the class schedule. However, she quickly realizes that she has too much time devoted to individual instruction and not enough time for child directed activities. She extends the morning free play time and adds two additional small groups during the morning center rotation. She plans to lead one and Janelle, the school's Speech Pathologist, will lead the other one with several of the children with IEPs. Her co-teacher, Monae, will be assigned to lead a rotating art activity during the same time. Jessie noticed that the frequency and intensity of challenging behaviors have increased during the transitions into and back from the outdoor playground. She plans to monitor these transitions and consider using transition-based learning or changing the transitions to reduce down time.

Teaching During Activities, Routines, and Transitions

Most activities, routines, and transitions can occur in one-to-one, small group, or whole group instructional formats. Yet, certain types of goals might be more suited to specific contexts.

Activities. Activities are planned events during which the primary goals and materials will change across the day, throughout the year. These likely include: circle time, story time, other early literacy activities, play on the playground or in the gym, free play, center times, and planned instructional times. Child directed and small group planned instructional activities might be the most flexible and efficient for teaching a variety of skills. Generally, activities should be planned and designed based on the skills children need to learn. Teachers should limit one-to-one instruction, given it is so resource intensive; most skills that professionals teach in individual arrangements can actually be effectively taught in small groups. Likewise, the amount of class time spent in whole group instruction should be limited, avoiding activities that require long wait times and activities that result in unclear expectations. In fact, children with disabilities are less engaged during circle time than any other typical activity (McWilliam, Trivette, & Dunst, 1985). Moreover, circle time is generally associated with low-quality interactions (Bustamante, Hindman, Champagne, & Wasik, 2018) and may often include activities (such as calendar time; Beneke, Ostrosky, & Katz, 2008) that are not developmentally appropriate.

Routines. Routines are regularly occurring, predictable events that usually have a clear beginning and end. These activities usually involve caring for basic needs (e.g., handwashing, toileting, mealtimes, nap). Social, communication, and adaptive skills (e.g., self-care, appropriate behaviors) are often essential to the completion of a routine. Thus, instruction targeting the development of these types of skills is often naturally embedded into routines that occur throughout the day. Some routines are ideal for social skills (e.g., mealtimes, arrival/departure), whereas other routines involve individual interactions (e.g., diapering, handwashing) and teaching more discrete skills. Support should be scaffolded so that children successfully complete the activity while increasing their level of independence as skill use develops. Sometimes teachers might inadvertently provide too much support in an effort to complete the routine quickly (e.g., washing a child's hands for them, dressing a child after diapering). Thus, strong teachers must balance the amount of time required for the completion of a routine, while remembering that the objective is to use this routine as an opportunity for children to begin to use targeted skills with greater independence.

Transitions. Children spend a good portion of their days in transitions from one activity or routine to the next. Transitions provide ideal opportunities for children to learn to independently transition across the day. For example, teachers might teach children to use a visual schedule, use visual or auditory cues to signal the next activity, or use response prompting procedures to support children through transitions. As with routines, teachers should always support a child's independence within the transition. Transitions also can provide opportunities for the teaching of other skills using response prompting or reinforcement-based procedures. Additionally, teachers should plan transitions so that the amount of down time (i.e., non-teaching time) is minimized. The use of small group transitions, adult zone defense scheduling, and peer-mediated interventions all help to reduce the amount of teaching time lost to transition.

Types of Early Childhood Classroom Activities, Routines, and Transitions

The following section describes what target skills might be taught during typical **activities**, **routines**, and **transitions**, and how to teach during these contexts including difficulties that might occur. Table 14.1 provides an overview of which types of strategies and formats should be used for which goals when teaching during activities, routines, and transitions. There will generally be three types of instruction: class-wide instruction, direct teaching, and individual adaptations.

Arrival

Although arrival routines occur across early childhood programs, they can differ depending on the overall schedule and format of that school. For example, the day might start early for children if the program has on-site early care or before school drop-off. Further, formats for drop-off may also vary: some schools use a car line system such that staff take children directly from the cars to the classroom, while other schools require parents or bus attendants to walk children into the classroom. Regardless of the type of routine, the arrivals should be predictable and structured.

When? The arrival routine typically marks the start of the school day but can also vary depending on family schedule and program needs.

What skills? Arrival is an ideal time to reinforce a child's independence, and to teach name identification, social interactions, dressing and undressing.

How? Arrival is the typical time to learn appropriate greetings, which can be taught using PTD or CTD, visual cues and positive reinforcement. Arrival is also an ideal time

Table 14.1 How and When to Teach

Strategy	System of Least Prompts	Graduate Guidance	CTD/PTD/SP
Types of Goals	Play skills, social skills, discrete skills	Chained and adaptive skills	Discrete skills, social skills
Types of Trials	Embedded, distributed	Embedded, massed, distributed	Embedded, massed, distributed
Format	Small groups, one-to-one	one-to-one	Small groups, one-to-one
Context	Activities, routines, transitions	Routines, transitions	Activities, routines, transitions
Example	Teaching play in a small group format with embedded trials	Teaching the transition from washing hands to mealtime using distributed trials	Teaching preschool sight words using PTD during a small group setting with massed trials

to provide responsive interactions to build rapport with children and support a collaborative relationship with their families. Children, their parents or caregivers, and their siblings should always be warmly greeted by name. Graduated guidance will be effective for teaching chained skills such as independently hanging up backpacks, dressing, and handwashing. PTD or CTD might be effective for teaching name identification or other discrete skills embedded into the arrival routine. Visual cues also can support children in learning and independently following the routine. Peers also can be taught to support each other during the routines, thus increasing social interactions. For some children, separating from caregivers might be difficult. When this occurs, teaching the child to respond appropriately to his parent's departure becomes the primary goal.

Free Play and Center Time

All early childhood contexts should include opportunities for children to engage in play activities that are self-directed and preferred.

When? Free play or center time will be structured differently across classrooms depending on the ages and needs of the children. Teachers should carefully arrange this time to include multiple activities and learning opportunities. There should be a mix of child-directed and small group activities. Each center (or activity) should have a specific purpose with clearly identified goals and teaching strategies identified for each child. A teacher might plan specific procedures such that children rotate through activities or centers on a schedule. Conversely, children might be given the opportunity to make their own choices about centers. Regardless of type of rotation used within a classroom, teachers should carefully monitor a child's progress to ensure that they are making adequate progress on goals and should support engagement and engage in active teaching rather than passive supervision.

What skills? A wide variety of skills can be taught during free play or centers (e.g., social, play, communication, motor, and adaptive), and it is particularly appropriate to embed teaching related to social, play, and engagement behaviors given these are the contexts in which children typically engage in these behaviors. Centers and activities should be rotated often enough to support child engagement and participation; materials should not remain static in any center for the entire duration of a school year. Centers should be designed such that multiple goals across children can be addressed, and these goals and adult expectations for teaching should be explicated (see information later in the chapter about matrix planning).

How? Activities will be both adult and child directed. Small groups should be the primary instructional format used to ensure children receive a sufficient number of learning opportunities. Trials should be embedded, massed, and distributed.

Gym or Outdoor Time

All children should spend an adequate amount of time engaging in physical activity, including outdoor play. Given the amount of time children should spend engaging in these activities, teachers should consider these activities as part of the instructional day.

When? The National Association for Sport and Physical Education (NASPE, 2009) recommends 60 minutes of moderate-to-vigorous physical activity each day for preschool-aged children. However, some research suggests that less than 10 percent of outdoor playground time is spent participating in vigorous activities (Hannon & Brown, 2008; Pate et al., 2008). Consequently, many children engage in MVPA for far less than the recommended 60 minutes. Research suggests that children in preschool get an average of less than 15 minutes of MVPA per day (Dolinsky et al., 2011). Gym and outdoor time are often underutilized and not likely to be viewed as an instructional time for young children (Davies, 1996; Gossett, 2017). Outdoor play should occur every day for all children and should include systematic instruction for a range of goals.

What skills? Activities in the gym or on the playground can facilitate physical well-being, gross motor development, communication skills, engagement and play skills, and social competence. Instruction should be planned, systematic, and closely monitored.

How? Teachers should carefully plan the outdoor play times, arrange the schedule and physical environment during outdoor play, and consider individual child needs. For example, in full-day programs, outdoor play should occur multiple times per day rather than once per day. Also, rather than requiring that children immediately transition from a low-structure and high-movement free play playground activity to the classroom, the teachers might arrange the transition to include structured small groups (e.g., small group Simon Says, seated games or sidewalk chalk) prior to transitioning inside. Teachers should monitor times at which children are most likely to be active (likely during the first few minutes of outdoor play time) and arrange that certain outdoor areas or centers are open or closed to facilitate moderate to vigorous physical activity. Structured and teacher-led activities, providing different or additional playground equipment, video modeling, and the use of environmental arrangement strategies have led to improvements in child physical activity (DeMarco, Zeisel, & Odom, 2014; Hannon & Brown, 2008; Ledford, Lane, Shepley, & Kroll, 2016; Ridgers, Stratton, Fairclough, & Twisk, 2007; Scruggs, Beveridge, & Watson, 2003). For example, teacher interactions designed to promote physical activities might include races, team sports play, obstacle courses, and other common games that require movement (e.g., Simon Says, Red Light Green Light, musical chairs; Brown, Googe, McIver, & Rathel, 2009; Brown, Pfeiffer et al., 2009). Teachers also should consider what individual modifications are needed to facilitate engagement and support participation for all children.

Large Group Activities (Circle, Story, or Music time)

For preschool children, circle time often requires children sit, listen, and attend to a teacher. For infants and toddlers, large group activities such as circle time should be active and not require that children sit, listen for extended periods of time, or wait. Circle time should always include music, movement, lots of opportunities for participation and social interactions, as well as activities that allow children to move around near each other. As children learn to participate in large groups, sit, and listen, the amount of circle time spent listening to stories and committed to activities that require listening and watching may be extended. Practitioners should always consider whether activities that are traditionally conducted in large group arrangements could be feasibly conducted as small groups instead (e.g., splitting the class into two groups, with one adult leading each). This allows for reduced wait time and increased opportunities to respond.

When? Circle time should occur when children are most likely to be quiet and attentive. The transition to circle time should occur in small groups such that teachers can support a few children at a time in finding a seat. As children enter circle time, the teacher can get started with some songs or other engaging activities to reduce wait time. For example, circle time might be scheduled immediately after center time so that children clean up then transition to the circle time area. Circle time should not require that children sit quietly for longer than is developmentally appropriate—no more than 10 to 15 minutes. Circle time should occur after the same activity/routine each day and should follow its own routine so children know what to expect. For example, circle time might always start with a few interactive songs, continue with a story, and end with a song. Holding circle time at a predictable time every day, in the same classroom area, and with consistent routines helps children understand the expectations.

What skills? Circle time might be ideal for teaching social routines, expectations, social interactions, and peer imitation.

How? When children do not understand the routine or expectations, they are less likely to engage or participate in circle time activities. Children will need to learn how long to stay at circle time and how to participate. If children are leaving circle time before it is over, a visual timer and a picture schedule of the circle time routine can be introduced so that children know how long circle time will last, can anticipate the order of the routines, and realize when it is over. Using children's interests and preferences when selecting songs and books is likely to increase their participation. Carefully planning seating arrangements such that children who are more competent and know the routine are sitting near children who might need more support can also be helpful. Peers can be taught to support and prompt children who need additional help participating. If children have the skills to participate and engage, but are not doing so, a planned reinforcement system should be used to increase their participation. The adults should be arranged such that the child(ren) who need the most intensive supports are in their proximity.

Transitions

Transitions are a necessary part of every school day; they are often associated with increased amounts of problem behavior and little teaching. However, with careful planning and systematic implementation, transition duration can be minimized and necessary transitions can be used as teaching opportunities.

When? Transitions occur multiple times each day. The schedule should be designed to minimize time spent in transitions. For example, moving afternoon outdoor time to right before departure reduces the need for a transition back into the classroom. Using a staggered transition, in small groups, to mealtimes ensures children are not waiting in line at the sink to wash hands. Likewise, the arrival transition might include specific tasks (i.e., hang up coat and backpack, find name, move name to the "here" board, and sit and read books quietly). Teaching this routine might involve intensive supports at the beginning of the year but eventually children can independently transition as they learn the routine and expectations. Teachers also need to monitor the schedule and transitions, making changes as needed. For example, if the transition from free play clean-up to circle time is taking too long and children are unengaged, the teacher might intentionally transition children in small groups and start singing a familiar song or reading a familiar book as soon as the first children sit down. When planning transitions, it is important to ensure all children transition successfully, which might involve material, adult, or peer support. Smooth, successful transitions set the stage for success in the activity that follows.

What skills? Transitions can be used to teach independence across routines and activities. However, a range of other skills can be embedded into transitions. For example, sight word or letter sounds can be embedded using massed trials during transition wait time.

How? Response prompting procedures such as CTD and PTD can be used to embed learning opportunities across transitions. Although transitions occur multiple times per day, they can be challenging for both children and adults. Transitions can involve both motivation and performance issues for children. That is, children might not be motivated to stop what they are currently doing, engage in the next activity, or engage in the transition itself. Children also might not understand what is expected, nor have the skills required to engage in the transition. A key to successful transitions is keeping children engaged during transitions. Challenging behaviors are most likely to occur during wait time. Thus, teachers should carefully plan for transition times such that both children and adults understand their roles and responsibilities. The schedule should be designed such that there are as few transitions as possible and that adults are available to support children during transitions.

Routines—Toileting and Mealtimes

When? For infants, toddlers, and young children, bathroom and mealtime routines should occur at the same time each day. It will be very important to carefully schedule bathroom time to ensure children are not waiting excessively and that they minimize disruptions to other routines. Children should have time to wash hands afterwards (or for infants and toddlers, teachers should be available to support handwashing immediately afterwards). As children become potty trained, they should be able to use the bathroom as needed. During potty training, children will have to go to the bathroom at regular intervals, which are sometimes very frequent and tightly spaced (e.g., every 20 minutes, every 30 minutes). Schedules might need to be revised when children are potty training. Teachers may consider potty training a couple of children simultaneously to facilitate peer modeling and imitation, and ensure that a sufficient number of adults are available. Likewise, mealtimes should be scheduled at a time of day when children are likely to be sufficiently hungry. If children are unengaged or mostly play with their food rather than eat it, they may not be hungry. Thus, a change in the meal time should be considered. Lunch time might be best scheduled after more active routines such as outdoor play.

What Skills? Social, communication, and self-help skills are particularly well suited to mealtime routines. Mealtimes are social events for individuals of all ages. Children should be given the supports necessary to engage in meaningful conversation and interactions during meals. Mealtimes might last anywhere from 15–30 minutes depending on setting, are regularly occurring, and often require children to remain near one another. Thus, mealtimes provide an ideal opportunity to deliver social communication interventions and embed social skills instruction (Lee & Lee, 2015; Locchetta, Barton, & Kaiser, 2017; Spohn, Timko, & Sainato, 1999). Given that mealtimes also involve washing hands, feeding, and cleaning up, several self-help or adaptive skills can also be taught during mealtimes.

How? Toileting and mealtime routines can be hard for children when they do not know the routines. When initially teaching the routine, teachers might need to use intensive supports such as full physical prompting and modeling. For mealtime routines, teachers can teach peers who know the routine to support other peers who are still learning the routine. Peer modeling can be effective during mealtimes as all children are typically engaged in the same or similar mealtime behaviors. Also, the mealtime routine should have routines within the routine. See Table 14.2 for an example of a mealtime routine.

Teaching Your Schedule and Setting Expectations

Good instruction is always intentional. Teachable moments are excellent for teaching a few skills, but good teachers do not wait for teachable moments to teach most skills. Further, the onus is not on the child to prompt instruction. Good teaching begins with careful planning, good assessments, and intentionally designing the schedule such that all children have a sufficient number of learning opportunities across the day to make adequate progress. This does not mean that good teachers do not *also* follow the lead of

Table 14.2 Mealtime Routine within Routines

Routines within the Mealtime Routine	
Transition to handwashing	Transition children in small groups to avoid delays and wait time at the sinks
	Intentionally select children to transition in small groups so that there are children fluent with the handwashing routine transitioning with children who need support with the routine
Handwashing routine	Respond to verbal cue and go to sink
	Turn on water
	Get soap
	Rub soap on hands
	Rinse hands
	Turn off water
	Get paper towel and dry hands
	Toss paper towel in garbage
Identify chair and sit down	Find name
	Pull out chair
	Sit down
Mealtime routine	Serving self
	Independently eating
	Passing to others
	Asking for more food or drink
	Talking to peers (social skills)
Clean up dishes	Identify cues that mealtime is over
	Pick up dishes and take to bin
Transition to quiet book reading	Go to carpet
	Select book
	Sit down
	Open book and read

the children in their class and know and use their interests, preferences, and reinforcers. Across any given day, three types of instruction should be planned and provided: class-wide, universal instruction; targeted instruction focused on a specific skill or skill set for a few children; and individualized instruction and adaptations. This is often referred to as a tiered system of support. Table 14.3 provides examples of the types of instruction typical to early childhood classrooms.

Planning Instruction

Good instruction is planned and intentional and always starts with appropriate goals. Once you have identified appropriate goals (i.e., what to teach), the next step for planning instruction involves identifying evidence-based practices to teach the targeted goals (how to teach, see Chapters 6–11). Further, identifying when to teach (including what adults are available), where to teach, and how often to teach are also important steps in a teacher's planning. *Matrices* are a critical tool used for planning instruction. There are generally multiple types of matrices that teachers use to define and specify the important aspects of instruction: goals, contexts, adults, program, center rotations, etc. Matrix planning is a long-standing approach for scheduling instruction across the day (Grisham-Brown, Pretti-Frontczak, Hemmeter, & Ridgley, 2002; Raver, 2004; Sandall, Schwartz, & Joseph, 2001). Matrices are a tool for planning and communicating to a variety of adults (teachers,

Table 14.3 Example of a Tiered System of Support and the Types of Instruction

Class-wide, Universal	Targeted Instruction	Individualized Instruction
Teaching classroom expectations and rules	Social skills instruction in small groups	Using behavior support plans
Teaching the class schedule (using predictable routines, activities, and transitions)	Peer-mediated instruction	Individual schedules (or modifications)
Behavior-specific praise	Small group transitions	Graduated guidance to teach self-help skills or routines
Responsive, nurturing interactions	Providing an additional reminder or cue to a small group of children	Individual supports during large group instruction (e.g., circle time)
Non-contingent reinforcement	Teaching problem-solving skills to two children	Adapting materials
Group contingencies	Adapting expectations for multiple children	One-to-one discrete trials to teach pre-academic skills (CTD/PTD)

paraprofessionals, practicum students, related service providers) what their responsibilities are for each activity, when and under what conditions to intervene, and how to intervene and use reinforcers to promote future occurrences of a target behavior. In addition, matrices can "serve as the classroom team's visual support" (Sandall, Schwartz, & Gauvreau, 2016, p. 358). That is, it can serve as a cue to adults to engage in planned intervention across the school day. Matrices should be considered a living document, modified as children make gains on goals and master objectives, and include input from all involved parties (e.g., paraprofessionals). Three of the most common types will be discussed in the next section: (a) objective-by-strategy matrices, (b) objective-by-activity matrices, and (c) activity-by-instructor matrices (see Appendix 14.1 for sample matrices).

Objective-by-Strategy Matrices

Goal matrices are created for individual children and their unique goals. The teacher uses them to plan *how* and *when* to teach the child's goals across multiple activities using multiple strategies. They often are created for all children who have IEPs or for multiple children who have common goals within a classroom. They should be easily accessible to all adults who enter the classroom to ensure teaching can occur all day and across multiple adults.

The **objective-by-strategy matrix** is a concise way to summarize which procedures should be used to teach each child all of their targeted behaviors (see Table 14.4). The objective-by-strategy matrix may be helpful for planning intervention for a single child and for identifying the procedures for which adults should receive training. It is less helpful for ongoing cues to staff because it is not organized by activity. For example, if graduated guidance is used at lunch and snack times to teach self-feeding, at toileting time for teaching handwashing, and during free play to teach simple object play, it is critically important that all classroom staff learn to use graduated guidance accurately, in a variety of contexts. It is also helpful for maintaining parsimony. For example, given the situation above, it is possible that the teacher considered the use of SLP to teach simple object play; however, given the use of graduated guidance in the other contexts, using

Table 14.4 Objective-by-Strategy Matrix

Goals	Social Problem-Solving	Pretend Play	Independence during Transitions	Letter–sound Identification
Strategy/ Activity #1 (implementer initials)	PTD labeling solutions during small groups (T1)	SLP during free play (T2)	GG (all transitions, T3 am, T2 pm; ST Wed)	PTD during small group (am and pm, T3)
Strategy/ Activity #2 (implementer initials)	Visual cues, Sr+ during free play (T1)	SLP on play-ground (T2)	EM (handwashing to meals, playground to departure, OT Th, T3)	RI (across meals, book reading, T1, T2)
Strategy/ Activity #3 (implementer initials)	PTD and Sr+ on playground (T3); Peer-mediated with planned opportunities	Peer-mediated during small groups (T1)		Arrival (letters and sounds from first name, PTD, T1)

Note: T1, T2, T3 = teacher 1, 2, or 3; ST = speech therapist; OT = occupational therapist; PTD = progressive time delay; SLP = system of least prompts; GG = graduate guidance; Sr+ = positive reinforcement; EM = environmental modification; RI = responsive interactions.

graduated guidance simplifies training needs. The steps for developing an objective-by-strategy matrix are:

1. Record *each objective* across the top row.
2. Record *potential teaching procedures* in the leftmost column.
3. In cells that correspond with a planned strategy use (e.g., the cell that aligns with lunch and graduated guidance), indicate that the procedure should be used, along with any supplemental information.

Objective-by-Activity Matrices

Another type of matrix is the **objective-by-activity matrix** that can be used to plan instruction for multiple children and their goals (see Table 14.5). This type of matrix is helpful for identifying both when to teach and for planning sufficient learning opportunities across the day. Teachers should ensure that children receive multiple learning trials across context and implementers using at least two different strategies. These matrices should be closely monitored and adaptations should be made regularly to ensure children are making adequate progress toward goals. This matrix is more helpful as a cue to adults to teach certain behaviors during specific classroom activities. The steps of completing an objective-by-activity matrix are:

1. List the daily schedule, including the location and the anticipated duration of each routine, activity, and transition.
2. Record *each objective* across the top row.
3. In each cell, record if a behavior should be targeted during a routine, activity, or transition and, if so, indicate which instructional procedure should be used during that time period.

Table 14.5 Objective-by-Activity Matrix

	JA, MW, CB: *Social problem-solving*	JA, CB, SC: *Pretend play*	JA, MW, SC: *Transition independence*	JA, CB, AA, SC: *Letter–sound ID*	MW, AA, SC: *Initiate social interactions*	MW, CB, AA: *Request items*
Arrival						EA, IT, VC
Free play/ Centers rotation	VC, Sr+, PTD-SG	SLP, PM-SG	VC, GG	PTD-SG	PTD-SG, VC	EA, RI
Circle time			VC	EM		
Transition			VC, GG		PTD-SG	
Outdoor time	VC, Sr+	SLP			VC, Sr+	PTD
Transition	VC, Sr+		EM	PTD-SG		
Lunch					VC, Sr+	EA, IT, VC

Note. VC = visual cues; PTD = progressive time delay; SG = small groups; PM = peer mediated; SLP = system of least prompts; GG = graduate guidance; Sr+ = positive reinforcement; EA = environmental arrangement; IT = incidental teaching; RI = responsive interactions.

Activity-by-Instructor Matrices

A third type of matrix is the **activity-by-instructor matrix,** which should be designed to indicate where each adult will be and what they should be doing (see Table 14.5). These can be aligned with a zone defense system (ZDS) scheduling system or just simply used to identify adults' roles. ZDS is a zone-based system where teachers are assigned to specific areas of a classroom to establish roles and responsibilities (Decker, 2013; Casey & McWilliam, 2005). The ZDS is recommended to increase child engagement in classroom settings over teacher-to-class or a one-to-one procedure in which teachers supervise specific children or groups of children (Lelaurin & Risley, 1972; Decker, 2013). However, the research on ZDS is limited and more research is needed. Regardless of the type of system used to define adult roles, matrices are critical for ensuring instruction is both efficient and sufficient. Adult matrices allow teachers to carefully plan adult roles (or zones in a ZDS system) to ensure children are receiving systematic instruction across *all* activities, routines, and transitions. Table 14.6 provides an example of an adult matrix. The steps of completing an activity-by-instructor matrix are:

1. List the daily schedule, including the location and the anticipated duration of each routine, activity, and transition.
2. Record *each adult's name* across the top row.
3. In each cell, record the roles and responsibilities for the adult by activity. In addition, if an adult is responsible for targeting a specific objective for a child or multiple objectives across children, corresponding target behaviors, instructional procedures, and modifications should be noted.

In classroom settings, it is often optimal if some roles are rotated or systematically changed over time. For example, it might be that in one 15-minute activity immediately preceding playground time, roles are as such: (Role A) Adult 1: reads books with one group of children; (Role B) Adult 2: leads a small group activity with a second group of children; and Role C) Adult 3: assists children to complete toileting and handwashing routines. So that each adult has the opportunity to engage in a variety of teaching tasks and each child learns

Table 14.6 Example Activity-by-Instructor Classroom Matrix

Time	Teacher 1	Co-teacher	Para-professional	Student Volunteer
Arrival	Greet children and parents	Prepare snack; guide children to sink; receive children at snack	Wash hands and guide children to snack tables	Help with handwashing and receive children at snack
Morning Snack	Sit with children and eat; support Ami, Thom, and Maggie	Prepare centers	Sit with children and eat; support Charlie and Devonte	Help prepare centers; Wipe down chairs as children finish
Transition to centers	Support Ami, Thom, and Maggie	Wash hands as children finish	Support Charlie and Devonte	Receive children at centers
Center time *(see separate center time rotation schedule)*	Implement SG at table	Sensory table and puzzle table	Implement SG at table	Support SG at table
Free play	Move with final group; receive in art area	Move with final group; receive children in reading area	Move with final group; receive children in dramatic play area	Receive children in block area

to engage in tasks with a variety of adults, it might be that the role assignments change based on the day of the week (e.g., Role A is assigned to Adult 1 on Mondays and Thursdays) or on a rotating weekly schedule (e.g., Role A is assigned to Adult 1 during week 1).

As mentioned above, optimally, each objective is targeted during multiple activities. This matrix allows teachers to easily identify which behaviors should be taught during which activities; this results in the objective-by-activity matrix serving as a useful reminder for adults.

Matrices are meant to guide adults in intervening on individual and class-wide objectives. In addition, data sheets should be readily accessible to all adults. Class-wide data sheets provide areas for adults to code presence or absence of target behaviors and the type of support required to ensure a correct response.

Jessie makes several minor changes to the schedule as children learn new skills and as adaptations are needed. For example, she changed two transitions from large group to small group, staggered transitions to reduce down time. Challenging behaviors rarely occur during these transitions when staggered. She created an adult matrix to identify where each adult should be across the day; she also included the specific skill goals to focus on and the strategies adults should be implementing during the routines, activities, and transitions.

References

Alger, H. A. (1984). Transitions: Alternatives to manipulative management techniques. *Young Children, 39,* 16–25.

Beneke, S. J., Ostrosky, M. M., & Katz, L. G. (2008). Good intentions gone awry. *Young Children, 13,* 12–16.

Brown, W. H., Googe, H. S., McIver, K. L., & Rathel, J. M. (2009). Effects of teacher-encouraged physical activity on preschool playgrounds. *Journal of Early Intervention*, 31, 126–145.

Brown, W. H., Pfeiffer, K. A., McIver, K. L., Dowda, M., Addy, C. L., & Pate, R. R. (2009). Social and environmental factors associated with preschoolers' nonsedentary physical activity. *Child Development*, 80, 45–58.

Bustamante, A. S., Hindman, A. H., Champagne, C. R., & Wasik, B. A. (2018). Circle time revisited: How do preschool classrooms use this part of the day? *The Elementary School Journal*, 118, 610–631.

Casey, A. M., & McWilliam, R. A. (2005). Where is everybody? Organizing adults to promote child engagement. *Young Exceptional Children*, 8, 2–10.

Daugherty, S., Grisham-Brown, J., & Hemmeter, M. L. (2001). Effects of embedded skill instruction on the acquisition of target and nontarget skills in preschoolers with developmental delays. *Topics in Early Childhood Special Education*, 21, 213.

Davies, M. M. (1996). Outdoors: An important context for young children's development. *Early Child Development and Care*, 115, 37–49.

Decker, J. (2013). Enhancing supervision on the preschool playground. Unpublished Master's Thesis. Vanderbilt University, Nashville, TN.

DeMarco, A. C., Zeisel, S., & Odom, S. L. (2014). An evaluation of a program to increase physical activity for young children in child care. *Early Education and Development*, 26, 1–21.

DEC (Division for Early Childhood). (2014). *DEC recommended practices in early intervention/early childhood special education*. Washington, DC: DEC.

Dolinsky, D. H., Brouwer, R. J. N., Ostbye, T., Evenson, K. R., & Siega-Riz, A. M. (2011). Peer reviewed: Correlates of sedentary time and physical activity among preschool-aged children. *Preventing Chronic Disease*, 8(6), A131.

Gossett, S. (2017). *The Effects of Video Modeling on the Outdoor Play of Children with Disabilities* (Doctoral dissertation, Peabody College of Vanderbilt University).

Grisham-Brown, J. L., Pretti-Frontczak, K., Hemmeter, M. L., & Ridgely, R. (2002). Teaching IEP goals and objectives in the context of classroom routines and activities. *Young Exceptional Children*, 6, 18–27.

Hannon, J. C., & Brown, B. B. (2008). Increasing preschoolers' physical activity intensities: An activity-friendly preschool playground intervention. *Preventive Medicine*, 46, 532–536.

Ledford, J. R., Lane, J. D., Shepley, C., & Kroll, S. M. (2016). Using teacher-implemented playground interventions to increase engagement, social behaviors, and physical activity for young children with autism. *Focus on Autism and Other Developmental Disabilities*, 31, 163–173.

Lee, S. H., & Lee, L. W. (2015). Promoting snack time interactions of children with autism in a Malaysian preschool. *Topics in Early Childhood Special Education*, 35, 89–101.

LeLaurin, K., & Risley, T. R. (1972). The organization of daycare environments: "Zone" versus "man to man" staff assignments. *Journal of Applied Behavior Analysis*, 5, 225–232.

Locchetta, B. M., Barton, E. E., & Kaiser, A. (2017). Using family style dining to increase social interactions in young children. *Topics in Early Childhood Special Education*, 37, 54–64.

Luke, S., Vail, C. O., & Ayres, K. M. (2014). Using antecedent physical activity to increase on task behavior in young children. *Exceptional Children*, 80, 489–503.

McWilliam, R. A., Trivette, C. M., & Dunst, C. J. (1985). Behavior engagement as a measure of the efficacy of early intervention. *Analysis and Intervention in Developmental Disabilities*, 5, 59–71.

National Association for Sport and Physical Education. (2009). *National standards & guidelines for physical education teacher education*. National Association for Sport and Physical Education.

National Association for Sport and Physical Education. (2011). *National standards & guidelines for physical education teacher education*. National Association for Sport and Physical Education.

National Association for the Education of Young Children (NAEYC). (2009). NAEYC standards for early childhood professional preparation programs.

Neely, L., Rispoli, M., Gerow, S., & Ninci, J. (2015). Effects of antecedent exercise on academic engagement and stereotypy during instruction. *Behavior Modification*, 39, 98–116.

Pate, R. R., McIver, K., Dowda, M., Brown, W. H., & Addy, C. (2008). Directly observed physical activity levels in preschool children. *Journal of School Health*, 78, 438–444.

Pate, R. R., O'Neill, J. R., Brown, W. H., Pfeiffer, K. A., Dowda, M., & Addy, C. (2015). Prevalence of compliance with a new physical activity guideline for preschool-age children. *Childhood Obesity*, 11, 415–420.

Price, J., & Just, D. R. (2015). Lunch, recess and nutrition: Responding to time incentives in the cafeteria. *Preventive Medicine*, 71, 27–30.

Raver, S. A. (2004). Monitoring child progress in early childhood special education settings. *Teaching Exceptional Children*, 36, 52–57.

Ridgers, N. D., Stratton, G., Fairclough, S. J., & Twisk, J. W. (2007). Long-term effects of a playground markings and physical structures on children's recess physical activity levels. *Preventive Medicine*, 44, 393–397.

Sandall, S., Schwartz, I., & Gauvreau, A. (2016). Using modifications and accommodations to enhance learning of young children with disabilities: Little changes that yield big impacts. In B. Reichow, B. A. Boyd, E. E. Barton, & S. L. Odom (Eds.), *Handbook of early childhood special education* (pp. 349–362). Switzerland: Springer International Publishing.

Sandall, S. R., Schwartz, I. S., & Joseph, G. (2001). A building blocks model for effective instruction in inclusive early childhood settings. *Young Exceptional Children*, 4(3), 3–9.

Scruggs, P. W., Beveridge, S. K., & Watson, D. L. (2003). Increasing children's school time physical activity using structured fitness breaks. *Pediatric Exercise Science*, 15, 156–169.

Spohn, J. R., Timko, T. C., & Sainato, D. M. (1999). Increasing the social interactions of preschool children with disabilities during mealtimes: The effects of an interactive placemat game. *Education and Treatment of Children*, 22, 1–18.

Tandon, P. S., Saelens, B. E., & Christakis, D. A. (2015). Active play opportunities at childcare. *Pediatrics*, 135, 1425–1431.

Wolery, M., & Hemmeter, M. L. (2011). Classroom instruction: Background, assumptions, and challenges. *Journal of Early Intervention*, 33, 371–380.

Appendix 14.1

Sample Matrices

Date: _____

		AB	ZB	CG	AH	EP	RT	AW
Activity	**Time**							
Arrival	7:30–8:00							
Transition	8:00-8:05							
Whole Group	8:05-9:20							
Transition	9:20–9:25							
Snack	9:25–9:40							
Transition	9:40–9:45							
Free play	9:45-10:30							
Transition	10:30-10:35							
Playground	10:35-11:00							
Transition	11:00-11:05							
Small Group	11:05-11:20							
Transition	11:20-11:25							
Lunch	11:25-11:55							
Transition	11:55-12:00							
Nap/Rest	12:00-1:00							
Transition	1:00-1:05							
Small Group	1:05-1:20							
Transition	1:20–1:25							
Playground	1:25-1:50							
Transition	1:50–1:55							
Free play	1:55-2:25							
Departure	2:25-2:30							

Key

T=Teacher	CTD=Constant Time Delay	M=Modeling
P=Paraprofessional	PTD=Progressive Time Delay	MM=Mand-Model
R=Practicum Student	GG=Graduated Guidance	NTD=Naturalistic Time Delay
	SLP=System of Least Prompts	IT=Incidental Teaching

Classroom Activity Matrix

Date: _____

		Teacher	Para-Pro.	Para-Pro.	Practicum Student	Practicum Student
Activity	**Time**					
Arrival	7:30–8:00					
Transition	8:00-8:05					
Whole Group	8:05-9:20					
Transition	9:20–9:25					
Snack	9:25–9:40					
Transition	9:40–9:45					
Free play	9:45-10:30					

Date: _____

Activity	Time					
Transition	10:30-10:35					
Playground	10:35-11:00					
Transition	11:00-11:05					
Small Group	11:05-11:20					
Transition	11:20-11:25					
Lunch	11:25-11:55					
Transition	11:55-12:00					
Nap/Rest	12:00-1:00					
Transition	1:00-1:05					
Small Group	1:05-1:20					
Transition	1:20–1:25					
Playground	1:25-1:50					
Transition	1:50–1:55					
Free play	1:55-2:25					
Departure	2:25-2:30					

Key

CTD=Constant Time Delay	M=Modeling
PTD=Progressive Time Delay	MM=Mand-Model
GG=Graduated Guidance	NTD=Naturalistic Time Delay
SLP=System of Least Prompts	IT=Incidental Teaching

Activity-by-Instructor Matrix

	Objective 1	Objective 2	Objective 3	Objective 4	Objective 5
Strategy 1 (Whole Group)					
Strategy 2 (Small Group)					
Strategy 3 (Free Play)					

Objective-by-Strategy Matrix

Activity	Time	Objective 1	Objective 2	Objective 3	Objective 4	Objective 5
Arrival	7:30–8:00					
Transition	8:00-8:05					
Whole Group	8:05-9:20					
Transition	9:20–9:25					
Snack	9:25–9:40					
Transition	9:40–9:45					
Free play	9:45-10:30					
Transition	10:30-10:35					
Playground	10:35-11:00					
Transition	11:00-11:05					
Small Group	11:05-11:20					
Transition	11:20-11:25					

		Objective 1	Objective 2	Objective 3	Objective 4	Objective 5
Lunch	11:25-11:55					
Transition	11:55-12:00					
Nap/Rest	12:00-1:00					
Transition	1:00-1:05					
Small Group	1:05-1:20					
Transition	1:20–1:25					
Playground	1:25-1:50					
Transition	1:50–1:55					
Free play	1:55-2:25					
Departure	2:25-2:30					

Key

CTD=Constant Time Delay M=Modeling

PTD=Progressive Time Delay MM=Mand-Model

GG=Graduated Guidance NTD=Naturalistic Time Delay

SLP=System of Least Prompts IT=Incidental Teaching

Objective-by-Activity Matrix

15 Working with Professionals in Early Childhood

Key Terms

Coaching *Collaboration* *Performance-based feedback*
Modeling *Behavior skills training* *Practice-based coaching*

Chapter Objectives

After completing this chapter, readers should be able to:

- Define and explain coaching and collaboration.
- Characterize and identify approaches likely to be successful when planning and working with other professionals.

Michelle is ready to begin her second year in an inclusive public-school classroom for four-year-old children with and without disabilities. She feels confident in her ability to structure centers, activities, and routines. Further, she is confident in her ability to provide effective instruction across the day. However, last year she struggled with supporting and effectively utilizing her assistant teacher and the two paraprofessionals who were assigned to work with specific children with disabilities in her classroom. Her classroom could be more effective if the other adults could embed instruction into activities, run small groups, or provide individualized instruction. She will have the same assistant teacher, Chelsea, and two new paraprofessionals, Sasha and Malia. She begins to review the research regarding how to coach and support adults.

The primary purpose of this chapter is to describe the collaborations among adults that are necessary for facilitating child success. We will describe professional partnerships across early childhood settings. We will delineate effective strategies for coaching professionals to use evidence-based practices in typical early childhood settings. We will describe empirically validated coaching practices with specific examples. Refer to Chapter 16 for specific strategies used to coach families and caregivers in homes or other natural environments.

Introduction to Collaboration and Coaching in Early Childhood

Effective collaboration between early childhood professionals is a ubiquitous indicator of quality in early childhood programs. Further, characteristics of effective collaborations have been delineated to guide these often-complex partnerships (see Division for Early Childhood [DEC] Teaming and Collaboration Recommended Practices; DEC, 2014). Effective collaboration practices facilitate ongoing interactions and relationships among practitioners and families to ensure children receive effective services and supports. For children with disabilities, these collaborations also include practitioners across a range of disciplines (e.g., ECSE, speech, occupational, or physical therapists) who provide EI/ECSE services to children and their families in schools, classrooms, homes, or other natural environments. There is a clear understanding that service provision is most effective when there is meaningful collaboration among professionals and families.

The nature of collaboration is often driven by the age of the child, the location of services, and the types of services provided. Effective collaboration in early childhood centers or schools is characterized by team-based decision-making whereby professionals and families jointly develop IEP goals and plan for services. In these ECSE contexts, families are key team members, are engaged in the decision-making processes, and are kept up to date on child progress. However, parents are not directly involved in service provision. ECSE teachers and related service providers (e.g., speech, occupational, or physical therapists) might provide services to the child directly in the classroom or in separate rooms outside of the classroom. Although the former (i.e., "push-in" services) are preferred, the type of preschool setting or the type of goals targeted might dictate the type of collaboration. ECSE practitioners might work with and coach classroom teachers to provide supports and target specific goals for the child with disabilities directly in the classroom. A key component of most collaborations in early childhood settings will involve some form of professional development. The importance of effective professional development has been recognized in recent years given its relation to both improved practitioner and child outcomes. Although research in this area is burgeoning, ongoing support and follow-up—often referred to as coaching—have been identified as necessary components of effective professional development (Artman-Meeker et al., 2015). ECSE teachers need job-embedded coaching to use effective practices with fidelity (Barton, Pribble, & Chen, 2013; Shepley, Lane, Grisham-Brown, Spriggs, & Winstead, 2017; Strain and Bovey, 2011). Thus, across settings and service provision models in early childhood (i.e., EI/ECSE), effective collaboration involves coaching.

What is Coaching?

Rush and Shelden (2008) defined coaching as "an adult-learning strategy that is used to build the capacity of a parent or colleague to improve existing abilities, develop new skills, or gain a deeper understanding of practices for use in current and future situations" (p. 1). Coaching has emerged as an effective, empirically supported method for supporting adult use of effective practices that in turn support improvements in child outcomes (Snyder, Hemmeter, McLaughlin, 2011). Coaching is goal directed: collaborative, interactive, and focused on skill building. Coaching should not be limited to just one strategy (e.g., feedback, modeling), use a one-size-fits-all approach, or be inflexible—individual, data-based adaptations should be expected. Traditional trainings in the form of workshops and didactic lectures are *insufficient* and *ineffective* for changing adult instructional behaviors in real-life contexts. Conversely, effective coaching directly impacts adult implementation and thus supports child learning and development. Effective practitioners use coaching to facilitate instruction that promotes child learning (DEC, 2014).

Coaching has been effectively used with both certified ECSE teachers (Fox, Hemmeter, Snyder, Binder, & Clarke, 2011), non-certified early childhood teachers (Barton, Pribble, & Chen, 2013; Barton et al., 2018; Hemmeter, Snyder, Kinder, & Artman, 2011), pre-service teachers (Barton, Chen, Pribble, Pomes, & Kim, 2013; Barton, Fuller, & Schnitz, 2016), and paraprofessionals (Ledford et al., 2017). This is important given children with disabilities in inclusive early childhood contexts are often served by a range of professionals including certified and non-certified adults. Further, a lead classroom teacher might be coaching her assistant teacher or an itinerant ECSE provider might be coaching a lead classroom teacher. Thus, hereafter the term "coach" will be used to refer to any adult who is engaged in teaching other adults to use new skill(s).

There is an emerging, albeit strong, body of research focused on identifying effective coaching components (Artman-Meeker et al., 2015; Snyder et al., 2012). The early childhood coaching research asserts four main conclusions: (a) coaches should use research-based strategies to support adult learning; (b) coaching must be ongoing and directly linked to effective instructional practices; (c) the use of evidence-based coaching strategies increases teachers' fidelity of implementation of effective practices; and (d) the teachers' use of effective practices leads to improved child outcomes (Sheridan, Edwards, Marvin, & Knoche, 2009; Snyder, Hemmeter, & McLaughlin, 2011). This chapter will delineate research-based strategies that support early childhood professionals. Although a *coach* can refer to an expert, a peer, or the teacher (self), in early childhood contexts, coaches are primarily experts or colleagues who have knowledge and experience in the teaching practices being coached. Comprehensive approaches to coaching have been developed and studied in early childhood contexts in recent years. Behavior Skills Training (BST) and Practice-Based Coaching (PBC) have empirical support in early childhood contexts and will be described in the next section.

Comprehensive Coaching Models

Trivette, Dunst, Hamby, and O'Herin (2009) conducted a review of four adult learning strategies: accelerated learning, coaching, guided design, and just-in-time training. They selected these four methods because they have established empirical support and have received considerable attention. They identified 79 studies to determine the relation between adult learning methods and learner outcomes. They found six characteristics of coaching strategies to be consistently related to adult learning: *to introduce*, *to illustrate*, *to practice*, *to evaluate*, *to reflect*, and *to master*. These are described in Table 15.1. Results of their meta-analysis indicated that the presence of any of the six characteristics resulted in adult learning. The most robust adult learning occurred when (a) multiple methods were used, (b) methods were used with smaller groups, and (c) methods were used for more than 10 hours. Although the settings and populations included in their review were not exclusively education related, their findings are relevant and have implications for coaching in early childhood contexts. Two comprehensive coaching approaches—BST and PBC—utilize these characteristics and have been effective in early childhood settings. BST and PBC will be delineated in the next sections.

Behavior Skills Training

BST is an approach to teaching new skills developed by Miltenberger (2012). Although BST was developed to support skill development across populations and skills, it has been widely used to teach educational staff instructional strategies that support skill development in their students. For example, behavior skills training (BST) includes knowledge provision, expert modeling, practice opportunities, and performance-based feedback (Miltenberger, 2012). BST has been used to teach adults to implement behavior support plans and instructional programs (Chazin, Barton, Ledford, & Pokorski, 2018; Lerman, Vorndran, Addison, & Kuhn, 2004; Love, Carr, LeBlanc, & Kisamore, 2013) and to make instructional decisions (Matthews & Hagopian, 2014). Further, BST can be used individually or with groups of professionals, although individual supports should be provided as a follow-up.

Table 15.1 Comprehensive Models and Characteristics of Adult Learning[a]

Effective Adult Learning Characteristics		Comprehensive Coaching Models and their Components	
		BST	PBC
Introduce	Provide a preview of the materials, knowledge, and practices that are related to the target skills. For example, this might be provided through a face-to-face workshop, online module, or written manual.	*Instruction*	*Shared goals and action planning*
Illustrate	Demonstrate or model the use of the target skills with the relevant materials. This might be a live model, video demonstrations, or self-models.	*Modeling*	
Practice	Provide opportunities for the learner to practice the target skills and deliver performance-based feedback. Practice opportunities might initially occur in contrived settings (e.g., role play), and should eventually occur in the settings in which they are intended to be used.	*Practice*	*Focused observations*
Evaluate	Evaluate the outcomes of the use of the target skills. For example, teachers' frequent use of language elicitation strategies might result in improvements in child language.	*Feedback*	*Reflection and Feedback*
Reflect	In collaboration with the learner, evaluate progress and set goals for next steps.		
Master	Support the learner in examining how the target skills fit within a broader conceptual framework to support ongoing monitoring, self-assessment, and continual self-improvement.		

[a] Definitions were adapted from Trivette, Dunst, Hamby, and O'Herin (2009).

There are four primary components of BST: instruction, modeling, rehearsal, and feedback. Initially, the *instruction* is provided by the coach (who is an expert in the procedures being taught) regarding the rationale for the procedures, descriptions of the specific steps or strategies involved, and when and how to use the strategies (as well as when not to use the strategies, if relevant). Instruction might be provided in a lecture or didactic training format, although the coach should model the skill and the learner should have multiple opportunities to practice during the instructional component. In BST, *modeling* is then provided in situ, that is, with the students/children and in the context where the learner is expected to implement the strategy. *Modeling* gives the learner an opportunity to observe an expert implementing the strategies as intended. The learner then should have opportunities to *practice* using the strategies in situ. *Practice* should occur immediately after the coach models the skills. The coach then provides performance-based *feedback* while the learner practices. The coach should provide both supportive feedback related to the correct use of the strategy and corrective feedback, as needed, to improve the learner's use of the skill. The coach should continually collect data regarding the learner's performance (i.e., use of the target strategies) and adapt coaching as needed to facilitate correct implementation. Using the data to make decisions, the coach might need to repeat the *instruction-model-practice-feedback* cycle multiple times across multiple days or sessions before the learner accurately and independently uses the strategy. This might be particularly true for more complex instructional procedures. For multi-component interventions (e.g., behavior support plans) the coach may need to provide individual instruction on each component.

Practice-Based Coaching

Similar to BST, PBC involves shared goals and action planning, focused observations, and reflection and feedback in the context of a collaborative coaching partnership (Snyder, Hemmeter, & Fox, 2015). Practice-based coaching (PBC) is an approach to professional development that uses a cyclic process of planning goals and action steps, focused observations, and reflection and feedback (Snyder, Hemmeter, & Fox, 2015). PBC supports occur within the context of collaborative coaching partnerships, but can be implemented in several different delivery formats (e.g., live, from a distance, using videos) and provided by experts, peers, or self-guided. Collaborative partnerships are developed over time through two-way interactions that involve intentionally building rapport, developing shared understandings, and identifying achievable outcomes. PBC has primarily been used in early childhood contexts to support teacher use of practices that support social competence of young children (Fox et al., 2011; Hemmeter, Snyder, Fox, & Algina, 2016), embedded instruction (Snyder, Hemmeter, McLean, Sandall, McLaughlin, & Algina, 2018), and strategies for preventing challenging behaviors (Artman-Meeker, Hemmeter, & Snyder, 2014; Conroy, Sutherland, Algina et al., 2014; Conroy, Sutherland, Vo et al., 2014; Sutherland, Conroy, Vo, & Ladwig, 2015).

Although professional development research to date has included researcher support, the components of PBC have been shown to be effectively implemented in authentic early childhood contexts. The initial component—goal setting and action planning—is driven by a needs assessment. The coach and teacher create an action plan based on initial needs assessments (e.g., observations, structured assessments, fidelity tools) and review and update it regularly as part of the cyclic process. During focused observations, the coach gathers and records information regarding the teacher's target behaviors. In addition, the coach also can provide support, as needed, to guide the teacher's use of target behaviors as part of the focused observation component. Reflection and feedback are then used to provide supportive and constructive feedback to improve or refine the teacher's use of target behaviors. The goals and action plan are continually reviewed, updated, and refined to ensure improvements in teacher behavior(s) and high fidelity implementation of effective teacher practices. For more detailed information on PBC see: https://eclkc.ohs.acf.hhs.gov/professional-development/article/practice-based-coaching-pbc.

Michelle comes across a few studies using Behavior Skills Training to teach paraprofessionals to use response prompting procedures during small groups. She meets with Sasha and Malia to discuss the two small groups that she thinks they might be running. They agree on the target skills for the children—peers names, sight words, and letter sounds—and Michelle indicates they should use Progressive Time Delay (PTD). Michelle creates a brief presentation to review tips for running small groups, how to implement PTD, and how to collect data on the target skills. She sets up a time to review the materials with them and they role play with each other to practice using PTD while Michelle delivers feedback. Sasha and Malia then start practicing their small groups during the school day. Michelle provides immediate and brief performance-based feedback during and after each small group session for the first two weeks, but then fades feedback as they demonstrate mastery. As suspected, Michelle finds she has more instructional time in her classroom when Sasha and Malia can implement small groups.

Individual Coaching Practices

Although the aforementioned approaches to professional development have been shown to be effective, the approaches use multiple components; many of these components can be effectively used in isolation or with one or more of the other components. Several individual coaching practices are evidence-based and related to improved use of instructional behaviors. Decisions about which strategies or approaches to use should be driven by the educational levels and experience levels of the recipients of the professional development (e.g., experienced teachers, pre-service teachers, paraprofessionals), the target behaviors (e.g., complex procedures, discrete behaviors), resources available (e.g., smart phones for texting, videos), and the context (e.g., early childhood classroom, playground, clinic). Coaching should be individualized using multiple methods as needed, delivered one-to-one or in small groups, and the dosage should be sufficient to ensure sustained learning (i.e., for more than 10 hours).

Performance-based Feedback. One critical component of effective coaching is performance-based feedback (Barton, Kinder, Casey, & Artman, 2011; Casey & McWilliam, 2011; Shepley et al., 2017). Performance-based feedback is information provided to a teacher regarding a specific aspect of her behavior. Performance-based feedback helps the person being coached understand exactly how and what they did relative to the target skills from the coach's perspective. Performance-based feedback, by definition, includes feedback related to the target behavior. The content, delivery method, and context for delivery can and should vary based on the skills being taught. Further, performance-based feedback is flexible and can be adapted to meet the unique needs of the teacher, target behaviors or skills, the specific needs of the children, the context, and available resources. When providing performance-based feedback the coach should consider: (a) methods of collecting information to generate performance-based feedback, (b) the target skills relevant to the feedback, (c) methods of delivering feedback, and (d) types of feedback.

Collecting information to generate performance-based feedback. In early childhood contexts, performance-based feedback is most likely to be provided based on observations of an individual's performance. This can be live or video-recorded observations. The coach should carefully consider ideal times and contexts for observing the target behavior(s). For example, if a coach was supporting early childhood teachers in using more descriptive praise, s/he might observe during free play when there are multiple opportunities to deliver descriptive praise. Likewise, if a coach was supporting early childhood teachers in implementing individualized behavior support plan procedures for a child with challenging behaviors, the coach might observe at a time when challenging behaviors were likely to occur. Carefully planning observation times is critical to ensuring the coach has sufficient and relevant information to provide within the performance-based feedback.

Feedback delivery methods. Performance feedback has been delivered in a variety of ways: verbally during observations (Schepis, Ownbey, Parsons, & Reid, 2000; Schepis, Reid, Ownbey, & Parsons, 2001; Tate, Thompson, & McKerchar, 2005), using bug-in-ear technologies during observations (Coogle, Rahn, & Ottley, 2015), face-to-face feedback immediately following observations (Schepis, Reid, Ownbey, & Parsons, 2001; Shepley et al., 2017), via written forms and checklists following an observation (Barton et al., 2013; Casey & McWilliam, 2011), and through the use of technology to provide email feedback (Barton, Pribble, & Chen, 2013; Hemmeter et al., 2011). Performance-based feedback has generally focused on an individual's current and previous performance, but a few studies have examined group-based feedback (Casey & McWilliam, 2008). The specific characteristics of feedback should be selected based on the learners, their current repertoires, and targeted skills. Generally, when teachers are learning complex skills or instructional procedures (e.g., constant time delay during small groups) feedback might need to be provided during the session to support accurate use of the skill and immediately after the session to review what happened during the session and how to make improvements for the next session. Although a brief discussion after the observation session might be important for building rapport with the person being coached, allowing questions, and facilitating reflection, this might not be feasible for all teachers given classroom schedules. Ultimately, the timing of the feedback should be intentional such that the learner can attend and focus on the content.

Types and content of feedback. The focus of performance-based feedback is always to improve behavior. Thus, the feedback should be helpful and directed toward the identified target skill(s). Feedback should always include positive, constructive language such that the tone conveys a message of support. Although in some cases general feedback might be sufficient for improving behavior, more specific feedback should be used when teachers are initially learning new skills. General feedback (e.g., "You did a great job managing transitions today" versus "You effectively used 5 precorrections and 10 descriptive praise statements during transitions today") might be effective for skills that the teacher already has in her repertoire but is expected to use more often, across different children, or during different activities and routines. Specific feedback might be more useful for teaching new skills or procedures. Specific feedback might include implementation data from the session (e.g., frequency of a target skill, ratios of positive to negative statements, the percentage of correct use) or child outcomes (e.g., transition duration, frequency of challenging behaviors, engagement duration). Feedback should always be balanced such that it includes both positive, supportive statements about what went well and constructive statements to enhance future performance. Constructive feedback should be objective and non-judgmental in that the focus is on skill improvement rather than just on what went wrong.

Modeling. Modeling is an antecedent coaching strategy that can be used to show learners how to implement skills or strategies. Several different types of modeling have been identified in the early childhood coaching research (Artman-Meeker et al., 2015). Live modeling is when the coach shows the learner how to implement the target skill(s). Live models are usually conducted in the context and setting in which the learner is expected to use the target skill(s). For example, a coach might model how to use the system of least prompts to facilitate a child's play skills during free play with the child. Another type of modeling, video modeling, includes video recordings rather than live demonstrations of an adult implementing the skill(s). Demonstration video models often include adults with similar roles implementing the target skill(s) in similar contexts with similar children. Conversely, self-video models show clips of the learner practicing the skills in their own context. Video models may require more preparation time, but they can be beneficial because skills can be observed multiple times, examples and non-examples can be carefully planned and executed, and non-relevant parts of an activity can be excluded from the video via editing. Modeling is often paired with a discussion regarding the implementation of the skills and should include opportunities for the learner to ask questions about his/her implementation.

Role Play. Although role play was reported by Artman-Meeker and colleagues (2015) as the least reported coaching practice used, role play can provide an opportunity for learners to practice new skills in controlled contexts. Coaches can use role play to provide learners with an opportunity to practice new skills and receive performance-based feedback related to the skill. Role play might be particularly successful when teaching multistep and multicomponent interventions whereby the coach can break down the intervention into single steps, give learners opportunities to practice each step in settings without distractions, and provide performance-based feedback. This might increase initial fluency with complex interventions and increase the likelihood of success in typical contexts.

Practice. Modeling and role play are often followed by opportunities for the learner to practice the use of the target skills(s) in a contrived or in situ setting. The sole purpose of practice sessions is for learners to receive performance-based feedback from coaches related to their use of the targeted skill. Practice without feedback might lead to inappropriate use of a recently acquired skill. However, as learners increase their fluency with skills, the coach can provide less intensive or less specific feedback and focus the feedback on generalization of the skills across children, settings, or materials.

Checklists and Manuals. Checklists and manuals might be provided to introduce an intervention or to support ongoing implementation; however, they should not be used alone. Checklists, for example, were effectively used to provide performance-based feedback for teaching early childhood teachers to use zone defense scheduling for organizing adults (Casey & McWilliam, 2011). Likewise, manuals have been included as one of many components in effective coaching interventions (Artman-Meeker et al., 2015). Similar to performance-based feedback, checklists and manuals should be developed based on the target skills and learner characteristics. Checklists should be brief, focus directly on the skills at hand, be easy to complete, and structured to support the ongoing implementation of the skill(s). Manuals might be lengthier, but also should focus on target skill(s) and support ongoing implementation.

Michelle wants to teach her assistant teacher, Chelsea, to support the social interactions between specific children with disabilities and their peers with typical development. Chelsea occasionally attempts to do this when on the playground, but has struggled with follow through and providing feedback and reinforcement. Michelle also wants to teach her to do this across routines during the day. Michelle has a brief meeting with Chelsea before school one morning to discuss ways to facilitate social interactions, the children that are likely to benefit from this support, optimal times during the day to use this intervention, and a coaching plan. Chelsea says she already knows how to facilitate social interactions, but she would like support remembering when to do it and making sure she does it well. They develop a brief, written checklist outlining when and how to facilitate social interactions and they decide that Chelsea and Michelle will use the checklist each day; Chelsea will use it to self-monitor her implementation and Michelle will use it to give Chelsea feedback. They decide to briefly touch base at the end of each day to review their checklists. After five days, Chelsea indicates she feels more confident facilitating social interactions on the playground and Michelle indicates she notices improvements. However, Chelsea still struggles with using these techniques during other routines and activities. They decide to make some minor changes to the checklist to emphasize when and how to facilitate social interactions during specific routines such as morning center time, snack and meal times, and during transitions. They continue to complete the checklist, but Michelle also gives Chelsea performance-based feedback during these activities regarding her use of the strategies. After a couple weeks, Chelsea shows clear improvements and Michelle fades her in vivo performance-based feedback. They continue to complete the checklists each day, but adapt them over time as different needs arise in their classroom.

Research Abstract

Chazin, K. T., Barton, E. E., Ledford, J. R., & Pokorski, E. A. (2018). Implementation and intervention practices to facilitate communication skills for a child with complex communication needs. *Journal of Early Intervention*, 40, 138–157.

The authors designed a coaching package using a behavior skills training approach to teach four teachers from the same inclusive classroom to implement a comprehensive behavior intervention plan for a child with self-injurious behaviors and complex communication needs. Prior to starting the study, a functional analysis was conducted and a comprehensive behavior support plan was created in collaboration with the classroom teachers and two board certified behavior analysts. The behavior intervention plan included several components such as the use of an individual visual schedule, verbal transition warnings, having the child's AAC device within reach, blocking self-injurious behaviors, withholding attention for self-injurious behaviors, and responding to communication attempts. The coaching package included a didactic training with a presentation regarding the behavior intervention plan components and a basic overview of behavioral function, modeling, and opportunities for practice and feedback. The coaching occurred in two phases: the first phase included verbal and model prompts to the teacher and behavior-specific feedback, and the second phase only included behavior-specific feedback. Results indicated that the teachers did not show sustained increases in the implementation of the behavior support plan following the brief didactic training, but improved to consistent, high fidelity implementation with coaching.

Planning and Implementing Coaching

The previous sections reviewed the rationale for coaching, two comprehensive coaching models, and specific coaching strategies. This section will provide an overview of how to plan for and implement coaching. The following steps should be taken when planning coaching.

Establish rapport. It is the coach's job to establish strong, positive rapport with the learner/ teacher. Ideally, this is an ongoing process that takes time. However, in many contexts coaches do not have a lot of time on site to build rapport. Thus, coaches should develop several different strategies for building relationships with teachers and use them efficiently. This might include discussing shared teaching or educational experiences, establishing a commitment to a common goal (e.g., reducing challenging behaviors for a specific child, improving early math skills for the children in a classroom), and identifying the teacher's specific strengths. Coaches also might build rapport by helping out behind the scenes (e.g., making visuals or other materials for the teacher); wiping tables or helping with other obvious tasks; or stepping in when the teacher requests help with a specific child or activity. If opportunities for in-person contact are limited the coach can check in via email, text, or phone, depending on the teacher's preferred communication method. Starting coaching without building rapport might result in limited adult behavior change due to a lack of motivation or engagement by the teacher.

Identify target behaviors. While building rapport, the coach should start to identify the focus of the coaching—the specific target behavior(s) or intervention(s). Sometimes, the coach's primary role involves coaching a discrete skill, complex teaching strategies, or multi-component interventions. Whether the coach is focused on one skill (e.g., a teacher's use of the system of least prompts to teach play, a paraprofessional's use of constant time delay to teach pre-academic skills) or a comprehensive intervention (e.g., the teacher's use of Pyramid Model practices; Hemmeter et al., 2016), the coach and the learner should identify and operationalize a target behavior. Also, the target child behaviors hypothesized to be impacted by improvements in teacher behaviors should be identified. For example, if the coach is using BST to train a teacher to use progressive time delay (PTD) embedded into a small group play context to teach pre-academic targets, the targeted behaviors for the teacher are PTD, embedded instruction, and small group instruction, while the targeted behaviors for child are specific pre-academic skills. Table 15.2 lists coaching strategies that are likely to be effective for different types of target behaviors.

Identify coaching strategies. Depending on the target skills and the available resources, the coach might use a comprehensive coaching approach (i.e., PBC or BST) or select from the menu of coaching strategies. PBC or BST might be more effective when teaching complex or multi-component interventions and when the coach has adequate time and resources. Further, a comprehensive approach might be helpful as coaches are initially learning how to coach. When teachers are learning a discrete skill, a comprehensive approach may not be needed, as one or more individual coaching strategies might be effective. For example, performance-based feedback with and without didactic trainings have been effective for teaching discrete verbal skills such as descriptive praise and the use of language and play expansions to early childhood professionals (Barton et al., 2013; Hemmeter et al., 2011). Table 15.3 lists coaching strategies and components.

Identify intensity of timing and supports needed. The intensity of the coaching will be dictated by the availability of the coach, the teacher's schedule, available resources, the teacher's current skill level related to the target behaviors, and the complexity of the target behaviors. Coaching might occur on a continuum, from the coach modeling the skills with the children and in the intended context to the coach observing and providing specific feedback. The intensity and duration of coaching should be discussed and agreed upon by the coach and the learner prior to the start of coaching.

Identify coaching delivery formats and communication type. Coaching can be delivered in person (face-to-face) or remotely (e.g., via FaceTime, Skype, Zoom). There are a plethora of new technologies that can be used to deliver coaching remotely and several have been used and tested in early childhood contexts (Artman-Meeker, Hemmeter, & Snyder 2014; Pianta et al., 2008). Current research suggests distance coaching might be a cost-effective and efficient option when resources are limited or distance and travel preclude on-site coaching. However, the delivery format will be dictated by the availability of the coach, the teacher's schedule, the resources, the teacher's current skill level related to the target behaviors, and the target behaviors. For example, distance coaching might be ideal for situations where location or travel times are a challenge. However, distance coaching might not be ideal when you are training teachers to use complex or multicomponent interventions in which teachers will likely need in situ modeling and feedback. Regardless of the delivery format, the communication type should be decided upfront and coaches should use the learner's preferred means of communication if possible. Email or text communication might be effective for skills that can be counted, timed, or briefly summarized. Verbal face-to-face or distance communication (via Skype, Facetime, or telephone) is effective for many different types of target behaviors and might be particularly useful when supporting teachers in using new or complex skills.

Identify feedback type and content. Performance-based feedback is an essential aspect of coaching and can be delivered alone, with other coaching strategies (e.g., modeling, practice), or as part of a comprehensive coaching intervention (e.g., PBC). Specific types of performance-based feedback are discussed in the previous section. The type (e.g., verbal, graphical, email, checklists) and the content (e.g., verbatim examples, constructive feedback) should be identified based on the available resources and the target instructional behavior. Graphical feedback could be useful for skills that can be counted or timed. Checklists will be useful for identifying the correct implementation of specific steps or components of complex interventions. Multiple types of feedback also might be useful for complex target behaviors or multi-component interventions. Also, the coach might ask the teacher/learner for their preferred communication format (e.g., email, text, verbal, written). Complex behaviors might require more detailed and specific feedback, whereas discrete behaviors might improve with simply brief supportive and constructive statements.

Commence implementation and monitoring. Once the coaching intensity, delivery, and strategies have been identified, coaching can commence. Although the coach should establish rapport prior to commencing, the coach can continue to build rapport during coaching. Coaches should monitor their coaching, the teacher's use of target behaviors, and relevant child outcomes.

Additional Coaching Considerations

Generalization. Coaching should be designed to focus on generalized skills. Effective coaching ensures teachers can implement evidence-based practices across children, settings, materials, and target behaviors. From the start, coaching must be systematically planned such that learners receive performance-based feedback regarding their use of the targeted skills in more than one setting and across different learners.

Maintenance. There is some evidence of observer effect in the early childhood coaching research (Barton et al., 2018). This means teachers might be more likely to implement specific skills when they know they are being observed. To avoid this and facilitate the maintenance of skills implementation, coaches might make a specific plan with the teacher regarding their use of the target instructional behaviors outside of the observation times. Coaches also might develop self-monitoring systems (e.g., checklists, tallies) such that teachers can record their own use of the target instructional behaviors when the coach is not there. Finally, coaches should plan the intensity (i.e., dosage) of coaching such that maintenance observations can be conducted at regular intervals (e.g., 2 weeks, 6 weeks, 10 weeks, etc.) after teachers master the implementation of the target instructional behaviors.

Lack of progress. When teachers are not making adequate progress, coaches should review their coaching plan to ensure they are delivering the coaching as intended. If they are coaching as intended, coaches might review their specific coaching plan and make adjustments based on the data. For example, the coach might provide more frequent or more specific performance-based feedback if the teacher needs minor adjustments. If more significant improvements are needed, the coach might have to provide more intensive in situ modeling and more opportunities for practice with feedback. Coaches also should review child outcome data and adapt coaching or the target practices as needed if children are not making adequate progress.

Table 15.2 Types of Targets and Specific Coaching Strategies

Professional Development Components		Performance feedback	Live Modeling	Video Models	Role Play	Manuals/ Checklists
Types of Target Behaviors	Discrete	√		√		
	Complex	√	√	√	√	√
	Multi-Component	√	√	√	√	√

Table 15.3 Coaching Strategies and Components

Coaching Strategies	Frequency	Intensity of Support [a]	Delivery	Communication Format	Timing	Feedback Type	Feedback Content
• Performance-based feedback • Modeling • Role Play • Checklists • Manuals • Practice	• Multiple times per day • Daily • Several times per week • Weekly • Several times per month	• Coach provides video models of the target instructional behavior prior to observation • Coach models the target instructional behavior and teacher observes • Coach prompts and provides performance-based feedback while teacher practices the target instructional behavior with adults • Coach prompts and provides performance-based feedback while teacher practices the target instructional behavior with children • Coach provides performance-based feedback while teacher implements the target instructional behavior (without coach prompts) with children • Coach provides performance-based feedback after teacher implements the target instructional behavior with children and does not prompt during the session • Coach observes and provides general feedback	• Face-to-Face • Distance	• Email • Text • Written narrative • Verbal, face-to-face • Verbal, from a distance	• Immediately after • Live • Delayed	• Supportive • Constructive	• Frequency data of the adult • Verbatim examples • Frequency data for the child • Checklists • Graphs

[a] Adapted from Rush and Shelden (2011).

After a few months, Michelle reflects on the progress of the adults and children in her classroom. She successfully used BST with Sasha and Malia and now they are effectively running three small groups per day. As a result, the children with disabilities are making adequate progress toward several IEP goals. Her assistant teacher, Chelsea, has been using a variety of strategies to facilitate social interactions across the school day. All four of the teachers have observed that the children with disabilities are engaged in more frequent social interactions across multiple activities. Recently, a new child with disabilities, who uses an AAC device to communicate, started in the classroom. Michelle plans to use BST to teach Chelsea to teach this child to communicate functionally using her AAC. Michelle is quite pleased how efficiently the adults in her classroom are working and looks forward to supporting the learning and development of all children in her classroom.

Research Abstract

Ledford, J. R., Zimmerman, K. N., Chazin, K. T., Patel, N. M., Morales, V. A., & Bennett, B. P. (2017). Coaching paraprofessionals to promote engagement and social interactions during small group activities. *Journal of Behavioral Education*, 26(4), 410–432.

In this single case research design study, the authors used a behavior skills training approach with coaching and feedback to teach effective small group instruction to three paraprofessionals working in inclusive preschool classrooms. The coaching and feedback specifically targeted their use of environmental arrangement, prompting, and praise. The paraprofessionals learned to implement the target skills accurately after a relatively brief coaching session and small number of sessions. Also, children had some improvements in the engagement and social interactions.

References

Artman-Meeker, K. M., Fettig, A., Barton, E. E., Penney, A., & Zeng, S. (2015). Applying an evidence-based framework to the early childhood coaching literature. *Topics in Early Childhood Special Education*, 35, 183–196.

Artman-Meeker, K. M., Hemmeter, M. L., & Snyder, P. (2014). Effects of distance coaching on teachers' use of Pyramid Model practices: A pilot study. *Infants & Young Children*, 27, 325–344.

Barton, E. E., Chen, C. I., Pribble, L., Pomes, M., & Kim, Y. A. (2013). Coaching preservice teachers to teach play skills to children with disabilities. *Teacher Education and Special Education*, 36, 330–349.

Barton, E. E., Fuller, E. A., & Schnitz, A. (2016). The use of e-mail to coach preservice early childhood teachers. *Topics in Early Childhood Special Education*, 36, 78–90.

Barton, E. E., Kinder, K., Casey, A. M., & Artman, K. M. (2011). Finding your feedback fit: Strategies for designing and delivering performance feedback systems. *Young Exceptional Children*, 14, 29–46.

Barton, E. E., Pokorski, E. A., Gossett, S., Sweeney, E., Qui, J., & Choi, G. (2018). The use of e-mail to coach early childhood teachers. *Journal of Early Intervention*, 40, 212–228.

Barton, E. E., Pribble, L., & Chen, C. I. (2013). The use of e-mail to deliver performance-based feedback to early childhood practitioners. *Journal of Early Intervention*, 35, 270–297.

Casey, A. M., & McWilliam, R. A. (2008). Graphical feedback to increase teachers' use of incidental teaching. *Journal of Early Intervention*, 30, 251–268.

Casey, A. M., & McWilliam, R. A. (2011). The characteristics and effectiveness of feedback interventions applied in early childhood settings. *Topics in Early Childhood Special Education*, 31, 68–77.

Chazin, K. T., Barton, E. E., Ledford, J. R., & Pokorski, E. A. (2018). Implementation and intervention practices to facilitate communication skills for a child with complex communication needs. *Journal of Early Intervention*, 40, 138–157.

Conroy, M. A., Sutherland, K. S., Algina, J. J., Wilson, R. E., Martinez, J., & Whalon, K. J. (2014). Measuring teacher implementation of the BEST in CLASS intervention program and corollary child outcomes. *Journal of Emotional and Behavioral Disorders*, 23, 144–155.

Conroy, M. A., Sutherland, K. S., Vo, A. K., Carr, S., & Ogston, S. (2014). Early childhood teachers' use of effective instructional practices and the collateral effects on young children's behavior. *Journal of Positive Behavior Interventions*, 16, 81–92.

Coogle, C. G., Rahn, N. L., & Ottley, J. R. (2015). Pre-service teacher use of communication strategies upon receiving immediate feedback. *Early Childhood Research Quarterly*, 32, 105–115.

DEC (Division for Early Childhood). (2014). DEC recommended practices in early intervention/early childhood special education 2014. Retrieved from www.dec-sped.org/recommendedpractices.

Fox, L., Hemmeter, M. L., Snyder, P., Binder, D. P., & Clarke, S. (2011). Coaching early childhood special educators to implement a comprehensive model for promoting young children's social competence. *Topics in Early Childhood Special Education*, 31, 178–192.

Hemmeter, M. L., Snyder, P., Fox, L., & Algina, J. (2016). Evaluating the implementation of the Pyramid Model for promoting social-emotional competence in early childhood classrooms. *Topics in Early Childhood Special Education*, 36, 133–146.

Hemmeter, M. L., Snyder, P., Kinder, K., & Artman, K. (2011). Impact of performance feedback delivered via electronic mail on preschool teachers' use of descriptive praise. *Early Childhood Research Quarterly*, 26, 96–109.

Ledford, J. R., Zimmerman, K. N., Chazin, K. T., Patel, N. M., Morales, V. A., & Bennett, B. P. (2017). Coaching paraprofessionals to promote engagement and social interactions during small group activities. *Journal of Behavioral Education*, 26, 410–432.

Lerman, D. C., Vorndran, C., Addison, L., & Kuhn, S. A. C. (2004). A rapid assessment of skills in young children with autism. *Journal of Applied Behavior Analysis*, 37, 11–26.

Love, J. R., Carr, J. E., LeBlanc, L. A., & Kisamore, A. N. (2013). Training behavioral research methods to staff in an early and intensive behavioral setting: A program description and preliminary evaluation. *Education and Treatment of Children*, 36, 139–160.

Matthews, K., & Hagopian, L. (2014). A comparison of two data analysis training methods for paraprofessionals in an educational setting. *Journal of Organizational Behavior Management*, 34, 165–178.

Miltenberger, R. G. (2012). *Behavior modification: Principles and procedures* (5th ed.). Belmont, CA: Wadsworth Cengage Learning.

Pianta, R. C., Mashburn, A. J., Downer, J. T., Hamre, B. K., & Justice, L. (2008). Effects of web-mediated professional development resources on teacher–child interactions in pre-kindergarten classrooms. *Early Childhood Research Quarterly*, 23, 431–451.

Rush, D. D., & Shelden, M. L. (2008). Common misperceptions about coaching in early intervention. *CASEinPoint*, 4(1), 1–4.

Rush, D., & Shelden, M. (2011). *The early childhood coaching handbook*. Baltimore, MD: Brookes.

Schepis, M. M., Ownbey, J. B., Parsons, M. B., & Reid, D. H. (2000). Training support staff for teaching young children with disabilities in an inclusive preschool setting. *Journal of Positive Behavior Interventions*, 2, 170–178.

Schepis, M. M., Reid, D. H., Ownbey, J., & Parsons, M. B. (2001). Training support staff to embed teaching within natural routines of young children with disabilities in an inclusive preschool. *Journal of Applied Behavior Analysis*, 34, 313–327.

Shepley, C., Lane, J. D., Grisham-Brown, J., Spriggs, A. D., & Winstead, O. (2017). Effects of a training package to increase teachers' fidelity of naturalistic instructional procedures in inclusive preschool classrooms. *Teacher Education and Special Education*, 41, 321–339.

Sheridan, S. M., Edwards, C. P., Marvin, C. A., & Knoche, L. L. (2009). Professional development in early childhood programs: Process issues and research needs. *Early Education and Development*, 20, 377–401.

Snyder, P., Hemmeter, M. L., McLean, M., Sandall, S., McLaughlin, T., & Algina, J. (2018). Effects of professional development on preschool teachers' use of embedded instruction practices. *Exceptional Children, 84*, 213–232.

Snyder, P. A., Hemmeter, M. L., & Fox, L. (2015). Supporting implementation of evidence-based practices through practice-based coaching. *Topics in Early Childhood Special Education, 35*, 133–143.

Snyder, P., Hemmeter, M. L., & McLaughlin, T. (2011). Professional development in early childhood intervention: Where we stand on the silver anniversary of PL 99-457. *Journal of Early Intervention, 33*, 357–370.

Snyder, P., Hemmeter, M. L., Meeker, K. A., Kinder, K., Pasia, C., & McLaughlin, T. (2012). Characterizing key features of the early childhood professional development literature. *Infants & Young Children, 25*, 188–212.

Strain, P. S., & Bovey, E. H. (2011). Randomized, controlled trial of the LEAP model of early intervention for young children with autism spectrum disorders. *Topics in Early Childhood Special Education, 31*, 133–154.

Sutherland, K. S., Conroy, M. A., Vo, A., & Ladwig, C. (2015). Implementation integrity of practice-based coaching: Preliminary results from the BEST in CLASS efficacy trial. *School Mental Health, 7*, 21–33.

Tate, T. L., Thompson, R. H., & McKerchar, P. M. (2005). Training teachers in an infant classroom to use embedded teaching strategies. *Education and Treatment of Children, 28*, 206–221.

Trivette, C. M., Dunst, C. J., Hamby, D. W., & O'Herin, C. E. (2009). Characteristics and consequences of adult learning methods and strategies. *Practical Evaluation Reports, 2*(1), 1–32.

16 Specific Considerations for Coaching Families

Key Terms

Coaching   Teach-model-coach-review   Routines-based model
Behavioral skills training   Family-guided routines-based intervention

Chapter Objectives

After completing this chapter, readers should be able to:

- Identify effective strategies for coaching with parents.
- Name strategies that have been successfully used by parent implementers.

After having their morning coffee, Raphael and Yvonne grab their girls' shoes and coats in preparation for the morning commute. Getting the girls out of the door each morning has become a daunting process. After repeatedly reminding Livy that she will lose her iPad time after school if she doesn't get her shoes and coat on, both parents become frustrated. Livy's behavior escalates; she runs out of the room with only one shoe only half way on. When the timer on the microwave starts to beep, Raphael and Yvonne look at each other exhaustedly and proceed to put both kids in the car without shoes and coats. They decide that this daily morning chaos has got to stop and they need professional help.

The primary purpose of this chapter is to describe effective family coaching strategies. We will describe several comprehensive approaches to family coaching including for whom they have been effective. We also will delineate effective family coaching strategies.

Family Coaching Overview

In 2016, the U.S. Department of Health and Human Services and the U.S. Department of Education recently released a joint policy statement on family engagement. The policy statement purports that all early childhood systems should recognize and support family engagement in children's learning, development, and wellness. They outlined several specific family-focused practices such as respecting families, focusing on strengths, and being flexible and collaborative. They emphasized the importance of building a supportive and reciprocal relationship with families that demonstrates value and respect for the caregiving role. Their position statement was based on the wealth of research that supports the relation between strong family engagement in the early years and positive outcomes for children including their overall development, academic success, and long-term health and wellness.

For example, families of infants and toddlers with disabilities often receive early intervention (EI) services in their homes (i.e., natural environments). Effective collaboration in this context is characterized by team-based decision-making whereby professionals and families jointly identify IFSP goals and services, and EI practitioners support and coach families to enhance their children's learning and development in natural settings (e.g., homes, child care). A different type of collaboration might occur for preschool children with disabilities who receive services in the least restrictive environment (e.g., inclusive preschool classrooms; see Chapter 15).

The Division for Early Childhood Recommended Practices include an entire topic area focused on family practices guided by three themes: family-centered practices, family capacity building, and family and professional collaboration (DEC, 2014). There also are specific practices across other topic areas focused on working with families. For example, family coaching practices align with the DEC Instruction-Recommended Practice #13: "Providers use coaching or consultation strategies with primary caregivers or other adults to facilitate positive adult–child interactions and instruction intentionally designed to promote child learning and development" (2014, p. 12).

Relatedly, an emerging body of research supports family-coaching or consultative approaches that focus on supporting parents, particularly on supporting parent–child interactions (Powell & Dunlap, 2010). These approaches maximize children's opportunities for learning by teaching caregivers to be responsive adults during typical daily routines and interactions with their children (McWilliam, 2010). Supporting caregivers in enhancing their child's learning and development is associated with positive benefits for both the children and parents (Dunst et al., 2007) and might be particularly important in the early years to mediate long-term impact related to preventing deleterious outcomes (Fettig & Barton, 2014).

In recent years, several specific family coaching practices have been identified (Friedman, Woods, & Salisbury, 2012; Powell & Dunlap, 2010; Salisbury et al., 2018) along with strategies for training practitioners to use these practices (see Chapter 15; Brown & Woods, 2012; Marturana & Woods, 2012). Family coaching practices, like practitioner coaching practices, are based on principles of adult learning, which assert that adults learn when they are actively engaged; have multiple opportunities to practice in the immediate, relevant context; participate in self-reflection and assessment; and are taught using a variety of methods (Dunst & Trivette, 2012). When practitioners coach families, they use practices while also focusing on parent–child interactions and daily routines (Rush & Sheldon, 2011). The goal of family coaching is to support parents' confidence and competence in supporting their child's learning and development (Allen & Huff, 2014). The practitioner works directly with the parent—rather than the child—to support the parent's use of effective strategies across daily routines. In this manner, the child receives substantially more learning opportunities than would be provided if the practitioner alone worked with the child (McWilliam, 2010). Family coaches adapt and match practices taught to the needs of the family. The coach's primary focus is on the family's participation in their child's development and learning. Although family coaching is a primary method of service provision in EI, family coaching can occur for children of all ages. In the following sections we will outline existing family coaching approaches and specific family coaching characteristics and practices.

Routines-based Models

Teach-Model-Coach-Review

Teach-Model-Coach-Review (TMCR) is a manualized approach to family coaching. TMCR was developed specifically for teaching parents to use language elicitation strategies (Kaiser & Roberts, 2013) and has been shown to be effective for teaching parents to use Enhanced Milieu Teaching (EMT). The four elements of TMCR were developed based on the synthesis of adult learning strategies by Trivette et al. (2009), which are described in the previous section. The first element—**Teach**—involves both initial didactic teaching regarding the rationale and steps for each strategy and a review of each specific strategy prior to each coaching session. The didactic training might occur in a group or one-to-one workshop in which the trainer (e.g., therapist, coach) provides an overview of the specific intervention (e.g., EMT) and each specific strategy (e.g., time delay, language expansions), a rationale for the intervention, and examples of each strategy. During the pre-session review, the trainer reviews one specific strategy (e.g., language expansions), models the strategy, and practices with the parent during a role-play scenario. This gives the parent an opportunity to review and practice and provides the trainer with an opportunity to observe how well the parent understands the implementation of the strategy. The second element—**Model**—occurs immediately after the review component. The therapist models the strategy directly with the child and remains focused on the child, but occasionally makes comments to the parents regarding specific aspects of the strategy. During the third element—**Coach**—the parent interacts with the child and uses the strategy while the trainer provides performance-based feedback (i.e., both praise and constructive feedback). During the fourth and final element—**Review**—the trainer summarizes the parent's use of the strategy. The trainer also asks several open-ended questions to elicit parent reflection.

Research Abstract

Wright, C. A., & Kaiser, A. P. (2017). Teaching parents enhanced milieu teaching with words and signs using the teach-model-coach-review model. *Topics in Early Childhood Special Education*, 36, 192–204.

   In this study, the authors used the Teach-Model-Coach-Review model to teach enhanced milieu teaching words and signs to parents of children with Down syndrome. The authors conducted an hour-long workshop for parents and provided handouts with strategy summaries. Following each workshop, the parents practiced the strategies with their coach and child in the home and clinic until fidelity criteria were met. Parents' fidelity increased to levels higher with coaching.

Family-Guided Routines-based Intervention

Family-Guided Routines-based Intervention (FGRBI; Cripe & Venn, 1997; Woods, Kashinath, & Goldstein, 2004) has been primarily used to teach parents of toddlers and young children with communication delays to use practices that support language development. FGRBI includes seven different processes that are implemented in a step-wise fashion. The first process is introducing the concept of the natural environment, which can be unfamiliar to both providers and families. This allows providers and parents to set the stage for the intervention; the providers can explain the importance of active family participation. The second process is routines-based assessments in natural environments during which the priorities and concerns of the family are discussed. During the third process, the coach works with the parents to link assessment to intervention. Through discussion of the child's assessment outcomes, a functional and meaningful intervention plan is developed. Given that the first two processes focus on routines, outcomes are identified that reflect the skills necessary to function in the routines and activities identified as important to the family. Further, opportunities to embed learning are identified which consider the needs, preferences, and interests of the child and must involve adults in the child's life. The process accommodates the priorities and concerns of families by encouraging family members to share information about their family routines including the strategies that they have previously tried that have worked well and those that have not worked well. The fourth process includes involving caregivers in teaching and learning in ways that match their learning history and participation in the routine. The fifth process is monitoring progress. This is critical for identifying the effectiveness of family coaching. Data should be collected from a variety of sources and should directly reflect the family's concerns. The sixth process, coaching, involves the provider supporting parent–child interactions during routines. The seventh and final process is sharing Family Stories. Family Stories are examples of how FGRBI has worked well with other families for a range of outcomes.

Routines-based Model

Over the past 30 years, McWilliam (2010) has developed the **Routines-based Model** for working with young children with disabilities and their families. The whole model consists of 17 components, organized by (a) intervention planning, (b) providing supports, and (c) the Engagement Classroom Model. The practitioner uses the Routines-based Interview (RBI) to start the process (McWilliam, Casey, & Sims, 2009). The RBI is a semi-structured interview that asks caregivers to describe their daily routines and their child's participation in those routines, and helps caregivers identify priority outcomes. This model emphasizes the child's engagement and independence within the family's routines and caregivers' satisfaction with their routines. The child's engagement in specific, targeted routines becomes the primary outcome. The practitioner focuses his/her coaching on supporting the caregivers to facilitate their child's engagement during each routine. All intervention strategies are embedded into routines.

Behavioral Approaches

Several researchers have successfully used behavioral approaches to teach parents to prevent their child's challenging behaviors and support social-emotional competence. For example, behavior skills training is described in detail in Chapter 15 with a focus on working with early childhood professionals. **Behavior skills training** also has been used to teach parents to conduct functional assessments using direct observations and implement behavioral interventions based on functional assessments (Shayne & Miltenberger, 2013). The BST approach is similar for parents and teachers. The primary components are: didactic training, modeling, practice, and systematic feedback. Other researchers have used similar behavioral procedures, including describing the procedures (didactic training), modeling, and role play (practice) with feedback (McIntyre, 2008). Behavioral approaches have primarily been used to support parents in reducing their child's challenging behaviors. Additional research is needed supporting parents' use of strategies that support child skills acquisition and competence across domains.

Livy's parents, Rapheal and Yvonne, set up a meeting with Ebony, the behavior specialist at Livy's school, to discuss the challenges at home during morning routines. With the support of Ebony, Rapheal and Yvonne created a visual schedule for Livy to follow during the morning routines, similar to the one Livy follows at school. Ebony role-played with Rapheal and Yvonne regarding how the visual schedule might be implemented at home. She modeled how to use the visual schedule, how to provide frequent positive attention and praise to Livy for appropriate behaviors, and how to avoid providing additional attention to Livy for not complying with the morning routine. Ebony also sent them follow-up texts every week to provide ongoing support and checked-in regularly at school.

Family Coaching Characteristics

Family-centered practices. Family centeredness is a term used to define how practitioners should consider and support families (DEC, 2014). Family centeredness can be conceptualized as two distinct categories—(1) relationship between practitioners and families, and (2) the extent to which parents meaningfully participate in planning and implementing interventions. Family-centered practices demonstrate an awareness and respect for individual family values and beliefs and support the developing relationship between the practitioner and the family. Family-centered practices are responsive to families' priorities, resources, and concerns. Practitioners using family-centered practices show an awareness and appreciation of each family's unique needs, support individual families in making informed choices, and enhance their capacity to support their child's development. Practitioners may be more likely to establish rapport with families, but may display difficulties allowing families to actively and meaningfully participate in planning and implementation (Dunst & Dempsey, 2007). Thus, practitioners need to collaborate with families across interactions and related sessions.

Capacity building. A primary component of family-centered practices is family capacity building. This means practitioners support the family's capacity (i.e., knowledge and skills) to support their child's development and their family's well-being. Capacity building practices include, for example, coaching the family rather than providing direct services to the child, focusing on the family's routines (and minor changes to their current routines), using materials from the natural environment (e.g., family's home) during intervention, and developing an appreciation for the family's beliefs and values. Practitioners facilitate the parent's acquisition of new skills, which improves their confidence and competence in supporting their child's development.

Routines. A key component of family coaching includes operationalizing learning opportunities that occur during daily routines with the family's own materials. The family coach should plan to support families in using specific strategies that involve *minor changes* to what they are already doing. As described in the previous section, many of the family coaching approaches focus on embedding instruction into the family's daily routines. Embedding intervention within daily routines and activities has been effective for enhancing parents' use of effective practices and communication outcomes for children with communication delays (Woods, Kashinath, & Goldstein, 2004). For infants and toddlers with disabilities, who by law have to be served in the natural environment, routines provide a naturally occurring context for embedding instruction.

Self-reflection. Self-reflection is a critical component of the coaching process as it provides an opportunity for the practitioner and caregivers to examine progress and adjust implementation strategies accordingly. Practitioners support caregivers in engaging in regular *self-reflection* regarding their child's progress, their sense of competence, and their satisfaction with routines, their child's behaviors, or their use of specific interventions. Practitioners should engage in self-reflection to ensure they are (a) using family-centered and capacity building practices, (b) effectively communicating with families particularly when there are disagreements or difficult conversations, and (c) seeking support from peers or other experts as needed.

Family Coaching Practices

The research on adult learning clearly points to the need for ongoing supports to ensure caregivers are confident and competent in supporting their child's development. Several specific, evidence-informed family coaching practices have emerged from the research on family supports. Although a good proportion of this research relates to supporting families with children with language delays and challenging behaviors (Barton & Fettig, 2013; Fettig & Barton, 2014; Roberts & Kaiser, 2011), the practices are applicable for supporting caregivers with children with a range of needs (e.g., autism spectrum disorder; Lane et al., 2016).

Modeling. Modeling can be done live by the practitioner, or using videos. Modeling directly demonstrates specific instructional strategies during specific routines. Live models should accurately represent the exact use of the strategy with relevant materials and within relevant routines. Modeling is used to show caregivers how to use specific skills and should be used along with opportunities for practices and performance-based feedback.

Practice. Practitioners should ensure caregivers have multiple and varied opportunities to practice new skills and receive feedback and support to improve competency with new skills. Practice opportunities can occur during relevant routines with the family materials and the child. Practitioners and caregivers can plan multiple opportunities for practice during coaching sessions and outside of coaching sessions during typical routines.

Performance-based feedback. When caregivers practice and use new skills, practitioners should provide performance-based feedback. Feedback should be based on specific skills the caregiver is learning to use and should include both supportive feedback and corrective feedback. Supportive feedback highlights what the caregiver did well, while corrective feedback gives specific suggestions for improvement. Feedback should always be specific enough that it tells the caregivers exactly what they did accurately and what they might change to improve outcomes for their child.

Collaborative progress monitoring. The coach and caregivers should work together to identify primary outcomes and a method for monitoring progress toward those outcomes. The caregivers and provider regularly collect and review data to make decisions about goals or changes to routines.

Using novel technologies. Family coaching practices might be time intensive and most families receive limited time with coaches. However, the burgeoning use of internet and mobile technologies to support families is promising for reaching families in rural areas, communicating with families in between visits, and providing increased intensity of supports. Mobile technologies are widely accessible and can be used to provide ongoing support to caregivers when providers cannot be physically present (Baggett et al., 2010; Meadan & Daczewitz, 2015; Meadan, Meyer, Snodgrass, & Halle, 2013). For example, text messaging has been effectively used in many areas of education and healthcare (Bigelow, Carta, & Lefever, 2008). For example, providers might send daily or weekly text reminders to caregivers to check in regarding child progress, or use mobile technologies to connect caregivers with each other to facilitate support systems.

After a few weeks Livy started using the visual schedule without prompting and Rapheal and Yvonne were quite satisfied with the routines. However, they had moved Livy into a new bed and the bedtime routine was taking longer and longer. Ebony problem solved with them regarding how they might be able to make the process more efficient. Ebony supported them in outlining the bedtime routine and then modifying the visual schedule used for Livy's morning routine. They were excited to try it out and confident they could teach Livy to use it successfully.

Research Abstract

Brown, J. A., & Woods, J. J. (2015). Effects of a triadic parent-implemented home-based communication intervention for toddlers. *Journal of Early Intervention*, 37, 44–68.

In this study, the authors coached nine parents of toddlers with disabilities to implement communication strategies during family-identified routines. Parents demonstrated increased responsive and modeling strategy use, and children exhibited higher rates of targeted communication forms from baseline to intervention phases. The coaching consisted of observation, opportunities for practice, and problem-solving within routines and across the session to build the parents' capacity to embed effective strategies into their routines. With coaching, parents increased their use of the strategies, and most children had increases in their communication targets.

Research Abstract

Fettig, A., Schultz, T. R., & Sreckovic, M. A. (2015). Effects of coaching on the implementation of functional assessment-based parent intervention in reducing challenging behaviors. *Journal of Positive Behavior Interventions*, 17, 170–180.

In this study, the authors coached three parents of young children to implement function-based interventions to reduce their children's challenging behaviors at home. Coaching consisted of an initial parent training session on implementing the FA-based strategies. This included a strategy review, modeling, and corrective and supportive feedback. With ongoing coaching, parents implemented the strategies at a high level and children's challenging behavior decreased, which maintained when coaching was withdrawn.

References

Allen, K., & Huff, N. L. (2014). Family coaching: An emerging family science field. *Family Relations*, 63(5), 569–582.

Baggett, K. M., Davis, B., Feil, E. G., Sheeber, L. L., Landry, S. H., Carta, J. J., & Leve, C. (2010). Technologies for expanding the reach of evidence-based interventions: Preliminary results for promoting social-emotional development in early childhood. *Topics in Early Childhood Special Education*, 29, 226–238.

Barton, E. E., & Fettig, A. (2013). Parent-implemented interventions for young children with disabilities: A review of fidelity features. *Journal of Early Intervention*, 35(2), 194–219.

Bigelow, K. M., Carta, J. J., & Lefever, J. B. (2008). Txt U ltr: Using cellular phone technology to enhance a parenting intervention for families at risk for neglect. *Child Maltreatment*, 13(4), 362–367.

Brown, J. A., & Woods, J. J. (2012). Evaluation of a multicomponent online communication professional development program for early interventionists. *Journal of Early Intervention*, 34(4), 222–242.

Cripe, J. W., & Venn, M. L. (1997). Family-guided routines for early intervention services. *Young Exceptional Children*, 1(1), 18–26.

Division for Early Childhood (2014). DEC Recommended Practices. Arlington, VA: DEC. Retrieved from https://divisionearlychildhood.egnyte.com/dl/tgv6GUXhVo .

Dunst, C. J., & Dempsey, I. (2007). Family-professional partnerships and parenting competence, confidence, and enjoyment. *International Journal of Disability, Development and Education*, 54, 305–318.

Dunst, C. J., & Trivette, C. M. (2012). Moderators of the effectiveness of adult learning method practices. *Journal of Social Sciences*, 8(2), 143.

Dunst, C. J., Trivette, C. M., & Hamby, D. W. (2007). Meta-analysis of family-centered helpgiving practices research. *Mental Retardation and Developmental Disabilities Research Reviews*, 13(4), 370–378.

Fettig, A., & Barton, E. E. (2014). Parent implementation of function-based intervention to reduce children's challenging behavior: A literature review. *Topics in Early Childhood Special Education*, 34(1), 49–61.

Friedman, M., Woods, J., & Salisbury, C. (2012). Caregiver coaching strategies for early intervention providers: Moving toward operational definitions. *Infants & Young Children*, 25, 62–82.

Kaiser, A. P., & Roberts, M. Y. (2013). Parent-implemented enhanced milieu teaching with preschool children who have intellectual disabilities. *Journal of Speech, Language and Hearing Research (Online)*, 56(1), 295–309.

Lane, J. D., Ledford, J. R., Shepley, C., Mataras, T. K., Ayres, K. M., & Davis, A. B. (2016). A brief coaching intervention for teaching naturalistic strategies to parents. *Journal of Early Intervention*, 38, 135–150.

Marturana, E. R., & Woods, J. J. (2012). Technology-supported performance-based feedback for early intervention home visiting. *Topics in Early Childhood Special Education*, 32, 14–23.

McIntyre, L. L. (2008). Parent training for young children with developmental disabilities: Randomized controlled trial. *American Journal on Mental Retardation*, 113(5), 356–368.

McWilliam, R. A. (2010). Routines-based early intervention. *Supporting Young Children and Their Families*. Baltimore, MD: Brookes.

McWilliam, R. A., Casey, A. M., & Sims, J. (2009). The routines-based interview: A method for gathering information and assessing needs. *Infants & Young Children*, 22, 224–233.

Meadan, H., & Daczewitz, M. E. (2015). Internet-based intervention training for parents of young children with disabilities: a promising service-delivery model. *Early Child Development and Care*, 185(1), 155–169.

Meadan, H., Meyer, L. E., Snodgrass, M. R., & Halle, J. W. (2013). Coaching parents of young children with autism in rural areas using internet-based technologies: A pilot program. *Rural Special Education Quarterly*, 32(3), 3–10.

Powell, D., & Dunlap, G. (2010). Family-focused interventions for promoting social-emotional development in infants and toddlers with or at risk for disabilities. roadmap to effective intervention practices# 5. *Technical Assistance Center on Social Emotional Intervention for Young Children*.

Roberts, M. Y., & Kaiser, A. P. (2011). The effectiveness of parent-implemented language interventions: A meta-analysis. *American Journal of Speech-Language Pathology*, 20, 180–199.

Rush, D. & Shelden, M. (2011). *The early childhood coaching handbook*. Baltimore, MD: Brookes.

Salisbury, C., Woods, J., Snyder, P., Moddelmog, K., Mawdsley, H., Romano, M., & Windsor, K. (2018). Caregiver and provider experiences with coaching and embedded intervention. *Topics in Early Childhood Special Education*, 38, 17–29.

Shayne, R., & Miltenberger, R. G. (2013). Evaluation of behavioral skills training for teaching functional assessment and treatment selection skills to parents. *Behavioral Interventions*, 28, 4–21.

Trivette, C. M., Dunst, C. J., Hamby, D. W., & O'Herin, C. E. (2009). Characteristics and consequences of adult learning methods and strategies. *Winterberry Research Syntheses*, 2(2), 1–33.

Woods, J., Kashinath, S., & Goldstein, H. (2004). Effects of embedding caregiver-implemented teaching strategies in daily routines on children's communication outcomes. *Journal of Early Intervention*, 26, 175–193.

Index

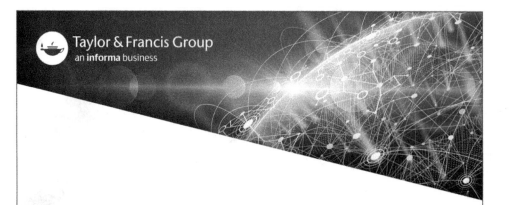

Printed in the USA
CPSIA information can be obtained
at www.ICGtesting.com
LVHW082336140823
755255LV00011B/402